REBALANCING THE E

CW01081740

Photo by Miriam Kennet

Edited by Christopher Brook and Miriam Kennet

The Green Economics Institute (GEI)

REBALANCING THE ECONOMY ©
September 2014
Published by The Green Economics Institute
Registered Office: 6 Strachey Close, Tidmarsh, Reading RG8 8EP
greeneconomicsinstitute@yahoo.com

Typeset by Christopher Brook

Printed on FSC approved stock by Marston Book Services Ltd.

The Green Economics Institute

Photo: Bogusia Igielska (Poland)

The Green Economics Institute has been working to create and establish a discipline or school of Economics called "Green Economics" and seeks to reform mainstream economics itself into a well-defined goals-based discipline which provides practical answers to existing and future problems by incorporating all relevant aspects, knowledge and complex interactions into a truly holistic understanding of the relevant issues. It uses complexity, holism, pluralism and interdisciplinary working in order to widen the scope of economics, adding the science from the green aspects, and the social ideas from economics discourses. This new scope for the first time avoids partial explanations or solutions and also biased and partial perspectives of power elites.

The Institute has begun to influence the methodology of mainstream economics, according to Professor Tony Lawson of Cambridge University's Economics Department (2007). It uses trans-disciplinary and interdisciplinary methods so that it can factor in the complexity of nature into economics. It seeks to provide all people everywhere, non human species, the planet and earth systems with a decent level of well-being based on practical and theoretical approaches targeting both methodology and knowledge and based a comprehensive reform of the current economic mainstream. It can, for example, comfortably incorporate glacial issues, climate change and volcanic, seismic and earth sciences into its explanations and thus in this, and many other ways, it is far more complete and reflects reality much more closely than its predecessors on which it builds. The current narrow conventional economic approach using purposely designed methods, is challenged to bring areas and concepts into its scope which have been until now   neglected. Existing outdated or inappropriate propositions and solutions are examined and revised to provide a realistic and more comprehensive understanding of the subject.

The Green Economics Institute argues for economic development based on economic access and decision making for all, including respect for cultural diversity and normative freedom. It does this by bringing together all the interested parties, who want to help in developing this progressive discipline, by inviting them to its events, and conferences and by means of such activities as writing books and publications and using its research, its campaigns and its lobbying and its speeches and lecturing all over the world.

The Green Economics Institute created the first green academic journal *International Journal of Green Economics* with publishers Inderscience.

The Green Economics Institute has its own delegation to the Kyoto Protocol, and is a recommended UK government reviewer on the Intergovernmental Panel on Climate Change (IPCC). Members of the Green Economics Institute have lectured or worked in governments and Universities around the world, for example receiving invitations from Surrey University, the Schumacher College, The University of Bolzano, the

Tyrollean Cabinet, via Skype in Thessaloniki, FYRO Macedonia, Turkey, the National Government School in the UK with top Cabinet Officials, at University in Cambridge and Oxford, Transition Towns, Oslo, Norway, Liverpool University, Lancaster University, Abuja, Nigeria and Gondar, Ethiopia, Shillong, and Gujerat, in India and attended conferences in many places including Cancun, Mexico and Riga, Latvia and appeared on TV and radio in Italy and Tallin in Estonia and the UK and Bangladesh amongst many others and received invitations the President of Russia and from the governments and several universities in China and from several governments and Princes in several Gulf States as well as several parts of the United Nations and the International Labour Organisation!

The spread of Green Economics is accelerating and hence The Green Economics Institute is pleased to bring these ideas to a broader group of readers, students, policy makers, academics and campaigners in this ground breaking volume and to begin to offer its Green Economics Solutions to help rebalance the economy.

The Directors
Miriam Kennet, UK,
Volker Heinemann UK, Germany,
Michelle S. Gale de Oliveira UK, USA, Brazil

Contents

The Green Economics Institute Publications

Leading thinkers now publish with The Green Economics Institute with over 50 titles.

Titles available from The Green Economics Institute ©:

Economics Books
Handbook of Green Economics: A Practitioner's Guide (2012). Edited By Miriam Kennet, Eleni Courea, Alan Bouquet and Ieva Pepinyte, ISBN 9781907543036

Green Economics Methodology: An Introduction (2012). Edited By Tone Berg (Norway), Aase Seeberg (Norway) and Miriam Kennet, ISBN 978190754357

The Green Economics Reader (2012). Edited By Miriam Kennet ISBN 9781907543265

Rebalancing the Economy (2014). Edited By Christopher Brook & Miriam Kennet, ISBN 9781907543845

An Alternative History of Economics and Economists for students (2015). Edited by Miriam Kennet

Finance Books
The Greening of Global Finance: Reforming Global Finance c (2013). Edited By Professor Graciela Chichilnisky (USA and Argentina), Michelle S. Gale de Oliveira (USA and Brazil), Miriam Kennet, Professor Maria Madi (Brazil) and Professor Chow Fah Yee (Malaysia),ISBN 9781907543401

The Reform and Greening of Global Banking (2014). Edited by Miriam Kennet, Professor Maria Madi and Stephen Mandel, ISBN 9781907543203
Islamic Banking from our team in Bangladesh (2015)

Geographies of Green Economics
Greening the Global Economy (2013). Edited by Sofia Amaral (Portugal) and Miriam Kennet , ISBN 9781907543944

Green Economics: The Greening of Asia and China (2012). Edited by Miriam Kennet (UK) and Norfayanti Kamaruddin (Malaysia), ISBN 9781907543234

Green Economics: Voices of Africa (2012). Edited By Miriam Kennet, Amana Winchester, Mahelet Mekonnen and Chidi Magnus Onuoha, ISBN 9781907543098

Green Economics: The Greening of Indonesia (2013). Edited By Dr Dessy Irwati and Dr Stephan Onggo (Indonesia), ISBN 9781907543821

The Indigenous Women of Bangladesh: Shifting Livelihoods and Gender in the Matrilineal Garo Community of Madhupur (2014) Dr. Soma Dey, ISBN 9781907543807

The Greening of Latin America (2013). Edited By Michelle S. Gale de Oliveira (USA and Brazil), Maria Fernanda Caporale Madi (Brazil), Carlos Francisco Restituyo Vassallo (Dominican Republic) and Miriam Kennet , ISBN 9781907543876

Africa: Transition to a Green Economy (2013). Edited By Dr Chidi Magnus (Nigeria), ISBN 9781907543364

The Greening of the Indian Economy: The Economic Miracle (2014). Edited by Associate Professor, Dr Natalie West Kharkongor (India), Dr Indira Dutta (India), Kanupriya Bhagat (India), Odeta Grabauskaitė (Lithuania), Miriam Kennet (UK) & Professor Graciela Chichilnisky (Argentine, USA), ISBN 9781907543500

European Books
The Greening of Europe (2014). Edited by Miriam Kennet, ISBN 9781907543463

The Greening of Eastern Europe (2013). Edited by Miriam Kennet and Dr Sandra Gusta (Latvia), ISBN 9781907543418

Green Economics: Policy and Practise in Eatern Europe (July 2014). Edited by Professor Dr Dzintra Astaja (Latvia), Miriam Kennet and Odeta Grabauskaitė (Lithuania), ISBN 9781907543814

Greening of the Mediterranean Economy (2013). Edited by Miriam Kennet, Dr Michael Briguglio and Dr Enrico Tezza, ISBN 9781907543906

Green Economics: Potential for the Italian Recovery: The Greening of Italy. Edited by Alberto Truccolo and Miriam Kennet, ISBN 9781907543920

The Greening of Norway and the future economy. Edited by Miriam Kennet (2014)

Europe, an analysis for the future of its economy. Edited by Martin Koehring Senior Editor of the Economist Magazine, Miriam Kennet, Volker Heinemann (2015)

Social Policy Books

The Greening of Health and Wellbeing (2013). Edited by Michelle S. Gale de Oliveira, Miriam Kennet and Dr Katherine Kennet, ISBN 9781907543760

The Vintage Generation, the Rocking Chair Revolution (2014). Edited by Miriam Kennet and Birgit Meinhard – Siebel (Austria), ISBN 9781907543517

Citizen's Income and Green Economics (2012) By Clive Lord, edited by Judith Felton and Miriam Kennet ISBN 9781907543074

Green Economics: Women's Unequal Pay and Poverty (2012). Edited by Miriam Kennet, Michelle S Gale de Oliveira, Judith Felton and Amana Winchester, ISBN 9781907543081

Young People: Green Jobs, Employment and Education (2012). Edited by Miriam Kennet and Juliane Goeke (Germany), ISBN 9781907543258

Garment workers in Bangladesh (2014). Soma Dey (Bangladesh) and others

The Philosophy of Social Justice (2015). Edited by Miriam Kennet and others

Ending the War against women (2015). Edited by Miriam Kennet, Michelle S Gale de Oliveira, Professor Graciela Chichilnisky and Professor Maria Madi

Memories of India by Lynden Moore (2015). Edited by Odeta Grabauskaitė

Migration, Refugees and Population (2015). Edited by Miriam Kennet and others

Mental Health (2015). Edited by Miriam Kennet and Dr Katherine Kennet

Energy and Climate Policy

Green Economics and Climate Change (2012). Edited by Miriam Kennet and Winston Ka-Ming Mak, ISBN 978190754310

Green Economics: The Greening of Energy Policies (2012). Edited By Ryota Koike (Japan) and Miriam Kennet, ISBN 9781907543326

Renewable Energy (2014). Edited by Miriam Kennet and a team of writers, ISBN 9781907543784 . Forthcoming in 2014

Fracking, Black Swan Events and Risk (2014). Edited by Miriam Kennet and Paul Mobbes ISBN 9781907543791. Forthcoming in 2014

Food, Farming and Agriculture

Green Economics & Food, Farming and Agriculture (2013). Edited by Michelle S. Gale de Oliveira and Rose Blackett-Ord and Miriam Kennet, ISBN 9781907543449

Green Economics & Food, Farming and Agriculture: Greening the food on your plate c (2013). Edited by Michelle S. Gale de Oliveira, Rose Blackett-Ord and Miriam Kennet, ISBN 9781907543654

Towards Sustainable Regional Food Systems: The Langenburg Forum c (2013). Edited By Miriam Kennet, by kind permission of Joschka Fischer and HRH Prince Charles Prince of Wales Forthcoming in 2015

Organic Food (2015)

Biodiversity, conservation and animal protection Books

Biodiversity, Animal Welfare and Protection (2014). Edited by Anna Wainer, Compassion in World Farming and others, ISBN 9781907543227

Forests and Trees (2015) Edited by Miriam Kennet and others

Lifestyle Books

The Green Transport Revolution (2013). Edited By Richard Holcroft and Miriam Kennet, ISBN 9781907543968

Green Poetry, Art and Photography (2013). Edited by Dr Matt Rinaldi, Rose Blackett-Ord, Friedericke Oeser Prasse and Miriam Kennet, ISBN 9781907543784
The Green Built Environment: A Handbook (2012). Edited By Miriam Kennet and Judith Felton, ISBN 9781907543067

Fairtrade in Europe (2014) Jessica Boisseau. Edited by Christopher Brook

Philosophy Books
Integrating Ethics, Social Responsibility and Governance (2013). Edited by Tore Audin Hedin (Norway), Michelle Gale de Oliveira and Miriam Kennet, ISBN 9781907543395

The Philosophical Basis of the Green Movement (2013). Edited by Professor Michael Benfield, Miriam Kennet and Michelle Gale de Oliveira (Brazil), ISBN 9781907543548

Books about Resources and Basic Needs
Water, Flooding and sea level rise (2014)

Technology and Technical Books
The Greening of IT (2014). Forthcoming

Engineering and Technological Solutions to current problems (2015)

List of Contributors

Helene Albrecht holds a Bachelor in Music from Musikhochschule Köln, Germany and an LLP and LLM Specialist degree from Westminster University, London and University College London respectively. Following an intensive career as teacher and performing artist her recent research interest is dedicated to the current entanglement and progressive humanization of law and economy.

Joyce Appleby is an American historian. She is Professor Emerita of History at University of California, Los Angeles (UCLA). She served as president of the Organization of American Historians (1991) and the American Historical Association (1997).

Joel Bakan, a professor of law at the University of British Columbia, wrote the award-winning and widely-translated book and film (co-created with Mark Achbar) The Corporation, as well as, more recently, Childhood Under Siege. Highly regarded as a teacher, scholar, and social commentator, Bakan makes his home in Vancouver, Canada

Christopher Brook is an economist at the University of Cambridge. His interests lie in sustainable development and poverty alleviation. He worked in Nicaragua on a sustainable watershed management project where he began to understand the needs and challenges that those in poverty face. He hopes to use this gained knowledge in the future to help relieve poverty sustainably all over the world. He currently works for the Green Economics Institute and ran the 9th Annual Green Economics Institute Conference at Oxford University in July 2014 and is a deputy editor of the International Journal of Green Economics

Professor Graciela Chichilnisky, (USA and Argentina) has worked extensively in the Kyoto Protocol process, creating and designing the carbon market that became international law in 2005. She also acted as a lead author of the Intergovernmental Panel on Climate Change, which received the 2007 Nobel Prize. A frequent keynote speaker, special adviser to several UN organisations and heads of state, her pioneering work uses innovative market mechanisms to reduce carbon emissions, conserve biodiversity and ecosystem services and improve the lot of the poor. She is a Professor of Economics and Mathematical Statistics at Columbia University and the Sir Louis Matheson Distinguished Professor at Monash University.

Chuck Collins is a senior scholar at the Institute for Policy Studies (IPS). He co-edits the web resource, www.inequality.org, an online portal for analysis and commentary. He is author of the book, *99 to 1: How Wealth Inequality is Wrecking the World and What We Can Do About It* (Berrett Koehler Publishing, 2012).

Richard Cooper is a Maurits C. Boas Professor of International Economics at Harvard University. He has published widely and has served as chairman of the Federal Reserve Bank of Boston and as Under-Secretary of State for Economic Affairs in the US State Department

Dr Craig Duckworth is head of the department of Economics and International Business, and principal lecturer in Economics and Business Environment at Anglia Ruskin University. His research interests lie at the interface of economics and ethics.

Aart Heesterman has a degree in political and social sciences of the University of Amsterdam. After four years as a civil servant in The Hague he moved to the University of Birmingham, UK. He has published a number of books related to economic forecasting ands planning. In retirement he started what eventually became a joint publication with his wife Wiebina: the more environmentally orientated book *Rediscovering Sustainability*.

Wiebina Heesterman is also Dutch by nationality, living in the UK since the mid 1960s. She has a PhD in Law on children's rights from Warwick University as well as degrees in information science and IT. She read extensively on biodiversity and climate change while writing *Rediscovering Sustainability* jointly with A. R.G. Heesterman, then wrote a chapter on climate change denial for a book aimed at engineers and followed a climate change course.

Hazel Henderson, D.Sc.Hon., FRSA, president of Ethical Markets Media (USA and Brazil), is a futurist, evolutionary economist, author of award-winning *Ethical Markets:*

Growing the Green Economy and many other books. She has advised the U.S. Office of Technology Assessment, the National Academy of Engineering and the National Science Foundation. She founded the EthicMark® Awards for Advertising, created the Green Transition Scoreboard® and the Principles of Ethical Biomimicry Finance®, and co-developed with Calvert the Ethical Markets Quality of Life Indicators. In 2012, she received the Award for Outstanding Contribution to ESG & Investing at TBLI Europe; was inducted into the International Society of Sustainability Professionals Hall of Fame in 2013, and in 2014 was again honored as a "Top 100 Thought Leader in Trustworthy Business Behavior" by Trust Across America.

Manan Jain, An economist from India, specialising in the Gift Economy. Manan addressed the Green Economics Institute's Conference at Oxford University in 2012 (India)

Miriam Kennet, is a specialist in Green Economics, she is the Co-Founder and is CEO of the Green Economics Institute. She also founded and edits the first Green Economics academic journal in the world, the International Journal of Green Economics, and she has been credited with creating the academic discipline of Green Economics. Green Economics has been recently described by the Bank of England as one of the most vibrant and healthy areas of economics at the moment. Having researched at Oxford University, Oxford Brookes and South Bank University, she is a member of the Environmental Change Institute, Oxford University. She has taught, lectured and spoken at Universities and events all over Europe, from Alicante to Oxford and Bolzano, and to government officials from Montenegro and Kosovo to The UK Cabinet Office, Transport Department, National Government School and Treasury and spoken in Parliaments from Scotland to Austria and The French Senat and Estonia. She is also a regular and frequently speaks at public events of all kinds, and after dinner speaker.. She has a delegation to the UNFCC COP Kyoto Climate Change Conferences and headed up a delegation to RIO + 20 Earth Summit: Greening the Economy in RIO Brazil. She regularly speaks on TV around Europe, most recently in Belgium, and Estonia and this year the BBC has made a special programme about her life and work. She runs regular conferences at Oxford University about Green Economics Publishing regularly and having over 100 articles, Chapters and other publications. She has been featured in the Harvard Economics Review and Wall Street Journal as a leader.

Recently she was named one of 100 most powerful unseen global women by the Charity One World action for her global work and won the Honour Award from the Luxembourg Ministry for her work.

Martin Koehring is a senior editor in the Content Solutions team of the Economist Intelligence Unit (EIU), where he works on bespoke research programmes with a focus on sustainability and healthcare. Previously he was Europe editor in the EIU's Country Analysis team. Prior to joining the EIU, Martin worked as a senior Economist at business intelligence provider D&B. He studies International Politics in Wales, European Studies in Belgium and Economics in London

Professor Dr Maria Alejandra Madi, holds a PhD in Economics. She works at the intersection between macroeconomics, finance and socio-economic development. Retired Professor at the State University of Campinas, Brazil, she is currently Director of the Ordem dos Economistas do Brasil and Counselor at the Conselho Regional de Economia–SP. Besides her participation as co-author in chapter books edited by the Global Labor University, she is a regular author with the Green Economics Institute.

Alastair McIntosh is an independent scholar, poet and broadcaster who holds or has held honorary fellowship or professorial positions at the universities of Ulster, Strathclyde, Glasgow and Edinburgh, as well as the Centre for Human Ecology. Best know for his books Soil and Soul, Hell and High Water and Rekindling Community, his writing has been described as "world changing" by George Monbiot, "life changing" by the Bishop of Liverpool and "truly mental" by Thom Yorke of Radiohead.

Kari Marie Norgaard is Associate Professor of Sociology and Environmental Studies at University of Oregon. Her research on tribal environmental justice and gender and risk and climate denial has been published in Sociological Forum, Gender and Society, Sociological Inquiry, Organization and Environment, Rural Sociology, Race, Gender & Class, and other journals, as well as by the World Bank. Her research has also been featured in The Washington Post, National Geographic, High Country News, and on National Public Radio's "All Things Considered." Her first book "Living in Denial: Climate Change, Emotions and Everyday Life" was published by MIT Press in 2011.

Norgaard is recipient of the Pacific Sociological Association's Distinguished Practice Award for 2005.

Vandana Shiva is world-renowned environmental leader and recipient of the 1993 Alternative Nobel Peace Prize (the Right Livelihood Award), Shiva has authored several bestselling books, most recently Earth Democracy. Activist and scientist, Shiva leads, with Ralph Nader and Jeremy Rifkin, the International Forum on Globalization. Before becoming an activist, Shiva was one of India's leading physicists.

Rosamund Stock is completing a PhD in the social psychology of distributive justice. She has worked within NGOs developing ideas about the nature of social relationships and recasting the economic narrative. She has worked for the ILO on their Socio-economic security survey providing the social psychological underpinning for the project. She has also advised research teams on the relevant social psychology for their project as well as publishing in the International Journal of Green Economics.

Joss Tantram is a founding partner at Terrafiniti LLP, a pioneering sustainability and systems consultancy. He has 20 years private and not for profit experience in the UK, Europe and world-wide. He leads Terrafiniti's strategic services and their R&D and innovation initiative, Towards 9 Billion.

Sir Crispin Tickell is a former British Diplomat who worked for several organisations including President of the Royal Geographic Society, Warden of Green College Oxford, Chancellor of the University of Kent and is currently director of the Policy Foresight Programme.

John Weeks is Professor Emeritus of the University of London, School of Oriental & African Studies. He is author of over 100 scholarly publications including 12 sole authored books. He has consulted for many international organizations and advised numerous governments on economic policy

Part 1 The Path We Are Travelling

1.1 A History of Capitalism

Joyce Appleby

Elements of our modern capitalist economies emerged first in 17th century England when domestic traders began going further and further away to enlarge their markets. Taking advantage of the political turmoil of the period, individuals cheerfully broke the laws which directed economic activities into narrow, policed channels until finally their innovations appeared more customary than the old laws.

Larger markets called forth greater productivity. Working interactively, these forces slowly replaced the traditional ways of working the land, fabricating goods, and circulating products and profits. When the French looked across the Channel and saw the prosperity generated by the new economic habits, they dubbed it the English miracle. European rivals emulated England as quickly as their own traditions and political regimes allowed.

The great expander of these new economic routines was of course the introduction of steam power which could be and was - quickly adapted to all kinds of mining and manufacturing ventures, especially cloth factories. In the 18th century practical applications of scientific knowledge succeeded in getting steam to drain mine pits, power factories and drive locomotives.

Looking at all the factors which greased the steady evolution of a traditional economy into a capitalistic one, many scholars have found the origins of capitalism much earlier in such practices as double-entry bookkeeping and the global trade that developed at the discovery of the New World and the creation of new trade routes to the Orient. But commerce was as old as human society. It happily existed within the interstices of a traditional society, involving a small percentage of the population. Manufacturing, particularly after the introduction of steam-powered machines, required more and more workers whose lives changed dramatically.

When Europeans traversed routes to the Indies, they found exotic Asian ports where they could buy silks and spices. Going in the other direction, the encountered a new world with two continents bracketing dozens of tropical islands. Lucrative trades sprang up, demonstrating that Europeans already had impressive savings to invest in foreign ventures.

The aristocracies which supported European monarchies in the 16th and 17th centuries looked down upon merchants because of their absorption in making money, but they liked the challenge of expanding European influence and power. They believed unquestioningly in human inequality. Some few were born to head diplomatic missions, serve the law or the church, advise kings, and lead armies; the remainder were the hewers of wood and drawers of water, not to mention the farmers and servants who lived lives of drudgery. As an urban group, merchants fell somewhere in between these categories, respected for their skill and money, but demeaned for their lack of distinguished family ties.

These attitudes began to change as buying and selling things became more prevalent. The aristocrats and gentry who were the landholders were also affected by the economic innovations because of an increased demand for food and the profits to be made from larger harvests achieved with fewer agricultural laborers. The old, customary agricultural system yielded to improved techniques for raising food. Over time, agricultural improvements led to lower food prices. When ordinary people no longer spent the lion's share of their income on food, they could buy other goods. Instead of having one or two shirts or blouses, they could indulge in what seemed like superfluous consumption.

At the same time many of the farmers' children were no longer needed on the farm and moved into rural industries or left to pick up city trades or thicken the distribution networks of England's unified market. By the end of the 17th century England had the largest integrated market in the world. Elsewhere on the globe special privileges, monopolies, and regional antagonisms prevent the free circulation of goods. Even in England, these changes ran athwart personal expectation. They also challenged the mores embedded in the laws, religion, and popular lore of the day.

In cities, buyers found objects of delight and usefulness from maps and travel books to jewelry and clothing decorated with precious stones, exotic foods like sugar, coffee, and cocoa and fascinating contrivances like eye glasses, scientific instruments, and pocket compasses. The exultation at human inventiveness that had become part of the spirit of capitalism started to take hold of the public imagination. Invidious comparisons between the West and the rest of the world entered public discourse.

Scarcities continued to characterize Western societies in the 18th century because population began to grow in the 1730s and 1740s. But in prosperous England, there were no more famines, and they became less severe elsewhere in Western Europe. The dreaded plague which had revisited Europe with regularity since the Black Death of the 14th century also made an exit after its 1723 visit. That sense of life's precariousness which justified the invasive authority of fathers, magistrates, and kings would now slowly fade. Calls for greater political participation, religious toleration, and personal mobility grew louder as market participants acquired – or seized - the freedom to move outside the skein of social prescriptions. Short term individual goals replaced old worries about the future. The aggregation of such decisions set prices and rates without anyone taking responsibility for their consequences.

The celebration of the individual inventor – homo faber – gained ground as the initial experiments with steam turned into a revolution in production processes. The industrial era began in earnest in the 19th century gaining momentum as it moved out from England to France, Germany, and the United States. By the end of the century, the magic of steam engine was overtaken by the wizardry of electricity. Chemistry joined physics as a handmaiden to industry. Eager investors promoted a sustained search for new inventions which led in time to organized research. This meant a constant delving into the qualities of the natural world and its elements, as they studied reactions to heat, cold, stress, compression, tension, and gravitational force. This work infused a wondrous quality into the material universe as it was replacing an earlier spirituality. Some called it the disenchantment of the world. While this constant bombarding of nature with questions began with natural philosophers, inventors came right behind them to commercialize their findings and diffuse their impact.

The social world that wound around the repetitions of each year's seasonal tasks and holidays morphed into one of constant variation. Change, always something to be feared, acquired a Janus-like quality. It could actually bring improvements; it could also obliterate long-standing ways of being in the world. To keep the economy developing required men and women to take risks, think innovatively, and accept changes that made their lives very different from those of their parents. New too was the idea of people earning their place in society regardless of family origins. Social mobility, which seems so ordinary a concept to us, was an abomination in a society structured around the statuses of nobility, gentility, commoner and servant – the dependent many and the independent few.

The ambition that played an essential role in inducing people to be more productive could only be sustained if there was room on the higher rungs of the social ladder. While statuses had supported stasis, striving promoted expectations of moving up and fears of moving down or being pushed there. Once uprooted from the old agrarian order, men and women learned crafts like shoemaking, worked in construction, formed the human ligaments of commerce, or were drawn into factory work. Two new classes emerged to take the place of the old ranks: those of workers and employers. Working with your hands was further distinguished from working with your brains. While these positions were open to all claimants as the old statuses were not, social mobility had its limits. But geographic mobility increased as farm people found work in rural industry and then in the cities. The more adventurous left Europe altogether to find a place and perhaps a fortune in South and North America. Capitalism benefited enormously from its association with political freedom, even as it created new forms of control. Factories replaced the home and the shop as work sites.

This account of the emergence of capitalism smooths over all the rough edges, failed ventures, and harmful dislocations that accompanied the new investment practices and work routines. Economic entrepreneurs had to defend their practices from those who wanted to maintain the status quo. Those who built, ran, and invested in them acquired power, and they used their power and influence to promise the ideology of individualism, independence, and human rights that accompanied their rise to predominance.

By the middle of the 17th century some people began to analyze the capitalist economy that was emerging. They ceased upon its naturalism as a defining characteristic. People acted on their own economic impulses untutored by laws and customs. These observations slowly turned into economic theories that emphasized what Adam Smith at the end of the 18th century called "the invisible hand of the market. These ideas were very congenial to those who built, ran, and invested in the new ventures whether they were manufacturers, merchants or improving landlords. As they acquired power, they held fiercely to the ideology of individualism, independence, and human rights that accompanied their rise to predominance.

As domestic consumption became more important to the national economy, it undermined the social distinctions that were so important to the old order. There was as great a divide between the very rich and the very poor as ever, but there was now a middle class increasingly disdainful of old customs that dictated their lives. Manufacturers wanted to keep wages low and hours long when making goods, but they needed to have customers, well-paid and interested in shopping, when it came time to sell them.

Theorists began making this point explicitly as they put together their observations of the new economy.

Simultaneous with the economic changes within England and elsewhere, was the new trade in the often addictive tropical plants like sugar, tobacco, tea, and cocoa. Rather than import these products from Asians and Africans, Europeans organized a system of plantation agriculture to raise these appetizing novelties in the New World. This trade was made possible because they could buy slaves by the millions from Africa and ship them to the Caribbean islands and Atlantic coasts of North and South America. The European exploitation of vulnerable people began with slavery in the 16th century and moved to on-the-site exploitation in distant countries, especially Africa in the 19th century. Then Germany and Italy joined Spain, Portugal, Great Britain, and France in building empires with capital investments directed to developing their colonies' natural resources. In treating colonial laborers and their societies as so many aspects of production, capitalists dehumanized their relations with the people outside their continent.

While the belligerent rivalries of Europe were very old, the wealth generated by capitalism changed the terms of engagement in the 20th century, enabling the countries to sustain hostilities for years. Surprisingly no one expected this outcome in 1914 when war broke out. Most people thought it would end in months; instead it dragged on for four bloody years. Since the competition was in part over imperial holdings, colonies and their neighbors all over the world were dragged into the conflict. Two decades after World War I, the Second World War began. Perhaps no greater contrast has existed than that between the sense of accomplishment at the opening of the 20th century and the despair that reigned when the Second World War ended in an explosion of ferocious energy in 1945.

1900 opened with the marvels of the automobile, electric power, and reconfigured city centers dotted with skyscrapers. Life expectancy got longer, and public health measures checked the spread of diseases that had once ravaged populations. Four decades later the war had killed millions of men and women, expelled millions of others from their homes, and utterly demolished thousands upon thousands of city blocks. Men and women who had been young for the First World War entered middle age chastened. Hard times promoted serious thought. After a second world war, capitalist nations recognized the need for cooperation and created templates for international organizations of lasting value.

Between the two world wars, the United States and Europe suffered a massive decline in commerce. Known as the Great Depression just as the First World War was originally known as the Great War, this sudden deceleration of the capitalist tempo left experts in a state of shock. Dozens of economies fell into shambles. Despite efforts at ameliorating the loss of jobs and savings, most government policies proved ineffectual. It took the massive spending of the Second World War to get the capitalist system humming again, a result that vindicated the theory of John Maynard Keynes. Keynes argued that private investments alone could not pull economies out of depression. Like the biblical reference to seven fat years followed by seven lean ones, capitalism has oscillated between good and bad times, though with less predictability. The pent-up demand after World War II and the great wealth which the United States was willing to spend to help in the recovery of Western Europe and then Japan, led to a golden age of a quarter century. A generation later, a new matrix for recession brought to an end the bounteous prosperity of the postwar era.

People began in the 1970s to take notice of the environmental toll taken by the accelerating levels of fossil fuel consumption, a fact driven home by the emerging power of OPEC, the association of oil producing countries. Exercising something of monopoly power, OPEC voted a dramatic rise in oil prices, making noticeable several other problems in the homelands of capitalism. The most prominent was that for the first time rising prices did not signal a period of growth, but rather one of stasis or stagnation or, in the term of the hour, stagflation. The income equalizing of the postwar period reversed into a four-decade long stretch of the gap between low and high incomes in the United States. The mutually beneficial agreements among big business, big labor, and big government grew weaker. Organized labor, the beneficiary of depression despair and postwar growth, lost its purchase on the popular imagination. Stagflation also broke up the consensus of opinion that Keynesian solutions would work for all of capitalism's problems. As labor power waned, that of employers waxed.

While capitalist nations were taking in these troubling facts, capitalism moved into high gear with a cascade of new technologies that brought in the age of the computer, the transistor, and the Internet. Schumpeter's creative destruction went to work again.

The history of capitalism doesn't repeat itself; but capitalists do. The fact that rarely does any one register surprise when a crisis arrives even though few had done anything to prevent it points to a quality that capitalism cultivates: an optimism that denies reality. The "spirit" of capitalism is that of the salesman who exudes confidence. When no one is in charge, and most participants are searching for new (and, if possible, easy) ways to make money, panics, crises, and meltdowns become inevitable. People worldwide can be counted on to seek out lucrative deals outside the patrolled precincts of regulation. When the good deals tank, governments rush in to fix what's wrong, with varying results.

Before the world recession of 2008-2009, the market's stumbles had grown ever more frequent and painful, starting with the crash of 1987, followed by the junk bond crisis of the late 1980s, the 1989 sinking of the savings and loan industry, the Japanese depression, the Asian fiscal crisis of 1997, the Long-Term Capitol Management near-default of 1998, the bursting of the dot.com bubble of 2000, the Enron and WorldCom debacle of 2001, climaxing with the rippling losses from the mortgage-based securities debacle in 2008. Mounting foreclosures, beginning in 2007, put the brakes on the subprime mortgage joy ride, but the problems went deeper. China's great savings had made borrowing cheap. American consumers apparently decided to let the Chinese do the saving while they spent in a grand style. At the same time, low interest rates drove the managers of capital to seek new ways to get more for their money, even if they had to invent new stratagems to do so.

The 2008 financial crisis had two underlying causes roiled by a wild card. The first predisposing cause was set in place in the late 1970s when a recession stirred interest in eliminating the regulations that formed a legacy of the Great Depression of the 1930s. Writers began depicting capitalist enterprise as a Gulliver tied down by a thousand Lilliputian strings from environmentalists, safety monitors, and the like. Business people argued that an economy became robust when its participants had the freedom to act freely and quickly. This era of deregulation, associated with English Prime Minister Margaret Thatcher and President Ronald Reagan, was completed in the United States in 1999 with the Gramm-Leach-Bliley Financial Service Modernization Act signed into law by President Bill Clinton.

A boon to banks, brokerage firms, insurance companies, and high-flyers generally, the law permitted banks to merge with insurance companies and liberated investment banks from many of the restrictions that applied to regular commercial banks of deposits. The Securities and Exchange Commission unanimously voted to exempt America's biggest investment banks – those with assets greater than $5 billion - from a regulation that limited the amount of debt they could take on.[1] The rest, as they say, is history.

While legislatures were busy deconstructing the regulation of banks, brokerage houses, and insurance companies, an unusual amount of money was sloshing through global markets. Financial assets had been growing faster than real economic activity. High rates of saving among people in Asia's developing nations combined with governmental efforts to stimulate their economies had considerably reduced interest rates.[2] Unhappy with rates in the 2%-3% range, the mavens of finance began thinking up ways to increase that return. A boom in housing in the United States gave them the opportunity they were looking for. They contrived a dicey array of new financial investments. Bank mortgages were divided up and turned into derivative securities, a term that refers to assets with value derived from other assets. Soon these securitized mortgages passed from commercial to investment banks which were not regulated as were commercial banks. Investment banks repackaged and sold the securitized mortgages to investors or

---

1
"Agency's '04 Rule Let Banks Pile Up New Debt, and Risk," *New York Times*, October 3, 2008.
2   Willaim Greider, *One World Ready Or Not: The Manic Logic of Global Capitalism* (New York, 1996), 316, 310-311.

other banks. Lots of other individuals and institutions looking for places to park their money bought them too. Once commercial banks had sold their mortgages, they were free to write new ones in what became a jolly round of growth for those in the know. The actual mortgage payments from home-owners sustained the value of the securities. Alas, bankers underestimated the risks which grew exponentially as the number and dubiousness of the mortgages increased.

The unintended consequences of perfectly rational, individual decisions can help explain how the world's financial centers skidded into disaster in 2008. When Asian families decided to build nest eggs after their 1997 financial crisis, they didn't intend to stimulate American consumption with the cheap credit their savings created. When Republican and Democratic administrations endorsed home-ownership as sound social policy, they didn't intend to set off a race among bankers to issue subprime mortgages so they could securitize them for eager investors. When CEOs at investment banks and hedge funds paid their star traders handsome year-end bonuses, they intended to reward and encourage superior performance. Totally unintended was the creation of a testosterone-driven competition so intense it kept at bay second thoughts, looking at the larger picture, or listening to naysaysers. The notion of unintended consequences doesn't lend itself to the mathematical models favored by economists, but the freer the market system the more widespread are individual initiatives which pull along in their train the unintended consequences of their actions.

Risk-taking is integral to capitalism, but it plays differently in the financial sector than in technology. Banks, like utilities, contribute most when they are dependable and efficient. Instead they became as ingratiating as sales people. The cold shoulder bankers used to give to incautious borrowers turned into a warm welcome for all comers. Of course if they never lent to risk-taking entrepreneurs, capitalism would suffer. Balancing stability with innovation eluded banks in the first decade of the 21st century. Investment banks even started buying the asset-based securities that they were selling to others, with disastrous results. Some say strategies of risk-taking changed for bankers when their institutions went public, allowing them to bet on other people's money instead of their own.

During the last ten years, financial services grew from 11% of our gross national product to 20%. Some otherwise sober men and women were able to leverage at a ratio of 1 to 30 for money invested, spreading risk without tracking it. More damaging to the nation in the long run, physicists, mathematicians, and computer experts were drawn away from their original work to join the high-earning financial wizards. At least 40% of Ivy League graduates went into finance in the early years of the 21st century. In retrospect, people who were making decisions affecting the economies of dozens of countries were responding to incentives that sealed them off from the consequences of their acts. In the immediate postrecession period, efforts to change these incentives have been only partially successful. That old optimism that capitalist investments depend on has returned only slightly modified in force.

Every economic downturn gives critics a chance to draft obituaries for capitalism, but they underestimate the fecundity of capitalism in promoting ingenuity and turning novel prototypes into great cash cows. Or more important: to lift people out of poverty. Since mid-1970s, capitalist developments in Korea, Taiwan, China, and India have brought 300 million people out of poverty. Millions of other men and women have moved themselves out of poverty by emigrating to more prosperous places.[3] For example, half a million Romanian immigrants are now supplying the labor of the missing youth in an aging Italy. And Italy is not the only European country losing population. France, Germany, Spain, and Greece are all dipping below the replacement rate.

Elsewhere, Middle Eastern oil fields, construction work, and domestic service in cities like Dubai are pulling workers, mostly young and male, from India and the Philippines. A wave of immigrants from Africa pushes its way through the European doorway of Spain every week. And prospective economic developments in Africa itself will reduce that continent's poverty.

---

3   Tina Rosenberg, "Globalization," *New York Times*, July 30, 2008.

Still, of the seven billion people living today, one billion live in countries with stalled economies.[4] World Bank figures for 2010 indicate that 1.22 billion people live below the poverty line, earning less than $1.25 a day. Unlike the backward, underdeveloped, Third World nations of yore, the bottom billion today live in particular countries – 57 in fact – that are treading water while the world around them is swimming towards development, even during a world recession.

What is needed is a capitalism that responds to more than profit impulses, one that serves important social needs, environmental imperatives, and humane values. Were one to make a list of that capitalistic qualities that need reshaping, it would include responding to short-term opportunities to the neglect of long term effects, dispensing power without responsibility, promoting material values over spiritual ones, commoditizing human relations, monetizing social values, corrupting democracy, capriciously unsettling old communities, institutions, and arrangements, and rewarding aggressiveness and – yes – greed.[5]

The first reshaping task has two aspects: to scotch for ever the theory that capitalism is natural rather than being a particular, historical development, and, secondly, to make a strong case that capitalism must serve society even if it relies on individual choices.

---

4   Paul Collier, *The Bottom Billion, Why the Poorest Countries are Failing and What Can Be Done About It* (Oxford, 2007).
5   "Modern Market Thought has Devalued a Deadly Sin," *New York Times*, September 27, 2008; and Steven Greenhouse and David Leonhardt, "Real Wages Fail to match a Rise in Productivity, *Ibid., August 28, 2006.*

1.2 The Economics of the Anthropocene

By Sir Crispin Tickell (UK)

What is the Anthropocene? Briefly it is the idea that humans have so transformed the land surface, seas and atmosphere of the Earth since the beginning of the industrial revolution some 250 years ago that we need a new geological epoch to describe it. Our not so little animal species has changed the character of soils, the chemistry of the oceans and atmosphere, the selective breeding of species of all kinds and their movement round the Earth to produce a world substantially different from what preceded it. Hence the Anthropocene.

It has fallen to this generation to try and measure the impact on society, and work out what might be done to mitigate or adapt to change in the interest of humans as well as of other forms of life. Little is more difficult than learning to think differently. Yet it is hard even to define the principal problems without upsetting longstanding traditions, beliefs, attitudes and the often unspoken assumptions on which we build our lives. It took a long time for previous generations to accept the antiquity of the Earth, the mechanisms of evolution, the movement of tectonic plates, the shared genetic inheritance of all living organisms, and the symbiotic and to some extent self-regulating relationship between the physical, chemical, biological and human components of the Earth system, known by some as Gaia. Some still reject the whole idea.

The impacts which together constitute the Anthropocene can be defined in many ways. In broad terms we are exploiting and in some respects running down the Earth's natural capital, including the biosphere, and damaging the ecosystem services on which we directly or indirectly depend. This is hard to reconcile with our experience of the bonanza of inventiveness, exploitation and consumption since the industrial revolution. All successful species, whether bivalves, beetles, pigeons or humans, multiply until they come up against the environmental stops, reach some accommodation with the rest of the environment, and willy-nilly restore some balance. Are we near to those stops?

In September 2009 the magazine Nature published an article by Johan Rockstrom and others identifying nine scientific stops or boundaries which humans would cross at their peril. Three had already been crossed: climate change; loss of biodiversity; and interference with nitrogen and phosphorus levels. The other six were stratospheric ozone depletion; ocean acidification; use of fresh water; changes in land use; chemical pollution; and atmospheric aerosol loading.

But these stops, however important, are only half the story. There are six more general ones where the societal responses are critical. First we need to confront the effects of our own proliferation in all its aspects; next to work out new ways of generating energy; to manage and adapt to what is in effect climate destabilization; to give higher priority to conservation of the natural world; to create the necessary institutional means of coping with global problems; and not least to look at economics in the broadest sense and the way in which we measure things. As has been well said by Lord Rees former President of the Royal Society: in the future global village we cannot afford to have too many village idiots.

There is a lot to be said about all these issues, but today I want to focus on economics and what has been labelled socio-ecology. Much current economics is built on the assumptions of more than a hundred years ago. Resources then seemed limitless; shortages were more of labour and skills than of goods; technology could solve almost any problem: wastes could always be disposed of; the other organisms on which we depended could adapt to the demands we made on them; the good functioning of society was a product of what was called 'growth' (hence the increasing use of Gross National Product and Gross Domestic Product as measuring devices); and a kind of belief (I can think of no better word) in market forces as the main if not the only drivers of health, wealth and prosperity. With this comes the belief that economics are governed by reason (often mathematically expressed) rather than by animal - herd - instincts which otherwise rule.

It may be painful but indeed we have to think again. Our society, even our animal species, is in a unique situation: as the title of a recent book put it: we have *Something New Under the Sun.* Here are some broad propositions:

We should recognise that there is no such thing as a free market, and there never has been. All markets operate within rules, whether explicit or implicit. Together they constitute a framework which if it is any good should be in the public interest and to the public good.

The question, answered differently, in different societies is to determine the character of regulation, the nature of incentives and disincentives, how best to profit from enterprise, the avoidance of market failure, and in the long as well as the short term the stability and general health of society.

Somehow we have to bring in externalities (or true costs in social as well as economic terms). Indeed externalities could be more important than internalities. Markets are marvellous at fixing prices but incapable of recognising costs.

We should be ready to admit that human population increase is a major global problem, even if it is levelling off in some areas. Continuing multiplication of humans could be as disastrous as that of any other species of plant or animal. There is also the immediate prospect of human unemployment as technology enables us to produce more goods and services with fewer people.

We should challenge the current models of 'development' which underline the artificiality of the distinction between developed, developing, under-developed and even over-developed countries. The true distinction is between those who have set industrialization as an ideal within and between their countries, and those who look more widely and see the future in term of their people's resources and welfare.

In measuring health, wealth and happiness, we have to take into account the things we most value: safety, security, food, water, cleanliness and energy. Here we must recognise that despite continuing population increase we are producing more and more goods and services with fewer and fewer people. The social costs of unemployment are enormous, and we have to reckon properly with them.

Concepts of value are controversial. For example how do we value uncut rainforest, and reward those who do not cut it? Who should take the responsibility for human-driven climate change, and pay those who suffer most from it ? How are we to cope with the likely redistribution of water supplies as patterns of rainfall change?

None of these points is new. Change is already under way, even if sometimes obscured by the current economic crisis. In particular efforts have been made to establish new systems of measurement: for example through the Human Development Index, the Stern Review, and the recent report of the Stiglitz Commission. There is even a effort to measure GDH, or Gross Domestic Happiness, I suppose as part of the Big Society. But we are still far from the changes of attitude that are required.

Supposing, as I hope, that the message does eventually become more widely received and understood, what would be the implications? Frankly they go so wide that I hesitate to be very specific. Individuals, local authorities, corporations, government at all levels would need to set very different priorities and human behaviour generally would change as a result.

A pivotal factor would be the ways in which we generate and use energy. The flow of energy affects economics, indeed life itself, every minute. It was the uses to which we put the stored energy or sunlight known as coal, oil and gas, which directly caused the industrial revolution and the consequent transformation we now label the Anthropocene. I take energy as an example of how we need to think differently.

First we must recognize that supplies of energy from fossil fuels are limited. Estimates vary all the time as technologies develop, but deposits of oil, gas and coal are by their nature finite, and the environmental penalties paid in their exploitation will become higher than society can expect. There is also a changing balance of consumption between them. There is increasing fear of dependence on certain suppliers, whether they be in the Middle East or Russia. Energy security is now high politics. In the meantime demand continues to increase worldwide. In China energy use doubled between 1990 and 2006, and is likely to double again by 2025. The development of alternative sources still has a long way to go.

The second new factor is better understanding of the cumulative effects of fossil fuel use and combustion on the chemistry of the atmosphere and the environment generally. The general relationship between greenhouse gases and the surface temperature of the Earth is well established, and although strenuous debate continues on the degree of public responsibility for the current increase in carbon dioxide in the atmosphere, many think that the consequences of our continuing dependence on fossil fuels are more serious than the prospect of their depletion.

Hence the increasing interest in making more effective use of what fossil fuels remain, and such measures as sequestration of carbon or global auctions of permits to emit greenhouse gases. But the main interest has been in developing alternative sources of energy. They include nuclear power, whether fission or fusion; solar energy on the ground or through geo-engineering; power from biofuels; tidal and ocean power; a return to wind and hydro power; geothermal power using the heat beneath our feet; and a range of new electrification technologies.
Of course there are many uncertainties and complexities. We can rarely identify tipping points until we have passed them. So far the societal responses have been mixed and uncertain with wide variations between countries.

The economics of the Anthropocene demand not just a new approach but a whole new methodology. Out of date economics should be recognised as a dangerous mental condition which is driving the world in an alarmingly wrong direction. In natural terms we are tiny parts of a gigantic system of life to which we are doing increasing injury. The human superorganism has to learn its place among other superorganisms. So far it has failed to do so. The impact of our species has been so great that the term Anthropocene is more than justified. Let economists reckon with the implications.

1.3 Global Systems Shifting

Hazel Henderson, D.Sc.Hon., FRSA, RichardSpencer, Tony Manwaring
Excerpt from *Mapping the Global Transition to the Solar Age*
(ICAEW and Tomorrow's Company, 2014)

The 'Titanic' phenomena

Back in 2012, widespread interest in the hundredth anniversary of the Titanic's sinking offered a deeper metaphor for incumbent industrial giants and paradigms of power. Lessons from brain science illuminated beliefs that the Titanic was 'unsinkable': the same consequences of theory-induced blindness, cognitive illusions, confirmation bias, and herd behaviour we see in many elites.[6] Social inequality on board the doomed ship was evidenced in the shortage of lifeboats and the prevention of escape routes for the 700 steerage passengers trapped on the lower decks. Blindness to ecosystem realities made collision with icebergs likely, just as today's science-denying politicians and special interests are leading legacy fossil-fuelled industrial societies toward collision with self-inflicted climate disasters. An influential global NGO, the World Business Council for Sustainable Development used similar themes in its many reports,[7] and its founder Stephan Schmidheiny made the same point in *Changing Course* (1992).

Systems analysts term such 'Titanic' phenomena as 'overshoots' where a conventional goal of scaling-up a technology for greater efficiency and economic returns instead creates a dysfunctional dinosaur. Examples include too-big-to-fail banks, oversized nuclear-powered electric utilities' cost-overruns and the latest monster container ships which require the current $5bn widening of the Panama

---

6   See for example, Kahneman, Daniel, *Thinking Fast and Slow*, Farrar, Straus and Giroux, New York, NY, 2012.

7   See for example, 'Vision 2050: the new agenda for business', World Business Council for Sustainable Development, February 2010.

Canal, and the Chinese proposal for a $50bn new canal in Nicaragua to accommodate them – all to handle forecasts of a quadrupling of world trade.[8]

The need for a new story

Most human learning comes from environmental challenges and those crises that are self-inflicted through our behaviours, beliefs and dogmas, which lead to conflicts, repression, injustice or misguided over-exploitation of resources, overshoots and ecological collapse.[9] Exploration of how human struggles for power throughout history are exposed in *Why Nations Fail* (2012).[10] I predicted three zones of our current global transition in 1986: Breakdown, Fibrillation-Bifurcation, Breakthrough. Today, the over seven billion member human family has reached another teachable moment. To avoid further disasters, humanity needs a new story of how our still-growing population can live together cooperatively, interdependently, sharing our planetary home with each other and other living species.[11] These are the lessons nature teaches As we learn them, we adopt new values based on the realities of our current situation, envision goals, creating innovations as we transition from the late-stage, fossil-fuelled industrial era to what I have termed the solar age[12] (see for example, 'Statement on Transforming Finance Based on Ethics and Life's Principles'[13] at and Ethical Markets Principles of Ethical Biomimicry Finance™, co-developed with our partner company, Biomimicry 3.8[14]).

Tidal waves of change

We see a global, whole-system shift underway as societies, corporations, academic and other institutions, face tidal waves of change due to accelerating

---

8   Zakaria, Fareed, 'GPS: The Global Public Square', CNN, 16 June, 2013.
9   Tainter, Joseph, *The Collapse of Complex Societies*, Cambridge University Press, NY, 1988, and Jared Diamond, *Collapse*, Viking Press, 2004.
10   Acemoglu, Daron and James Robinson, *Why Nations Fail*, Crown Business, 2012.
11   See for example, Henderson, Hazel, *Paradigms in Progress*, 1991, and *Building a Win-Win World*, Berrett-Koehler, San Francisco, 1996; ebook, 2008.
12   Henderson, Hazel, *Politics of the Solar Age*, Doubleday, NY, 1981, 1988.
13   www.transformingfinance.net
14   www.ethicalmarkets.com/2013/05/16/ethical-markets-rolls-out-ethical-biomimicry-finance/

interconnectedness driven by communications technologies, air travel, global networks and infrastructure. More than 50% of humans now live in cities, and our numbers are projected to grow to nine billion or more by 2050. An earlier wave of globalisation occurred during the colonial expansion of European powers in the seventeenth and eighteenth centuries. The second wave went into high gear in the 1980s when the USA and the UK and their leaders Ronald Reagan and Margaret Thatcher embraced laissez faire economics, deregulated global markets and finance and promoted widespread privatisation of government-led companies and public infrastructure.[15] Thus unleashed, market forces spread these changes and led to the financialization of economies and the domination of money centres, too-big-to-fail banks, Wall Street and the City of London over governments, politicians and local economies worldwide. A UK government report on curbing banking and finance in June 2013 called for new reforms.[16] Such global interlinked complexity cannot be modelled or managed with the simple computable general equilibrium (CGE) models of economics, which try to control only for inflation, unemployment, budget deficits and interest rates. Efforts to re-think economics, such as that led by Wendy Carlin at University College, London, aim to reform curricula, examine what went wrong and re-introduce the history of economic thought. Such laudable initiatives will need to go far beyond the box of economic theory and incorporate all the recent scientific knowledge from other fields into a systems approach.[17]

International fora

The first responses to military globalisation were the short-lived League of Nations following the first World War in 1918 and after the second World War, the subsequent founding in 1945 of the United Nations (UN), which now has 193 member states The premise was that with all their sovereignty under the Treaty of Westphalia in 1648, nation states were now facing each other competitively in an interconnected world which required them to cooperate, share knowledge and

---

15 Henderson, Hazel, *Building a Win-Win World*, op. cit.
16 'Changing banking for good', Report of the Parliamentary Commission on Banking Standards, House of Lords, House of Commons, UK, 19 June, 2013.
17 "Keynes' New Heirs," *The Economist*, November 23, 2013, p. 58.

manage access to the oceans, atmosphere, electromagnetic spectrum, Antarctica and outer space.

Psychologist Stephen Pinker's historical global research indicates that violence actually has declined due to five trends in human societies: the expansion of governance, gentle commerce, feminisation, expanding empathy and the escalation of reason.[18] The Global Peace Index measures trends in 162 countries, ranking them on 22 indicators, costs of containing violence and a Positive Peace Index.[19] In spite of the horrors of internal conflicts such as in Syria, major wars between nations have decreased. While their citizens want peace, civilian prosperity and security, military-industrial interest groups lobby for bigger arms budgets, dwarfing those for human needs. Only an international forum, the UN, provides these nations with a venue to gather, negotiate and address the new global issues which no individual country could solve alone. This has led to another teachable moment: countries can pool their sovereignty![20]

The special agencies of the UN became drivers of new planetary awareness, new memes and norms which spread among member countries.[21] Since 1945, under UN mandates, treaties and protocols were enacted on environmental pollution, protecting oceans, forests, biodiversity, migrating birds, and curbing the hydrofluorocarbons that created the hole in the Earth's protective ozone layer. Clearly, norms and values were changing. Summits were convened on population, social conditions (poverty, education, health), women's empowerment promoting human rights, happiness and well-being and on environment in 1972, 1992, 2002 and Rio+20 in 2012.

---

18 Pinker, Stephen, *The Better Angels of Our Nature*, Viking, NY, 2011.

19 'Global Peace Index 2013: measuring the state of global peace', IEP Report 21, Institute for Economics & Peace, visionofhumanity.org, 2013.

20 *The United Nations: Policy and Financing Alternatives*, eds. Harlan Cleveland, Hazel Henderson and Inge Kaul, Elsevier Science, UK, 1995.

21 Henderson, Hazel, *Beyond Globalization*, Kumarian Press, Focus on the Global South, New Economics Foundation, London, 1999.

The Bretton Woods institutions, the IMF, and World Bank were launched in 1945 and later, after many conferences on trade, the World Trade Organization was initiated in 1996. Alas, these institutions were based on the obsolete economic textbooks which allowed 'externalising' of social and environmental costs and the faulty scorecard of GDP to measure nations' 'progress.' These obsolete rules[22] collided with the need to reform finance and cross-border financial flows.[23] An expanded popular awareness was leading to new approaches. The anomalies of financialization and 'economism' were becoming clearer. NGOs led debates on transforming finance, the need to examine the politics of money-creation, the role of credit, debt and resource allocation.

The impetus for all the learning and cooperation between countries was also to prevent conflicts and the outbreak of wars. The UN General Assembly in its September 2012 debates illuminated the conflicts between religions, democracy, freedom of speech and respect for cultural diversity. Thus, peacekeeping has always been central to the UN. Its outdated Security Council is now the target of needed reforms: expansion beyond the five permanent members, victorious countries of the second World War: the USA, Britain, France, Russia and China and to abolish their veto.

A useful set of proposals is offered in *The Great Convergence* by Singapore's former ambassador to the UN.[24] An effort to de-militarise nations and UN peace-keeping was the proposal for a UN Security Insurance Agency (UNSIA), allowing countries to follow Costa Rica's lead in abolishing its military in 1946. Nations could purchase insurance policies from this UN agency, guaranteeing a response if the insured country was attacked.[25] UNSIA was backed by several Nobel laureates,

---

22 Henderson, Hazel, 'Time to Internalize Those Externalities', GreenBiz, December 24, 2012.

23 Kevin P. Gallagher, 'Trade Rules Should Not Constrain Fixing Global Finance', *Real World Economics Review*, 26 September, 2012.

24 Mahbubani, Kishore, *The Great Convergence: Asia, the West, and the Logic of One World*, Public Affairs, New York, 2013.

25 Kay, Alan F. and Henderson, H, 'United Nations Security Insurance Agency (UNSIA)', *Futures*, Elsevier Science, UK, 1994; assessed by Col. Dan Smith, Center for Defence Information in *The United Nations: Policy and Financing Alternatives* (op. cit.), debated in the UN Security Council in 1996. See also, Kay, Alan F. and Smith, Dan, *Eliminating War,*

including former Costa Rican President Oscar Arias and debated in the UN Security Council in 1996. The emerging countries of India, Indonesia, South Africa and Brazil need to join the five permanent members on the Security Council, along with Japan. Now that Britain and France are less influential, there is a good case for one seat representing them, and the other countries of the European Union (EU).

The EU is itself an important social innovation: an example of cooperation among 28 formerly warring countries along the lines of the social innovation of the UN. In spite of its limitations and right-wing opposition in the USA, if the UN did not exist, we would need to invent it.

Notwithstanding the problems with its ill-designed currency – the euro,– the EU is a key innovation in human affairs and still a model for many other countries. An interdependent world needs social innovations as much or more than new technologies. These associations of nations raise huge issues of which essential functions to centralise and which to decentralise.

Age-old tensions: individual v. society

At the heart of today's human efforts to face our current global issues of governance, there are the deeper issues of individual rights versus the rights of groups, societies, other species and ecosystems. Recent re-visiting of Charles Darwin's *The Descent of Man* and *The Origin of Species* reveals how his research was used in Victorian Britain to glorify 'the survival of the fittest' and competition,[26] even though the phrase was coined by Herbert Spencer, a writer for *The Economist*.[27] Darwin actually held that humanity's survival was based on our genius for cooperating, bonding and even altruism.[28]

2009.

26 The Darwin Project, www.thedarwinproject.com.

27 *The Economist* editorial apologized for this 'poisoned phrase' and how it focused too much on competition and less on cooperation, 24 December, 2005.

28 Loye, David. *Darwin's Lost Theory of Love*, 2000, and Pinker, Stephen op. cit.

New research finds that human babies exhibit empathy and even altruism.[29] Using DNA samples from diverse populations in the USA geneticist Bryan Sykes at Oxford University, finds that virtually all have mixed DNA from Africa, Asia, Europe and indigenous peoples.[30] Such research is upending older ideas about nature versus nurture and shows there is no biological basis for racism and other prejudices. Our greatest challenge as a species lies in our growing population which continues to rise in those countries where women cannot control their own fertility. One study indicates that if these women had access to cheap solar energy and micro-finance official population projections of 9-10 billion by 2050 could be lowered by some 3 billion avoided births.[31]

Participation in democratic decision making becomes more complex as populations increase and demographics change presenting new challenges as evident in the ideological contests in Europe and the Middle East and driving political gridlock in the USA. Social innovations, in response, include expansion of human rights, the principles of 'subsidiarity' (keeping decisions relevant to every level as close to its affected population as possible) and the 'precautionary principle' (placing the burden of proof on those who seek to change established conventions or introduce pollution or unknown substances into ecosystems). The principle of 'sustainability' was introduced in the UN's Brundtland Commission's 1987 report, *Our Common Future*, and needs additional definition since it originally related to intergenerational equity in use of natural resources – a vital issue in climate change. Today, the term has been hijacked by corporations, governments and financiers to serve narrower purposes, eg, 'sustainable economic growth', 'sustainable corporate profits', etc., rendering the term almost meaningless. The social implications of these new post-Cartesian principles: interconnectedness, redistribution, change, complementarity, heterarchy and indeterminacy augured the transitions we see more clearly today.

---

29 Tucker, Abigail, 'Born to be Mild', Smithsonian, January 2013.
30 Sykes, Bryan, *DNA USA*, Oxford University Press, UK, 2012.
31 Khosla, Ashok, Lecture at the Tällberg Foundation, Sweden, 2009, www.ethicalmarkets.tv Khosla.

Diving into money design

After the financial crises of 2007–8, which are still devastating millions in many countries, 2012 and 2013 saw further scandals in the global banks' manipulation of LIBOR interest rates and the exposures of dark pools and high-frequency computerised trading.[32] No issues are more important than those of money creation, credit allocation, financial architecture and prudential regulation, monitoring and oversight – including offshore finance, tax avoidance and criminality.[33] These deeper issues are the focus of many NGOs, including the Public Banking Institute, the American Monetary Institute, the Center for New Economics, in the USA and the Finance Innovation Lab, Positive Money, BankTrack, New Economics Foundation (nef), the Green Money Working Group and others in Europe. Our manual for asset managers, Principles of Ethical Biomimicry Finance™ is now available for licensing.

Beyond traditional economic textbook definitions of capital, efficient markets, rational actors and property rights, new definitions emerged: social and human capital, ecological assets, amenity rights and recognition of the domains beyond markets, the commons (oceans, atmosphere, biodiversity, culture, information and electromagnetic spectrum).[34] Ethical Markets foresaw today's dilemma of structural unemployment due to automation and technology and why this causes collapsing aggregate demand in mature economies, and examined alternative access to purchasing power: guaranteeing minimum incomes, contingent cash transfers, employee stock ownership and cooperatives.[35] Contingent cash transfers in Brazil and Mexico have brought millions out of poverty and contributed to that country's recent successes – now leading their youth to demand farther social progress.

---

32 Arnuk, Sal L. and Joseph C. Saluzzi, *Broken Markets*, FT Press, 2012; Patterson, Scott. *Dark Pools*, Crown Business, New York, 2012.
33 Shaxson, Nicholas, *Treasure Islands*, Palgrave MacMillan, 2011.
34 As covered in the 13-part TV series 'Ethical Markets,' carried on PBS stations in the USA in 2005-2006 and available for college use at www.films.com.
35 www.ethicalmarkets.tv 'Transformation of Work', episode 2004.

Some economists adopted ecosystem perspectives and terms from biology, but with little effect on mainstream models.[36] The UN's programme on The Economics of Ecosystem and Biodiversity (TEEB) incorporates ecosystems services into the price system which has engaged the business community.[37] Global finance was first recognised as a part of the global commons at Bretton Woods in 1945 and subject to international rules and oversight of the IMF, World Bank and later the WTO.[38] These earlier rules are inadequate to prevent the unregulated risk-taking, exotic new instruments and leverage that led to the financial collapse of 2007–8 and the continuing social devastation it caused.

High frequency trading (HFT) by computers and algorithms will no doubt hasten the next financial blow-up, as discussed in 'Global Finance Lost in Cyberspace,' (2011)[39].

Throwing sand in the gears of financialization
The financial transaction taxes (FTT) I have advocated since 1996 have now been endorsed by the European Commission despite vigorous opposition from financial sectors and are in place in many countries. The most focused approach is as 'cancellation fees' since HFT traders enter many thousands of orders and cancel most of them in milliseconds.[40] Most types of FTT, all under 1%, are fiercely opposed by market players while their projected revenues to governments mired in budget deficits make them quite popular, particularly among NGOs. These FTTs are a better way to curb the excesses of high-frequency traders than, for example, economist Joseph Stiglitz's proposal that HFT positions in any stock must be held

---

36 See for example, *Ecological Economics*, the Journal of the International Society for Ecological Economics, Elsevier Science, UK.
37 Kumar, Pushpam; Pavan Sukhdev (Ethical Markets Advisory Board), et al, *The Economics of Ecosystems and Biodiversity: Ecological and Economic Foundations*, Pushpam Kumar, ed. Earthscan, 2010.
38 Transforming Finance, www.ethicalmarkets.tv and at www.transformingfinance.net for additional co-signers.
39 Henderson, Hazel, 'Global Finance Lost in Cyberspace', InterPress Service, 2011.
40 Henderson, Hazel, 'Transforming Finance Still a Top Priority', CSRWire, 8 February, 2013.

for at least one second![41] Computer expert in electronic markets Dave Lauer, refutes the claims of HFT traders that their practices improve markets.[42] Meanwhile, NGOs, ATTAC and those promoting FTT as the 'Robin Hood Tax' are joined by Occupy activists and intellectuals including Brett Scott, author of *The Heretic's Guide to Global Finance*.[43]

The subsidy barrier to transition

The 'elephant' blocking more rapid progress has been clearly identified: the powerful, incumbent fossil fuel sectors which finance 10 major US 'think tanks' and media campaigns against green energy.[44]

The resurgent fossil fuels in shale-based natural gas and oil, Canada's tar sands, as well as the nuclear industry (even after Fukushima-Daichi) – all still enjoy outsize subsidies from most governments. Global subsidies to fossil fuels in 2012 exceeded $520bn.[45] The resulting incorrect pricing, together with still uncounted negative externalities, continues driving mis-investing: for example, new coal plants in Europe which are unjustified on both economic and environmental grounds.[46] In the Rio+20 Declaration[47], these subsidies were identified as the key barriers to the level playing field required to fully utilise existing renewable energy technologies and speed the transition to green economies.

Pledges to reduce these subsidies, negative externalities, as well as shift government tax policies and procurement budgets to greener technologies at

---

41 Gore, Al, *The Future*, Random House, 2013; Henderson, Hazel. <u>Review</u> in SeekingAlpha.com.

42 Lauer, Dave, 'Confronting High-Frequency Trading: David vs. Goliath's Evil Twin', Huffington Post, 11 June, 2012.

43

44 Fossil Fuel Front Groups on the Front Page, <u>www.checksandbalancesproject.org</u>, December 2012.

45 World Energy Outlook, International Energy Agency, Paris, 2012.

46 'Europe's Dirty Secret', Briefing: Coal in the rich world, *The Economist*, 5 January, 2013, 54-56.

47 (<u>www.uncsd2012.org</u>)

Rio+20 were accompanied by commitments to reform finance and its conventional metrics. These included correcting national accounts by reformulating GDP indicators widely favoured by the public in 11 countries[48] and to internalise formerly externalised costs at all levels including corporate balance sheets and accounting practices. The UN report from Secretary-General Ban Ki-moon, 'Happiness: Toward a Holistic Approach to Development' outlines considerable progress by UN agencies, the OECD and many countries to shift beyond GDP to subjective measures of well-being, satisfaction, happiness as well as objective measures of education, health, poverty, social exclusion, adequacy of public welfare and services and environmental quality.[49]

In the private sector, a survey by Novethic found that nearly one-third of institutional investors managing €4.5bn use environmental, social and governance (ESG) metrics for long-term risk management.[50] A group of seasoned cleantech asset managers saw 2013 as an inflection point for the rise of the green economy.[51] A survey of 1,300 US companies in 2012 found growth rates for green business products and services rising faster than conventional goods.[52] The OECD's 2013 'Green Growth Papers' reviewed the rapid progress among its 37 member countries.[53]

---

48 (Globescan survey, 2013, www.ethicalmarkets.com Beyond GDP)

49 Ban Ki-moon, 'Happiness: Toward a Holistic Approach to Development', Note by the Secretary-General, United Nations General Assembly Sixty-seventh Session, Agenda Item 14, 16 January, 2013.

50 'Asset owners using ESDG for long-term risk management', IPE, 11 December, 2012.

51 Konrad, Tom, 'A Clean Energy Inflection Point in 2013?', AltEnergyStocks.com, 6 January, 2013.
    Jabush, Garvin. '2013: Green Economy Inflection Point', AltEnergyStocks.com, 6 January, 2013.

52 Marcacci, Silvio, 'The Big Green Business Opportunity for America's Economy', Cleantechnica.com, 15 June , 2013.

53 'What have we learned from attempts to introduce green-growth policies?', Green Growth Papers, OECD, March 2013.

Part 2 The Role of Economics

2.1 How Neo-classical Economics Became the Mainstream and why it matters

John Weeks

Economic Fakery[54]

Many if not most people feel a certain uneasy awe when confronted by economic issues and economists themselves. The awe results from a belief that economists hold profound knowledge of society. Just as physics provides the knowledge to unravel the mysteries of the universe, economics reveals the esoteric workings of finance, production and distribution. And in common with physics, the knowledge that allows economics and economists to understand the hidden workings of markets is far too complex and specialized for the public to understand.

This perception of incomprehensible complexity of markets leads people to view economic policies as a field for experts, which produces the unease that accompanies the awe. The informed citizen may reach an opinion on economic issues, then frequently find that it conflicts with expert assessment of economists. The latter frequently seems extremely conservative and occasionally contrary to basic human sentiments.

---

54 The issues addressed in this chapter are discussed in more detail in John Weeks, *Economics of the 1%: How mainstream economics serves the rich, obscures reality and distorts policy* (London: anthem Press, 2014), and for a technical presentation, *The Irreconcilable Inconsistencies of Neoclassical Macroeconomics: False Paradigm* (Oxford: Routledge, 2012).

For example, the concerned citizen may feel that an international convention to prohibit child labour is essential to providing children with a decent life,[55] only to discover from economists in the mainstream media that the convention would be "counter-productive". Far from helping children, such a prohibition would drive families deeper into poverty by eliminating this source of income. Two mainstream economist tell us in an article in the prestigious *Economic Journal*, "although intuitive and morally compelling, a ban on the worst forms of child labour in poor countries is unlikely to be welfare improving".[56] Yet another example of do-gooders harming those they wish to help.

Much of the population in North America and Europe is also under the impression that paying women less than men for similar work is discrimination, as is paying minorities less. The common man or woman is wrong again -- three economists at the US National Bureau for Economic Research demonstrated in 2009 that what appears to be "discrimination" against women can be fully explained by differences in training, "career continuity" (aka, having children) and hours worked.[57] Many people also believe that the salaries paid to business executives are outrageous. The mainstream of the economics profession tells us that on the contrary these high salaries reward entrepreneurship that makes market economies dynamic.[58]

Confronted with these arguments the non-economist typically throws up her/his hands and declares, "I don't care if child labour, high executive salaries, etc, are good economics, it's just plain wrong". These justifications of anti-social outcomes are without doubt "just plain wrong". In addition, they are bad economics, from

---

55 The International Labour Organization has pressed for prohibition on child labour since its creation immediately WWI. Details of existing and proposed international conventions are found on its website, http://www.ilo.org/ipec/facts/ILOconventionsonchildlabour/lang--en/index.htm.

56 Sylvain Dessy and Stephane Pallage, "A Theory of the Worst Forms of Child Labour," *Economic Journal* 115, 500, 68-87 (2005).

57 The original study is here, http://www.nber.org/papers/w14681.pdf

58 The argument that high salaries are socially efficient is reviewed and demolished in Scott Elaurant, "Corporate Executive Salaries - the Argument from Economic Efficiency", http://ejbo.jyu.fi/pdf/ejbo_vol13_no2_pages_35-43.pdf

analysis based on nonsense. The consistent commitment of the global mainstream economics profession to a reactionary social ideology results from a right wing seizure of the profession, not from expertise, knowledge or understanding in matters economic.

Beginning in the 1970s, the right wing of the economics profession, the "neoclassicals", embarked upon an aggressive campaign to take ideological and institutional control of the discipline. And "discipline" loomed large in their successful seizure of the profession. They methodically purged it of even the mildest dissidents. This Inquisition-style ideological cleansing represented an intellectual regression to the pre-Enlightenment. Purged along with the dissidents were all arguments critical of "market forces" or supportive of public intervention to alter the outcomes generated by the "impersonal" forces of competition.

The loss of the economics profession to the neoclassicals is the equivalent of astrologers taking over astronomy departments, alchemists occupying the chemistry laboratories of the great research institutions, and creationists setting the syllabus for a genetics course. This defeat of rational thought might be viewed as a shocking but minor crime were it not that the neoclassical nonsense is viewed by politicians and the public as the source of economic wisdom. The neoclassicals successfully label the victims of the purge as ignorant and incompetent (whether they call themselves Keynesians, Institutionalists, Ricardians, Marxists or some eclectic mixture).

The neoclassicals, not the dissidents, are the incompetents, burdening a once-respectable profession with an intellectual dead weight of absurd inconsistencies presented as theory. Like astrologers and alchemists presented a barrier to interpreting the natural world, neoclassicals prevent understanding market societies. As a result of the neoclassical seizure of the profession, there is no policy or market outcome so reactionary or outrageously antisocial that some mainstream economist will not defend it. Among the more appalling of these reactionary absurdities is that income gaps due to gender and race discrimination are an illusion, unemployment is voluntary, and sweatshops are good.

The neoclassicals systematically sows confusion and ignorance by a false version of economic relations. They are *econfakers*, practicing a pseudo-scientific *fakeconomics*, just as astrologers practice astrology and alchemists alchemy. The neoclassicals achieved their domination of the profession by shamelessly serving the interests of the rich (Häring and Douglas 2012, chapter 1). These faithful servants of neoliberal ideology are not strictly speaking "economists", if by that term we mean "those who seek to understand and explain real economic phenomenon". Instead, the neoclassicals construct an imaginary world far from anyone's reality. They should be recognized as the fakes they are and so labelled, "econfakers practicing fakeconomics".

Foundation of Economic Nonsense
The central unifying element in the neoclassical mainstream is the assumption that market economies are always and continuously at *full employment*. All their theoretical and policy conclusions derive from that fanciful base. It is the unrelenting and unapologetic presumption of full employment, contrary to economic reality, that most qualifies the mainstreamers as "fakers" propounding and zealously defending a fake version of market society.

The ideology of fakeconomics derives from a major illogical inference or syllogism: the resources of each country and the world are insufficient to meet human needs, and, therefore, decisions on how to allocate those limited resources for human satisfaction dominates human existence. For the econfakers "economics" is the (pseudo)science of "the allocation of limited resources to achieve unlimited human needs".[59]

Can any sane person disagree that resources are limited? The effect of human activity on the global climate should alone make that obvious. Scarcity is equally obvious when you reflect on world population growth, meeting the basic needs of

---

59 The classic statement of this approach is, "Economics is the science which studies human behaviour as a relationship between given ends and scarce means which have alternative uses." Lionel (Lord) Robbins, *An Essay on the Nature and Significance of Economic Science* 1932, 16.

the increasing population, the possibility of natural resource limits ("peak oil"), and the aging of the population that leaves fewer workers to support more retirees. Because scarcity is real, economics must study how to set the guidelines for allocating our limited resources to best achieve the needs of all humanity. Isn't that what "rebalancing is all about"?

No, it is not. It is the intellectual virus that mutated economics into fakeconomics. Its power lies in its superficial appearance of truth. The belief that full employment is the normal state for market societies began to take hold in the profession in the second half of the nineteenth century, not present in the work of the founders of economics from Adam Smith through John Stuart Mill.

The analytical importance to fakeconomics of the generalization that scarcity rules human existence cannot be exaggerated. It is the necessary foundation of the market parables summarized in the phrase "supply and demand". The principle of scarcity underpins commonplace statements of the type, "executive salaries are determined by supply and demand", or "supply and demand dictate the prices at supermarkets".

"Supply and demand" statements serve as voodoo incantations, conveying compelling messages at several levels of consciousness, some of which we do not completely realize. These incantations attribute a naturalism to markets, their operations and their outcomes.. The commercial relationships we observe, and the prices associated with those relationships, do not result from the arbitrary actions of men and women, nor from the laws and regulations of governments.

Supply and demand stories preach that natural laws of economics control us and dictate specific outcomes. Because they arise from forces beyond individual discretion, tampering with these specific outcomes leads to an accumulation of economic maladies too disastrous to contemplate. The scarcity principle preaches that markets may appear as social institutions, but they result from nature, the unavoidable need to allocate what is scarce. The comparison to religious dogma should be obvious- God (or gods) are not social creations, they exist whether you believe in them or not.

Incantations of "supply and demand" also repel attempts by critics to regulate market. They expose critics as either ignorant dreamers of a communitarian Never-Never Land, or the nefarious purveyors of authoritarian collectivism. The naïve and the nefarious have ignorance in common, ignorance of basic human nature that manifests itself in the mundane setting of the supermarket: the prices we pay result from unlimited human wants and finite resources to satisfy them. Buying and selling are inherent in human nature like the instinct to mate. They may follow social conventions, but there are natural in origin. The authority for this economic naturalism is Adam Smith himself, the idol of econfakers, who wrote "the propensity to truck, barter and exchange one thing for another is common to all men" (*Wealth of Nations*, Book 1, Chapter 2, paragraph 1).[60] The human propensity to exchange implies that markets arise from human nature itself, just as nature brings forth the flora and fauna of the world. From this naturalism to the conclusion that regulating markets ("interfering") contradicts human nature is a short step.

While fakeconomics claims deep and impenetrable knowledge of markets, it is eager to put the matter simply -- we cannot have everything we want. But by balancing work and leisure, and allocating our expenditures rationally, we can achieve the best outcome consistent with the scarcity inherent in nature and infinity of human desires (also natural). Few people understand this subtle and sublime optimization process even as they act it out, similarly perhaps to the bird that constructs its nest without ever taking an engineering course in strength of materials.

---

60 Adam Smith, *An Inquiry into the Nature and Causes of the Wealth of Nations* (Book 1, Chapter 2, paragraph 1). This can be found in an online version on the website of the modestly named "Library of Economics and Liberty", http://www.econlib.org/library/Smith/smWN.html.

Little does the individual realize that each trip to the supermarket, excursion to a department store and stop to fill the tank of the car is but a small part of a grand scheme to resolve the tension between the scarcity of resources and the infinity of wants. Though individuals may grumble at the prices they pay to achieve their state of grace, those prices are the outcome of millions of people seeking bliss through market relationships.

This reactionary principle of scarcity is false. The inferences drawn from it are invalid. Resources are not scarce. Wants are not unlimited. There is no "law of supply and demand". It is all made-up nonsense that serves the interests of the rich and prevents the policies to build a better world.

Supply and Demand Fakery

To clear this fog of faux naturalism we must go back to basics. The "supply" of a commodity or service and the "demand" for it are theoretical constructions. These theoretical constructions exist only in an imaginary world in which no buyer or seller has power to influence market outcomes, what fakeconomics calls "perfect competition". No such "perfectly competitive" markets exist. Buying and selling, prices rising and falling, and gluts and shortages of commodities are not the operation of any economic law, and certainly not something that could legitimately be called the law of supply and demand, or the "law" of anything.

Commodities are produced and delivered to wholesale and retail distributors. People, companies and governments demonstrate how much they want of these commodities by purchasing them from the distributors. In this simple, everyday sense commodities have a supply and there is a demand for them. The words mean nothing more than "someone sells" and "someone buys". The real world activities of buying and selling are not the "law of supply and demand" made infamous by econfakers, and so eagerly misrepresented by free market ideologues in journalistic outlets such as the *Economist*.

Real world production, distribution and exchange are subject to manipulation through market power by both buyers and sellers. To take the obvious example, producers of petroleum do not passively accept prices. They manipulate prices directly through price fixing agreements or indirectly by adjusting what they offer for sale. Supply and demand do not determine oil prices. Quite the contrary, administered oil prices determine how much will be bought, and the petroleum producers match their "supply" to that demand.

As any first year student learns in introductory economics (more accurately, introductory fakeconomics), the "supply" to which the "law of supply and demand" does *not* mean an amount. The word refers to a list of quantities of a commodity that a producer would *offer* for sale at different prices. These are not actual sales or deliveries to the retailer. The quantities on the list or schedule are planned or anticipated amounts that might be supplied were various anticipated prices to appear in the market.

For example, a tailor might plan to produce and deliver five custom made shirts over a week at a price of fifty dollars each, eight if the price rises to sixty dollars, and so on. It might appear obvious to the untutored that a producer offers more when prices rise. This simple relationship proves extremely difficult for the econfakers to establish.

These offers and the anticipated prices cannot be observed. They are imaginary, sometimes called "notional" supply in the fakeconomics jargon. When producers match the imaginary quantities with prices, this matching has an extremely important property. The producer must believe that each planned quantity will be entirely sold at the anticipated price. Formally stated, the "supply" of "supply and demand" consists of the quantities of beer, computers, *etc.* that each company offers at each conceivable price, firm in the belief that sales are potentially unlimited. But if potential sales have no limit, from where come the quantities to match the prices? Why not increase "supply" until the tailor shop operates twenty-four hours with as many assistants that the master tailor can pack in?

If each item a company produced were the same, for example a DVD of the *Titanic*, we would expect each to have the same cost of production as output increases.

The problem comes when trying to combine this reasonable idea of constant unit costs with the improbable idea that companies decide their supply offers believing they have no sales limit.

The combination, constant unit cost and unlimited sales, implies that the DVD producer would run its machinery twenty-four hours a day, 365 days a year, producing all the digital disks it possibly could. We should observe producers, from the tailor to the multinational, operating continuously at maximum capacity. We do not observe this. Idle capacity shows itself frequently, even continuously. Either the logic is incomplete or it is fundamentally wrong.

What began as an apparently simple idea, markets themselves generate prices determined by the supply and demand, and producers and consumers act upon them proves exceedingly difficult to establish in logic, much less in practice. The solution to the "supply and demand" puzzle requires additional pieces unanticipated when we began, some with very strange shapes. With unlimited demand and constant unit costs, there would be only two levels of production ("supply"). If the selling price is below unit cost, the company makes losses and drops the product from its sales list (zero supply). If the price rises above unit cost, the company produces at full capacity output.

Any other production level, between zero and maximum, would mean that the quantity produced and offered came from an estimate of the company's anticipated sales. While this inference seems reasonable and realistic, it has a devastating impact on the "fundamental law of supply and demand". When anticipated sales determine production, the anticipated quantity demanded dictates the actual quantity supplied. *Supply and demand are the same thing*.

If "supply and demand" determine prices, then supply and demand must be independent of each other. To use common metaphor, the "scissors of supply and demand" must have two blades, not one. Buyers ("consumers") determine demand and sellers determine supply. If constant unit costs characterize a company's production, anticipated (predicted) sales determine supply, "supply" and "demand" coincide. Independence of supply from demand (predicted sales) requires that the company believe that the demand for its product is limitless. If demand is limitless and unit costs constant, supply is independent of demand, but we have only two possible outcomes, zero and maximum. The famous law of supply and demand seems to paint itself into a tautological corner.

An escape route exists if we can abandon constant unit costs. Doing so leads to intractable complications. If a company's unit costs continuously rise as output increases, then it will not continue to operate for long. Under pressure of price competition, the company managers would discover that in order to lower unit costs they must reduce the level of production continuously, driving output and sales down, down, until closure.

The opposite case is, if anything, even worse for the putative Law of Supply and Demand. Continuously declining unit cost leads to monopoly (as does the constant unit cost case). Each company will increase its scale of operations until one company can satisfy the entire market. Railroads during the nineteenth and first half of the twentieth century provide a clear example of falling unit costs, as the huge fixed investment spread over larger and larger scale of operation. As a result, the railroads in every country in the world are either a public monopoly or publicly regulated private monopolies.

What can salvage the Law of Supply from tautology? Constant unit costs cannot generate a meaningful supply curve, nor can falling or rising unit costs. A process of analytical elimination leads to a solution, albeit rather absurd. We require a plausible explanation of why unit costs might first fall, level off, then rise, resulting in "U-shaped" unit cost. If this unlikely sequence could be justified and generalized, it provides hope for the concept of "supply". A "U-shaped" company would have a minimum unit cost resting somewhere between the falling and rising portion.

A superficially credible supply and demand story might go as follows. On the belief that they can sell as much as they can produce, companies set their production at the cost level that maximizes profit. As the market price increases, this compensates for rising unit costs and induces the company to offer a larger quantity for sale. Over time, competition among producers forces companies to their lowest unit cost point. If the level of output for minimum unit cost contributes just a small fraction to total consumer sales, then the industry can support many companies.

The mechanism to avoid monopoly on the one hand and zero production on the other has been found, in the simple letter "U" applied to unit costs. An unfortunate difficulty remains. U-shaped unit cost structures do not exist in the real world. The "solution" requires a bold *ex machina* step. In the absence of a known mechanism for such a cost structure, econfakers make one up and repeat it endlessly as if it were credible. The inventive creation is the fakeconomics Law of Diminishing Returns. This new law states that if we combine more of a "variable input" (i.e. workers) with a "fixed input" (plant and machinery, "capital"), "output increases but at a diminishing rate". Out of thin air this "law" generates the U-shaped production story so desperately needed.

The famous Law of Diminishing Returns suffers from misnaming, because "diminishing returns" do not yield the necessary U-shape for costs. This magical shape requires that "returns" first *increase* (the declining or first part of the "U"), then begin to decrease or "diminish" (the rising or second part of the "U"). Mere "diminishing returns" leave the company with a fatal case of continuously increasing costs, discussed above. The Law of Increasing-then-Diminishing Returns is imaginary, a Rube Goldberg attachment to a Heath Robinson "Law of Supply".

The Law of Supply and Demand that determines market prices has no existence except in the feverish imaginations of econfakers. The "supply" part cannot be logically specified or empirically verified. If companies believe they have no sales constraint, they would always be at full capacity. If they estimate their sales constraint, then the amount offered and sold are the same. A little non-ideological common sense reveals that all the complicated stuff about supply and demand is nonsense, unnecessary obfuscation of how companies make decisions and markets operate.

Resources are Abundant

As illogical and contradictory as supply and demand may be, a more serious problem faces fakeconomics. The generalization that resources are scarce underpins its entire analytical structure. The problem is that resources are not scarce. To the contrary, they are abundant. The people of a country and their working capacity constitute the most important resource in every society. If labour is in excess supply, unemployment, it is not scarce.

During the Great Depression civilian unemployment in the United States reached a peak of twenty-five percent of the labour force in 1933, one out of every four working people. It persisted in double digits until 1941, the eve of United States entry into the Second World War (Congress declared war in early December). During 1943-45 the rate edged below two percent, and would never again fall so low. For the sixty-five years, 1950-2014, the annual unemployment rate dropped below four percent in only eight years, and not once after 1969. In Britain during the last fifty years, unemployment fell below four percent in only four, all consecutive (1971-1974). After 1974 unemployment averaged almost 7.5 percent of the labour force.

Has unemployment persisted because workers in Britain and the United States lazy? A more obvious answer presents itself. Some major change occurred over the last three decades to render society less capable of providing employment for those who seek it. That change occurred as a result of the implementation of fakeconomics policies by governments all over the world, policy imitating bad art. With an average unemployment rate over the last twenty years of six percent in the United States and seven in the United Kingdom, only econfakers and their business patrons see scarce resources (and probably not the patrons, who live in the real world).

When something is in surplus, it is not scarce. The remote possibility that labour could suffer from a shortage at some time in the future does not make scarcity economics plausible. If you cannot use all of something, there is no danger of running out of it. In most countries in most years we find no scarcity of labour or the machinery to employ that labour. Only rarely does the problem of how to allocate scarce resources arise in a market economy. How to mobilize and use productively the available resources plagues market economies. Mainstream economics offers no solution. It denies the existence of the problem.

Competitiveness and Globalization

"Globalization" provides the bottom line of the fakeconomics ideology. Whatever one's opinion of the post-war social democratic policies, the globalized economy has rendered them impossible to implement. Whether resources are scarce or abundant, global imperatives rule. The need to keep the economy competitive in world markets not only rules out most forms of public intervention, it dictates a set of national policies that every country must follow. These policies include balanced budgets, low inflation, free trade and unrestricted capital flows. Governments deviate from these policies at their peril.

This seems a compelling if disturbing argument -- no more progressive economic policies because of the reaction by "global financial markets". Therefore, whether the underlying theory is correct or incorrect, weak or strong, it accurately describes the world in which we find ourselves. This is the TINA defence of fakeconomics -- whatever its problems, There-Is-No-Alternative (TINA) but to embrace it, anti-social warts and all.

Like so many of the arguments in fakeconomics ideology, the TINA defence assumes what it seeks to prove. The ideology presents a hypothesis, that the current characteristics of the world economy are the inevitable result of forces beyond the control of individuals or governments. Most important among those characteristics are 1) international trade dictates that national labour market and social welfare policies must foster competitiveness, and 2) massive and rapid capital movements dictate the macroeconomic policies that governments can implement.

On the company and household level ("microeconomics") the TINA principle means that employers must have the right to hire and fire workers without constrain from bureaucratic regulations. Such "flexible" labour market policies facilitate lowering costs and raising productivity. Households must accept lower and fewer social support payments, because these prevent wage flexibility. In addition, unemployment support and payments such as housing benefits reduce the incentive to work. If the British, US or any other economy hopes to compete with exports from Asia, especially China, "reform" of social support programmes cannot be postponed, much less avoided.

As for macroeconomic policies, the lesson is clear -- balanced budgets, reduce taxes, and keep inflation low. Governments must balance their budgets to maintain the confidence of international investors. Public deficits, even modest ones, may provoke speculation on the national currency or government bonds. The experience of numerous countries in the euro zone provides clear evidence of the need to follow the balanced budget rule. There is no alternative to the sound policy of balanced budget, and UK citizens have George Osborne to thank for doggedly implementing austerity.

The TINA principle is another manifestation of the naturalistic misrepresentation of market relations, that their operation results from inevitable and inescapable forces beyond the control of human agency. Water runs downhill, budgets must be balanced. The first is dictated by the laws of gravity, the second by ideology.

On close inspection it proves to be nothing more than pro-business ideology. For Big Capital and its ideologues globalization means two things, "free trade" and "free capital flow". The enthusiastic globalizers treat the first as self-evidently desirable, bringing benefits to all. A media article or commentary critical of "free trade" is so rare as to make dentures in chickens common by comparison. However, it proves extremely difficult to establish the benefits of "free" or even "freer" trade.

Despite claims by the econfakers of analytical rigour, the key concepts in this "theory" are not and cannot be rigorously defined, and cannot be measured. The central claim is that countries with cheap labour will gain by specializing in labour-intensive commodities and exchanging them for capital intensive commodities produced in countries where capital is cheap ("comparative advantage"). For example, the United States should export things that use a lot of machinery and not much labour, and China should do the reverse.

This sounds reasonable. Poor countries export to rich countries things produced with a lot of labour, and rich countries do the reverse. This superficially reasonable proposition is gibberish, having the coherence of a random series of words. The first problem is the word "cheap". To the person in the street, the meaning of "cheap labour" seems obvious, lower wages (converted with the appropriate exchange rate and other adjustments). If this "cheap labour" were the basis of trade, no case could be made for it generating benefits for all. "Cheap labour" paves the road for the "race to the bottom", and does not bring "gains for all".

The trade imbalances in the euro zone early this century provide a case in point. The European Commission, International Monetary Fund and the German government offered wage reduction in the trade deficit countries as the solution. Whether or not this prescription would work, and it cannot bring benefits to all unless one considers descent into poverty a beneficial outcome.

In the trade theory of fakeconomics "cheap" is defined as "relatively abundant". For example, labour is cheap in China compared to the United States if the ratio of the total labour force to the total capital stock in China is lower than the same ratio in the United States. To put it simply, we find lots of workers for each machine in China, and lots of machines for every worker in the United States. Economists as well as econfakers have tried to measure that ratio for well over a century, without success.

Why construct such a convoluted definition of "cheap" when we have an unambiguously straight-forward definition? If we use the simple definition, it implies that *absolute* costs determine trade flows. If low costs make exporters "competitive", then a big country with good infrastructure and low wages would have the possibility of producing almost every commodity cheaper and overwhelming all its global competitors as Chinese exporters have done. The result is persistent trade imbalances and recurrent national and global financial instability.

Mainstream theory encounters a problem: logic and practice indicate that unregulated markets tend to generate unsustainable trade imbalances among countries. The theorist seeks a solution from this ideologically unpalatable result by creation of a concept consciously designed to resolve the difficulty, in this case "relative abundance" of labour and capital. The rescuing concept proves to be nonsense, as the "U-shaped" cost curve is. Strange as it may seem, we can find no sensible way to measure the ratio of labour to capital in or across countries.

A head count of workers will not serve the purpose, because of the variation in skills and training within and across countries. And the problem of measuring labour pales compared to difficulties with calibrating the capital stock with its quality differences due to variations in age and obsolescence. The "gains from trade" hypothesis consists of nonsense derivative from smoke and mirrors.

The entire globalization-TINA argument is based on a false premise, that changes in the world economy result from forces beyond human control. The two most important changes have been 1) the dramatic increase in international capital flows, and 2) the rise of China as the world's largest exporter. Neither resulted from forces beyond human control. On the contrary, policy changes drove both.

The "free trade" dogma seeks to disguise the reality of international exchange as a benignly competitive activity that brings goods and services to people in countries where those items are not or cannot be produced. Surely, that is a benefit, even if the theory upon which trade is justified is rotten to the core. What the ideologues of free trade never tell us is that it is an major source of environmental damage, mainly through pollution caused by transporting consumer and producer goods.

To take the worst example, food trade transported by air accounts for just one percent of all food trade, and 11% of world carbon emissions.[61] More goods moving across the globe, the goal of free trade ideologues, is bad for our health.[62] As John Maynard Keynes wrote, "let goods be homespun whenever its is reasonably and conveniently possible".[63]

The fervent defence of unregulated trade goes hand-in-hand with enthusiasm for more global capital flows. Prior to the 1980s international capital flows played a relatively minor role in the world economy. First, various types of regulations severely restricted capital movements in both advanced and developing countries. Among the most important were foreign exchange controls and regulations on the activities of commercial banks. For example, until Margaret Thatcher became prime minister, exchange regulations limited the amount of foreign currency that a UK citizen could purchase. In the United States the Glass-Steagall Act of 1933 prohibited commercial banks from engaging in a range of activities including speculation of all sorts, on currencies, real estate and derivatives of all sorts.

For the first seventy years of the twentieth century international practice or formal treaties determined the exchange rates among countries when the world was not at war. In the early decades national governments operated under the infamous "gold standard", which set each currency in relation to gold. In addition, government held their foreign reserves in gold, which was used to balance trade accounts across countries. At the end of WWII the victorious powers through the Bretton Woods agreement established a variation on the gold standard, with the US dollar playing the role of gold.[64]

---

61 Helena Stratford, "Food Miles: The environmental impact of food," *Pollution Issues*, 2 June 2014, http://www.pollutionissues.co.uk/food-miles-environmental-impact-food.html

62 This is elaborated in John Weeks, "Trade and the Triple Crisis," *Triple Crisis*, June 2014, http://triplecrisis.com/trade-and-the-triple-crisis/.

63 J. M. Keynes, "National Self-sufficiency," *The Yale Review*, 22, 4 (1933), 755-769. The major aspects of this extremely important New Deal legislation are explained at http://www.federalreservehistory.org/Events/DetailView/25.

64 The UK delegation to the 1944 Bretton Woods negotiations was led by John Maynard Keynes. I discuss the Bretton Woods system in John Weeks, "A Progressive International

Again, currency rates were fixed. Under the "Bretton Woods system" speculation on currencies occurred only when a government found that it could no longer maintain its fixed rate to the dollar. The combination of Bretton Woods fixed rates and national restrictions on private capital flows reduced "hot money" speculation to insignificance. All that changed in 1970s when gathering pressure on the US balance of payments prompted the government of Republican Richard Nixon to withdraw unilaterally from the "dollar standard" by ending the fixed dollar price of gold.[65]

The end of formally fixed exchange rates opened the possibility of wide spread currency speculation. It required financial deregulation to turn that possibility into reality.[66] From the 1970s onward governments in the advanced countries, especially in the United States and the United Kingdom (after the election of Margaret Thatcher), implemented a deregulation of financial capital.[67] The effect of this deregulation was the liberation of finance capital to speculate not only on currencies, but on everything bought and sold, public bonds, mortgages (the "sub-prime crisis"), commodities including food, and every conceivable type of financial asset (and some invented just for speculative purposes – "derivatives").

Beginning in the late 1980s speculative capital could claim authorship of disaster after disaster: the US stock market collapse of 1987 ("Black Monday"), the US "savings and loan" crisis (1989-1991, cost $90 billion), Mexican *peso* crisis (1994), the Asian financial crisis (1997), the Russian financial crisis (1998), and the "dot-com"

Monetary System: Growth-Enhancing, Speculation-Reducing and Cross-country Equity," in *Economic Policies, Governance and the New Economics*, Philip Arestis and Malcolm Sawyer (eds) (Basingstoke: Palgrave, 2013).

65 My doing so the Nixon government broke the international treaty agreed and signed just after WWII.. The end of the dollar standard is described on the web site of the International Monetary Fund, https://www.imf.org/external/about/histend.htm.

66 John Weeks, *Economics of the 1%: How mainstream economics serves the rich, obscures reality and distorts policy* (London: anthem Press, 2014), Chapters 3 & 10.

67 Deregulation in the United States is explained in non-technical language in Ismael Hossein-zadeh, *Beyond Mainstream Explanations of the Financial Crisis* (Oxford: Routledge, 2014), Chapter 4.

speculative bubble (2001-2002, wiping out $5 trillion in papers "assets"). These provided the prelude to the biggest of them all, the Global Financial Crisis of 2008, which would send tens of millions of people throughout the world into unemployment and poverty.

What possible defence or justification could there be for the continued deregulation of finance capital in light of its habitually destructive nature, to the point of criminality and beyond? The answer, is "none", but the Lords and Ladies of Finance give it a try. The best they can offer is that the global "free flow" of capital lowers borrowing costs and thereby contributes to global growth and prosperity. To put it crudely (and the apologists for financial disasters are nothing if not crude) -- if free trade in commodities is good, free flow of money must be even better.[68]

The ideologues of finance augment this rather lame abstract justification, free capital flow results in cheaper borrowing, with an allegedly practical one. Whether or not free capital flow brings benefits to all, regulating global financial movements proves impossible in practice, TINA (there-is-no-alternative).

There is an alternative to the despotic rule of global finance capital. The removal of domestic regulations on international trade and capital flows liberated capital to impose its rule. Re-introduction of previous and new regulations will return finance capital to its previous constrained role in the world economy. The enthusiasts for globalization dismiss re-regulation of capital by the public sector as an anachronistic pipe dream, "we have moved on from that", one frequently reads or hears from the media.

Officials at the International Monetary Fund are rarely accused of being dreamers, yet the organized officially endorses re-introduction of national capital controls

---

68 This argument is found in one of those ultra-neoliberal articles that no critic of globalization could make up as a straw ma. See, Shailendra J. Anjaria, "The Capital Truth: What works for commodities should work for cash," *Foreign Affairs* , November/December 1998.

(albeit it took the IMF a very long time to reach that position).[69]   The same technological changes that facilitate the rapid, indeed instantaneous, movement of hot money serve to trace and regulate those movements. The same measures used to trace and prevent the "laundering" of money from criminal activities can be employed to control capital flows in general.[70]

The debilitating effects of "free trade" and the rule of financial capital are not the inevitable outcomes of a globalized world.   These maladies result from the conscious application of policies to liberate capital from social regulation. In other rich and poor countries the vast majority of the population suffer from unemployment, falling real incomes and a degradation of the environment as a result of the laws of politics not the laws of economics -- if it has the political power, the global 1% rules in its own interest.

Capitalism Fit for Human Life
The power of neoclassical/fakeconomics arguments comes from their repetition and serve to the rich, not from their theoretical or empirical validity. They are all based on a theory that is internally contradictory and ideologically driven. The fundamental issue in a democratic society is not whether inflation, foreign trade, public deficits or unemployment are too high or too low. The fundamental issue is, who decides?

The general rule in democratic societies is that experts advise and democratically elected representatives decide. Mainstream economics provides the ideological foundation for canceling that rule: elected representatives should enact laws that make the advice of neoclassical experts legally binding. This anti-democratic ideology sharply reduces the danger that the many will pressure for policy that limits the privileges of the few.

---

69 The IMF policy guidelines are summarized in the organization's online policy magazine, http://www.imf.org/external/pubs/ft/survey/so/2012/pol120312a.htm
70 A recent set of studies on capital flight from Africa show in detail how these measures can be effective. See S. Ibi Ajayi & Leonce Ndikumana (eds.) *Capital Flight from Africa: Causes, Effects and Policy Issues* (Oxford: Oxford University Press, 2014).

There is an alternative to the Hobbesian neoclassical world in which the capitalist minority defines and limits social and economic policy.[71] The economic crisis of the 2000s demonstrated that a range of government actions can be effective to rescue national economies from collapse, and others can make the crisis far worse. The experience of the United States and Western Europe after the Second World War, during the so-called golden age of capitalism, suggests the what the component parts of the progressive alternative must be.

First and foremost, converting capitalism into a system fit for human beings will require the reassertion of the strength of the trade unions in the advanced countries. In North America and Western Europe the trade union movement led the fights to introduce social support systems, full employment policies, and universal provision of health and education. The power of unions can no longer rest on workers in manufacturing. Central to the regeneration of the trade union movement will be the public sector, and in the private sector workers in services such as home care. This shift will necessarily require a more ethnically diverse workers' movement, in which all forms of discrimination, especially sexism, are overcome. Extremely positive signs are the selection of Frances O'Grady as General Secretary of the British Trades Union Congress in 2013 and the support of UNITE the Union for immigrant workers.[72]

The progressive programme to transform capitalism requires four fundamental reforms, whose purpose would be to severely restrict the economic and political power of capital.[73] First, because capitalist economies do not automatically adjust to full employment, governments must institutionalize an active countercyclical

---

71 Thomas Hobbes, with more insight than Adam Smith, recognized that pursuit of individual self interest result in a "state of war" and lives that would be "solitary, poor, nasty, brutish, and short" (*Leviathan* I, 13).

72 See the 2013 statement in opposition to the Coalition government's immigration bill, http://www.unitetheunion.org/news/unite-condemns-governments-immigration-bill-as-politics-of-hate-and-fear/.

73 The four measures are much the same as those in the program of the British Labor Party in 1945, which was more radical than what was actually implemented during 1945-1951. http://www.unionhistory.info/timeline/1945_1960.php

macroeconomic program. The active element in the countercyclical program would be fiscal policy, supported by an accommodating monetary policy, and, if necessary, with exchange rate management and capital controls to stabilize the balance of payments.

Countercyclical policies, and many other sensible and humane economic measures, are dismissed as impractical because of the alleged affect they might have on "financial markets". As I discussed above, this personification of markets is an essential part of the justification of a capitalist economy free from the constraints of democratic oversight. This personification is applied across all types of markets, as if the market itself were an independent actor in society. In the twenty-first century it became integral to the justification of a socially dysfunctional financial system, national and global.

This personification, an ideological abstraction from the real world of speculators and financial fraud, is an essential part of the mystification of financial behavior. It facilitates the mythology that the dysfunctional financial system is not the work of men and women (mostly the former) within institutions that have socially irrational rules and norms. It promotes the disempowering argument that financial dysfunction is a manifestation of the inexorable operation of the laws of nature that no government can change. It seeks to hide that a specific financial speculators wish to coerce governments to take actions in their narrow economic interests.

While it is in the interests of capital to exaggerate the power of finance, the dire warnings about the behavior of financial markets carry some truth. The solution to this threat to humane macroeconomic policies is to tame those markets. The manner to tame them is public control of the financial sector. In part this could be through direct nationalization, and in part by conversion of financial activities into non-profit or limited profit associations such as mutual societies and savings and loan institutions (building societies). Even in the United States, the heartland of minimalist public regulation, non-profit and limited profit financial institutions have been common in the past..

Third, government regulation of internal markets would be based on the principle of the International Labor Organization that "labor is not a commodity".[74]   The purpose would be to eliminate unemployment as a tool of labor discipline.   The most effective method to achieve this would be a universal basic income program.[75] A properly designed universal income program would facilitate labor mobility, by reducing the extent to which people were tied to their specific employer. Also, by reducing the volatility of household income, it would provide an automatic stabilizer at the base of the economy, the labor market. It would be similar to the automatic stabilizing effect of unemployment compensation, and more effective.

Fourth, and the basis for all of all others would be the protection of workers' right to organize. As explained above, the program of fundamental reform of capitalism would be based on the political power of the working class, in alliance with elements of the middle classes.

For two hundred and fifty years a struggle has waxed and waned to restrict, control or eliminate the ills generated by capitalist accumulation: exploitation of labor, class and ethic repression, international armed conflict, and despoiling of the environment. When a progressive majority has allied, this struggle has brought great strides. When capitalists, the tiny minority, have been successful in creating their own anti-reform and counter-revolutionary majority much is lost. The last thirty years of the twentieth century and into the twenty-first has been such an anti-reform period, during which capital achieved a degree of liberation it had not enjoyed since before the Great Depression.   A major ideological weapon in the fight to return to reform is the expose of mainstream economics as what it is, fakeconomics..

---

74 This principle can be found at http://www.ilo.org/ilolex/english/iloconst.htm. It is sometimes called the Declaration of Philadelphia, where it was adopted in 1944 at the twenty-six conference of the International Labour Organization.

75 A universal basic income would be paid to the employed as well as the unemployed. Possible specifications for such programmes are explained in detail at http://www.basicincome.org/bien/. .

2.2 The Bankruptcy of Conventional Economics

Hazel Henderson, D.Sc.Hon., FRSA, RichardSpencer, Tony Manwaring
Excerpt from *Mapping the Global Transition to the Solar Age*
(ICAEW and Tomorrow's Company, 2014)

Economics new challengers

Economics, never a science, has been largely invalidated by its own failures and defunct models now exposed.[76] Markets grew from village greens to national systems of resource-allocation, buttressed by the first political economists from Adam Smith onward. While game theory eclipsed many economic theories, behavioural science delivered the *coup de grace*! Brain researchers and endocrinologists discovered that economic textbook models of human nature were inaccurate, since they portrayed rational behaviour as that of individual competition for maximising of self-interest. Even though generations of critics have pointed out that humans also enjoy cooperating, sharing, giving gifts and caring for each other,[77] it took physical scientists to challenge economists.

Brain researchers discovered that humans are not always rational and that we are usually of two minds: with our decisions sometimes made emotionally and instinctively by our 'reptilian' brain, the amygdala, and at other times by our

---

76 See for example, Orrell, David, *Economyths: Ten Ways Economics Gets It Wrong*, Wiley, NY, 2010. Orrell, a mathematician and complexity scientist, provides a recent succinct critique.

77 See for example, Hyde, Lewis, *The Gift*, Vintage, 1983, 2007; Vaughan, Genevieve, *For Giving*, Plain View Press, 1997; and more recently Eisler, Riane, *The Real Wealth of Nations*, Berrett-Koehler, 2008; Bohtlingk, Louis, *Dare to Care*, Cosimo, 2011; Eisenstein, Charles, *Sacred Economics*, Evolver Editions (2011) and my own research of the Love Economy throughout my work.

forebrain, the prefrontal cortex which allows us to consider consequences and longer-term issues.[78]

Hormones: hidden drivers of trading and behaviour

Endocrinologists discovered testosterone and how this hormone governs aggression which in excess can lead to violent behaviour, lack of control and excessive feelings of omnipotence and thus risk-taking. Not surprisingly, as financial markets were deregulated, leverage increased and traders took ever-greater risks which led to the blow-ups of 2007–8. Endocrinologists taking cheek swabs of traders in the City of London found elevated testosterone levels,[79] while many books on these crises reported the same kind of heedless risk-taking by these often self-proclaimed 'masters of the universe.' Studies show that gender-balance improves companies' performance while others conclude that women manage financial assets better and less riskily than men.[80] Much psychological research shows how aggression, violence and risk-taking are related to males.[81] Economic theory is also male-focused and patriarchal. Many studies link economic and particularly monetary policy to wars. For example, John Maynard Keynes' *The Economic Consequences of Peace* (1919) warned about excessive demands in the Treaty of Versailles for payment of war debts by defeated Germans and Naill Ferguson's *The Ascent of Money* (2008) both document the role of bankers and speculators in wars.[82]

Meanwhile, endocrinologists were researching another hormone affecting human behaviour: oxytocin, secreted by women in pregnancy and elevated during the

---

78 Kahneman op. cit. and Moral Markets, ed. Zak, Paul J., Princeton University Press, 2008.

79 'Low testosterone linked with financial risk-taking', *New Scientist*, 24 March, 2011; Adams, Tim, 'Testosterone and high finance do not mix: so bring on the women', *The Guardian*, 18 June, 2011.

80 See for example, Lewis, Michael, *The Big Short*, W.W. Norton, 2010, and Coates, John, *The Hour Between Dog and Wolf: Risk-Taking, Gut Feelings and the Biology of Boom and Bust*, Penguin Press, London & New York, 2012.

81 See for example, Coates, John, op. cit.

82 Keynes, John M. *The Economic Consequences of Peace*, Harcourt Brace, NY, 1920, and Ferguson, Naill. *The Ascent of Money*, Penguin, 2008.

nurturing of children by men as well as women (women normally have many times more oxytocin than men, but it increases in men nurturing children). In *The Better Angels of Our Nature*, psychologist Stephen Pinker provides overwhelming evidence of how 'feminisation' of societies leads to more peaceable, better governed and educated, healthier and more prosperous societies.[83] Application of such behavioural research to public policy includes the widely used 'choice architecture' by corporations and governments designing prior 'opt-in' features to defined contribution retirement savings plans. These require employees to 'opt-out,' which leads to many more contributors staying in these plans. These are based on economist Richard Thaler and lawyer Cass R. Sunstein's work at the University of Chicago. Sunstein joined the Obama Office of Management and Budget in 2009 to oversee regulatory affairs, often relying unfortunately on conventional cost/benefit analysis.[84]

Science and new evidence trump economic theories

All this new science delivered body blows to economics, while its models were also in tatters due to their failure in financial markets. My interest in exploring economic assumptions grew as I documented the pseudo-universality its models claimed and how the power of its narrow methodologies purported to explain human behaviour and politics. The growing power of economists became evident in academia, dominating discourse in law, sociology and colonising political debates, as I saw in Washington in the 1970s while serving as a science-policy adviser. For example, all legislation under discussion since the late 1970s was made subject to 'economic impact statements' with blatantly biased cost-benefit analysis, omitting impacts on citizens, future generations and the environment.[85]

The textbook models of efficient markets, Pareto Optimality, rationality, Modern Portfolio Theory, Capital Asset Pricing models, Value-at-Risk, even the Bank of Sweden prizewinning Black-Scholes Options Pricing Model, are now all found

---

83 Pinker, Stephen, op. cit.
84 Thaler, Richard and Sunstein, Cass R., *Nudge: Improving Decisions About Health, Wealth and Happiness*, Yale University Press, 2008.
85 Henderson, Hazel, *Politics of the Solar Age*, op cit.

wanting and challenged by many market players themselves.[86] From critiques of economics core theories by other social sciences to those from the physical sciences, the economics profession was challenged with new research from both knowledge domains. Endogenous human-focused conventional research was challenged by psychologists, including Daniel Kahneman in *Thinking Fast and Slow* (2011), highlighting our subconscious biases, cognitive errors and theory-induced blindness, while endocrinologists pinpointed how our hormones drive behaviour and how our forebrains and their higher cognition get hijacked by the 'fight or flight' responses of our reptilian brain amygdala. Paul Zak in *The Moral Molecule* (2012), Robert Axelrod in *The Evolution of Cooperation* (1984) and David Loye in *Darwin's Lost Theory of Love* (2000) show how these new scientific discoveries invalidate economics and financial models of risk. Exogenous models in physics were similarly challenged by quantum mechanics demonstrating a non-local universe including Bell's Theorem and the work of Robert Nadeau, physicists David Bohm and Fritjof Capra, and in the non-linear mathematics, chaos models I described in *Politics of the Solar Age* (1981). While macroeconomics was discredited, accounting models at company levels were evolving to embrace broader issues, as described in this chapter, including the Value Driver Model, as well as the International Integrated Reporting Framework released in December 2013 which recognises six forms of capital: finance, built, intellectual, social, human and natural capitals. This shifts focus to knowledge and other intangibles and rates the performance of organisations and their business models in value-creation or destruction.[87]

As global issues from hunger, poverty and pandemics to desertification and climate change were debated in many UN forums and NGO conferences, they went unaddressed by obsolete paradigms. Yet another tenet of economic theory came under attack: the supremacy of markets postulated in the Arrow-Debreu

---

86 Taleb, Nassim, *The Black Swan*, Random House, 2007. Triana, Pablo. *Lecturing Birds on Flying*, Wiley, 2009. Bookstaber, Richard, *Demon of Our Own Design*, Wiley, 2007.

87 'Consultation Draft of the International <IR> Framework', International Integrated Reporting Council, April 2013; 'The Value Driven Model: a tool for communicating the business value of sustainability', PRI-UN Global Compact LEAD, 2013.

model seeing 'progress' as 'market completion' and favouring property rights in governing common resources.[88] Ever since biologist Garrett Hardin's 'The Tragedy of the Commons' (*Science*, 1968), policymakers and Hardin himself had become convinced by economists that common resources could best be managed sustainably by converting them into property. I was invited by Hardin and the other faculty of the University of California – Santa Barbara, as a Regent's lecturer in 1976, and challenged these notions.

Challenging Economics in the US Congress

By the 1980s, my alternatives to economics in multi-disciplinary policy tools such as those I helped develop for risk assessment[89] and for technology assessment, scenario-building, and normative futures research led me to many debates in Congress, testifying at hearings on why Congress needed its own budget research group, which became the CBO.[90] In my hundreds of lectures at business schools, I enjoyed challenging economists, but found few who would with debate me and many who banned my books as too radical. Students continued to invite me and often told how they had bought my books and put them in their college libraries – only to have their economics professors remove them. E. F. Schumacher advised me to 'stay under the radar,' advice which I have taken ever since. In 'New Markets and New Commons' (1995), I pointed out that a new paradigm from game theory based on 'win-win' cooperation was more appropriate than economics' focus on 'win-lose' competition.[91]

Not until 2010 did the Nobel economics committee recognise the work of political scientist Elinor Ostrom with its Bank of Sweden Prize. Ostrom, who died in 2012, had documented many examples of equitable, sustainable management of

---

88 Arrow, Kenneth. *Social Choice and Individual Values*, Wiley, 1951, 1963.
89 Geneva Papers on Risk, reprinted in *Best's Review*, Casualty Edition, May 1978.
90 Holden, C, 'Hazel Henderson: Nudging Society Off Its Macho Trip', *Science*, 28 November, 1975: 863–64.
91 Henderson, Hazel, 'New Markets and New Commons: Opportunities in the Global Casino', *Futures*, vol 27 no 2, 1995.

commons by cooperative decision-making processes.[92] The deeper story is that Alfred Nobel never gave or intended to give a prize in economics, which is a profession, not a science. So, the Swedish Riksbank lobbied the Bank of Sweden Prize for Economic Sciences in Memory of Alfred Nobel onto the Nobel committee in the 1960s in order to legitimise economics as a 'science' as part of the Cold War effort to de-legitimise Marxism and communism.[93] As economic theories were invalidated from all these directions, the Nobel committee resorted to giving its Bank of Sweden Prize to non-economists: including Elinor Ostrom, as well as game theorists Robert Aumann and Thomas Schelling, information theorist Herbert Simon, psychologists Daniel Kahneman and Amos Tversky. I helped expose this intellectual scandal in my editorials and found an ally in Nassim N. Taleb who met with the King of Sweden and called for this Bank of Sweden Prize to be withdrawn or abolished.[94] In 2011, Alfred Nobel's descendant and lawyer Peter Nobel, after many years trying to expose this misuse of the Nobel Prize name, persuaded the Nobel family to publicly dissociate from the Bank of Sweden and its prize.[95]

All this largely unreported intellectual history of the economics profession is now necessary if we are to face our current global conditions beyond theory-induced blindness regarding climate change and many other 'externalities' caused by the influence of these now defunct theories. The paradigm breakthroughs at Rio+20, other UN agencies, the G-20 and others reported in this chapter are welcome signs! While economics focuses on competition, the world now needs cooperation at every level and the contributions of other disciplines documenting the full repertoire of human behaviour (conflict, competition, cooperation and sharing). We also see how better information is needed to address our human purposes. Indeed, computer scientist Jaron Lanier explores the deeper philosophical and

---

92 Ostrom, Elinor, *Working Together: Collective Action, the Commons and Multiple Methods in Practice*, with Amy R. Poteete and Marco A. Janssen, Princeton University Press, 2010.

93 Nadeau, Robert, *The Non-Local Universe*, with co-author Menas Kafatos, Oxford University Press, 2001 (also see his article in *Scientific American* and the TV program 'Redefining Success', www.ethicalmarkets.tv).

94 Baker, Stephanie, ''*Black Swan*' Author Says Investors Should Sue Nobel for Crisis', *Bloomberg*, 8 October , 2010, and personal email exchange with author.

95 Henderson, Hazel, 'The 'Nobel Prize' That Isn't', *Le Monde Diplomatique*, February 2005.

political issues of the pervasive information revolution, its effect on unemployment, inequality in *Who Owns the Future?* offering deeper, more mature thinking than most of the sophomoric ideas and business models emanating from Silicon Valley.[96] Another internet pioneer Clay A. Johnson shows how watching our information intake is as important as our food diet.[97]

Revealing advice to economists by Britain's Department of Environment economist, John Corkindale urged them 'to capture the sustainable development agenda for the economics profession.'[98] This occurred in the skewing of the UN climate conference in Kyoto in 1998 by US insistence on 'market-based' approaches which focused on creating the ambitious complexities of designing a priori the global emissions-trading regime in the Kyoto Protocol. The better approach would have been the simpler market-based approach of pollution and carbon taxes. Pollution taxes are widely popular, as are financial transaction taxes. Instead, the influence of US economists led to the complicated creation of markets for trading carbon permits which were taken over by London and Wall Street financial firms, leading to the gaming, frauds and corrupt practices that have plagued these markets and the near-collapse of the Emissions Trading Scheme in Europe.[99] I have examined these issues and how traders profit while CO_2 emissions have increased since Kyoto.[100]

I had pointed out how economists had gained power in academic and political circles as apologists justifying elites and their political control through central banking, monetary policies, mass media and favouring the rise of corporations through their competition, 'free markets,' 'free trade' and property rights paradigms.[101] The flowering of the Industrial Revolution lauded by Adam Smith in

96 Lanier, Jaron, *Who Owns the Future?*, Simon & Schuster, New York, 2013, and his equally challenging *You Are Not a Gadget: A Manifesto*, Knopf Publishing, 2010.

97 Johnson, Clay A, *The Information Diet*, O'Reilly Media, Inc., Sebastopol, CA, 2012.

98 Henderson, Hazel, *Building a Win-Win World*, op. cit., page 56.

99 Henderson, Hazel, 'From Potemkin Carbon Markets to Direct Green Investments', Network for Sustainable Financial Markets, 12 July, 2011, and at www.ethicalmarkets.com.

100 'Extremely Troubled Scheme', *The Economist*, 16 February, 2013, p 75.

101 Henderson, Hazel, *Politics of the Solar Age*, op. cit., 'Economists as Apologists' Ch. 7.

Wealth of Nations in 1776 had produced leaps in human knowledge and technological advancement. However, after 2007–8 and a series of earlier financial collapses with orthodox advice for austerity measures,[102] rising evidence of the social and environmental impacts in 2012 became the time to move on to more multi-disciplinary systems approaches to today's urgent global problems. This requires a further look at how economics misled us: it's lack of understanding of energy and ecosystems as the basis of human life and survival. I realised this fatal flaw while serving on the Technology Assessment Advisory Council to Congress from 1974–1980. My fellow member James Fletcher, then president of the Midwest Research Institute, who became administrator of NASA, told us that if the US government had subsidised solar, renewables and energy efficiency by equivalent subsidies as those to oil, coal, gas and nuclear power that the USA could have been 100% powered with renewables by 1975. This led to my life-long study of green technologies.

Energy-blindness and the Illusions of Abstraction

Economic theory favoured energy and resource-extraction from the Earth's crust, following the fossil-fuelled Industrial Era. This led to the technological 'lock-in' and excluded all the earlier evidence of solar-based technologies in many societies beyond the Eurocentric industrial model. Thus, economics ignored the role of energy as a factor of production – subsuming it under 'land'. This is why economics did not fully understand or embrace the laws of thermodynamics, particularly the Second Law of Entropy as evident in economists' continuous recycling of the theories of Stanley Jevons regarding the use of coal in the 1850s that purport to show the futility of increasing energy efficiency.[103] Economic models of general equilibrium and prices, elasticity of demand and substitution still see human economies as able to pursue perpetual growth in their money-

---

102 Reinhart, Carmen and Rogoff, Kenneth, *This Time It's Different*, Princeton University Press, 2009.

103 Sorrell, Steve, *The Rebound Effect*, UK Energy Research Centre, October 2007. Sorrell reviews over 500 studies of these theories since Jevons, finding little evidence or agreement on assumptions, methods, concepts and results. Full-cost pricing, life-cycle costing and rising energy taxes could mitigate such apparent effects.

focused view, as in their cash-flow based GDP model which ignores 'externalities' just as corporate balance sheets have done over the past centuries.[104] It took OPEC's oil shocks of the 1970s for economic theories to recognize the primacy of energy, while still ignoring its source: photons from the Sun!

As economists embraced mathematics in their aspirations to scientific legitimacy, following the lead of Leon Walras, they also saw the economy, abstracted from its social embeddedness, as an equilibrium system, later buttressed by the Arrow-Debreu Model. This reinforced the mathematical illusion of compound interest-imposed on the real world economies - which has led to inevitable debt-based collapses over the centuries. These debt crises gave rise to the tradition of 'jubilee' – that allowed debt-forgiveness to wipe away theoretical mountains of un-repayable debts,[105] most recently in the Jubilee 2000 campaign led by Ann Pettifor, author of *The Coming First World Debt Crisis* (2006), which wrote off HIPC debt in the poorest African countries. Robert Skidelsky, author of *The World After Communism* (1995), recently recommended the need for debt cancellation.[106] I drew attention to this mathematical illusion of compound interest:

Economists have set up an *a priori*, positive feedback system (based on the value system of private property and its accumulation), in which the interest earned on a fixed quantity of money (capital) will be compounded and the next calculation of interest added on cumulatively. But this 'runaway' accumulation process bears no relationship to the real world – only to the value system. However, it has profound real-word effect if enough people believe it is legitimate and employ lawyers, courts, etc., to enforce it![107]

---

104 See for example, Capra, Fritjof and Henderson, Hazel, *Qualitative Growth*, ICAEW, UK, 2009.
105 See for example, Brown, Ellen H, *Web of Debt*, Third Millennium Press, 2007, and Graeber, David, *Debt: the First 5000 Years*, Melville House, 2011.
106 Skidelsky, Robert, 'Down with Debt Weight', *Financieele Dagblad*, Netherlands, 18 April, 2012.
107 Henderson, Hazel, *Politics of the Solar Age*, op. cit., p 228.

Additional theory-induced blindness by early economists regarding the laws of thermodynamics was first scientifically challenged by Nobelist chemist Frederick Soddy in *Cartesian Economics* (1922), when he asked what drove a steam-engine:

In one sense or another the credit for the achievement may be claimed by the so-called engine-driver, the guard, the signalman, the manager, the capitalist, or the shareholder – or, again, by the scientific pioneers who discovered the nature of fire, by the inventors who harnessed it, by Labor, which built the railway and the train. The fact remains that all of them by their united efforts could not drive the train. The real engine-driver is the coal. So, in the present state of science, the answer to the question how men live, or how anything lives or how inanimate nature lives, in the senses in which we speak of the life of a waterfall or of any other manifestation of continued liveliness, is, with few and unimportant exceptions, BY SUNSHINE.[108]

Soddy was ridiculed by the economists of his day, as so many other challengers had been before him.

This blindness of economics was exhaustively examined by Nicholas Georgescu-Roegen in *The Entropy Law and the Economic Process* (1971). He was also ignored and became alienated. Georgescu-Roegen taught at Vanderbilt University and his best-known student is Herman Daly.[109]. Daly has at last found the following his work deserves. Amory Lovins, Jeremy Rifkin and I[110] all discovered the entropy problem simultaneously and discussed its implications for our common human future many times in the 1970s and 1980s. I postulated that three basic resources: information, energy and matter were key to human development and that the quality and accuracy of information controlled the efficiency of our economy and our prospect for progress.

However, by this time, 'economism' had been entrenched in academia, business schools and most problematically in finance, where it has caused such harm as

---

108 Henderson, Hazel, *Politics of the Solar Age*, op. cit., p 225. A new edition of Soddy's
   Cartesian Economics is published by Cosimo Books, NY, 2012.
109 Daly, Herman, *Toward a Steady-State Economy*, W.H. Freeman,1973.
110 Rifkin, Jeremy, *Entropy*, Bantam, 1981.

described by Britain's senior financial regulator Lord Adair Turner and others. At a lecture at London's Cass Business School, Lord Turner broke ranks and called for an end to allowing private banks to create the nation's money, turning this vital function over to government as money-creator. Politicians and media were caught up in these power politics as Wall Street, the City of London and other financial centres began controlling even the most democratically elected politicians through the power of money and credit creation.

Currency units track real wealth
Money is a useful unit of account and if well-managed can be a store of value, but it became equated with the real-world wealth it tracks and measures, rather than recognizing how such units of account have changed over millennia. As powerful money-centres grew, financialization began to trump democratisation as investment banks controlled ratings agencies, helped governments raise bond issues, hide indebtedness with creative accounting and special-purpose vehicles and bail out excessive risk-takers in their banking sectors, while allowing their central banks to create interest-free money to bail out those banks and insurance companies deemed too-big-to-fail.

The latest financial 'products' being offered to investors are infrastructure funds, where distressed cities and states are persuaded to sell or lease public infrastructure built with taxpayer funds, to consortia of investment banks which then package these public assets e.g., toll roads in Indiana, parking meters in Chicago and state-owned public buildings in Arizona, and sell them based on their income streams from tolls, fees and rent.[111] Yet new, more efficient infrastructure is vital as societies shift to solar-based green economies. Promulgating new designs for cities and sustainable infrastructure is the focus of UN agencies and NGOs,

---

Turner, Adair, *Economics After the Crisis*, MIT Press, 2012; Henderson, Hazel, 'Review of Economics After the Crisis', www.seekingalpha.com, 11 September, 2012; and lecture at Cass Business School, 6 February, 2013 – Kalesky, Anatole, 'A breakthrough speech on monetary policy', *Reuters*, 7 February, 2013.

111 See for example, Niquette, Mark and Hart, Jerry, 'The Governors' Garage Sale', *Bloomberg BusinessWeek*, 28 February, 2011; 'The Big Sell: Asset-leasing in Chicago', *The Economist*, 18 September, 2010.

including Global Energy Basel, Switzerland. Financiers had forgotten that they do not provide capital, but are intermediaries, serving their clients whose savings they purport to direct to the most efficient uses among borrowers and entrepreneurs. Their failures and conflicts of interests with their clients helped cause the blow-ups of 2008.[112] This agency–principal conflict has been studied in corporations but only recently applied to finance, notably by former banker Paul K. Woolley who founded the Paul Woolley Centre for the Study of Capital Market Dysfunctionality at the London School of Economics.[113]

The circle has now closed, as governments assumed private bank debts, compromised the value of their sovereign bonds and imposed often un-repayable levels of debts onto their own taxpayers. As if these betrayals of public trust were not enough, politicians at the behest of their financial sectors then imposed cuts and 'austerity' on their taxpayers, leading to today's widespread revolts and mistrust of government and business elites. As one Spanish protest group complained, 'we now have market dictatorship!' Indeed, it is not lost on the worldwide Occupy Movements that in Europe, such appointed 'technocrats' in Italy, Mario Monti; in Greece, Lucas Papademos; the Bank of England's Martin Carver; and the European Central Bank's Mario Draghi, are all alumni of Goldman Sachs, and this same company provides many US senior officials, including Treasury Secretaries Robert Rubin and Henry Paulson, former New Jersey Governor, then Senator Jon Corzine and many in the Obama administration.

These 'technocratic' policies of imposing austerity are mostly driven by financial interests that refuse to take the necessary write-downs on their toxic assets.[114] They can only survive by enforcing their economic paradigm. This has, so far, worked through invoking fear of even greater cuts to social safety nets, pensions, wages

---

112 Taft, John, *Stewardship*, John Wiley, NY, 2012, and Woolley, Paul, 'The Future of Finance', London School of Economics, 2010.

113 Woolley, Paul K, *The Future Of Finance: And The Theory That Underpins It*, London School of Economics Press, UK, 2010; Henderson, Hazel, 'Book Review: The Future of Finance', www.seekingalpha.com, 20 July, 2010.

114 See for example, as described by Gillian Tett in *Fool's Gold*, Free Press, 2009, and former chair of the FDIC, Sheila Bair in *Bull by the Horns*, 2012.

and jobs, combined with threats of national bankruptcy,[115] eroding value of currencies, fears of Chinese creditors, and 'fiscal cliffs,' etc. In both the USA and Europe, budget battles are becoming deadlocked by political infighting over such manufactured crises by these 'scarcity of money' paradigms. Lord Turner instead proposed that governments can create new fiat money, interest-free, to re-start economies mired in private debt,[116] much as Milton Friedman once suggested: 'throw money out of helicopters for citizens to pick up'! 'Helicopter Ben' Bernanke instead used this idea to throw free money at banks rather than citizens.

Politics of money-creation and credit-allocation

At last, in 2011, all this theory-induced blindness and the pain it has imposed on average citizens and Main Street economies was exposed by the Occupy Movements,[117] which began in Europe and spread across the USA, echoed in the student revolts in Chile and elsewhere. These widely diverse movements, often led by the young, finally forced recognition of the inequalities imposed by the 1% and made fairness for the 99% their rallying cry. The politics of money-creation and credit-allocation has now emerged as well as its long history.

The Occupy Movements at last allowed focus on how money had taken over, even in democracies, and the secretive role of central banks and their Bank of International Settlements, often called the central bankers' central bank. No conspiracy theories were needed, as the role of central banks was clear in bailing out the perpetrators of the 2007–8 and on-going crises. In today's Information Age, many TV shows feature currencies rolling off printing presses. Central banks are being forced to account for the trillions they create and have given to prop up their failing big banks. Instead of creating interest-free fiat money, these liabilities foisted onto taxpayers. In the USA, the $700bn Troubled Asset Relief Program, was

---

115 See for example, *IOUSA*, a film produced by the Peterson Foundation, funded by hedge fund billionaire Peter G. Peterson to promote cuts in US entitlement programs and government budgets.

116 Turner, Adair, 6 February, 2013, op. cit.

117 See for example, *The Debt Resistors' Operations Manual*, Strike Debt and Occupy Wall Street, www.strikedebt.org, 2012.

a part of the total estimated by the Treasury's Inspector General at $23.7tn.[118] Law suits by Bloomberg and other news groups required the US Federal Reserve to disclose which banks received the $16tn it dispensed between December 2007 and June 2010. The General Accountability Office audit listed the largest recipients of this zero interest loan programme: Citigroup, Morgan Stanley, Merrill Lynch (now part of Bank of America), Bank of America, Barclay's PLC, Bear Stearns, Goldman Sachs, Royal Bank of Scotland, JP Morgan Chase, Deutsche Bank, UBS, Credit Suisse, Lehman Brothers and BNP Paribas.[119]

With the increase in whistle-blowing, corporate investigating is now big business with firms, including Kroll, FTI Consulting, Corporate Resolutions, Palantir and accounting firm Deloitte and others pursuing corporate, banking and other financial crimes.[120] Offshore tax havens and money laundering are now exposed by civic groups' research. The Tax Justice Network's estimate is $21tn, among other estimates in the 2013 special *Economist* report , which focuses on the US tax havens of Delaware and Nevada and Britain's City of London, as well as the usual black-listed OECD regimes.[121] NGO campaigners picket tax-avoiding corporations and others focus on firms speculating in food, while banks fought back.[122] The World Development Movement helped Barclays Bank to decide to stop speculating in food,[123] while BankTrack, Global Financial Integrity and other watchdogs spurred the focus on re-instating public banks, moving money to credit unions and cooperative banks and the coalition Global Alliance for Banking on Values.

---

118 SIGTARP Quarterly Report, July 31, 2009, Office of the Special Inspector General for the Troubled Asset Relief Program. (www.sigtarp.gov)

119 'Federal Reserve System: Opportunities Exist to Strengthen Policies and Processes for Managing Emergency Assistance', GAO Audit of the Federal Reserve, http://www.gao.gov/new.items/d11696.pdf, 21 July, 2011.

120 'The Bloodhounds of Capitalism', *The Economist*, 5 January, 2013, 47-48.

121 'Tax havens: The missing 20 trillion', *Economist*, 16 February, 2013.

122 Clapp, Jennifer, 'Banks on Counter-Attack in Food and Finance Debate', www.triplecrisis.com, 15 February, 2013.

123 Ross, Miriam, 'Barclays Stops Speculation on Food – Campaigners Demand Regulation', World Development Movement, www.wdm.org.uk, 12 February, 2013.

In the USA, as in Europe, by 2012, the issues of inequality and the need for fairness exploded across the political spectrum from Republican Congressman Ron Paul[124] and his Tea Party followers to Democrat Congress member Marcy Kaptor and Independent Senator Bernie Sanders of Vermont. The issue of fairness underlay the re-election of President Barack Obama by more than five million votes. A bill to reform US money-creation has been introduced into Congress by the American Monetary Institute together with a detailed plan and a systemic model by Japanese complexity theorist Kaoro Yamaguchi.[125]   Monetary reformers include the American Monetary Institute (www.monetary.org) led by former mutual fund manager Stephen Zarlenga, author of *The Lost Science of Money* (2002); William Krehm in Canada, founder of the Committee on Monetary and Economic Reform, COMER; lawyer Ellen H. Brown, author of *The Web of Debt* (2007) and *The Public Bank Solution* (2013) and president of the Public Banking Institute; James Robertson, author of *Future Money* (2012); Bernard Lietaer, a former currency trader, co-author of *Money and Sustainability* (2012); Tom Greco, author of *The End of Money* (2009); Australia's Shann Turnbull and New Zealand's Dierdre Kent, author of *Healthy Money, Healthy Planet* (2007), Riane Eisler's *The Real Wealth of Nations* (2008) focusing on gender equality and a new care-based economy; Louis Bohtlink's *Dare To Care* (2012), among others.

Inequality: the Invisible Hand's winners and losers

To understand why economics overlooks inequality, we need to examine how unfairness is generated by the way money and credit are created by private banks and how tax codes are often shaped to favour special interests. These debates went public in the USA in the 2012 elections. We also see the focus on markets and Adam Smith's belief in an 'invisible hand' whereby individuals striving competitively for their own self-interest benefited the community and the common good. This theory propagated the view of markets as moral and any government effort to distribute those individual benefits more widely would reduce the market's efficiency.

---

124 Paul, Ron, *End the Fed*, Grand Central Publishing, 2009.
125 Yamaguchi, Kaoru, 'Workings of a Public Money System of Open Macroeconomies – Modeling the American Monetary Act Completed', Doshisha University, October 2011.

But, we must ask 'efficiency for whom and over what time frame?' Adam Smith himself was clear that markets could only allocate resources efficiently if buyers and sellers had equal power and information and that no harm from their transactions be imposed on innocent bystanders. Research by political scientist Gar Alperovitz documents the ways in which all individuals rely on groups and society in *Unjust Deserts* (2008), debunking the idea of the usually male 'rugged individual' portrayed in novels.[126] Yet, the rhetoric in the USA 2012 election still returned to these old debates as 'business versus government'; 'makers' versus 'takers'; 'job creators' versus 'dependents' and which groups were most responsible for avoiding taxes and 'gaming' the system.[127]

Yet the power of this meme of the 'invisible hand' lives on in laissez-faire economics at the Chicago School, in business schools, corporate boardrooms, on Wall Street and in the revolving door 'technocrat' politicians installed in many countries by financial interests. Economic models portray a trade-off between equity and efficiency, reinforcing the theories that any government effort to balance the rewards of their economies is immoral, inefficient and that re-distribution is unfair to the most enterprising and hard-working citizens. Furthermore, these theories see them as the pre-eminent 'job-creators' in their model of trickle-down economics. Some go so far as to say that only the private sector creates jobs, despite widespread obvious evidence to the contrary that government does indeed create jobs (current government jobs in the USA total 21,862,000[128]) as well as redistribute incomes.

I pointed out the absurdities of these laissez-faire theories and how automation would require new ways of maintaining levels of essential aggregate demand for basic needs in the face of growing structural unemployment.[129] Computer scientist Jaron Lanier documents how the digitisation and automation of retailing,

---

126 Alperovitz, Gar and Daly, Lew. *Unjust Deserts*, The New Press, NY, 2008.
127 Henderson, Hazel, 'Celebrating Redistribution: Backbone of a Great Nation', CSRWire October 2012.
128 US Bureau of Labor Statistics, www.bls.gov, 17 June, 2013.
129 Henderson, Hazel, 'The Ethics of Job Creation: Let's Get Real!' CSRWire 6 February, 2012.

publishing, manufacturing and other sectors of the US economy are driving unemployment, inequality and eroding the middle class in *Who Owns the Future?* (2013). Similar conclusions are found by Adam Arvidsson and Nikolai Peiterson in *The Ethical Economy* (2013)[130] and by two courageous MIT economists, Erik Brynjolfsson and Andrew McAfee in *Race Against the Machine* (2011).[131]

Inequality hidden in obsolete metrics

Yet these theories are missing in many countries' budget debates since they contradict orthodox economic models. The *Economist's*, June 1-7, 2013 cover 'Toward the End of Poverty,' trotted out research on poverty from the World Bank, the IMF and its own Economic Intelligence Unit. These were all cited in an exploration of various scenarios, 'The Final Countdown: Prospects for Ending Extreme Poverty by 2030.'[132] Its authors clearly explain its speculative hypotheses and wide range of possible outcomes. All these studies are based on highly aggregated global data and cede that China has contributed most to poverty reduction in the world, using its own socialist market model.

As income inequality grew along with financialization, globalisation, de-regulation and privatisation, as well as trade deals driven by corporate and financial interests, poverty gaps between and within nations became obvious – even though masked in GDP, which averages incomes. Health, education and welfare statistics began to show the correlations between widening inequality (as measured by GINI Coefficient) and declining health, failing education and the rise of soup kitchens, homelessness, crime, suicide and other signs of social distress.[133] The financial blow-ups of 2007–8, rising joblessness, foreclosures, homelessness, poverty, lack of

---

130 Arvidsson, Adam and Peiterson, Nikolai, *The Ethical Economy*, Columbia University Press, 2013.

131 Brynjolfsson, Erik and McAfee, Andrew, *Race Against the Machine*, Digital Frontier Press, 2011.

132 Chandy, Laurence, Natasha Ledlie and Veronika Penciakova, 'The Final Countdown: Prospects for Ending Extreme Poverty by 2030', Brookings Institution, Washington, DC, April 2013.

133 Pickett, Kate and Wilkinson, Richard, *The Spirit Level*, Bloomsbury Press, 2009; Galbraith, James K. *Inequality and Instability*, Oxford University Press, 2012.

medical care and other social pathologies contributed to alarming rises in inequality in many OECD countries, particularly in the USA as described by Joseph Stiglitz,[134] as well as that continuing worldwide.

IMF, World Bank and official reports using averages, often mask inequality, while it became the focus of some courageous economists and social scientists.[135] These inequality researchers examined how inequality bred instability and resulted in less efficient, less productive societies. Another study estimated the social costs of such instabilities in rising levels of violence.[136] Psychologists Joe Griffin and Ivan Tyrrell of Britain's Human Givens Institute point out the basic conditions for optimal human functionality.[137] The UN 2013 report 'Happiness: Toward a Holistic Approach to Development' by Ban Ki-moon underlines all this research.[138]

Economists justifying laissez-faire correctly cited reasons for the jumps in inequality due to globalisation, trade pacts and competition from cheaper labour; or the job losses due to technology and automation.[139] Their prescriptions beyond 'allowing the markets to work' were for re-training the unemployed which assumes that economies are structured for full employment – when clearly they are not. A report on higher education and student loan debt reaching $1tn in the US in *Bloomberg Business Week* found more than 116,000 college graduates were working as janitors and parking lot attendants.[140] The idea that a whole-system transition was underway has barely entered the debate. Yet, restructuring away from legacy

---

134 Stiglitz, Joseph, *The Price of Inequality: How Today's Divided Society Endangers Our Future*, W.W. Norton & Company, 2012.

135 These social statistics were displayed at ICONS, the First International Conference on Implementing Indicators of Sustainability and Quality of Life, Curitiba, Brazil, 2003. Henderson, Hazel, 'Statisticians of the World Unite', IPS, November 2003.

136 'Violence Containment Spending in the US', Institute for Economics and Peace, 2012.

137 Griffin, Joe and Tyrrell, Ivan, *Godhead: the Brain's Big Bang*, HG Publishing, Human Givens Institute, Chalvington, Sussex, UK, 2011.

138 Ban Ki-moon, op. cit.,www.un.org/ga/search/view_doc.asp?symbol=A/67/697

139 , I also explored this in Henderson, Hazel, *Building a Win-Win World*, op. cit., Ch. 4 'The Jobless Productivity Trap', 1996.

140 Coy, Peter, 'Debt for Life', *Bloomberg BusinessWeek*, September 2012.

sectors and incumbents from the nineteenth and twentieth centuries was proceeding, and this, along with emerging sectors, was largely un-reported in mainstream media. Similarly, asset allocation models used by security analysts obscured the rise of these new sectors.[141]

The Occupy Movements focused on the 40–50% levels of unemployment among even well-qualified graduates in Spain and other countries. These young people were also often burdened by huge student loans – clearly un-repayable if no jobs were available. Bills in the US Congress based on lawyer Ellen Brown's proposal,[142] similar to that of Lord Turner, would have had the Fed take these securitised loans onto its balance sheet and forgive them to stimulate the US economy or allow students to borrow at the same 0.75% rate that banks get at the Fed's discount window as proposed by Senator Elizabeth Warren.

An even deeper fairness issue is that unpaid work, usually performed by women, is deemed 'uneconomic' in economic theory and therefore missing from GDP, even though 170 countries pledged to correct this in Agenda 21 Article 40 of the UN Earth Summit, Rio de Janeiro, 1992. The UN Human Development Report estimated this unpaid productive work at $16tn in 1995, but missing from the global GDP total of $24tn. An estimated $11tn was performed by women and $5tn by men. All these social symptoms of dysfunctional economies are clear indications of the need for a whole system transformation – beyond economic measuring. The 300 years of the fossil-fuelled industrial era is shifting toward a global restructuring of human production, redesigned for the common good and mimicking nature's 3.8 billion years of successful life on Earth powered by the Sun. This requires new accounting and asset-valuation models that start with earth systems science and how our planet utilizes the regular shower of photons from

141 Henderson, Hazel, 'Updating Fossilized Asset-Allocation Classes: Here comes the sustainability sector!' EthicalMarkets.com, 2008.

142 Brown, Ellen, 'Indentured Servitude for Seniors: Social Security Garnished for Student Debts', WebofDebt.com, 9 May, 2012.

the Sun, processing them through the atmosphere, ocean currents and their harvesting by our living biosphere.[143]

---

143 NASA's and other earth-sensing satellites provide this daily information, which now must be the basis of all financial models.

2.3 Social-ecological Transformation and Green Economics: New perspectives for solutions to the most pressing problems of today.

Miriam Kennet

Introduction

This chapter will examine why we need a socio- ecological transformation and introduce some of the global scale problems we are facing. These include climate change, species extinction and threats to the natural systems upon which we depend.

It then discusses neo – classical economics roots and causes of this situation, and what kind of economics transformations are needed. The contributions of Rosa Luxemburg are discussed including her work on international production, consumption, property rights and enclosure of the commons which are important elements today.

Finally there is a discussion of the characteristics of an economics which could produce such a socio – ecological transformation, which the chapter suggests could be a Green Economics with different attitudes to nature, inclusive of feminist perspectives and compatible with modern science, with a long term perspective. A focus on equity is in keeping with sharing the planet's resources with each other and with other species. This would also provide for wider involvement in economics.

Why we need a socio-ecological transformation in order to solve the most pressing problems of today

The world is currently experiencing crises of a magnitude and a type unseen in the 10,000 years of "civilisation." Our "civilisation" arose after the last ice age and was founded upon the particular climactic conditions of the Quaternary interglacial period. We now have the challenges of human induced climate change with sea level rise, and millions of environmental refugees predicted Lohachara Island was the world's first populated island, to be lost to climate change 5 years ago and left 7,000 people homeless. Sagar the largest island, houses 20,000 refugees from other islands along with many rare species and is also disappearing fast. This illustrates how people, planet and biosphere are intricately connected.

One fifth of humankind is in life threatening poverty, and three quarters of mammal species are predicted to be extinct by the end of this century, according to the IUCN Red List report (Barker 2007). There has never been a more pressing need for a simultaneous social and ecological transformation, which needs to now take on board that poverty is an environmental issue and the environment is a poverty issue.

Dr Rajendra Pachauri, the chair of the Intergovernmental Panel on Climate Change, warns that " the very survival of the human species is at risk," (Lean, 2005).

The polar ice caps are contracting and sea level rise could permanently displace up to 200 million people, (Stern 2006). With predicted global warming of between +2 to +4.5 % or up to + 6C by 2100, (Lynas 2007), extinctions, desertification and reduction in agricultural yields are anticipated. The Millennium Ecosystem Services Assessment, (2005) found that ecosystem services are being degraded and an increase in 'non-linear events' brings increased disease, collapse of fisheries and other threats, in particular to fragile ecosystems which are also hosts to rapidly growing human populations.

These changes make our task urgent and compelling. Further, our current economic system perpetuates poverty, inequality and social injustice. The economic system fails to meet even many wealthy people's needs. A UNICEF report, (2007) about the well –being of young people in the UK, shows that a country which has the fifth largest economy in the world, simultaneously has the worst rankings among the 25 richest nations, in terms of the well- being and happiness of its young people when analysing indicators such as relative poverty and deprivation, relationships with family and peers, health and safety and feelings of well being. The report raises significant questions about how the pursuit of economic wealth, as current attained and measured, may actually detract from broader measures of well being. Seventy per cent of the world's 1.2 billion people in life threatening poverty, according to a UN Report, (UN 2006) are women and children. Every day 6,000 children in developing countries die for lack of acess to clean water (Sullivan 2000, Crisis in water). Only 1 per cent of the world's titled land belongs to women,(Firth ,2006).

Gendered domestic violence is the single largest global cause of female morbidity, more than war, traffic accidents, and cancer (Smith, 2006). It is therefore vital to redress the balance of poverty and power between men and women on the planet. Wangari Maathai, likens the things that matter in society to an African stool, *"The three legs represent three critical pillars of a just and stable society. The first leg stands for democratic space, where rights are respected, whether they are human rights, women's rights, children's rights, or environmental rights. The second represents sustainable and equitable management of resources. The third represents cultures of peace. The seat represents society and its prospects for development."*

These three pillars have got lost in the drive for global economic success defined as ever increasing profit, industrial productivity and trade flows which has brought the risk of destruction of much of our habitat.

Neo – classical economics roots and causes of this situation and what kind of economic transformation do we need?

Today's economics discourse has become almost unrecognisable from its origins as provisioning for the needs of the household or the estate. Its root is the word *oikia*, ancient Greek for a house. The root of the word, Eco-nomics is the same as that of eco-logy. Green Economics reverts it to its original and useful beginnings: the provisioning of needs for all of us and the biosphere within the household we all share, which is actually the earth.

Neo-classical economics has come to mean the exact opposite, which is, everything formal, mathematical and external to the household sphere which has assumed superiority over the earth believing itself to be some how outside its systems and limitations. Examining our resource needs and working out how to share them fairly among the people of the world is a major task. In 1890 Marshall described economics as "it examines the part of individual and social action which is most closely connected with the attainment and with the use of the material requisites of well-being." (2005:57.Hogdson). However Samuelson (1948) the father of neo-classical economics, argued that "economics is the allocation of scarce means between alterative uses, as a universal matter of choice for every individual in a world of scarcity. Instead of the whole system of production and allocation of the means of life, the choosing individual alone became the foundation stone of economic theory (2005:57) in Hogdson.

Economics which purports to be value free science, is in fact practised in the main by white middle class men and outside the home sphere. The discipline of economics has to some extent been subsumed by business schools which aim to "grow" companies. There are very few women economics professors, just 23 in the UK in 2003(RES Report: Humphries). Economics has become mathematically oriented and exclusive with a fixation on " economic growth" as the key indicator of progress, conceived as more important than indicators relating to the health of people, well being or ecosystem integrity.

Economics, the provisioning for needs, is done by all of us. Every creature and every ecosystem has an "economic" or resource need and impact. We need to broaden the scope of economics in order for it to helpful in solving today's socio – and ecological problems. The emerging discourse of Green Economics reclaims economics for all people everywhere, aiming for all people and the biosphere to be beneficiaries rather than inputs. Green Economics rejects the short term timescales of business cycles in favour of geological lengths of time as only archaeological and palaontological explanations can illuminate what is happening.

Green Economics has arisen from the need for an framework which can encompass social and environmental insights and does not factor out "life- world" evidence but instead embraces the complexities of people, nature and their dynamic inter-relationships. Green economics logic is built upon an interdisciplinary range of philosophies and methodologies from human learning, from the economics of Aristotle and Xenophon, through the enlightenment to post-modern illustrations of difference and power relationships. Its world view is that everything happens within the earth's boundaries and so no longer theorises economics as being separate from but rather within the earth's systems. There are no resources which don't come from nature.

Socio- ecological transformations and Revolutions: The relevance of Rosa Luxemburg's analysis for today's solutions

Luxemburg made a number of analytical observations which are useful in starting us on the path to transformation. An updated environmental definition of such transformation is given by Olsson, Folke and Hahn (2004). They define it as resilience, in social – ecological systems, the ability to cope with environmental variability and disturbance events. Characteristics of such a system might include property rights, environmental ethics, public accountability and reciprocal exchange systems. These are all pertinent to learning to live with change and uncertainty and elements can be found in the ideology of indigenous peoples. The industrial revolution brought benefits according to mainstream economics definitions. However Luxemburg correctly predicted some of the drawbacks.

Enclosure and the transformation of property rights

Concurrent with the industrial revolution, the commons began to be enclosed for the benefit of the few who made money out of them and prevented the rest of humanity or other species from accessing them. This has been followed most recently by the enclosure of knowledge with intellectual property rights and patents. (Shiva in Biopiracy). Luxemburg argued that three things were aimed for: to coerce labour power into service, to impose a commodity economy and to separate agriculture and trade and drive farmers off the land and into towns. She showed how colonizers created a fiction that land had always belonged to the political ruler- rather than being owned in common.(Luxemburg 1913 :352.). These ideas have largely been implemented.

Everything has been commodified including, including land, knowledge and ecosystems services which are a new way of defining the role of nature.

Capitalism and the transformation of wealth and power

A new system of economics, capitalism, emerged, whereby the rich could increase their wealth or capital. In theory the poor would benefit as wealth trickled down. There was a theoretical justification for periods of enduring hardship with the Kuznets curve which showed that theoretically less developed countries could take off into an accelerated growth, after a period of hardship. The view that more development along capitalist lines will provide the socio-economic transformation required has pervaded development theories such as sustainable development. It became accepted that the rich should enjoy so-called free trade with no constraints or trade barriers for the good of society, as the invisible hand of the market would ensure their decisions ultimately benefited everyone.

Corporations grew in this laissez faire environment into huge monoliths and many of them are larger and more powerful than governments. Luxemburg argued that it was the very dispossession of the peasants of their common land which provided both the property, and also the labour with which to keep this system going, and hence that poverty is part of the engine of the capitalist system. She foresaw that this system needed previously non industrialised areas, beyond the spatial scope of the capitalist consumption or democratic area, to provide cheap international production but that this would ultimately reach limits of expansion. Encroachment for international production is a little explored area but is extremely pertinent to the issue of democracy. Corporations find an area of potential cheap labour and then set about creating favourable market conditions before entry, being complicit in combinations of civil instability, displacement of people, regime change, economic instability and military action.

Luxemburg realised that expanding capitalism would need new markets, and that there was ultimately a limit to them. Advanced capitalism's requirement of ever expanding rich consumer markets for its products and lower and lower paid, poor workers for its production must eventually must reach a saturation of possibilities, including finite physical limits of resources. Consumption is a battle ground. People are manipulated to consume more by government including infrastructure for global trade corridors and demand is artificially stimulated by activities such as corporate advertising.

Transformations in attitudes to nature, civilisation and agriculture
Luxemburg identified a struggle against the natural economy. Just when humans thought they had tamed nature, largely by means of economics and technology, climate change has forced a rethink of our position in the universe and our role as stewards of nature. We are beginning to realise that rather than using science to control nature, we are going to have to use our knowledge to live within and respect it. The power of nature was pivotal to elements of early belief systems and religions which we can learn from.

Transforming the limits of civilisation- 10,000 years of town dwelling-An audit.
We need to assess the viability of agriculture, and urbanisation during this period of rapid global environmental change and to establish the best course of action. The issues of population growth, people displacement and scarce resources raise important economic questions. Agriculture enabled cities to develop, but the project of "civilisation" itself is under threat. Civilisation derives from *civis*, the Latin word for townsman or citizen, *civis*, adjectival, *civilis*, which implies

urbanisation. Mega-cities surpass human-scale communities, their own local ecosystem services and the carrying capacity of their immediate hinterland. There is an urgent task, fundamental to Green Economics, to reanalyse "civilisation" and to develop strategies for how human living and economic patterns can adapt for survival.

Transforming the human habitat and ecosystem services crisis and the current mass extinction. This is affecting the ability of our habitat to sustain us all, as a species. It is becoming clear that our economics is running into limits of expansion and we need therefore to re-think the whole premise of our economics to limit further human induced global environmental damage. If the consumption rate of the rich countries continues and is adopted by poorer countries we would require the resource of three planets, so we have reached the limits of possible ecological footprints within this earth and the natural world.

Transformations in international production

The internationalisation of production in globalisation is little understood, but is one of the most pertinent phenomena identified by Luxemburg. Large TNCs outsource production across sectors, firms and countries, (Ietto –Gillies 2005 :48) and workers rights are eroded by casualisation. The arms trade has grown rapidly and everything and everyone is commoditized and a growing slave trade including even in children.

Three quarters of world trade originates with multinationals and over a third is internal to the firm precluding regulation or scrutiny or competition from other companies. (Ietto -Gillies UNCTAD 1996).

The globalisation of international production and effects on national and local economies has been described by Dicken (2007). "There has been a huge transformation in the nature and the degree of interconnection in the world economy, and especially in the speed with which such connectivity occurs, involving both the stretching and the intensification of economic relationships. There is today a deep integration organised primarily within and between geographically extensive and complex transnational production networks and through a diversity of mechanisms. There are changes are not so much in volume as in **composition**. There has been a huge increase in intraindustry and intra – firm trade. Both of which are indicators of a more functionally fragmented and geographically dispersed production processes. Dicken (2007: 7)

Flows of material and non material processes are organised into relational structures and processes in which the power relationships between key actors such as firms, states, individuals, and social groups are uneven. (Dicken 2007: 8). States, labour unions and even NGO's compete to attract TNC's. Vertical dimensions of transnational production networks, intersect with territorially defined political and economic systems and horizontal dimensions of territorial systems of different geographical scales. Firms have global reach according to Ohmae,in The end of the nation state. According to the World Trade Report (2005a) 4/5ths of global manufacturing and 2/3rds of agriculture are concentrated in 15 countries, and outward FDI is similarly concentrated with 30% emanating from the US and the UK.

The Surmounting of democracy and government by TNCs and the transformation of existing power structures

Gillies explains that *"transnational companies can and do play governments of different countries or regions against each other with the objective of raising the offer of financial incentives for the location of inward investment FDI . Thus the TNC has a strong element of bargaining power towards both governments and labour force in that it canrelocate to different countries with relatively low costs of change."* .(2005:293 Ietto-Gillies)

This is a concern as there are several countries where democracy is under serious threat. Large MNC's can influence government. For example Shell is widely suspected of this in Nigeria, and Burma Oil in Burma, both of which are repressive regimes. In many cases corporate regulations are created in the same department that ought to be regulating their activity. Regulation has become the subject of lobbying at extra national level in order to resist the impositions and limitations governments place on corporate activity.

Differing currency and taxation laws give firms the opportunity of developing location and intra firm transfer strategies that give them the benefit of transfer pricing manipulation and therefore higher profits. With outsourcing and the transfer of rules and regulations environmental dumping is facilitated.

New markets reflecting environmental and other concerns are hijacked by larger firms buying up more ethical trading houses, for example the Body Shop was bought by L'Oreal. Large family owned organic dairies are bought up by global firms who retain the family name and marketing.

Large firms use their market power to avoid complying with usual labour standards. Lidl has been investigated as a firm with geographical variation in working conditions. In the case of Lidl this affects workers' human dignity such as very limited toilet breaks and pressure on women not to have children to discouraging unions.

The economics system needs to be fed by increasing consumption, and according to Rostow the final state of economies must be a stage of "high mass consumption." Here it has come up against the limits to growth (Meadows et al) . Furthermore, production is oncentrated into large scale operations to create "efficiency," or " lean supply" with a consequent reduction in diversity of suppliers.

Inequalities are widening between and within countries, with key indicators of infant mortality and life expectancy becoming increasingly divergent. Dicken points out that the benefits of trade, are limited in the poorest countries. This is due to dependence on a narrow economics base and exacerbated by downward pressure and lack of stability in the price of traded goods. Combined with a market mechanism that fails to share the benefits equitably (Dicken 2007: 519) this has resulted in the terms of trade worsening considerably between 1990 and 2000.

The characteristics and scope of an economics for socio – ecological transformation

a) Moral and Spiritual aspects of economics for transformation

Satish Kumar, (2007) suggests that we need a transformation in our attitudes to each other, and to other living things on the Earth. He suggests that we have lost the idea of spirit and become wedded to materialism," identifying the roots of this in the views of Descartes and Newton who looked upon the Earth as an object of human dominance. He reminds us that Nature rights are equal to human rights, Kumar suggests we need a *"geo centric world view"*- which is in fact how green economics is constructed with the earth at the center or foot of all activity and observations. Kumar says that we cannot solve a problem in the mindset that caused the problem in the first place and "we need to realise the subservience of economics to ecology."(Kumar 2007:33).

Green Economics recognizes poverty as a moral issue, yet the application of neo-liberal logic appears to be making matters worse for the world's poor. Neo-classical economics views world poverty as offering opportunities for further exploitation as a vast untapped market offering cheap resources and labour for revenue growth (Prahalad and Hammond, 2003, p.1). In Green Economics wealth and power are recognised as inextricably intertwined, so an appropriate level of decision-making is encouraged, which allows access and transparency for everyone. New indicators, rather than just GDP (which only measures the activity, throughput and quantity as monetary value of goods exchanged) show what the social and environmental justice targets could be, analysing trends and identifying risks such as in education, work, consumption, relative distribution of wealth and health of people, species and ecosystems (Anderson, 1991) .

b) Eco – ecological/economic transformation

It is recognised that all these elements need to be reworked, and particularly that power structures need to be changed as economic power is often concentrated in the same hands as political power. Lack of democracy appears to be a factor in several parts of the world where there is unrest or extreme poverty where a small ruling class hold the economic power and control the government

c) Economic objectives for transformation

The objectives of Green Economics are indivisible from its methodoloy:

i) To create economic conditions where social and environmental justice thrives and benefits all people everywhere, non human species, the planet and its systems.

ii) To reform mainstream economics into a discipline which no longer supports or accepts that only a minority can be wealthy, but which works towards a fair and equitable society which lives within its means in all senses. Further Green Economics seeks to re-examine broader versions of reality, beyond the views of the rich and powerful, rejecting the idea of rational economic man "homoeconomicus" as a benchmark in order to hear different voices, as proposed for example by feminist theory (Ghilligan,1982).

A key reason for mainstream economics' failure is its lack of influences and learning from other areas. Green Economics attempts to combine trans- and inter-disciplinary studies to counteract this narrow thinking, As Welford exhorts, *"if we were to emphasize moderation and sufficiency rather than maximisation of output, consumption, incomes and profits, this would have a radical and fundamental impact on the way we lead our lives and the way we treat the environment."* (Welford, 2007)

iii)To enable all people everywhere to participate in the economy with equal power, equal rights and with equal access to decision making. Green Economics methodology brings new perspectives to conventional economics tools and enables it to reveal the power relationships and vested interests in the global economy. It also reincorporates political economy and the moral and transformational aspects of the economics of Smith (1776). It offers new solutions to 'managing the commons', which has been restricted to theoretical models (von Neumann and Morgenstern), and exercises based on the prisoner's dilemma (Arrow, 1951) which perpetuate assumptions of self interest as the key motivation of human activity.

Learning from this broad range of wisdom is essential to enable our economic systems to adapt to operating within a 'carrying capacity' of the earth. Pegging the level of that capacity should be a pressing subject for economic debate. Green Economics re-embeds the economy within ecological and social structures. Economic growth, progress and development are measured by indicators that aim towards 'creation' mimicking the abundance of nature, not 'annihilation' of resources (Goldsmith, 2005). Profit, prices and markets are regarded as incidental, rather than drivers of the economic system. Green Economics treats people, the planet, nature, non-human species, and the biosphere as beneficiaries, not just resources or economic factors of production.

This new discipline operates on the principle that the needs of people and natural systems must be satisfied simultaneously. The purpose of economic activity is to satisfy needs, not to enhance the power of people, corporations or states. Global industrialism, according to Dobson (2000, p.27), is regarded with suspicion. The welfare value of products is questioned, as well as their transformation into forms of identity through marketing.

The concept of equilibrium is reclaimed from price concerns to encompass impacts and effects in political, social, moral and ecological terms reflecting concern for people, society, non-human species, nature and the biosphere as a holistic whole. In this way, Green Economics acts as a filter for other systems as it is does not seek to impose one system globally, as in capitalism or socialism, but rather advocates diversity using a Green Economics analysis for each situation. Many practitioners of conventional economics are critical of their own discipline, according to Medena and Samuels (1996) and Ormerod (1994). "The subject has become so obscure that even orthodox economists are bemoaning its intellectual poverty," says Kitson (2005). Mainstream economists observe that their work has little bearing on the real 'life-world' or on important concerns such as ending poverty (Kitson, 2005). However, disciplinary insurgence is rare because of the limited professional progress that usually follows. Unfortunately, many well-known economists, for example, Pasinetti (2005) continue to advocate a more intensified business as usual approach, fixated on growth, more profit, which entails increasing economic hegemony of global corporations and is framed by increasingly elaborate theory,.

Green economists argue that these blinkered and alienating positivist dogmas cannot solve the problems of today.

d) Transformation in attitudes to economics and its relationship to science and earth science

Mainstream economics employs a set of positivist, modern tools to produce the desired simplified logic that is vital for the picture of the world that is its basis. It produces results that contradict insights from other sciences such as the urgency of human induced climate change. It is focused on an infinite growth assumption and supposedly innate individual preferences in our prescribed role as passive consumers.

Green Economics can integrate the world's big ideas, such as those presented by The Big Bang, Evolution, Quantum Mechanics, Risk Theory, New System Theory, Relativity and Climate Change. Green Economics incorporates the ideas of progress in scientific thinking and in scientific methodology such as natural science, ecology and social science rather than econometrics. reen Economics therefore challenges the reductionism and supposed objectivity of mainstream economics which is based on the supremacy of unadjusted market solutions at the expense of people and the planet.

e) A Transformation from short termism to long termism

Green Economics takes a view that is much longer-term than the short business cycles of neoclassical and economics. Due to its consideration of the effects of a transaction on the 200 000th generation and beyond (Myers, 1985), Green Economics can draw from history, paleontology and archaeology. As a consequence, Green Economics does not simply discount the future. Intergenerational equity is investigated by such writers as Alderson (2006) who is greatly influenced by Chong (2006). Instead of mobilising the resources of the planet in support of human kind, we must surely mobilise the resources of human kind in support of the planet. This postulates a revision of our value systems, social paradigms and consumption culture (Myers, 1985).

f) An inclusive transformation including women and men together, using a feminist economics discourse

There are two realms of economic activity, that of competitive production and exchange in markets and that of direct production such as subsistence agriculture, care and reciprocity. Feminist economics contributes the notion that production does indeed occur in the home or 'okia'. Mies (1994) concentrates on methodology in economics and has been in integral influence on the development of green economics along with Mellor (1992) and Henderson (1983). Their approaches warn against theories that legitimise a single-gendered *homo economics* (rational economic man) version or 'story' of reality that excludes *gynaika oikonomika,* (*economic woman)* from the public economic sphere. Feminist methodologies allow us to dig into the foundations of a discipline and expose them as particular and contingent. It reveals the placing of boundaries in economics as an intensely political act.

Feminist economics has opened debate about the role of women in the global economy (Mies, 1994) and found evidence of patriarchy and exploitation. Women have provided unpaid, nonvalued, invisible work and the discipline of economics has excluded their experience. There has, been a recognition of the power of nature, due to human induced climate change and this has challenged the belief of man's domination over nature, which is embodied in patriarchal culture.

There is an urgent need to design an economics which helps to limit further ecological devastation, and to design an economics which can work under some of the radically changed environmental conditions predicted in some scenarios, such as agriculture being limited to smaller regions of the world. Major climatic and other shifts could bring a lack of availability and viability of natural resources impacting on our basic needs such as food and water and the likelihood of major displacement of people. Our economics must be able to deal with such severe problems and the inherent uncertaintyof climate change.

Conclusion

Humanity has come to a crossroads where we have reached the limits to the economic logic on which its agrarian, industrial, and technological revolutions were based. Economic growth sustained by resources in furtherance of this aim have been discovered to be finite. Yet supply chains have become more globalised and wasteful of resources. Furthermore, the natural world has turned out to be extremely complex and fragile whilst at the same time enjoying the ultimate power to wipe us out as along with many other species. In order to preserve a natural world which we could reasonably call home- and an economics based in that home- or oikia, we need to undertake a rapid socio-ecological transformation and to re-align our entire economics systems.

Luxemburg also pointed out the need for grassroots democracy and co-operation. Recent primate studies indicate that co-operation is an important aspect of society, De Wal (2005), contradicting economic theories like the prisoner's dilemma and the tragedy of the commons. De Waal suggests that reciprocity arose from sharing of food within the group, in prehistoric times. This, he suggests involves keeping a balance of good deeds which we expect them to be roughly equal and reciprocal.

Main stream neo classical economics has been based on inequalty between rich and poor, between men and women, between man and other species, between man and the planets natural systems. Our economic system has allowed for one fifth of humankind to go to bed hungry at night and there is no justification for this. If we want to call ourselves *civilised,* it's time to transform in a peaceful and positive way to a caring and sharing culture where everyone and everything counts, and into a Green Economics system of abundance and growth in nature shared by all and richly embedded in the natural world.

The ideas in this chapter were first published in German and in English by the Rosa Luxembourg Foundation in Germany in 2008, in a book edited by Kraus G. and Delheim J.

Part 3 Measuring Progress

3.1 Sensational! Against the tide of shallow value

Joss Tantram

"What does the world weigh? Its scales are crooked. It weighs life and labor in the balance against silver and gold. That will never balance, it spills a lot of life that way."
Walter M. Miller Jnr "A Canticle for Liebowitz"

We need to campaign for real value

Real value refers to those things which have meaning in sustaining and supporting life, whether human or otherwise.

Shallow value refers to value priced beyond its worth; where value is the product of hype, glitter and market hysteria rather than of human and ecological need or meaning.

It is time to value what is precious to us all. The water, food and air that give us life, the shelter and warmth that allow comfort, the security of place, equitable income, education and communication that allow us to plan for our and our children's future and the ability to develop, share, discuss and distribute ideas about the world and our existence.

Swamped by shallow value

Shallow value dominates our media, our discourse and our markets.

Shallow value is the triumph of sensation over meaning, surface over depth and gratification over satisfaction. It is by no means restricted to the obvious and literal elevation of image over substance in the media but has increasingly pervaded the everyday, becoming the base currency of capitalism itself and influencing the very core of how we understand and value what is worthwhile.

Capitalism has come to depend upon sensation to sell its products; brand has become the medium for translating a set of corporate behaviours, undertaken to maximise private profit, into a set of implied emotions and sensations. Buying a product or wearing a brand, capitalism implies, will help us to be who we want to be, to be happier, more beautiful, better and more fulfilled people.

Of course this is nothing new, sensational bubbles have been a feature of markets for many hundreds of years. More explicitly, the foundations of modern advertising consciously used and adapted the then emergent science of psychology for the purposes of linking products to a buyer's sense of self and self-worth.

Alastair McIntosh, the scholar and activist, has written extensively on the issue, related to tobacco marketing and the pornography of consumerism. In his logical and emotional tour de force "Hell and High Water" (2008) McIntosh summarises consumerism's deliberate "hacking" of psychological circuitry as follows *"Could this be the core dynamic by which consumerism sustains itself? Addictions are powerful precisely because they taunt us with our heart's longing. But they fake it. They short-circuit and actually block off the real thing – the focus of our ultimate concern."*

Building upon McIntosh's thesis, I would argue that this sensationalist agenda has gone far further than merely representing the (now) unspoken design principles of advertising and marketing, it has also become unconsciously embedded within the very DNA of every facet of economic and financial activity, warping our conceptions of what is valuable, mistaking shallow economic price for real value.

The fetishisation of financial markets

One of the main reasons financial markets struggle with real value is due to the problem of economic externalities. These are the environmental, social and economic costs and benefits which either take place "outside" institutional accounts or occur across the balance sheets of multiple actors, stakeholders or proxies. The reconciliation and adequate pricing of economic externalities has become a major source of activity for environmentalists and economists seeking to address systemic and unpriced risks and market failures.

The problem of externalities becomes much, much more problematic when we consider the active disinterest of modern financial markets in their original, fundamental purpose. Financial markets first grew as a way of providing financial resources to agricultural and mercantile enterprise, allowing endeavours to be undertaken in expectation of future reward. For instance, to allow a farmer to buy next year's seed on the promise of this years' crop or a merchant to invest in stock for the next sea voyage in the expectation that the current one would land and its cargo be sold.

Financiers supporting such endeavours would of course need to make an assessment as to whether the investee in question was likely to be able to make good on the debt – and the way that they organised and conducted their business was therefore a key area of judgement for investors.

Today's markets in listed companies are theoretically no different – representing a set of companies seeking investment and requiring a judgement on behalf of investors as to whether those companies have the strategy, risk management and staff capabilities to execute that strategy and deliver a return on investment.

It may therefore be presumed that an interest in, and analysis of, the fundamental viability, utility and longevity of those companies would be an essential area of interest for investors. While this is certainly the case for a wide range of individual investors, it is not necessarily true for the market as a whole. Market movement and the behaviours and inferred intentions of other market actors have become more important than the analysis of company fundamentals.

Market movement has become king, coupled with the rise of automatic, sub-second trading technologies, investors have become more interested in making sure they are not left stranded by market hysteria than acting as financiers and stewards of companies.

The UK economist John Kay entertainingly explores this fetishised market in his Parable of the Ox, which describes the perverse development of a market focussed solely upon market actors (experts in the art of Ox weighing) rather than upon its original purpose (weighing an actual Ox).

I would additionally argue that beyond the pornography of marketing and advertising, beyond the mistaken belief that price equals value, beyond a focus upon the market rather than the investee, there is one further perversion of real value that we have allowed to take place, the belief that just because a thing can be traded, that it should be.

The calculated sensationalism of price

The grand champions of sensation over meaning are not peddlers of sex or even of products but those in financial markets who have mistranslated the real, underlying sources of social, ecological and economic value into abstracted price.

Price is not value itself, it is a signifier of value. However, it is one which largely omits the value of externalities.

In sustainability terms this is a problem because the major means of determining behaviour in our capitalist world is the price signal. We continue to knowingly explore and exploit dwindling and dangerous sources of non renewable fuel because price perversely pushes us to, telling us that the use of free energy from the wind and the sun is somehow more expensive overall. Renewables are often currently more economically expensive, but the price of such fuels is not the same as their value to us.

Ceteris non paribus – all things are not equal

Efforts to define the price and value of natural capital can equally fall prey to confusion between price and value. We are easily lulled into the notion that if we price something we can make a rational decision to trade it and that it is somehow fungible (capable of mutual substitution) – that the money we receive in return for a trade can be used to obtain a substitute which is functionally useful in the same way as the property traded in the first place.

Yet there are some areas where such fungibility just does not apply. If you could achieve a price that you were happy to receive in order to sell your mother, could you use that money to buy yourself another?

Trading the stuff of life

"…intellects vast and cool and unsympathetic, regarded this earth with envious eyes, and slowly and surely drew their plans against us."
H. G. Wells

Financial markets have become obsessed with shallow value and too remote from anything that resembles real life for too long. Recent years have shown us just a fraction of the dangers of exotic financial instruments, of bundling up a range of debts, and labelling them as risk free investments for trading long after we have forgotten the underlying value of the asset (or absence of asset) upon which they were originally based.

Such abstraction goes far beyond the re-packaging of potentially bad debts. Financial markets have, in recent years, undertaken trading in food – the fundamental components of human survival – for purposes far removed from the allocation and distribution of those assets to those in need of them. This trade has become a sensational distortion of the purpose of markets in food stuffs, focused merely around the idea that the thing traded can give rise to profit, rather than that the thing traded can give rise to adequate nutrition.

Can life arise from poisoned markets?

"Capitalism is the astounding belief that the most wickedest of men will do the most wickedest of things for the greatest good of everyone."
John Maynard Keynes

In such a fetishised market, can the trading of environmental and natural value, through Carbon Credits, Conservation Banking Credits, Transferable Development Rights and other such theoretically "sustainable finance instruments" possibly give rise to the sort of long term, strategic outcomes that our planet needs or will they merely become just another means by which common value can be turned into private profit?

Surely if we are to truly use the mechanisms of capital markets and international trading to deliver environmental and social good then those markets need to be fundamentally reformed, such that they are capable of truly valuing a common future as more valuable than a private present.

Such markets must have both the incentive and capability to deliver the required strategic outcomes. They must rise to the challenge of valuing activities and behaviour which pay off over the long term, to compound rather than discount the value of a more sustainable future and to start to value decisions that allow the growth and stability of ecosystems and societies as an outcome of value to the market as a whole. Allowing sustainable decisions and behaviours to be inherently valued and prioritised rather than considered as an afterthought.

Truly sustainable markets, those dedicated to the discovery, trading and distribution of *real value* would therefore, naturally:

Value thermodynamically optimisation – such that their use of energy and materials would be in alignment with the physical characteristics and limits of the planet with a focus upon 'entropic efficiency'.

Value abundance rather than scarcity – prioritising technologies and behaviours which deliver either *natural* (e.g. biologically-based) or *managed* (e.g. through closed loop stewardship) abundance.

Enhance natural vitality – valuing technologies and processes which make use of the planet's natural rejuvenative and productive abilities, learning from and utilising natural production techniques as the basis for their technological and industrial models.

Balance their interdependence – recognising and balancing the web of social interdependencies they exist within, seeking mutual equity within all relationships.

It is time for real value. It is time to value the abundance, vitality and interdependence of all that exists on this precious, irreplaceable planet. To move beyond the surface, sensational value of current market price and start to define and trade the real value which sustains us all.

3.2 Entropic Overhead – measuring the circular economy

Joss Tantrum

"Errors using inadequate data are much less than those using no data at all."
Charles Babbage

The broken hourglass
Do you break the timer when your boiled egg is cooked?
Our economy does, it is like a broken hourglass. We collect together valuable materials, apply energy and labour, put them into products that have yet more added design and brand value and spew them out into the world before starting again (mostly), from scratch.

This of course would all be fine if scarcity was not a problem: if the materials, energy and inputs we rely upon for industrial production were either eternally abundant or safe to distribute and use. However in our current industrial models this is simply not the case.

To pursue the disposable hourglass metaphor, instead of merely turning it over when the sand has run through (a cradle-to-cradle, or circular industrial model), we smash it, buy another hourglass (a cradle-to-grave industrial model) – and maybe pop the old one in the recycling if we're feeling virtuous.
This is all fine until the raw materials, energy and skills to make more hourglasses start to get scarce or expensive. Then we would have to start to pick over the remains of the broken one to collect these now valuable raw materials for remanufacture and reuse.

How much easier is it to retain the investment that has gone in to making an hourglass than to smash it and start again every time we want to boil an egg?

Measuring the performance of different models

The performance difference between a broken and unbroken hourglass economy is easy to sum up simply – "a lot". However, in practice more marginal differences can be crucial. A metric would allow us to measure the difference between potential courses of action and help determine the processes and activities most effective in achieving a circular, sustainable economy. But given the complexity of modern industrial processes and the fact that a well-functioning circular economy would add further convolutions, how do we develop a suitable measure?

The common denominator for all industrial activities is energy, therefore a metric which refers to the energetic characteristics of systems and processes is required. We believe this is entropy.

Entropy applies without exception to all activities and processes. Given that universality, it might be used to measure the overall efficiency of our economy and the transition to a circular economy.

Entropy applies primarily to energy and not to matter – something we are fundamentally concerned with in the circular economy. However, matter is of little use until we organise, process, manufacture and distribute it in products and services – all these activities require energy.

We therefore propose the metric of Entropic Overhead.

What is Entropic Overhead?

Entropic Overhead is a relative lifecycle measure of the energetic efficiency of maintaining the utility of a product or service, or reusing its constituent materials.

It can be used to assess the energetic efficiency differences between alternative pathways: for example the energy required to either make a new product or retrieve its resources to original utility, versus the energy that would be spent on retaining the original products' use. It can also be used to assess the efficiency of alternative uses of constituent resources, beyond the original utility, in different products and processes within a circular economy.

In terms of the hourglass metaphor, it is the energetic performance difference between:

-obtaining a new timer with virgin materials;

-obtaining a new timer and making some further use of the constituent materials of the old one for other purposes;

-remaking the broken timer by retrieving and reprocessing all the constituent materials (and supplementing with new materials where needed), and;

-avoiding breakage and simply turning the hourglass over.

Entropic Overhead is therefore a measure of the differential energy costs we would bear because we failed to make full use of the initial investment we have made in creating a functioning object with long term utility.

Why we need a metric for the circular economy

Humans seek simplicity, and we value simple measures to tell us whether we are moving in the "right" direction and to help assess marginal choices.

However, this desire does cause us problems, such as an over reliance upon metrics that are so abstracted as to be meaningless or even dangerous. GNP was famously condemned by Senator Robert Kennedy as a metric which "*measures everything in short except that which is worthwhile*".

The dictum "If you can't measure it, you can't manage it" might be trite and one dimensional (and often wrong), but in this case it is useful. How do we measure progress towards a circular economy and, is there one measure, rather than a million, that we can use?

"Essentially, all models are wrong, but some are useful"
George E. P. Box

Finding a metric that applies everywhere is difficult. In order to do so, we must look to universal principles which apply to all, without exception. The <u>laws of thermodynamics</u> are a good candidate as they represent a fundamental framework for physical existence.

What about zero impact energy and materials?

Entropic Overhead is an ideal measure to indicate the difference between varying production approaches because, in our current unsustainable economy, energy is a useful proxy for environmental efficiency.

However, it would theoretically be possible to have an economy that used only zero impact energy sources and materials. In this utopian situation, Entropic Overhead would be less suited to indicate the sustainability or otherwise of processes.

Therefore the metric is a transitionary one – useful until we achieve a circular economy which uses zero impact energy. Before this occurs, we can rate the Entropic Overhead of different processes using carbon intensity factors to allow for different means of production.

What scale can Entropic Overhead be applied to?

Any scale we like: from a product level, comparing the performance of a leased product to a "disposable" one; to the level of a value chain; for comparing business models, or comparing national & international economies.

Who else has explored this?

"It is not once nor twice but times without number that the same ideas make their appearance in the world." Aristotle

Various people have explored the concept of entropy in different fields from economics to social dynamics, including Frederick Soddy in the 1930s and more recently Nicholas Georgescu-Roegen. Many have caught the imagination and many have foundered, possibly because the concept of entropy has been misunderstood or misappropriated – often stretched to apply to social organisation or economics.

However, this doesn't mean the concept is without value, particularly if we don't over extend our interpretation of the underlying science. Entropic Overhead is seeking to avoid the pitfalls that misappropriation of the concept can create by focusing upon the fundamental energetics of different industrial and economic processes and not over extending the application of the second law.

Measures that matter

Truly useful measures are required if we are to assess and drive towards a sustainable world. At the physical level, sustainability requires us to find ways to exist and thrive in a system which is closed to matter – though open to energy.

This existential context should define our ways of measuring and managing performance yet we have effectively <u>ignored</u> the reality of life on this planet for too long.

As we start to recognise and push against the hard limits of existence we need measures which tell us, meaningfully, how we are performing and the value of doing so.

3.3 Growth Creates Poverty

Dr Vandana Shiva
theme of her talk at Sydney Opera House for the Festival of Dangerous

GDP, or Gross Domestic Product, has emerged as both the most powerful number , and dominant concept in our times. It is supposed to measure the wealth of nations. Limitless growth is the fantasy of economists, businesses and politicians. It is seen as a measure of wealth and progress.

However, economic growth hides the poverty it creates, both through the destruction of nature ,and nature's ability to provide goods and services, as well as through destroying the self provisioning capacities of societies and communities.

"Growth" was created as a measure to mobilize resources during the war. GDP is based on creating an artificial and fictitious boundary, and then assuming that if you produce what you consume, you do not produce. In effect , "growth" measures the conversion of nature into cash, and commons into commodities.

Thus nature's amazing cycles of renewal of water and nutrients are defined into non-production,. The peasants of the world who provide 72% of the food do not produce, and women who do most of the work do not work in this paradigm of "growth".

A living growing forest does not contribute to growth, but when trees are killed and cut down and sold as timber, we have growth. Healthy societies and communities do not contribute to growth, but disease creates growth through hospitals and sales of patented medicine.

Water available as a commons shared freely and protected by all provides water for all. However ,it does not create "growth". But when Coca Cola sets up a plant , mines the water and puts it into plastic water bottles , there is growth of the economy. This growth is based on creating poverty for nature and local communities. Water extracted beyond nature's capacity to renew and recharge creates a water famine. Women walk longer distances looking for drinking water. In the village of Plachimada in Kerala, when the walk for water became 10 kms, Mylamma, a local tribal woman said enough is enough. We cannot walk further. The Coca Cola plant must shut down. The movement that the women started eventually led to the closure of the plant.

Evolution has gifted us the seed, and farmers have selected, bred, and diversified is the basis of food production. Seed that renews itself and multiplies in the commons produces seed for the next season, as well as food. However farmer bred and farmer saved seed is seen as not contributing to growth. It creates and renews life . But it does lead to profits. Growth begins when seed is genetically modified and patented, farmers are prevented from saving seeds and must buy seed every season.

Nature is impoverished as biodiversity is eroded. Farmers are impoverished as seed, a free, open source resource, is transformed into a patented commodity. Buying seed every year is a recipe for debt for India's poor peasants. And as seed monopolies have been established, farmers debt has increased. More that 284000 farmers caught in a debt trap in India have committed suicide since seed started to be privatised and monopolized in 1995.

Poverty is also created when public systems are privatized. Thus privatization of water, electricity, health, education does generate growth through profits . But it also generates poverty by forcing people to spend large amounts of money on what was available at affordable costs, as a common good. When every aspect of life is commercialized and commoditized, living becomes more costly, and people become poorer.

Both ecology and economics have emerged from the same roots -- "oikos" -- the Greek word for household.

As long as economics was focused on the household, it recognized and respected its basis in natural resources, the limits of ecological renewal. It was focused on providing for basic human needs within these limits. Economics as based on the household was women centered.

Today, economics is separated from, and opposed to both ecological processes and basic needs. While the destruction of nature has been justified on grounds of creating growth, for the majority of people poverty and dispossession has increased. While being non-sustainable it is also economically unjust. While being promoted as "economic development", it is leading to underdevelopment, while projecting growth, it is causing life threatening destruction.

The dominant model of "economic development" has in fact become anti-life. In fact when economies are measured only in terms of money flow, inequalities grow, the rich get richer, the poor get poorer. And the rich might be rich in monetary terms – but they too are poor in the wider context of what being human means.

The resource demands of the current model of the economy are leading to resource wars – oil wars, water wars, food wars. There are three levels of violence involved in non-sustainable development. The first is the violence against the earth, which is expressed as the ecological crisis. The second is the violence against people, which is expressed as poverty, destitution and displacement. The third is the violence of war and conflict, as the powerful reach for the resources that lie in other communities and countries for their limitless appetites and limitless growth.

I have witnessed again and again that as people's resources are commoditized and people's economies are commercialized, money flow does increase in society, but it is mainly outflow from nature and people to commercial interests and corporations. The money economy grows but nature's economy and people's economy shrinks.

Increases of money flow through GDP has become totally disassociated from real value, but those who accumulate financial resources can then stake claim on the real resources of people – their land and water, their forests and seeds. "Hungry"

money is predating on the last drop of water and last inch of land on the planet. This is not an end to poverty. It is an end to human rights and justice. People are being made disposable in a world where money rules and the value of money has replaced the human values that lead to sustainability, justice and human dignity.
This is why countries like Bhutan have adopted the Gross National Happiness in place of Gross National Product as their measure of well being. Even economists like Joseph Stiglitz and Amartya Sen have admitted that GDP does not capture the human condition

We need to create measures beyond GDP, economies beyond the global supermarket ,to rejuvenate real wealth and authentic well-being. We need to remember that the real currency of life is life itself.

3.4 It Can't Just be the Economy, Stupid

Christopher Brook

'It's the economy, stupid' is one of the most well-known phrases in politics and it perfectly highlights the problem with politics today. However, you cannot blame the politicians that they prioritise the economy over everything else; the problem lies in how we measure their success. GDP is the most quoted statistic about any country's economy with economic policies being judged mainly by their effect on GDP. Most other policies are heavily judged on their effect on this one statistic. Governments have risen and fallen on the back of this one statistic. In 1934 Kuznets warned against equating GDP with well-being. However, for the last 70 years that is what it has become.

The official GDP we know today was created in the 1940's in response to World War 2 planning needs in the USA. It was then strengthened as a globally-used measure due to the Bretton Woods conference. GDP is a measure of economic activity; it measures the total output of goods and services of an economy.

An earlier version of GDP was created by Simon Kuznets in the 1930's in response to the information gap revealed by the great depression. He would have been horrified by the latest adjustments to GDP. Statisticians have begun to include the value from drugs and prostitution in GDP. Kuznets only wanted to include activities that contributed to society's well-being. He argued it was pointless to count things that detract from human welfare. I doubt today he would have been thrilled by the notion that the more prostitutes visited and the more drugs consumed, the healthier the economy. It signals desperation on the part of governments trying anyway to mould the statistics to indicate a stronger economy. GDP also fails to account for leisure time and so again fails at measuring well-being. Much of the recent growth has come about due to people working longer hours and so, although GDP is now at 2008 levels, again we are not actually better off. A famous speech by Robert F Kennedy at the University of Kansas in 1968 highlights the ineptitude of GDP as a result of including 'regrettables'.

"Gross National Product counts air pollution and cigarette advertising, and ambulances to clear our highways of carnage. It counts special locks for our doors and the jails for the people who break them. It counts the destruction of the redwood and the loss of our natural wonder in chaotic sprawl. It counts napalm and counts nuclear warheads and armoured cars for the police to fight the riots in our cities. It counts Whitman's rifle and Speck's knife, and the television programs which glorify violence in order to sell toys to our children. Yet the gross national product does not allow for the health of our children, the quality of their education or the joy of their play. It does not include the beauty of our poetry or the strength of our marriages, the intelligence of our public debate or the integrity of our public officials. It measures neither our wit nor our courage, neither our wisdom nor our learning, neither our compassion nor our devotion to our country, it measures everything in short, except that which makes life worthwhile. And it can tell us everything about America except why we are proud that we are Americans."

However, some argue that GDP was never intended to measure well-being and so this critique is no different to criticising a thermometer for not telling us how comfortable we are. But there is far more wrong with GDP.

GDP helps to fortify the largest 2 problems facing us today. The first is environmental degradation and climate change. GDP is a measure of flow and not stock. This means it takes no account of capital depreciation, either natural or physical (although Net National Depreciation (NNP) includes physical depreciation). Therefore GDP ignores the effects of depleted resources and the services that ecosystems provide. In 1997 it was estimated that the world's ecosystem provides benefits valued at $33 trillion per year (Constanza et.al 1997). This means cutting down a tree or extracting oil adds to GDP far more than it should, because cutting down a tree for lumber is valued at more than the service of that tree to the eco-system - currently measured as 0. GDP will not help us reach a more sustainable level of resource use. Neither does it account for the externalities, the by-products of our growth. According to the World Bank 2013 report Diagnostic Assessment of Select Environmental Challenges in India, the annual cost of environmental degradation in India is 5.7%. Given that in the last 2 years India's growth has been close to 5% per annum, then India is actually shrinking in terms of its long term development. If GDP does not begin to include these costs then it will never account for the trade-off between the present and the future.

The second problem is inequality. GDP takes no account of how income is divided between people. This has led to trickle-down economics being the main method to grow the economy. Income tax rates on the highest earners have been slashed to help promote this growth where the benefits slowly trickle down. Even though we are wealthier, and probably all better off, the gross inequalities this has created are unjustified. A little inequality is needed, but the levels we are reaching today are becoming dangerous to society and damaging social capital (trust), which is vital to society. These costs to inequality lead to a threshold effect. Beyond this threshold increases in GDP are offset by the costs of inequality, lost leisure and natural capital depletion. (Cobb et.al, 2007; Max-Neef,1995). There is an increasing body of research that shows that further increases in material well-being have the negative side effects of reducing community cohesion, healthy relationships, knowledge and other dimensions of happiness. Inequality has other associated costs such as poorer overall health, decreased worker productivity, greater social unrest and lower levels of investment (Anna Bernasek, 2006). Furthermore, unequal growth counts less towards overall improvements in welfare. This is because conspicuous consumption by the rich is less beneficial than those who are poorer; families being fed is more beneficial than one man in a Ferrari. It would be far better to use the median, rather than mean income as this measures the increasing income of the middle man in society.

Despite these problems that GDP causes, as a measure it is becoming outdated in the new world and struggles to measure what it is here for, economic activity. It was hard enough to avoid the problems of double counting, when most things produced were physical goods. Diane Coyle calls 'GDP an artefact of the age of mass production'. GDP is terrible at capturing the value of services. This was not a problem when service sectors were small but in modern developed societies the service sectors account for up to two thirds of GDP. Intangible goods by nature are hard to calculate as they have no direct value. Only a few people, deep in the statistics department, understand the concept of 'financial services indirectly measured'. Some may argue the solution is that a service is worth what the market is willing to pay for it. However there is a greater issue here. GDP gives no way to differentiate between the quality and quantity of services. For instance the best example is health care in the USA. According to the World Bank data, US spending per capita on healthcare in 2012 was $8,895, compared to $3,647 in the UK and $5,741 in Canada, whereas life expectancy in 2012 was 78.7, 81.5 and 81.2 respectively. Yes, there will be other reasons for lower life expectancy, but given they spend well over twice the amount that is spent in the UK, you would expect life expectancy to be higher, if more spending meant a better service.

A major aspect of current economies is innovation. However GDP does not account for this. If your computer is twice as powerful as 10 years ago then you are, in reality, better off, as the price per power has fallen. However GDP is very bad at capturing this idea of 'hedonic accounting'. Even if the market value of what is produced does not increase, people can still be better off.

The internet also has large implications for GDP. The internet means that the marginal cost of many goods is tending to zero. This leads to complications of how to measure the value of goods such as online music that do not have a price, because their marginal cost is 0.

GDP then misses a whole section of the economy. It takes no account of non-marketed activity. The most commonly cited example is housework. This work is hard to calculate. As Keynes pointed out, when a man marries his housekeeper, GDP declines. This is because when he pays his housewife that increases GDP, as a transaction has taken place. Conversely if a family member does it for free, no transaction is recorded and so GDP does not increase.

GDP can also exaggerate the benefits of globalisation. Gross National Product (GNP) was used up to 1990. The difference between GDP and GNP is tiny and many thought would be insignificant. It turns out that it makes a great deal of difference for many countries. GDP looks at the output within the country. GNP looks at the income of the people, in the country. As countries began to adopt the policies of the Washington consensus, they started to privatise and become more open to trade and globalisation. Economic activity in many countries increased. However more and more of the income was going outside the country. For example, if you have a foreign owned mine, the company takes the resource, degrades the environment, with royalties in some cases of 1 or 2 percent, so almost none of the income from the mine goes to people in the country. So GDP is going up, but any measure of Green GNP would show the country declining. There are some really dramatic examples like in Papua New Guinea, where Green GDP would actually fall.

These concerns over GDP are being realised and governments and statisticians are looking into new ways to measure our progress. The report, *Mismeasuring Our Lives: Why GDP Doesn't Add Up by Amartya Sen and Joseph Stiglitz*(2009) concluded that our standard metric of economic wellbeing was not up to the job. Worse, they thought too much focus on GDP could send policy makers in the wrong direction – for example, expanding their banking industries and ignoring more basic things such as access to education or health. "If we have the wrong metrics, we will strive for the wrong things," they concluded. This summarises the largest problem of all with GDP. While government success is measured by increasing the level of GDP, then that is what governments will strive to do. This will mean a continuation of trickle down economic policies which will increase the earnings for the rich and marginal increases for the rest. It will lead to the continued destruction of our planet and ecosystems as governments prioritise GDP over the planet. How many environmental policies are rejected because they may hamper growth? However, if governments were not judged by GDP then they would be freer to follow the sustainable policies we need.

But is GDP the lesser of 2 evils, is it just the best we have and just need to use it more wisely? No, there are many other measures of well-being and the environment that better capture our lives.

A few methods have looked at adjusting GDP by expanding what us included. These include Green GDP and the Genuine Progess Indicatro (GPI)

Green accounting has become almost a sub-field in itself in recent years, with many scholars estimating different versions using different classifications. Green GDP requires that net natural capital consumption, including resource depletion, environmental degradation, and protective and restorative environmental initiatives, be subtracted from traditional GDP.

While GDP measures current income, GPI is aimed at measuring the sustainability of that income. GPI makes deductions for income inequality, costs of crime, environmental degradation and loss of leisure and adds in services from consumer durables, public infrastructure and benefits of volunteering and housework. Basically, GPI includes economic activity than enhances or diminishes social capital. Kuznets would approve. Yes, the GPI does have problems too, they all will. For example, the GPI would increase if we reflooded the fens, although in reality we are better off. However this is a nitpicky example and, in areas without malaria, preserving wetlands does improve well-being. For GPI to be a more precise guide to policy, these broad categories — "net forest change," "net wetlands change," "net farmland change" — could be disaggregated. This would easily be solved by more funding.

Others measures use GDP and other indicators to create composite indicators.

The most famous composite measure of development is the Human Development Index (HDI). The HDI is a composite measure of income, education and health. Health is measured by life expectancy, education by both mean years of schooling and expected years of schooling, and income by the logarithm of GNI(log so the marginal benefit falls). However even better is the Inequality Adjusted HDI (IHDI). In the IHDI all 3 variables, income, health and education are discounted to account for inequality. I will not bore you with the statistics here but to those interested the paper is *lkire, S. & Foster, J. (2010) Designing the Inequality-Adjusted Human Development Index (HDI)*. In their report they rightly comment on the issues of collecting the data. Obviously they cannot find the exact distribution of life expectancy or educational level as in many developing countries this data is not recorded, although they do make a good attempt to estimate it.However picking out inequalities for a large number of variables in a composite measure of well-being would not be possible. Even so it would not have to be, as the inequality could be just estimated on a few measures that are easily accessible.

The Happy planet index, another composite measure created by the New Economic. The index is an efficiency measure, it ranks countries on how many long and happy lives they produce per unit of environmental input. – It is calculated using the following formula.

$$\text{Happy Planet Index} \approx \frac{\text{Experienced well-being} \times \text{Life expectancy}}{\text{Ecological footprint}}$$

Well-being is calculated using the 'ladder of life' from the Gallup World Poll. This asks respondents to imagine a ladder, where 0 represents the worst possible life and 10 the best possible life, and report the step of the ladder they feel they currently stand on . The HPI uses the Ecological Footprint promoted by the environmental charity World Wildlife Fund (WWF) as a measure of resource consumption. It is a per capita measure of the amount of land required to sustain a country's consumption patterns, measured in terms of global hectares (g ha) which represent a hectare of land with average productive biocapacity. The result is a number between 0 and 100 for each country. By 2050 they want each country to achieve a score of 89 by 2050. Their results show currently no country is able to combine success across the three goals of high life expectancy, high experienced well-being and living within environmental limits. Whilst many high-income countries score low because of their large Ecological Footprints, the lowest income countries in sub-Saharan Africa tend to rank even lower because of low life expectancy and low well-being. Interestingly, High and medium development Latin American countries score highest in delivering fairly long and happy lives with a relatively low Ecological Footprint.

The OECD Better Life Index is a first attempt to bring together internationally comparable measures of well-being after the Stiglitz-Sen-Fitoussi Commission

(2009). It includes 11 dimensions of wellbeing from work-life balance to community to environmental quality. This index is still evolving and is responding to early criticisms; they are going to include inequality in future indices.

The Legantham Institute Prosperity Index defines prosperity as both wealth and well-being and finds that the most prosperous nations in the world are not necessarily those with a high GDP, but those with happy, healthy, and free citizens. The Prosperity Index identifies the building blocks of prosperity and assesses how 104 nations around the world perform in each area. A lack of comprehensive data on dozens of countries means they cannot be assessed. Nevertheless, the index does account for countries that contain 90 percent of the world's population. Its database consists of 79 different variables, each of which fits into one of nine different sub-indices, identified as the foundations of prosperity. A country's performance on each sub index is assigned a score, and the overall Prosperity Index rankings are produced by averaging the scores of the nine sub-indices for each country. Those countries that perform well across each sub index score highest in the overall ranking. The first four sub-indices are made up of variables that contribute to economic growth, measured in per-capita GDP. While the last 5 are indicators that contribute to the quality of life.

For full details of the variables that make up this list and the findings, refer to the Legatum Prosperity Index report. It is worth taking a look at these results as they often ask more questions than they answer.

Arrow et.al (2012) discuss an idea of comprehensive wealth. They define sustainability in terms of the capacity to provide wellbeing to future generations. The indicator of this capacity is a comprehensive measure of wealth, one that includes both marketed and non-marketed assets. The sustainability criterion is satisfied if this comprehensive wealth measure is increasing on a per capita basis. Their framework incorporates human and environmental capital as well as population growth and technological change. It assesses an economy's income-flows in the context of its stocks of assets. In other words, it accounts for the economy's productive base, rather than just its monetary wealth. This was developed into the Inclusive Wealth report. Simply, the basic formula is:

Wealth (IWI) = Produced capital + Natural capital + Human capital

Gross national happiness is often cited as an alternative to GDP. Suggested by the King of Bhutan in 1980, it is not actually an index but a principle for guiding Bhutanese development. However, a specific methodology has not yet been defined and many commentators think Bhutan use this measure to hide its terrible economic performance and to hide the levels of poverty in the country.

National statistics offices are starting to listen. The UK Office for National Statistics has embarked on a programme to measure National Well-Being and Italy's Statistics Office is working on Benessere Equo e Sostenibile (sustainable and equitable well-being)

However, it does not appear that creating new measures is the challenge; it is getting them introduced. It would be naïve to think all governments were ignorant of these new indicators or were completely blind to the issues of GDP. Therefore, it is important to look at why GDP is still the flag bearer for measuring progress today.

Barriers

There are methodology barriers due to standardization and values- which items are to be chosen. This is the problem of trying to measure well-being. Well-being is subjective and so many measures are criticised for this. People seem disgusted by the notion that a statistician can decide what makes them better off. The OECD better life index means statisticians do not have to. Countries could hold votes to decide the relative importance of each factor for that country. Yes, this would mean they would not be directly comparable but why should they be? If one country values leisure time, why should another country that values healthcare and education be measured by an identical stick. Measures of well-being are criticised often for their, however, I convinced whatever is used it will be a better measure than GDP on its own.

Many people criticise Green accounting, saying that we cannot value nature correctly. I do not disagree and I imagine most statisticians would not either.

Obviously these statisticians will not get the value perfectly correct. However I would suggest the value of $33 trillion is closer to the truth than the 0 we currently measure the environment by.

Data Barriers consist of problems with data availability, reliability and timeliness. Data availability is a problem in many developing countries when it comes to using more indicators. In many countries with poor infrastructure and little reporting there is often no way of reporting deaths and so even basic data, like life expectancy, are estimates. It would be nearly impossible to collect survey data in many of these countries.

Data reliability is whether a change in an indicator is an accurate signal. GDP data is very reliable, explaining why it is still used, whereas alternative measures based on the environmental or social data and subjective outcomes are less reliable.. Others point to the need to create a system to evaluate data and grade them on quality.

Data Timeliness relates to the frequency the data is available. GDP is reported at least annually for nearly every country and in more developed countries it is reported quarterly, whereas some of these measures are reported every year or less. It is a problem as governments cannot create policies based on last year's data when economies move so fast.

These problems are due to a lack of funding. Thankfully, several indicators have received enough support from government sand NGO's to begin reporting more frequently. These include the HDI and the GPI and so these measures will be refined and improved and more data collected.

Finally, there are social and institutional barriers:
The first is the dominance of the Growth is Good paradigm. This argument can take two strands. The first version is that growth is supremely important and environmental legislation is just a barrier to this. These politicians are set on the advancement of growth and openly reject goals that are inconsistent with this

(Lawn, 2001). Here, growth will always trump other objectives and so these politicians only want to measure growth. This has become even more relevant since the recession, when many governments have focused on growth. Governments are voted in on their short term agenda and sustainable development is just not a priority in the short term.

The second view is that growth is just one of many desirable outcomes, but there is a belief that the market can deliver these optimal outcomes, except to the extent specific market failures are identified. Welfare economics would support this view (1st welfare theorem states market allocation will be pareto efficient). In the case of identified market failures, governments do intervene (for instance redistributing wealth). Governments can correct these market failures without a new indicator.

There is also a lack of political leadership for two reasons. Firstly, a lack of public interest and attention in the issue means it is not a political concern. This is due to there not being a strong narrative that engages the public on needing new measures and also confusion about indicators amongst officials. Secondly, due to the perceived danger to political power- governments are worried the new indicators would reflect badly on past policies. The best example is in China. In 2004 the government commissioned the creation of Green GDP. In 2006 the initial report estimated 20% of China's growth was counterbalanced by environmental degradation (Liu, 2006) and in 2007 the project was cancelled. Moving beyond GDP represents innovation which entails a certain amount of risk, which policy makers are generally very averse to. At the OECD, policy recommendations are based on careful assessment of the impact specific policies have had in the past, and the organisation's reputation depends on the robustness of this kind of analysis. However, policy innovation typically involves new combinations of policies, which, as likely as not, have not yet been tried. Its impact is therefore difficult to predict. This represents a real dilemma for an organisation with OECD's reputation for impartial rigour.

There are many industries and institutions with vested interest in maintaining the status quo, such as large businesses. In an interview at the Asia Society in new York Joseph Stiglitz said *'When we tried to push for this (Green GDP), and people in the*

Department of Commerce were excited about doing this, the coal industry basically threatened to pass a proviso to take away funding for any research that would support these alternative measures. Because they knew that Green GDP would not be good for the coal industry'. In addition, the opposition to GDP waste time and resources arguing between themselves over the minutia of methodology and data. The advocates of GDP have managed to divide and conquer.

Creating Change

Before new measures can be introduced, goals have to be created to establish what it is we want to measure. There is already international capacity for consensus on this, for instance the Millennium Development Goals. There has to be an international agreement and recognition that GDP does not measure these goals. The new measure needs to be emphasised; it is not a way to compare countries, who is happiest, healthiest or poorest, but a way to define and measure common goals and how a country is contributing to these goals.

A paradigm shift will be needed to achieve this change. The discussion will have to change from growth to progress and from economic to sustainable.

As mentioned earlier, progress to this new measure is hampered by experts on what is the best and correct measure of economic, social and environmental progress. Each advocate of a certain measure shoots down the others for its subjectivity or difficult data collection. However, these academics need to realise this is not an exercise in finding the perfect indicator but a discussion on improving on what we have. All the new indicators discussed above are proxies and so limited. None can measure all economic, social and environment aspects that are significant. New indicator research has been on-going for 25 years but is constantly being stalled by arguments over their relevant criticisms, leaving GDP in the limelight.

GDP is the incumbent in the industry for measuring progress. Due to this it currently has advantages over the infant measures that want to replace it. GDP has been refined over and over for 70 years and so is now a good measure. These new measures have been around for fewer than 15 years and rely on a lot less funding than GDP. Just like large incumbents, it has the power to lobby in government (via industry) and so protect its own interests. For GDP to be replaced we need governments and international organisations to be strong and remove the advantages to this inefficient incumbent and allow new measures that are more competitive to develop.

When GDP was created it did what it was meant to do. It measured the economic activity in a mostly- manufacturing country. To its credit it remains a simple, easily reported measure. However, due to countries having evolved into service based economies and new technologies having been introduced, the economy today is very different from what it was 70 years ago. GDP has begun to fail even in measuring economic activity in this modern age. However, the emphasis on growing GDP and economic activity is leading the planet to destruction. GDP has created an emphasis on material growth ignoring the costs and balance of this growth. It has created serious distortions in our perceptions of development to the point where we value nothing but production. GDP being easy is no longer a strong enough justification for its continued use.

One fundamental truth must be recognized: the planet cannot accommodate high-income status for all 7 billion plus of its inhabitants. For every country to attain per capita GDP of $13,000 (the World Bank's definition of high income), global GDP would need to rise to $91 trillion. If, however, we already use the equivalent of 1.5 Earths to provide the resources we consume and to absorb our waste, how can we? The planet can sustainably support a GDP of around $50 trillion. If the planet already exceeds its sustainable carrying capacity, we need to be reducing our demands on it – not adding new ones. Simply put, we can no longer depend on GDP growth, and the limitless wealth accumulation that it implies, to solve our social and economic problems.

References-

Arrow K.J., P. Dasgupta, L.H Goulder, K.J Mumford, and K. Oleson (2012) 'Sustainability and the Measurement of wealth', Environment and Development Economics, 17: 317-353.

1997, Costanza et al. The value of the world's ecosystem services and natural capital World bank data on Health Expendiute per capita:

http://data.worldbank.org/indicator/SH.XPD.PCAP

Sen.A; Stiglitz,J (2009) Mismeasuring Our Lives: Why GDP Doesn't Add Up

http://forumblog.org/2014/05/growing-disconnect-gdp-wellbeing/ (2014) Zakri Abdul Hamid & Anantha Duraiappah

Diagnostic Assessment of Select Environmental Challenges in India 2013 World Bank report

-http://wwwwds.worldbank.org/external/default/WDSContentServer/WDSP/IB/2013/07/16/000442464_20130716091943/Rendered/PDF/700040v10ESW0P0box0374379B00PUBLIC0.pdf

Kuznets, Simon. (1934). "National Income, 1929-1932".

Part 4 Incentivising the 'Homo Oeconomicus' – Market Based Solutions to Climate Change

4.1 The Missing Signal

Graciela Chichilnisky

Climate change is a new phenomenon in human history. It is an extreme case of large-scale negative external effects, harmful effects of one party on another which are external to and hence not mediated by the market mechanism. Indeed according to Nicholas Stern (2007) it is "the largest externality in the history of humankind" By the emission of CO_2 a country increases the risk faced by all countries, itself included, of a harmful change in climate. Hence the existence of a negative external effect

Climate change is also completely new in economics. The concentration of CO_2 in the atmosphere is a *global public good par excellance,* as it is one and the same for everyone in the world due to physical reasons. This global public good – or bad –defies classic notions of public goods. For example, it is not produced by governments as are classic public goods. CO_2 is produced in the course of private consumption and private production: in using one's car, heating one's home, and using electricity for industrial production. Unlike the conventional public goods defined by Lindahl, and studied by Bowen and Samuelson, emissions of CO_2 create a privately produced public good. As we just saw it is a private good at the level of production, while it is a public good at the level of consumption, a combination that was discovered and explained for the first time by Chichilnisky (Chichilnisky, OECD 1993) see also Chichilnisky and Sheeran (Saving Kyoto 2009), Chichilnisky and Heal (1994) and Chichilnisky Heal and Starrett (2000). Privately produced public goods had not been studied before in economics and do not fit the description nor the properties of classic public goods. . The global commons which are at risk today are all of this nature: biodiversity, water bodies including the level of the seas, and the quality of the atmosphere. They are all privately produced public goods. They are often called the global commons.

There are two principal approaches to the control and correction of external effects—control and correction via taxes and subsidies, in the tradition established by Pigou, and control and correction via the introduction of property rights, as suggested by Coase. Neither fits the global public good represented by the concentration of CO_2 in the atmosphere, since this is a privately produced public good that is private at the level of production but public at the level of consumption. This observation is critical to understand the solutions to the problems of the global environment that we face today. By their own nature markets that involve privately produced public goods merge equity with efficiency in a way that private goods markets don't. This discovery was made in Chichilnisky (1993), Chichilnisky and Heal (1994) and Chichilnisky Heal and Starrett (2000) and has led to the creation of the carbon market of the Kyoto Protocol by the author, which gives more property rights to the atmosphere to poor nations. This has created a new literature on markets with privately produce public goods. It also led to new solutions that require both equity in the distribution of property rights to reach economic efficiency – quite the opposite from what Coase had in mind, since Coase explained that the distribution of property rights for environmental assets had no bearing on the efficiency of the solution. He was right of course, but only for environmental problems like particulates or water pollution that are private goods in the sense that one person's share of particulates in the air can be very different from another's. This is definitely not the case with the concentration of CO_2 in the atmosphere that is one and the same all over the planet.

Pigou described externalities as stemming from differences between the private and the social costs of an activity. In his vision, these differences between private and social costs were to be corrected by taxes or subsidies that alter the private cost of the activity until it equals the social cost. After correction, one has the relationship:

private cost + tax = social cost

So in the case of CO_2 emission, there is a private cost given by the costs of the fuel burned: the social costs include, in addition to the fuel costs, the costs of an increased likelihood of harmful climate change. A Pigouvian corrective tax, when added to the private cost, will bring it into line with the social cost. A Pigouvian tax is however irrelevant for global climate change policy. Taxes are valid only inside nations: there is no taxation institution or authority for the world as a whole, and probably there will never be one. However we will see below that taxes can be a complement to global policy on climate change, operating at the national level.

Coase instead focused on the fact that goods and services can be bought and sold, and therefore brought within the orbit of the market mechanism, if they can be owned. Ownership of a good or service means that people can have property rights in these. Coase then saw externalities as arising from an absence of property rights: as a consequence of this certain economically important goods and service could not be bought or sold, and their provision could not be regulated by the market. Hence in particular the market could not ensure their provision at an efficient level. The natural policy prescription from this perspective is the introduction of property rights for the goods for which they are missing, so that these goods can be traded and their provision regulated by the market. The application of this view to climate change indicates that the services of the atmosphere are being used in the combustion of carbon-based fuels as a depository for CO_2, in a legal framework in which there are no property rights in the atmosphere and there is thus no opportunity for people to register a demand for it to be left unaltered. There are in contrast property rights over the ground, so that this cannot be used as a depository for waste without permission from the owner, which normally requires payment. Coase's insight is that we need to mimic this situation with respect to access to the atmosphere.

Indeed the Kyoto Protocol which was voted by 160 nations in 1997 has as its core a limit on industrial nations' rights to emit, which can be viewed as property rights on the use of the atmosphere. The carbon market introduced and written by the author into the Kyoto Protocol in 1997 is a natural result of the introduction of such property rights. This market is a flexibility mechanism, as it allows one nation that over emits carbon to buy rights to emit from another nation that under emits carbon with the total still remaining within the global limit. This is the actual wording that was written by the author in the 1997 Kyoto Protocol, introducing a flexibility mechanism that convinced the nations to agree to the stipulated limits (Chichilnisky and Sheeran, 2009). Hence the Kyoto Protocol came to existence in December 1997 – becoming the first international agreement based on the creation of a global market mechanism. The Kyoto Protocol was ratified in 2005 as international law and its carbon market is now trading known as the EU Emissions Trading System in Brussels, having reached trading levels in 2011 of about $300BN per year (see World Bank "Status and Trends of the Carbon Market, 2011). The key point is this approach is that before emitting a pollutant into the atmosphere, a firm or a nation must own the right to effect such an emission: such a right is conveyed by the purchase of a "carbon credit" or a "Trading Emission Quotas" or TEQ. The creation of these quotas establishes property rights in the atmosphere. What is unique and quite different from what Coase anticipated, is that, for market efficiency, this market requires preferential rights to be provided to poor nations (Chichilnisky 1993, Chichilnisky and Heal 1994). If a nation or a firm is forced to buy a quota before emitting a pollutant, then, in Pigouvian terms, this also raises the private cost of pollution, in this case by the cost of the quota. Once again, marginal private costs are changed so that they approach marginal social costs. In fact, in a competitive quota market, they will be equated exactly to marginal social costs by the inclusion of the costs of buying quotas.

The Carbon Market

What exactly is the object to be traded in a market for tradeable emissions permits? The fundamental source of possible climate change is the stock of CO_2 in the earth's atmosphere: the larger this is, the larger is the chance of a significant change in the climate. So the ultimate objective of economic policies is first to stabilize and then to reduce the stock of CO2 in the atmosphere.

The Gordian knot that must be cut is the link between natural resources, fossil energy, and economic progress. Only clean energy can achieve this. But this requires
changing a $US55 trillion power plant infrastructure, the power plants that produce. electrical power around the world (see IEA, 2012), because 87% of world's energy is driven by fossil fuels, and power plants produce 45% of the global carbon emissions. (IEA, 2012).

Energy is the mother of all markets. Everything is made with energy. Our food, our homes and ours car, the toothpaste and the roads we use, the clothes we wear, the heating of our offices, our medicines: everything. Changing the cost of energy, making dirty energy more expensive and undesirable and clean energy more profitable and desirable—changes everything.

The carbon market cuts the Gordian knot and makes change possible. The carbon market helps change the value of all goods and services in the world economy because the carbon market changes the cost of energy the world over: it makes clean energy more profitable and desirable and dirty energy unprofitable. This changes all the prices of products and services in the world—since everything is made with energy—it drives the economy to use cleaner rather than dirty energy sources. It is more profitable and less costly to use clean energy that reduces emissions of carbon now. The carbon market is not a way to escape emissions limits—it is only a way to rearrange who emits more and who emits less, as the overall lower limits remain in place. Now dirty power plants have to pay cleaner power plants for the rights to emit, creating an economic incentive that we all know we need for cleaner plants. It creates also an economic incentive for technology innovation and for investment in the crucial energy infrastructure and encourages economic growth without environmental destruction.

In net terms the world economy is exactly in the same position before and after the carbon market -there are no additional costs from running the carbon market, nor from its extremely important global services. The over-emitter nations are worse off, since they have to pay. But every payment they make goes to an under-emitter, so some nations pay and some receive, but in net terms the world economy is exactly in the same position before and after the carbon market is introduced. There are no costs to the world economy from introducing a carbon market, nor from the limits on carbon emissions and environmental improvement that it produces. It is all gain.

There is a period of transition where today's market cost of electricity could go up, but we all know that the low costs of dirty power can be illusory. An MIT study shows that the real cost of gasoline paid by the US tax payer is about $15 per gallon, more than three times of what we pay at the pump. Similarly the US taxpayer is paying today much more for dirty electricity than we appear to do, including health costs of coal plants, the scary risks of "fracking" for natural gas plants that contaminate drinking water, the defence costs and the political costs from importing gasoline from unstable regions, not to mention the environmental and health risks that are widely accepted from climate change damages such as increased frequency and violence of hurricanes and typhoons, increased costs of food from droughts that scorch the earth, and floods that destroy entire communities. The difference between illusory and real costs is exactly what the carbon market captures; the price of "carbon credits" evens up the computations. In any case, transitional costs of new technologies are just that—transitional. Our innovation-bent society understands that, and we invest enormous amounts of money on innovation in education and in risk capital every year for that reason. Transitional costs can also be covered by using the current subsidies to the fossil fuels to ease the transition thus avoiding all the risks and costs of fossil fuels already described. Finally, at the end of the day, as the scope of the clean technologies increases, when the built capacity of clean plants increases, the laws of innovation such as "learning curves" and increasing returns to scale kick in, and clean energy costs can emulate or even improve on existing ones.

The Carbon Market Experience

Does the carbon market work to reduce emissions? Yes, the European Union that was able to decrease its carbon emissions by about 37% since the Kyoto Protocol emission limits were imposed and the EU Emissions Trading System became international law in 2005. This market requires no external funding—it is self-financing—and it works well in economic terms, creating incentives for cleaner technology in industrial and developing nations. For example, China received about US$30 billion from the Kyoto Clean Development Mechanism to invest in clean technology, becoming since then the largest exporter of wind and solar power equipment in the world.

A global carbon market will change the way we measure economic progress in ways that many clamour for. It will create a new global system of economic values. With the carbon market, cleaner nations become richer and their economies grow faster than dirty nations, which have to pay the former and can be left behind. A new stick is created to measure economic progress—the GDP now measures the value of all goods and services at market value but now market value includes the value of a clean atmosphere and a stable climate for humankind.

The carbon market provides efficiency with equity. How? By making equity and efficiency the same side of the coin. Through its Clean Development Mechanism (CDM),the Kyoto Protocol provides a link between rich and poor nations as poor nations do not have emissions limits under the Kyoto Protocol and therefore cannot trade in the carbon market. But developing nations face steep opportunity costs if they do not reduce emissions, which strongly encourages reducing emissions—through the CDM of the carbon market. Developing nations have benefitted from the Kyoto Protocol. Since 2005, when it became international law, the Kyoto Protocol carbon market funded US$50 billion in clean technology (CDM) projects in poor nations (World Bank, 2005–2012). Its CDM projects have decreased so far the equivalent of more than 30% of EU emissions. The CDM works as follows. Private clean technology projects in the soil of a developing nation—China, Brazil, India—that are proven to decrease the emissions of carbon from this nation below its given "UN agreed baseline" are awarded "carbon credits" for the amount of carbon that is reduced that are themselves tradable for cash in the carbon market—so as to recognize in monetary terms the amount of carbon avoided in those projects and fill the role of shifting prices in favour of clean technologies. These CDM carbon credits—by law—can be transformed into cash in the Kyoto Protocol's carbon market. This is the role of the carbon market in the CDM and this is how the Kyoto Protocol has provided US$50billion in funding to developing nations since 2005(World Bank, 2005–2012).

Here is the background and a summary of the current situation. In 1997, the Carbon Market of the United Nations Kyoto Protocol was signed by 160 nations. The Kyoto Protocol became international law in 2005 when the protocol was ratified by nations representing 55% of the world's emissions—and the Kyoto Protocol and its Carbon Market have now been adopted as law by 195 nations, and four continents now have a Carbon Market. The United States is excluded from the Kyoto Protocol, because it signed it but did not ratify it, but its most populated state, California, introduced a similar carbon market in 2012.

The carbon market of the Kyoto Protocol is now trading carbon credits at the EU Emissions Trading System (EU ETS). The World Bank reports on its progress in its report "Status and Trends of the Carbon Market" which has been published annually since the carbon market became international law in 2005. The report documents that by 2010 the European the need for sustainable development and a carbon market Union Emissions Trading System (EU ETS) was trading $215 billion per year, and has decreased the equivalent of over 30% of EU's emissions of CO2. Through the carbon market, those nations who over-emit compensate those who under emit,—and throughout the entire KP process the world emissions' remains always under a fixed emissions limit that are documented in Annex I—(nation by nation emissions limits for OECD nations). A "carbon price" emerges from trading the "carbon credits" or rights to emit, which represents the monetary value of the damage caused by each ton of CO2. The carbon market therefore introduces a "carbon price" that corrects for the externality.

What is the status of the Carbon Market of the Kyoto Protocol today? Despite its success, its nation by nation carbon limits expired in 2012 but (what happened after) the Kyoto Protocol itself—its overall structure and the structure of the carbon market—do not expire; they are and continue to be international law. Furthermore in Durban South Africa at the United Nations Convention of the Parties COP 17, it was agreed to continue the Kyoto Protocol provisions to 2015 and to enlarge them to include the whole world by 2020.

In any case, all we have to do to keep the carbon market's benefits is to define new emissions limits nation by nation for the OECD nations, something that we should be doing in any case since they are the major emitters and since without limiting their emissions there is no solution to the global climate issue.

Perhaps the most exciting news on the carbon market comes from the USA and from China, the two largest CO_2 emitters in the world. China has established several carbon markets in the last two years, and with about $50Bn funding from the CDM of the Kyoto Protocol it became the world's largest exporter of clean energy equipment (solar and wind). In the US the State of California, the largest state in the Union, created a carbon market two years ago that is already trading. This has been challenged and nevertheless was ratified. On June 2, 2014 President Obama's administration created environmental law to cur carbon pollution from power plants by 30% from 2005 levels by 2030. These rules are important because power plants represent 50% of the US emissions – and also of the world's emissions. There is no solution to the climate change issue without reducing emissions from power plants, which in the long run means clean energy. President Obama's power plant emissions reductions were formally announced by the US Environmental Protection Agency and were confirmed on June 25th 2014 by the US Supreme Court, which also ratified the EPA's rights to limit carbon emissions at the federal level. This is the beginning of the federal carbon market in the USA. It is the way that the SO_2 market was created twenty one years ago, which has been trading successfully since then at the Chicago Board of Trade (BCT) and has successfully eliminated acid rain in the USA. SO2 markets are very different from the CO2 market since SO2 does not distribute uniformly and is therefore not a public good (or bad).

One frequently asked question is whether it suffices to create national or regional carbon markets or a global market for carbon emissions is required. The answer is eventually, yes. The limits on emissions must be established globally – the property rights on the use of the atmosphere must be established for all nations in the world since a single region – for example Africa – has enough coal to cause climate change the world over. But at the level of the carbon market there is hope due to the "no arbitrage" property of financial markets – and the carbon market is a financial market. No arbitrage implies that different markets trading the same commodity will eventually converge to share the same price. This is a market property and it means that the regional carbon markets will eventually converge embrace and identify with the Kyoto Protocol carbon market that we created in 1997.

Participating countries

How many countries, and which countries, have to ratify a global warming treaty for it to be worth implementing in the sense that it will make a real difference to the threat of climate change? Perhaps more important, how many countries have to ratify such a treaty for the signatories to feel that they will all gain from the treaty and that it justifies their support andcommitment'?

There are several analytical issues behind these questions. A global warming treaty is unlikely to have the participation of all countries as soon as it starts: it is likely to begin with limited participation and to gain support over time. The group of countries that starts the treaty must therefore be such that they all feel that the group is durable, and that the group will continue to abide by the treaty for long enough for widespread support to build up. Whether or not this condition is met, depends very much on the size and composition of the initial group.

A key issue here is that the gains to all countries from participation in a global warming treaty depend on and increase with the number and size of the participating countries. The costs to each country of participation also fall as the number of participants increases. There is a sense in which there are economies of scale in the formation of such agreements. There are two key points here.

One is that when a country cuts back its emission of CO2, it alone pays the costs of this abatement: however, benefits accrue to all other countries that would be negatively affected by climate change, because climate change, if it occurs, will be world-wide. It follows that if one country abates CO2emission on its own, it will clearly be a net loser from this: it will meet all of the costs, and many other countries will share the benefits with it. Suppose however that a group of countries agree jointly to abate carbon emissions: the costs of each co1mtry's abatement, as before, are borne by that country, but each country now gains not only from its own abatement but also from that of all of the other participating countries. The ratio of benefits to costs is now much more favourable: the costs to each country are unchanged, and the benefits to each country are multiplied by the number of participating countries.

In fact, and this is the second point leading to scale effects in the formation of abatement agreements, countries' costs may actually be reduced if the abatement is part of a simultaneous policy move by several countries. One of the main costs of CO2; abatement is the development of new technologies, and if this is done collaboratively by several countries each may face a lower individual abatement cost. There is clear evidence of this in the case of unleaded vehicle fuels: once refining practices and engine designs to cope with these had been developed in the United States (at considerable costs), these technologies could be deployed by the companies that developed them in other countries at little or no incremental cost.

It follows from this that there is a "critical mass" issue in forming the initial group of signatories of a CO2 abatement treaty": the group has to be big enough (size here is measured in terms of the fraction of global CO2emissions controlled) that the gains to each country from participation of the others are sufficient to outweigh the costs each country incurs. Once such an abatement configuration in place, problems of deliberate non-compliance at the national level should be greatly reduced. The Kyoto Protocol resolved this issue by requiring for its own ratification that nations constituting 55% of the global emissions should ratify it before the Protocol could become international law. This happened in 2005, when Russia ratified the Kyoto Protocol, which then became international law and continues today and into the future

Another analytical issue in evaluating the adequacy of a group of signatories to a global warming treaty is the phenomenon of "carbon leakage". This refers to the fact that if there is agreement by a group of countries which are major energy consumers to cut back the use of fossil fuels as part of a CO_2 abatement policy, then the consequent decrease in their demand for these fuels will decrease their prices on world markets, and so encourage other non-participating countries to consume more. This could partially offset the policies implemented by the signatories of the global warming treaty. There is as yet little agreement about the possible magnitude of the phenomenon of "carbon leakage" and indeed there are several other mechanisms throughwhich leakage can occur.

What are the implications of these issues for the group that should be targeted as the initial signatories of a CO;-abatement agreement? Such a group has to be sufficiently broadly-based to meet two conditions – and the Kyoto Protocol identified this by requiring ratification as already explained by nations representing over 55% of the world's emissions of CO_2:

1. it has to form a "critical mass" in the sense of being large enough to ensure that all members gain from membership and so have incentives to remain in compliance.

2. it has to be large enough that the "carbon leakage" phenomenon does not detract from its efficacy.

However, it need not contain initially all the countries who will ultimately have to join to make it a complete success. It should certainly contain the major industrial countries, the members of the OECD. The additional groups who will ultimately have to join for complete success are the economies of Eastern Europe and the Former Soviet Union, and the major developing countries such as India and China. It is probably not necessary for all of these additional countries to be full members of a global warming treaty as soon as it starts, as long as two conditions are fulfilled:1. that they will not pursue policies that will undo the efforts of the signatories of a global warming treaty, i.e., they will not increase their emissions of CO_2 to offset, fully or partially, the measures taken by signatories. In particular, they will neutralize carbon leakage, and
2. they express an intent to participate fully within a specified period of, say, ten years

In fact these aims could easily be achieved by all countries joining a TEQ regime if the OECD countries were allocated quotas which forced them either to reduce emissions or to buy from other countries, and the developing countries were allocated quotas sufficiently in excess of their current needs that they would not constrain their economic development in the near future.In effect the developing countries would then be sleeping members of the treaty for a period, but during this period would be able to benefit from the sale or loan of their excess quotas to industrial countries, which would provide them with an incentive to keep carbon emission low and maximize the revenues obtainable from quotas. Such a distribution of quotas is, consistent with their efficient allocation, under minimal assumptions. If all countries have similar preferences for private goods and environmental assets, similar technologies and there is a diminishing marginal utility to wealth then an efficient allocation will require developing countries receiving more emissions.

We can go further however. We can assume that environmental assets are necessary goods. This simply means that while the total amount spent on environmental assets increases with the level of income, the proportion of income a person is willing to spend on environmental assets increases as the income level drops. The assumption can be theoretically justified on the grounds that lower income people are more vulnerable to their environment than higher income people. From these facts it is possible to establish that a redistribution of income towards lower income individuals or countries will generally lead to an improvement in the world's emission levels, and generally in the world's level of environmental preservation. This is because when preferences are similar and the income elasticity of demand is less than one, a redistribution of income in favour of -lower income groups implies that relatively more income will be allocated to the environmental asset. If traders choose freely, the will choose more preservation: in our case higher abatement levels are to be expected when more resources are assigned to the lower income groups of countries.

There is another factor that must however be considered. This is that developing countries could be less efficient in terms of energy use and therefore lead to more emissions as they grow. This is certainly an important concern for the long run future, that is to say in fifty years or so. Indeed, it seems that such concerns should drive environmental policy today. Every effort must be made to help prevent developing countries from adopting the patterns of environmental overuse of industrial countries as they grow. Therefore as discussed earlier with the CDM, a carbon market can combine equity and efficiency.

Carbon Market or a Carbon Tax

The two approaches are formally equivalent in important ways, though not in all ways. A tradeable quota system requires a polluter to buy a permit before polluting, and this raises the private cost of pollution by an amount equal to the price of the permit: in this respect, it appears to the polluter like a tax: it imposes a tax equal to the price of a permit. Both approaches are consistent with the "polluter pays" principle, which has been adopted by the OECD: compliance with this is widely viewed as a prerequisite for fairness in the management of pollution. In theory the price of the tax should equal the price a permit if they fully account for the externality.

From the perspective of the policy-maker, however, there are differences associated with where the main policy uncertainties arise: we explore these below. There are also differences in the role of the government in each system: it plays a more central role, and of course raises revenue, under a tax regime.

Uncertainty about cost-benefit relation

One of the main differences between tradeable quotas and emission taxes is in the degree of assurance that they offer to the policy-maker about the aggregate level of pollution. The point here is simple, yet important. It is as follows. With a system of tradeable quotas, the aggregate level of pollution is determined to be the total number of quotas issued. If quotas are issued for the emission of, for example, six billion tons of carbon dioxide, then, if the system is enforced, the total of emissions will not exceed six billion tons. This much the policy-maker can be sure of in advance: the total amount of pollution is predictable. There is however an important aspect of the policy that is not known to her: this is the cost to polluters of the regulation of emissions to the specified level, as measured by the price of an emission quota. This price will be determined by the forces of supply and demand, and cannot in general be predicted with any accuracy.

Contrast this with the situation with a pollution tax: the cost to the polluter is now know with certainty and is of course given by the tax. But the aggregate amount of pollution cannot be predicted: this will now be determined in the market by the forces of supply and demand. To be precise, it will be determined for each firm at the level at which the marginal abatement cost just equals the tax on pollution.

So with quotas, the policy-maker is sure in advance of the aggregate amount of pollution that will result from her intervention, but is unsure of the resulting costs to industry and commerce. With taxes matters are exactly the opposite: the costs to polluters of policy are known, but the results, in terms of pollution levels, are not. This is a key difference, a key duality: in situations of great political sensitivity, knowing the cost of policy intervention to industry and commerce may be essential: this is an argument for taxes. In situations of great sensitivity of the environment to pollution, knowing the aggregate level of pollution that will result from a policy may be essential, an argument for a carbon market.

Threshold effects

This latter point is important in the context of certain types of environmental problem. Consider in particular a situation in which the effect of a pollutant on the environment is reversible up to a certain threshold level of pollution, which we denote L, and is irreversible after that. One can think of many examples: water bodies can cleanse themselves provided that they are not "too polluted", but they cannot cleanse themselves if pollution exceeds a certain level: threatened species can re-establish themselves provided that their stock is not "too low", but if their stock falls below this level, they are doomed to extinction: ocean currents and the climates dependent on them remain essentially the same provided that changes in atmospheric temperatures are not "too large", but may change in a major way if the temperature exchange exceeds a critical amount.

In each of these cases, there is a level of pollution below which the consequences of pollution are reversible, and above which they are not and there is a permanent loss of an environmental asset it is this threshold level that the symbol "L" denotes. In such situations, there is a premium on not exceeding L: the costs of pollution increase sharply beyond L. In such situations there is a strong argument in favour of quotas, for these can provide the assurance that the aggregate level of pollution will not exceed L. One does this by just issuing a total of permits that does not exceed L. The only way to reach such assurances with pollution taxes would be to consider the range of all possible marginal emission costs, and to pick a tax level which ensures pollution of less than L for any possible marginal emission abatement costs. If the uncertainty about possible marginal abatement cost schedules is great, such a tax may in fact be far greater than is actually needed. In contrast, the tax implied by tradeable quotas—the price of a quota when the total number of quotas is L —will be exactly the least needed to ensure aggregate pollution less than L.

In many contests, this may be an important consideration in favour of quotas: they guarantee that pollution will be within some predetermined limit. There is considerable scientific evidence of threshold effects in the damage that results from many pollutants. All of the examples alluded to above, have a real scientific basis.

A key aspect of carbon dioxide emission and global climate change is that scientific understanding of this phenomenon is continuously evolving. More is known now than ten years ago, and the next ten to twenty years will unquestionably bring even bigger changes. The problems of global climate change may come to be seen as much more, or much less, threatening than currently. As a consequence of such changes in scientific understanding, the tightness of CO_2 emission regulations will change, becoming more restrictive if the consequences of CO_2 emission are found to be more serious, and vice versa. This means there is uncertainty about the tightness of future policies. An advantage of TEQs relative to carbon taxes, is that they can naturally be developed in a way which facilitates hedging this kind of risk.

Hedging could occur via the trading of derivatives such as futures or options on TEQs. To elaborate, if a utility anticipates a sharp increase in the costs of CO_2 emission, it will choose the energy source that is least intensive in CO_2 emissions. This exposes it to the risk that scientific research will reveal CO_2 accumulation in the atmosphere to be less threatening than previously believed, with a consequent increase in the number of TEQs issued by regulators and a drop in their price. To offset the risk of being "wrong footed" in this way, the utility would either sell TEQs forward, or buy put options on them. In either event it would profit from a drop in quota prices, and this profit would in some degree of set the costs incurred unnecessarily by the selection of the least CO_2-intensive technology. In the Chicago market for SO_2 emission quotas, utilities have already demonstrated their ability to use such strategies. This is that derivatives help to achieve market depth and liquidity, and so improve market functioning. In the market they serve two important functions: they reallocate risks, as do all financial instruments: in addition they also function as substitute credit markets, allowing traders with limited liquid assets to trade extensively.

It is clear that some countries feel an unease at selling, parting permanently with, their rights to emit greenhouse gases, rights which they might need in the future at a different stage of economic development. In principle they can of course buy these rights back in the future when they are needed, although there is a risk that the price will then be excessive. The above can help mitigate this risk but another option is available. An alternative is to have a 'central bank' where emissions can be lended and borrowed. A country with a surplus of permits that it anticipated continuing for say five years would make a five year deposit in the bank, and be paid interest on this deposit. After five years, it could withdraw its permits, or roll over the deposit. Through this system, a country's total emission rights never change: it never gives them up permanently, but merely lends them while they are not needed. The interest rate payable on permits would of course depend on the balance of supply and demand for permit loans: a large number of would-be borrowers with few lenders would force up the interest rate, and vice versa. The interest rate would be affected strongly by the initial distribution of permits.

Taxes and quotas—alternatives or complements?

Although tradeable permits and carbon taxes are generally viewed as the main alternatives in the management of global CO_2 emissions, they are in fact not antithetical: they can be combined in several ways.

1. Mixed domestic policy regimes

A country could in certain cases find it attractive to employ a mixture of the two approaches. It could have a regime of tradeable CO_2 emission quotas, but allow firms to emit more than the CO_2 quotas that they hold in exchange for the payment of a tax on each unit of emission in excess of the quotas owned by the firm. For example, if a firm owned quotas to emit 100,000 tons of CO_2 and in fact produces 120,000, then it might be allowed to pay a tax on the 20,000 units by which its emission of CO_2 exceeds the quotas in its possession. In such a regime, a firm finding its quota allocation too restrictive would have three options:

1. to reduce emissions
2. to buy more quotas3. to pay a tax on emission in excess of the quotas possessed.

It would choose the least costly. This clearly implies that the market price of a quota would never exceed the tax rate, for if it did there would be no demand for quotas: one could always achieve the same efficient as buying a quota by paying a tax, so that at quota prices above the tax rate there would be no buyers. Hence the tax rate sets an upper bound on the market price of a tradeable emission quota. By setting a tax rate, the regulator bounds the costs to firms of its regulatory policies. This could reduce one of the main disadvantages of a tradeable quota regime, the unpredictability of the costs to firms, but at the cost reducing its main advantage, the predictability of the total level of CO; emissions. For to the extent that a firm can supplement its tradeable emission quotas by paying taxes, in can in effect create new quotas, making total emissions less predictable. In a situation where there is a need for a cap on the cost to industry of a regulatory policy, and where there is also a need for some predictability of the total level of emissions, this mixed system may have a valuable role to play.

2. Quotas internationally, taxes domestically
Another possible combination of the two approaches is to allocate trade-able quotas to countries, which can trade them internationally to alter their total allocations of emission quotas, and then have countries enforce the given total emission levels domestically either by tax or by command-and-control regimes. In such a system, a country allocated quotas allowing it to emit 500million tons of CO; might purchase additional emission quotas to bring its total allocation up to 550 million, and then implement the national target of 550 million tons domestically by any means that it chose. Of course, the commitment to emit no more that 550 million tons would, as already discussed, probably be

implemented most accurately by a domestic tradeable quota regime, but in principle any domestic policy regime is possible.

IPCC Fifth Assessment Report 2013: DAC and Carbon Negative Technologies are required for resolving climate change.

In 2013 the UN IPCC completed its Fifth Assessment Report and stated that reductions of carbon emissions are no longer sufficient to avoid our atmosphere reaching the 450 PPP (parts per million) threshold of concentration of carbon in the atmosphere. This is due to the fact that about 40% of the carbon emitted stays in the atmosphere for over 1,000 years, and we are already at the 400 PPM levels. The IPCC report went on to require carbon negative technologies ™ a concept created and trademarked by the author, which means technologies that can "scrub" or reduce the carbon that is already in the atmosphere in net terms. There are a few technologies that can achieve that and Direct Air Capture of CO_2 is the only form of carbon capture that can achieve carbon negative results. There exist technologies already patented and developed by the author in the company Global Thermostat LLC, and successfully operating in Silicon Valley (see www.globalthermostat.com) that can transform the global $55 Trillion power plant infrastructure into a fleet of "carbon negative power plants" (see Chichilnisky and Eisenberger, 2009 and 2011); these are power plants that produce electricity while they clean the atmosphere.

The Green Power Fund

In the Copenhagen Convention of the Parties COP 15 of the UNFCCC, the author introduced international legislation to create a $200Bn/year Fund that would draw existing funding from the Kyoto Protocol Carbon Market trading, which has reached $300Bn/year. The purpose of the Fund is to build 'carbon negative power plants' in Africa, Latin America and the Small Island States. See above. I also introduced the concept of carbon negative technology™ at the COP15 within the CDM, acting within the Papua New Guinea UNFCCC COP 15 delegation. US Secretary of State H. Clinton supported my concept and announced officially the Fund proposed two days later at the COP15. Following this it became international law, in part, under the slightly different name, Green Climate Fund, in Durban South Africa COP17. But at present the Green Climate Fund does not have a source of funding nor a purpose for the funding. The source intended was the Kyoto Protocol carbon market, and the purpose is the build carbon negative power plants that can bring development in Africa Latin America and Small Island States, while cleaning the atmosphere. The carbon negative properties of these plants is essential since without it these regions do not emit enough CO_2 by themselves to attract funds from the CDM of the Kyoto Protocol. With carbon negative technology these nations can reduce any amount of CO_2 from the atmosphere – 30% or more – even though the three of them together emit less than 8.5% of the global carbon emissions produced by humans.

The Green Power Fund is not emerging as the single financial solution to support the DAC and carbon negative technologies that the IPCC finds is needed to combat climate change. The future is not happening, in the making. After this article is published, we will see whether the Green power Fund will come to exist in COP 20 December 2015 in Lima Peru, followed by the important COP 21 in Paris 2015. It is not too soon to predict that it will, and with it a ray of hope for resolving climate change, the most intractable and immediate problem facing the human species now, and during the 21 century, together with water scarcity and the destruction of the world's biodiversity. All these three problems – each of them a global common – have in fact the same solution as the one that is proposed here for resolving climate change.

References

Chichilnisky, G. and P. Eisenberger "Energy Security, Economic Development and Global Warming: addressing short and long term challenges" Int. J. of Green Economics Vol --- No --- 2009 (Chris look this up and send me the correct volume and number and year)

Peter Eisenberger, Roger Cohen, Graciela Chichilnisky, Nicholas Eisenberger, Ronald Chance, Christopher Jones "Global Warming and Carbon Negative Technology: Prospects for a Lower Cost Route to a Lower Risk Atmosphere" Energy and Environment Vol 20, No 6, 2009

Chichilnisky G. and K Sheeran Saving Kyoto, North Holland, London UK 2009, Amazon.com

Chichilnisky G. "Economic Returns from the Biosphere" Nature, Vol 391, 12 February 1998, 629-630

Chichilnisky, G. "North South Trade and the Global Environment" American Economic Review Vol 84, No 4, 1994, 851-874

Chichilnisky G. and G.M. Heal "Who Should Abate Carbon Emissions" Economic Letters, Spring 1994, 443-449.

Chichilnisky, G. G.M. Heal Environmental Markets: Equity and Efficiency Columbia University Press, 2000.

Chichilnisky, G. and G.M. Heal "Markets for Tradeable CO2 Emissions Quotas, Principles and Practices", OECD Report No. 153, OECD Paris, 1995.

4.2　The Case for a Tax on Greenhouse Gases

Richard N. Cooper

This chapter argues for imposing a uniform charge on all emissions of greenhouse gases, insofar as practicable. It will focus for concreteness on carbon dioxide, the most prevalent and long-lasting greenhouse gas. It argues that such a charge would be superior to a system based on quantitative targets with provisions for trading emission rights, cap-and-trade for short.

Climate change is a global problem, not a localized one, and to be effective it therefore requires a global approach to reduction of GHG emissions. "Global" does not necessarily mean universal, although that would be desirable. It would be sufficient to engage the 30-40 largest emitting countries, at least for the next decade or two. These countries account for the overwhelming majority of fossil-fuel consumption, and also include countries covering the bulk of changes in land use that result in CO_2 emissions.

The case for a charge on carbon as opposed to a cap-and-trade scheme is based partly on the negatives associated with cap-and-trade, partly on the positives associated with the carbon charge. Let us take up the negative component first.

How well would a cap-and-trade system work at the global level? It would require allocating emission targets, covering many years, to states. To be effective, the total targets would have to be tight enough to cut emissions significantly from what they would otherwise be. In my view, it will be impossible to negotiate meaningful national targets. The reason is straightforward. Developing countries understandably place a higher priority on economic development than they do on mitigation of climate change, and they will not agree to binding emission targets that they believe will compromise their development objectives. Moreover, we now have several examples of countries that have grown 8-10 percent for two decades or more, and most developing countries will aspire to achieve such growth rates, even though most of them will fail to do so. But aspirations, not ex post realities, will shape their positions in international negotiations. And with generous targets allotted to the leading developing countries, the rich countries, especially the USA, will not agree to compensate with targets so stiff that they seriously threaten standards of living in those countries. In short, meaningful binding global targets are not feasible.

Even if this (decisive) argument is put to one side, there is another acute problem with a global system based on cap-and-trade. To work, the national targets (aka emission rights) must be allocated to the entities that actually make decisions about what kinds and how much fossil fuels to consume, that is, to electricity-generating firms and energy-intensive industrial firms. The idea of cap-and-trade is that each covered firm would be given an emission target for the coming year, perhaps declining from year to year, and each firm would either have to meet its target or purchase emission rights from other firms that had reduced emissions below their targets. This would require a market in emission permits, of which one has functioned in Europe since 2005. Although there were a number of glitches, Europeans have demonstrated that such a market can work. But the European system covers less than one half of European CO_2 emissions. For compelling practical reasons, Europeans have not yet extended the system to all or even most emissions, particularly those in the transport and heating sectors, and in much of industry.

Unless the permits are auctioned, raising the separate question of how a fair auction is assured, the permits are allocated to the covered firms free of charge. In countries with loose governance (i.e. most countries), this is an invitation to favoritism: the government is allocating permits that have significant financial value, and most governments are likely to do that in a biased way. Put more bluntly, it is an open invitation to corruption. This is a fatal flaw in a global cap-and-trade system, since well-governed democratic countries will be unwilling, and they should be unwilling, to impose burdens on their own citizens in order to enrich political favorites in less well-governed countries through international trade in emission permits. Concretely, no US Senator who understood the process would vote in favor of a treaty with this implication. In other words, the United States would not participate in such a global scheme, even if it had adopted a cap-and-trade system domestically.

This implication of unwholesome international transfers could be avoided if each participating country had its own national cap-and-trade system (EU-wide in the case of the EU). But that would vitiate much of the "trade" part of a cap-and-trade system, since we have reason to believe that emission reductions will be much less costly in many developing countries than they would be in many rich countries. Denying international trade in permits would reduce greatly the efficiency of the cap-and-trade system. High-cost emission reductions would yield to lower-cost reductions only on a national basis, not internationally.

That is the negative case for carbon charges: the main alternative, cap-and-trade, cannot be made to work effectively and efficiently at the global level. Yet a global solution is required.

The affirmative case for carbon charges contains a number of elements. First, it uses the price system, which is the only way to reach the billion plus decision-makers around the world who decide what and how much energy to consume. They will be encouraged either to consume less or to switch to less carbon intensive sources of energy.

Second, the charge can be applied to all fossil fuels at choke-points – oil refineries, main gas pipelines, principal coal transit points – with high confidence that the charge would affect downstream prices, that is, those faced by businesses and households. Separate provision could be made for the relatively few exceptions, e.g. a power plant located at a coal mine.

Third, the charge can and should (by negotiation) be made uniform (with perhaps a time lag of a few years for some developing countries), thus neutralizing the important issue of competitiveness of national energy-using industries in international markets. For example, the steel industry in all important steel-making countries would pay the same carbon charge, so none could complain that they were being put at a competitive disadvantage by a different GHG regime in other countries. It is noteworthy that many European countries levy much lower electricity charges to do business than they do to households, using "competitiveness" as the rationale; and they were disproportionately generous to some industries in the allocation of emission permits to some industries on similar grounds.

Fourth, a carbon charge would for many years generate revenues, badly needed by most governments these days (Norway and Qatar may be exceptions). These revenues could be used as each government saw fit, provided the use did not undermine the purposes of the agreement, viz. to reduce GHG emissions. Some would reduce deficits, some would finance needed expenditures, some (probably including the United States) would reduce other taxes, many would perhaps help adaptation to climate change in poor countries. Auctioning permits in a cap-and-trade system would also produce revenues, but if the legislative process in Europe and in the United States provides any guidance, auctions will be resisted strongly in favor of free allocation. The EU has agreed that in principle all permits will be auctioned by 2027 – 22 years after first introduction of its cap-and-trade system, and it remains to be seen whether this agreement will actually be carried out. The carbon charge can be phased in gradually, on a certain timetable, to limit any unwanted macroeconomic effects of a significant new tax.

The impact of a carbon charge on economic growth would be low, and could even be positive if the revenues are used in growth-enhancing ways, e.g. to reduce distortionary taxation or to finance research, development, and dissemination of new knowledge.

It will not be easy to negotiate a uniform tax rate among the major emitting countries. But "difficult" is much easier than "impossible," which I believe to be the case for a meaningful global cap-and-trade system. The current international negotiations through the conferences of parties to the Framework Convention on Climate Change cannot, in my view, lead to a meaningful mitigation of climate change. There are too many (193) participants, with too diverse interests and objectives, operating under a parliamentary rule of "consensus," which permits a small number of countries, even countries that are not relevant to GHG mitigation, to block action. And the focus has been on agreeing on binding quantitative restrictions on emissions, on only a subset of relevant countries, although the last restriction seems to be easing. To get somewhere, the negotiators need to shift away from quantitative emission targets to meaningful actions (such as a common charge on CO_2 emissions, although others are imaginable) by the relevant emitters, and initially only those emitters need to participate in the negotiations.

Some will object that a charge on carbon will leave the resulting reduction in emissions uncertain, since we do not know ahead of time how responsive businesses and households will be to the charge. That is entirely true. If the response is judged to be too slight, the charge can be raised in future years after an initial trial period of five to ten years. But the cap-and-trade system also has its uncertainties. As we learned from European experience, the permit price can decline to such a low level that conservation and fuel-switching is not encouraged at all, a result produced in part by two recessions that were not anticipated when decisions were announced on the permits to be allocated. Moreover, from basic principles it is preferable to have a stable emissions price than one that varies with macroeconomic conditions or other disturbances to supply or demand for energy. It is the stock of greenhouse gases in the atmosphere, not the current inflow, that influences the climate. The "externality" of emissions pertains to stock, not to flows, and is the same per tonne of CO_2 whether the flow is low or high. Thus the price on that externality should be relatively stable, not variable. Moreover, while European experience has been with unexpectedly low prices, it is a reasonable presumption that if the price had instead risen sharply to great heights, the political processes in Europe would have taken steps to limit the high price rather than see it generate an overall economic slowdown.

What about compliance? This is an issue for any international agreement that imposes unwelcome costs on the participants. The temptation to "free ride" – to shirk while others are (presumably) carrying out their obligations – is ever-present. That is as true of a global cap-and-trade agreement as of an agreement involving carbon charges. In either case monitoring would be required, made easier by constant improvements in long-distance sensors; but on-the-ground sensors and international inspections should also be introduced. In the case of carbon charges, the national legislation introducing such charges would be relatively easy to track. Harder would be the actual collection of emission charges. But the Fiscal Department of the International Monetary Fund is already familiar with the tax systems of all member countries (only Cuba, North Korea, and Taiwan and the smallest economies are not members, all except Taiwan being low emitters). It could be charged with monitoring the collection of carbon charges by each participant in the agreement, which could then be compared with the information from the sensors and inspections.

In summary, I conclude that a uniform carbon charge in all major emitting countries, revenues to be kept at home, is far superior to cap-and-trade as a global arrangement for mitigating climate change. This is partly because agreement on an effective and efficient global cap-and-trade regime is hard to imagine, both because the global "caps" would be too high and because the allocation of permits to domestic agents would invite corruption in a many of countries, leading other countries to decline to trade permits with them. Agreement on harmonized national carbon charges would not be easy, but at least agreement on common actions would have some chance to succeed if the relevant international community decided there needed to be a serious attempt to mitigate climate change. And it would have several advantages: providing an appropriate price signal to everyone to reduce consumption of fossil fuels, generating needed revenue, dealing directly with widespread concerns about international competitiveness, and even to stimulate growth.

Photo by Miriam Kennet. Green Economics Institute Speakers at Rio+20

Part 5 Incentivising the 'Homo Irrational'- The Psychology of Climate Change

5.1 The Social Psychology of Climate Change: A Rough Guide

Rosamund Stock

When discussions of rebalancing the economy take place, whether rebalancing from London to the northern regions or between conventional manufacturing procedures and power generation to renewable power and less wasteful processes, the considerations of what this means for the ordinary people on the ground can be neglected. In the end, though, rebalancing the economy means some jobs will disappear and newer ones develop. Making sure there are enough jobs to go around, especially in the already depressed areas of, for example, the north of England or Wales in the UK, and other will be an issue, and other countries will have similar problems. Less technologically developed nations may have an even bigger problem in that they may be asking their people to forego a style of consumption which has come to be seen as a benchmark of growth and development. In the wealthier nations people sooner or later must consume less, and differently.

Sooner or later, if our response to climate change is at all serious, people will have to face a shift in both employment and consumption. How to Public responds to this potential uncertainty will be key to whether efforts to efforts to rebalance the economy will have the support of those same ordinary people. By 'ordinary' is meant those who are neither practitioners, activists in NGOs (as opposed to those who are passive members). These people are not already wholeheartedly committed to efforts to combat climate change, it is still a value, but one of many which may conflict.

The first consideration those who seek to change minds, or to garner support for a campaign, or even to generate acceptance of a measure to rebalance the economy, is the need to understand what they world looks like to these same people. If you work in a green economics you are likely to spend most of your time talking to the like-minded or highly informed. It must always be remembered that other people do not see the world in the same way. There are also a wide range of views, but not infinitely so. However it looks to campaigners and politicians, the chances are that it will not look the same to the woman in the street, rushing home to get dinner for her children and the demands of whose situation mean that leaving the car at home is not an option, or more correctly, leaving the car at home is not *seen* as an option.

People respond to the situation they see, not one that politicians or even researchers specify: a well-known experiment showed that people play an online game quite differently when they believe they are playing with a person, to when they believe they are playing with a computer (Abric & Kahan, 1972). They will respond quite differently to a situation depending on how it is structured, are they treated as individuals or are they part of a group (Deutsch, 1987)? They will respond to others differently and want to distribute rewards differently.

However, they may respond to exactly the *same* situation in different ways depending on how they 'frame' them. One can think of it as a picture frame. How a painting appears can change drastically if it is in the wrong frame. This idea was developed by Tversky & Kahneman (1980, Kahneman & Tversky 2000 for the classic papers) in the context of how much people will risk: setting up the situation as a loss produces different responses to when the same situation is described as a gain: we are less risk averse when we contemplate gains. In justice research no one could not find any consistent links between how a resource was distributed and the way the situation was constructed, as had been theorised. However when you look at what people themselves see subjectively (Stock, 2003) there is a strong link between the social relations they see around them, and the way they want outcomes distributed between people. This suggests that communication should offer something, rather than demand to something be foregone.

Perhaps the most important thing to offer to people is security. Socio-economic security can affect how people interact with others, their commitment to an organisation, turnover, mental health issues, and productivity (for a review see Stock, 2001). Failing to do so can produce what is known as a 'threat-rigidity response in organisations., Providing some security e.g. in the shape of a basic income shows an improvemet in an individual's contribution to group output (Frohlich & Oppenheimer, 1992) and see ILO 2003 for its effects and some mitigating factors, including its effect on social justice issues.

But there are also factors which can improve someone's security: job security is usually characterised as:

(perception of threat) x (powerlessness)

and the threat is seen as:

(perceived probability) x (seriousness of consequences)
(see Greenhalgh, 1983 for the basic model).

This is similar to the psychological model of risk, usually characterised as probability x seriousness. The work by Tversky & Kahneman (see earlier), When we consider how the world looks to people who are being presented with a new policy that may balance the economy: what they will lose will be far more salient than the (possible) gains of controlling or mitigating climate change. There are many who dislike any change, even if the change turns out well (although they will probably never admit it!). Perceptions of risk/security are affected by the 'powerless' side of the equation in that more resources to lessen the seriousness of the consequences. If someone has savings behind them or their mortgage substantially paid losing a job is less financially serious than if they have multiple household debts, no family resources to turn to, and insurance. In the US it can be much worse, families lose their access to healthcare and the issue of access to an adequate pension scheme will be an issue in many Western countries.

It should also be borne in mind that the social consequences of losing a job may be as serious as the financial ones: the lost of a whole set of social relationships, a place in the world. 'You become nobody' would be a typical feeling. Depression and illness is just as likely to follow (Burchell, 1994) from the loss of, not merely personal friends, but a locus within the wider network of social relationships, each one being a confirmation of a person's membership of society, and often value. Some companies, on downsizing or closure or plant, do a great deal for the workforce and make genuine attempts to find alternative work, sometimes even providing retraining, others wash their hands of the situation. People sometimes report feelings not dissimilar to the end of a marriage or partnership. It is dissolving a relationship and not by mutual consent.

Moreover there are individual variations in how security is perceived: framing means that one person will look at the same situation and see it as difficult but they believe the solutions lie in their own hands. Whereas another will see only powerlessness In a classic work on job security (Hartley et al, 1991) showed that responses depended on the extent to which they saw causation/action as external or internal, controllable or not (known as attribution style). Those who saw the causes as external and controllable chose very different actions (involvement in collective action such as a strike or asking their union to come in and negotiate for them) to those who saw it as beyond anyone's control or even just beyond their control who showed denial, withdrawal from the work situation, hopelessness; depression can accompany job insecurity for some and extreme stress for most. Those who saw the situation in terms of their own abilities to act (individual factors) and controllable chose to pursue individual action (job search, retraining). If they see causes as internal and uncontrollable they are likely to take either no action, or sometimes precisely the action which would make it their failure a self perpetuating prophecy (called learned helplessness). If change in the nature of productive processes is to take place, reducing the seriousness of job loss for people has to be a primary concern. Well funded support for those whose jobs will be changing, through out of work benefits, good quality training and adequate job opportunities is a sine qua non of an adaptive economy.

These key factors need to be considered but there are a few more responses to risk that need to be considered: one is the social amplification of risk (Pidgeon, Kasperson & Slovic 2003). It refers to the repeating, either among a group of people or via wider social communication such as television news and the internet so that a problem or risk is presented as somewhat more risky each time it is dealt with by a new social actor. It is not hard to see how this can magnify risk out of proportion so the social context of situations may have a significant effect on perceptions of risk or security. Again, the availability of real rewards in an adaptive economy, emphasising the new and the positive contribution those in the new jobs will make, asking people to join something rather than suffering the loss of something. Social institutions such as public television services and unions need to be involved in both communicating the new opportunities, making the work seem worthwhile and providing platforms to recruitment for individuals to find their place in this new economy. If refusal to change is not to be met these opportunities and support must be in place first. Otherwise we are asking individuals to shoulder all the risk, not those with greater resources and deeper pockets.

One may also find 'stigma' being attached to an issue (Slovic, 2000): it comes to be seen so negatively that its threat is seen as so high or even infinite so that the threat is also infinite. Responses are often dominated by revulsion and emotional responses, and the threat is seen independently of actual risk. Nuclear power is seen in this light: for most people the response is a flat 'no' and that is the end of it. The extent of this stigma is illustrated by the emergence of magnetic resonance technology in healthcare. It was developed from the technique of nuclear magnetic resonance widely used in e.g. biochemistry. When its use was transferred to healthcare it was felt that to put the word 'nuclear' in the title would arouse anxiety and suspicion in patients perhaps leading to a refusal to participate, so the name was changed to the one we know: magnetic resonance imaging.

Another is false optimism: people see risk as less than it should be on the principle of 'it will never happen to me'. They also see it as more likely for others than themselves, and more likely still for outgroup members. (See Slovic, 2000 for many of the classic articles). This may mean that people see any changes that must take place as something for others to do, not themselves or of such low probability that it is unlikely ever to occur and their experience in seeing it happen to others including a tendency to remember confirming events and those become more salient in their own surroundings (called the hypothesis confirmation bias). You remember/see around you all those events which did happen, not the ones which didn't.

Such optimism also contributes to the 'silver bullet' approach: 'science will develop an answer, look at geoengineering: now they are going to put giant freezers in the Antarctic' (something which appeared in the New Scientist of 15th September 2012). They can do amazing things these days. They're going to put giant balloons in the atmosphere' (from the Guardian Newspaper of 1st September 2011). This is an example of seeing control of events as external, controllable by all means, but by others not oneself thus letting the individual off the hook from acting themselves.

Another factor arising from the internal/external locus of control (as it is known) is what you might term the 'we support you but...' response. This particular problem comes from the experiences of disabled people, particularly those in wheelchairs and reflects an external attribution of control. A wheelchair user may find herself entering somewhere where the access is poor or even non existent and, when challenged, the response is along the lines of 'oh we totally agree with providing access, of course we do, but there is nothing *we* can do because of the way the building is... (the mot usual but there are various others. The attitude of a lot of business leaders is that climate change is important and needs to be addressed but not now we are in a recession/it would be a burden on businesses/it's the government's responsibility/would cost in lost output (in spite of the Stern reviews),' Take your pick. People, whether in their work or their family and personal life, as part of organisations or voluntary groups will all need to contribute and need to know it; but it has to seem possible, the consequences near at hand, and rewarding opportunities need to be presented whether as career change or market opportunity, in the language that people from different backgrounds use.

Another is what might be termed the 'having your cake an eat it' response: people perform something which contributes to lower emissions but then return to other activities which contribute to raising emissions or just forget the issue, safe in the knowledge that they have done their bit. People rely on carbon offset to fly *more* often then they did before. This returns to question of cost; people's possible responses to the situations don't take place within silos in the mind, all these issues interact. The have your cake and eat it response is also a way to diminish risk (subjectively perceived) and reduces the seriousness of possible outcomes. Rather, in the short term, than suffering an inconvenient and onerous loss of the ability to travel by air freely, carbon offsetting reduces the cost (in that person's eyes) of contributing to emissions reduction. While we turn lights out and the heating down, we happily use larger fridges and flat screen televisions and leave our routers on.

There are other matters which help with the acceptance of adverse decisions: research on procedural justice is voluminous: people's responses to procedures are significantly influence by allowing people a voice in proceedings and better still, a voice in how the procedure was developed. One planning professional confessed surprise at the degree to which a two minute slot to talk at a local authority planning committee meeting increased people's satisfaction with the outcome. Such voice can increase compliance when the decision goes against someone.

A further factor in people's acceptance of adverse outcomes, even in the case of something like redundancy is the provision of explanations and justifications known in social psychology as 'accounts'. This is a question of taking people with you; decisions which appear arbitrary or arrived at without the proper consultation, decisions which appear insufficiently justified or simply don't use the explanations drawn from the same set of ideas as those who will lose out. If the justification is about the inevitability of market decisions, and the people on the shop floor reject this and believe that employers owe them for all their hard work then redundancies will provoke opposition. If on the other hand people accept the argument of the inevitability of the laws of supply and demand, there will be less. Obviously these kind of explanations feed into the attributions of control discussed above.

Once we start examining the wider issues of what repertoires of explanations are current in any society, the question of whose justifications are accepted becomes of issue. Justifications are usually derived from a socially available library of ideas, even though they will be adapted and modified by someone's individual ideas and according to their salience in the surrounding milieu. If a message can be communicated often enough and consistently enough the ideas of a minority can change those of the majority (Moscovici, et al., 1994). But then the question then arises as to who is able to dominate the airwaves, internet, or newspapers? They stand a better chance of getting their message across simply because they are heard more often. It is likely that the Drinkaware campaign by the Portman Group (a drinks industry funded body) will have more resources than is ever available to Action on Smoking & Health which was set up by the Royal College of Physicians, even though the latter has worked hard for 40 yrs and while it has excellent contacts with parliamentarians, its access to mass media is not necessarily as great. This kind of contact will affect those who have not previously given much thought to the matter: salience as a factor comes into its own in the case of 'lazy thinking' where, if the subject of climate change comes up in debate or conversation, someone will grasp the nearest (and likely to be the most prominent, frequent or most recently heard) idea to use. There is also the difference between 'hot' and 'cold' cognition: fast of the top of one's head, sometimes emotion driven think and slower, deliberate consideration using a wider range of cognitive resources.

If someone hears something often enough, by a trusted source whether that be a legitimate authority or by the professionals in a particular area, there will be an increased probability that the idea will be both adopted by an individual or group and used. Of course whether any particular source is accepted as trusted depends on the question. In Britain, the Met Office or the BBC is usually a trusted source for the changes in the weather pattern with climate change, and both institutions have worked hard to keep climate change on the agenda. But if sources can be discredited, as with the problems around temperature records which came to be known in British newspapers as 'ClimateGate', such explanations may be passed over, or discounted. Establishing trust is as important as establishing the message itself. (For more on the factors affecting social influence see the work of Cialdini (2001)).

While people most certainly can and do think for themselves, if they are in a hurry, talking casually in the pub, answering a question offhand, the most salient is likely be grabbed from memory. This tendency is then reinforced by the way in which we link information in memory: items linked in memory mean that when one item is used, its linked ideas also become more accessible so it is more likely they will be used. Alternative idea sets can underlie framing (see above) and also underlie the development of polarisation of debate or intractable conflict A recent example of both was raised in the press: government rangers want to cull wild boars to prevent them doing too much damage to a habitat; this is vehemently opposed by animal welfare campaigners. The two sides have become polarised and the newspaper article was headlined: 'Thrilling beast or feral pest'. (see Stock, 2009 for discussion of the clash of cultures involved in Green economics and standard economics).

What is needed is a situation where ideas about climate change, rebalancing the economy or simply greening the supply chain, are widely used and widely accepted; this will increase the probability that the people who will lose out either agree with the change however reluctantly, or they will recognise it as something legitimised by their society, even if they themselves disagree. One suspects this means access not just the national press, but the local; in the UK, for example, this means going to local meetings, talking to firms, to unions, going to branch meetings, talking to the Townswomen's Guild and the WI, the model railway club, teaching in adult education classes or the WEA, talking to churches, school governors, Older People's Forums, hospital trusts and their members (UCLH trust has an important patient involvement and education function). We need a groundswell of support, of making the assumptions about emissions reduction part of the social atmosphere, part of the wallpaper of people's lives.

References:

This paper has been a brief tour of some of the issues in social psychology which bear on the problems of rebalancing the economy. It has been written for an audience of non-psychologists and the references are relatively few. In the main those given have been introductions to or reviews of the area of research concerned or the key papers in the development. For more detailed or recent papers please contact the author.

Abric, J.C., & Kahan, J.P.,1972. The effects of representations and behaviour in experimental games. European Journal of Social Psychology 2. 129-144.

Burchell, 1994. Burchell, B.,The effects of labour market position, jobs security and unemployment on psychological health In Gallie, D., Marsh, C., & Vogler, C., (eds,) Social change and the experience of unemployment. Oxford: OUP. Pp 188-212.

Cialdini, R.B., 2001. Influence: Science & Practice. Needham Heights, MA: Allyn & Bacon

Deutsch, M., 1987. Experimental studies of the effects of different systems of distributive justice. In J.C.Masters & W.P. Smith (eds.) Social comparison, social justice and relative deprivation. Hillsdale, New Jersey:Erlbaum (pp.151-164).

Frohlich, N., & J. A. Oppenheimer, 1992. Choosing Justice: An experimental approach to ethical theory. University of California Press: Berkeley, CA.

Hartley, J., D. Jacobson, B. Klandermans & T. Van Vuuren, 1991. Coping with jobs at risk. Sage: London

ILO, 2004. Economic security for a better world. Geneva: International Labour Office

Moscovici, S., Faina, A.M., Maass, A., 1994. Minority Influence. Chicago : Nelson-Hall.

Pidgeon, N. F., Kasperson, R.E.,& P. Slovic 2003. The Social Amplification of Risk. Cambridge : Cambridge University Press

Slovic, P., 2000. The perception of risk. London: Earthscan.

Stock, R.E., 2000. Explaining the choice of Distribution Rule. Paper presented to the VIIIth Biennieal Conference of the International Society for Justice Research, Tel Aviv: September 2000

Stock, R.E., 2001. Socio-economic security, Justice and the Psychology of Social Relationships. Geneva: International Labour Office.

Stock, R.E., 2003. Explaining the choice of distribution rule: the role of mental representations. Sociological Inquiry, 73, 177-189

Stock, R.E., 2009. The clash between economics and ecology: frames and schemas. International Journal of Green Economics, 3, 285-296.

Tversky, A., & D. Kahneman, 1980. Causal schemes and judgements under uncertainty. in M. Fishbein (ed.) Progress in social psychology. Vol.1, Hillsdale, NJ: Erlbaum.

5.2 Encounters with the Inconceivable Climate Denial in Everyday Life

Dr. Kari Marie Norgaard

New evidence indicates that it is not just the radical right wing politics of those who don't believe that climate change is happening that slows action on the climate. Perhaps even more important for our lack of forward movement on climate change is the more everyday practice of the majority of people in the United States and other Western democracies who know about climate change but manage to just ignore it. For nearly three decades natural and physical scientists have provided increasingly clear and dire assessments of alteration in the biophysical world around which human social systems are organized. Just a few months ago the world atmosphere reached a carbon dioxide concentration of 400 parts per million. Yet despite these urgent warnings from the scientific community, human social and political response to ecological degradation remains wholly inadequate. Instead climate change is like a proverbial "elephant in the room." Climate scientists may have identified global warming as the most important issue of our time, but for urban dwellers in the rich and powerful Northern countries climate change is seen as "no more than background noise."

Americans are not alone in the act of everyday ignoring, this gap between the severity of the problem of climate change and its lack of public salience is visible in most Western nations. Indeed, no nation has a base of public citizens that are sufficiently socially and politically engaged to generate the level of change that predictions of climate science would seem to warrant. Instead we are confronted with a series of paradoxes: as scientific evidence for climate change pours in, public urgency and even interest in the issue fails to correspond. What can explain the misfit between scientific information and public concern? Are people just uniformed of the facts? Are they inherently greedy and self-interested?

My original and most extensive fieldwork on this topic was set in a small farming community in Norway. High levels of wealth, education, standard of living and political engagement, together with the nation's location in the northern latitude made Norway a very useful place to explore questions about the apathy and political silence in the face of climate change. If any nation can find the ability to respond it must be in a place such as this, where the effects are visible, the population is educated, cared for, politicized and environmentally engaged. In *Living in Denial* my book length description of these events, I use the voices of people in this one community in Norway during a recent very dry and warm winter in order to make visible the narratives and cultural constructions that can inform a larger story behind worldwide public paralysis in the face of predictions from climate scientists.

As it happened, in this rural community there was unusually warm weather during my stay. November brought severe flooding across the entire region. The first snowfall did not come until late January – some two months later than usual.
As a result of these conditions, the local ski area only opened in late December with the aid of 100% artificial snow – a completely unprecedented event with dramatic recreational effects and measurable economic impacts on the community. The local lake failed to freeze sufficiently to allow for ice-fishing. Casual comments about the weather, a long-accepted form of small talk, commonly included references to unusual weather, shaking of heads, and the phrase "climate change."

It was not just the weather that was unusual that winter. As a sociologist, I was perplexed by the behavior of the people as well. Despite clear social and economic impacts on the community, no social action was taking place. People could have reacted differently to that strange winter. The shortened ski season affected everyone in the community. In the words of one taxi driver: "It makes a difference if we move from five months of winter tourism to only three. It affects all of us, you know, not just those up on the mountain. It affects the hotels, the shops in town, us taxi drivers, we notice it too." Why didn't this awareness translate into social action? Community members could have written letters to the local paper, brought the issue up in one of the many public forums that took place that winter, made attempts to plan for the local effects of climate change, put pressure on local and national leaders to develop long term climate plans or short term economic relief, decreased their automobile use, or at the least, engaged their neighbors, children, and political leaders in discussions about what climate change might mean for their community in the next ten and twenty years. The residents of this town could have rallied around the problem of the lack of snow and its economic and cultural impacts. But they did not.

"We Don't Really Want To Know"

That winter I attended public meetings, read the newspapers, spoke with people on the street and conducted 46 interviews. Global warming was frequently mentioned and people seemed to be both informed and concerned about it. Yet at the same time it was an uncomfortable issue. People were aware that climate change could radically alter life within the next decades, yet they did not go about their days wondering what life would be like for their children, whether farming practices would change or whether their grandchildren would be able to ski on real snow. They spent their days thinking about more local, manageable topics. In the words of one person who held his hands in front of his eyes as he spoke, "people want to protect themselves a bit." Other community members described this sense of knowing and not knowing, of having information but not thinking about it in their everyday lives. As one young woman told me "In the every day I don't think so much about it, but I know that environmental protection is very important." As a topic that was troubling, it was an issue that many people preferred to avoid. Thus community members describe climate change as an issue that they have to "sit themselves down and think about," " don't think about in the everyday," "but which in between is discouraging and an emotional weight." Vigdis, a college age student told me that she was afraid of global warming, but that it didn't enter her everyday life:

> I often get afraid, like – it goes very much up and down, then, with how much I think about it. But if I sit myself down and think about it, it could actually happen, I thought about how if this here continues we could come to have no difference

between winter and spring and summer, like – and lots of stuff about the ice that is melting and that there will be flooding, like, and that is depressing, the way I see it.

Since members of the community did know about global warming but did not integrate this knowledge into everyday life, they experienced what Robert Lifton calls the *absurdity of the double life* (1982). In one reality was the collectively constructed sense of normal everyday life. In the other reality existed the troubling knowledge of increasing automobile use, polar ice caps melting and the predictions for future weather scenarios. In the words of Kjersti, a teacher at the local agricultural school in her early 30's: "We live in one way and we think in another. We learn to think in parallel. It's a skill, an art of living."

The term 'denial' is sometimes used to describe the phenomenon of outright rejecting information as true, as in the case of climate skeptics. But this is a very different, more literal use of the term denial. The denial metaphor of the elephant in the room is useful because it reminds us that ignoring a serious problem is not easy to do. Ignoring the obvious can be a lot of work. In her work on apathy in the United States, sociologist Nina Eliasoph observes, "We often assume that political activism requires an explanation, while inactivity is the normal state of affairs. But it can be as difficult to ignore a problem as to try to solve it, to curtail feelings of empathy as to extend them. . . If there is no exit from the political world then political silence must be as active and colorful as a bright summer shadow" (Eliasoph 1998, 6). Instead, people actually work to avoid acknowledging disturbing information in order to avoid emotions of fear, guilt and helplessness, follow cultural norms, and maintain positive conceptions of individual and national identity. As a result of this kind of denial, people describe a sense of 'knowing and not knowing' about climate change, of having information but not thinking about it in their everyday lives. Information from climate science is known in the abstract, but disconnected from, and invisible within political, social or private life. How did people manage to outwardly ignore what was happening in the community? Did they manage to ignore it inwardly as well?

I then traced the three disturbing emotions of guilt, fear of the future and helplessness, as well as how people in both Norway and the United States normalized the idea of climate change in order to avo id these emotions. I describe how people changed the topic of conversations, told jokes, tried not to think about it, and keep the concept off the agenda of political meetings all by following the "rules" of normal behavior. As a result, what happened in this one Norwegian town, and indeed what we can all observe in the public silence on climate change in United States and elsewhere, was not a rejection of information per se, but the failure to integrate this knowledge into everyday life or transform it into social action.

The view from this one town in Norway portrays global warming as an issue about which people cared and had considerable information, but one about which they didn't really want to know and in some sense didn't know *how* to know. Although individual people experience these emotions, this denial is not individual. Rather it is something that people do together as a community. I draw upon the work of sociologist Eviatar Zerubavel who coined the term "socially organized denial." Community members collectively held information about global warming at arm's length by participating in cultural norms of attention, emotion, and conversation, and by using a series of cultural narratives to deflect disturbing information and normalize a particular version of reality in which "everything was fine."

Many of the same emotions were at play in the United States, yet denial also looks different in the United States than it does in Norway. The United States is obviously a much larger and much less homogenous society. Also clearly different are some of the particular reasons for ignoring climate change (such as the fact that our greater carbon emissions make our involvement harder to face) and the extent of social structural support for us to ignore it. Denial in the United States also looks different due to the presence of corporate-funded campaigns of skepticism and the increasingly successful cultural challenge they have launched to the legitimacy of science in the public sphere (Jacques, Dunlap, and Freeman 2008; Jacques 2009)

One lesson from the American context concerns the hazard of individualism. The powerlessness and fear about the future described in both Norwegian and American interviews were exacerbated in the United States by a general discourse of individualism coupled with awareness that individual action was not enough. Another issue at play in the United States is mistrust of government. Both themes are present in the sense of helplessness articulated by one American student here:

> We'd hear all this information and get all riled up, and then they'd be, like, "contact your legislator," and I'd be, like, "Aw, really? Can't you give us a little more?" That's, like, where I feel the most helpless; it's like I know all this stuff, I have all this information, [but] what the hell do I do with it? I don't know where to turn, I don't know who to talk to. Yeah, I can write my congressman a letter, but in all honesty . . . I am not sure that one person can make such a difference.

It would seem that a combination of lack of trust in their political system (political alienation) and a culture of individualism leave Americans uniquely at a loss in terms of what to do about climate change. In many respects and for large segments of the population, however, denial in the United States looks and feels very much the same as it does in the small community in Norway. Many of the hopes and fears articulated by people in each country are remarkably similar. The widespread nature of the missing response to climate change itself indicates that there are cross-cutting, universal elements to people's experience of climate science. It is generally true, in the United States as well as in Norway and in many countries around the world, that despite new information about the fragility of our planet, life goes on "as normal." Across many sectors of U.S. society, people know facts about climate change that they believe to be true, but they live their lives without integrating this information into their decision making, political activities, or sense of daily reality. Thus, there appear to be lessons for all of us to learn from this one community in Norway. Life is different there, but for many of us around the world it is also very much the same.

Can such socially organized denial be overcome? And if so, how? One implication of socially organized denial of climate change is that as individuals we must struggle to imagine the reality of our current situation. With socially organized denial, the question becomes not how do we better educate and inform the public, but under what circumstances are people able to move beyond a sense of helplessness, guilt or fear of the future and take actions that are in their collective, long term survival interest? Climate change requires large-scale reduction of emissions, but our current political economic structure is intimately embedded in our petroleum- based economy. We need democratic engagement and response, yet individuals retreat out of a sense of helplessness. Part of what presently makes people feel helpless is an assessment of this very serious problem in a context where nobody else is acting, an assessment that political actions are socially unacceptable or politically unfeasible, and that larger international efforts are even more unlikely. How can we escape this circular pattern?

Must we go into the streets? Probably a lot more people do need to march with signs down the main streets of every town in Norway and the United States in order to break the cycle of invisibility around climate change. But for those with different instincts there are many other things that can and must be done to make climate change visible and to show each other and our political leaders that we demand action.

If socially organized climate denial is a cycle held in place by individual fear and silence, complicit cultural norms and a state logic based on fossil fuel extraction and economic profit at any politically acceptable cost, then the cycle can be interrupted at many places. In any political struggle there are key strategic possibilities. Individual people can get involved in local political efforts, even talking about it with family and friends is an important way to break the silence. For another kind of example: Norwegian farmers take seriously the politics of "local patriotism." Although they are not enough in isolation, local efforts to make climate change visible in the community, to plan for coming changes, to reduce emissions at the county and regional levels that are based on existing community ties and sense of place and identity may provide a key for breaking through climate denial from the ground up. There is already a global movement building for communities to uncover how climate change is manifesting in their local contexts. Local political renewal cannot be enough on its own. But it may be the important next step for individuals in breaking through the absurdity of the double life and for renewing democratic process. As people participate in thinking about what is happening in their own place and how they will respond, they will begin to see why the facts of climate change matter to them and to develop a sociological imagination at the same time as they reconnect the rifts in time and space that have constructed climate change as a distant issue. Working together may over time create the supportive community that is a necessary (though not sufficient) condition for people to face large fears about the future and engage in large scale social change. Facing climate change will not be easy. But it is worth trying.

References

Eliasoph, Nina. 1998. <u>Avoiding Politics: How Americans Produce Apathy in Everyday Life</u>. Cambridge, UK: Cambridge University Press.

Jacques, Peter. 2009. <u>Environmental Skepticism: Ecology, Power, and Public Life.</u> Burlington, VT: Ashgate.

Jacques, Peter, Riley Dunlap, and Mark Freeman. 2008. "The Organisation of Denial: Conservative Think Tanks and Environmental Skepticism." <u>Environmental Politics</u> 17 (3):349–385.

Lifton, Robert <u>Indefensible Weapons: The Political and Psychological Case against Nuclearism</u> New York: Basic Books, 1982.

Norgaard, Kari Marie <u>Living in Denial: Climate Change, Emotions and Everyday Life</u> Cambridge: MIT Press, 2011

Zerubavel, Evitar. <u>The Elephant in the Room: Silence and Denial in Everyday Life</u> New York: Oxford University Press, 2006.

5.3 Why my Mum doesn't recycle: The psychology of climate change action

Christopher Brook

Environmental problems have long been associated with numbness or apathy (e.g., Macy & Brown, 1998; Gifford, 1976; Searles, 1972). Dan Ariely in an interview with Axel said that if you wanted to create a problem people would not care about then climate change is it. One national representative opinion poll in the USA shows that 47% of people polled view global warming as a "very serious" problem, and another 28% view it as a "somewhat serious" problem (Pew Project, 2006). This level of concern—75% of people in the United States assessing global warming as a "very" or "somewhat" serious problem—is similar to the level in Russia (73%) and lower than that in many other nations: 87% of Canadians, 81% of Mexicans, 95% of French, 88% of Chinese, 97% of Japanese, 96% of Brazilians, and 94% of Indians assess global warming as a "very" or "somewhat" serious problem. Regardless of the stated level of concern however, few people in the United States or abroad see climate change as an immediate risk and tend to rank it as less important than many other social issues, like the economy and terrorism (Krosnik, Holbrook, Lowe, & Visser, 2006). But why do we not care. The majority of people accept it as a problem, but not many of us do anything about it. Yes there are the genuinely concerned people who go as far out of their way as possible to help; but for most of us, we do the bare minimum.

But why is that? Why do we not seem to care about such a large issue. One often cited reason is the cost of changing our behaviour. However if this was the case financial incentive schemes would have a much bigger effect. Behavioural Economists and Psychologists have come up with a large array of reasons.

Psychological Barriers to General Problems

Ignorance

Ignorance takes two forms. The first is not seeing climate change as a major issue and so these people remain unaware of the issue. The second dimension is a lack of knowledge about what to do and what actions to take. In 3 studies by Lorenzoni et.al (2007) participants mentioned ozone depletion in their discussion about climate change and said recycling was a solution to ozone depletion.

Uncertainty

People tend to interpret any sign of uncertainty (for example, the supposed stock of a resource) as sufficient reason to act in self-interest over that of the environment. Uncertainty about climate change probably functions as a justification for inaction or postponed action related to climate change. This not helped by the data is remote and distant and it being correlational data. People argued for ages against smoke and lung problems for ages as just correlation. Even though 97% of scientists agree over human caused climate change, the general public thought that it was around 50%. This is because of the exacerbated media portrayal of climate change, which tends to highlight scientific and political disagreement (Carvalho and Burgess, 2005)

Mistrust and Reactance

Ample evidence suggests that many people distrust risk messages that come from scientists or government officials (MacGregor, Slovic, Mason, Detweiler, 1994). Moreover the reaction against advice or policy that seems to threaten one's freedom, is based in part on a lack of trust of those who give the advice or set the policy (Eilam & Suleiman, 2004).

Denial

Uncertainty, mistrust, and reactance easily slide into active denial. This could be denial of the existence of climate change and/or the human contribution. Polls vary, but a substantial minority of people believes that climate change is not occurring or that human activity has little or nothing to do with it. In the case of climate change, some people actively deny that climate presents any problem.

The ideas of terror management theory (Goldenberg, Pyszczynski, Greenberg, & Solomon, 2000) suggest that people may deny the problem because it is a reminder of one's mortality and enhances efforts to validate one's beliefs and efforts to bolster self-esteem. Research applying this to concerns about the environment illustrated that increased mortality salience resulted in decreased concern about protecting the environment among those who did not derive their self-esteem from the environment and had the opposite effect on those who derived their self-esteem from the environment (Vess & Arndt, 2008).

Even within the group who accept human caused climate change many are still in denial. They locate responsibility for causing climate change with others (individuals, businesses and governments). (Lorenzoni et.al 2007)

Judgemental discounting
Behavioural scientists have emphasized that in their private lives, people sometimes display a form of myopia. They may neglect the future, seeing it as a kind of foreign country, one they may not ever visit. If the effects of climate change were on our doorstep then citizens would be rushing to the doors of parliament and congress and demanding protection. However as they perceive climate change as mostly a threat to future generations - if significant sea-level rises seem to be decades away - they are unlikely to have a sense of urgency.

Habit
Individuals exhibit what might be called behavioural momentum. William James (1890) called habit the "enormous flywheel of society". Habit may be one of the most important obstacles to the mitigation of climate change impacts.

Many habitual behaviours are extremely resistant to permanent change (e.g., eating habits), and others are slowly changed (e.g., use of seat belts) (Maio et al., 2007). Ensconced habits do not change without a substantial push; priming and even attitude changes often do not lead to behavioural change. For some people, behaviours that form part of the human contribution to climate change (e.g., the use of cars) are habitual and difficult to change (Aarts & Dijksterhuis, 2000), although not impossible. For example, temporarily forcing car drivers to use alternative travel modes has induced long-term reductions in car use (Jakobsson et.al, 2003). For many people car use is nearly essential because of the structure of human settlements. But very large numbers of people do a have choice, and choose not to purchase a low-carbon car or to take alternative transportation. For others, simple habit is the barrier to change.

Perceived Behavioural Control

We perceive our impact as a drop in the bucket when it comes to acting on climate change. Individually every time we recycle or choose not to drive it has a tiny effect. This reduces our motivation to act differently even though if everyone acted differently the difference would be huge. When people believe that they have no control over climate change, it facilitates such mechanisms as denial (Gifford, Iglesias, & Casler, 2009).

Because we are aware that we alone cannot effect climate change we are very self-conscience of people free-riding. People are reluctant to change their behaviour when they feel others will not follow suit. This personal distrust was also seen at a government level. Perceptions of limited political action by local, national, international governments were found to be a significant barrier to engagement amongst many of our participants. In particular, many referred to the lack of commitment to mitigate greenhouse gas emissions by the USA and lack of evidence of substantial action by the British government

Perceived risks from behavioural change

Potentially, changing behaviour of any sort holds at least six kinds of risk (Schiffman, Kanuk, & Das, 2006). First, functional risk refers to whether the adaptation will work: If one purchases, for example, a plug-in electric vehicle (PHEV) it may, as a new technology, have battery problems. Second, physical risk refers to the danger that one might face: Is this PHEV as crash-safe as the SUV traded in to buy it? Third, financial risk refers to the potential for costs that are not outweighed by benefits: The PHEV's purchase price includes a premium over equivalent gas-powered vehicles; will the money to buy and operate it be lost?

Fourth, social risk refers to potential damage to one's ego or reputation: If one buys a PHEV, will friends laugh? They may invoke any of the first three risks as my failure to reckon carefully. The fifth risk, which follows the fourth closely, is the psychological risk. Once rebuked, teased, or criticized by one's significant others, one's ego may suffer some damage. Sixth, time (lost) can be a risk. If the time spent planning and adopting the adaptation does not result in personal or environmental benefits, it would have been wasted.

Tokenism and the rebound effect

Even if people do believe they can make a difference many undertake low-cost actions. This has been called the low-cost hypothesis (Diekmann & Preisendörfer, 1992). Many of these effects have little effect in terms if mitigation. A further problem is the rebound effect, in which after some saving or effort is made, people erase the gains. For example, persons who buy a fuel-efficient vehicle may drive further than when they owned a less-efficient vehicle. It similar to dieting. Many people eat healthier foods, but then eat more.

Social Comparison, Norms, Conformity, and Perceived Equity

Social norms over the proper course of action are created by people comparing the actions with others. This has been recognized in the theory of planned behaviour (Ajzen, 1991), and applied to pro-environmental interventions (Cialdini, 2003). It can create a barrier to action. When any sort of inequality or inequity (real or perceived) exists, cooperation declines.

Ownership and consumption, for example of card and electronic goods are important status symbols in our society and people feel they are expected to achieve this. Some of the literature argues that once people become accustomed to a particular standard of living, their perceptions of needs and expectations change. Their revised expectations are perpetuated in discourses about quality of life, and once absorbed into daily routine become interpreted as "needs" rather than "wants" (Steg and Sievers, 2000)

Similarly, peer norms are a strong influence. For example, when homeowners are told the amount of energy that average members of their community use, they tend to alter their use of energy to fit the norm (Schultz, Nolan, Cialdini, Goldstein, & Griskevicius, 2007), increasing or decreasing their energy use accordingly. The increases can be prevented by giving low energy users positive feedback about using less energy.

Conflicting goals and aspirations

Everyone has multiple goals and values (Lindenberg & Steg, 2007), and goals that involve more production of greenhouse gases can trump goals that support using less. For example, many parents drive their children to school to protect them, when walking is an option. Many people want to relax and rest and do so after flying to an attractive vacation spot. The common goal of "getting ahead" often means engaging in actions that run counter to the goal of reducing one's climate change impacts: buying a very large house or flying frequently by choice.

Low Level Behaiours

Many everyday behaviours related to sustainable consumption occur at relatively low levels of of consciousness such as boiling a kettle.

One vs Many

An interesting human behaviour is that we care more about when it is one individual in trouble and we can see their individual suffering compared to if it is lots of people. In 1987 a girl fell down a well in the USA and this received more coverage on CNN than the Rwandan Genocide. We care more when there is one identifiable victim as opposed to many people. In this respect climate change is the worst problem as it effects all 7 billion of us. For all his errors Stalin had this one right when he said '1 death is a tragedy, 1 million is a statistic'.

The Invisible Enemy

We also care less when we cannot see anything happen. Yes we occasionally see videos of ice caps melting but we cannot see the pollution in front of us. We cannot see that small rise in sea levels. We cannot tell that the temperature is increasing due to natural fluctuations. These gradual changes have far less impact on our emotions than sudden changes. People tend to evaluate risks by way of "the availability heuristic," which leads them to assess the probability of harm by asking whether a readily available example comes to mind. Because the effects are happening slowly and it is difficult to pin any particular disaster on climate change we associate climate change with a lower level of risk. As we cannot detect climate change then for most people, their exposure to and experience of "climate change" has been almost entirely indirect and virtual, mediated by news coverage and film documentaries of events in distant regions (such as melting glaciers in Greenland) that describe these events in relation to climate change. Recent surveys conducted in Alaska and Florida (two states in which residents in some regions have increasingly been experiencing climate-change driven changes personally) show that such exposure greatly increases their concern and willingness to take action (Arctic Climate Impact Assessment, 2004)

Continual Effort

Another reason we do not act is because it is difficult. With helping charities we see the advert on tv, this inspires us to donate and we start a monthly membership. Effort over. However with climate change it requires us to be motivated constantly. Whether walking to work every day or recycling. It is continuous. It is hard for any of us to stay motivated permanently. It is for the same reason people find it so hard to diet.

Cognitive Processing

Our own processing systems also reduce our concern for global warming. Evidence from cognitive, social, and clinical psychology indicates that risk perceptions, in a broad range of domains, are influenced by associative and affect-driven processes as much or more than by analytic processes. Our associative processing system is evolutionary, automatic and fast, but our analytic processing system must be taught and works via algorithms and rules. The two types of processes typically operate in parallel and interact with each other. Analytic reasoning cannot be effective unless it is guided and assisted by emotion and affect (Damasio, 1994). In cases where the outputs from the two processing systems disagree, however, the affective, association-based system usually prevails, as in the case of phobic reactions, for which people know perfectly well that their avoidance behaviour is at best ineffective and possibly harmful to them, but cannot suspend it (Loewenstein et al., 2001). Global climate change appears to be an example where a dissociation between the output of the analytic and the affective systems results in less concern than is advisable, with analytic consideration suggesting to most people that global warming is a serious concern, but the affective system failing to send an early warning signal (Weber, 2006).

Perceived Barriers

Many of these barriers could be interpreted as perceived mechanisms to help cope with an internal discrepancy between the demands to engage and actual engagement. These strategies may be used to assuage their guilt or to cope with the anxiety brought about by the threats of climate change.

So we if we are not 'designed to care what can governments do?

Current policies for tackling climate change are based around the assumption that the optimal social outcome is achieved by rational agents responding mechanically to price signals. In this framework, prices are the incentive for achieving social responsibility.

But global warming is a physical problem involving the interaction between physical economic production and the physical characteristics of the atmosphere. While carbon taxes and cap and trade systems can be valuable economists should have more to say about public policy than assigning property rights and adjusting relative prices. The generalized Darwinism approach to policy recognizes that macro outcomes are the result of the action of individuals responding to behavioural incentives, but it also recognizes that incentives include more than prices, that they are embedded in cultural institutions, and that a broadly defined incentive structure should be part of public policy.

.

First to deal with the few who do care there is a need to provide information. For those willing to mitigate climate change, this will encourage them to channel their energies into appropriate activities (Kempton, 1997). The way information is communicated has been the focus of much research. The channels need to be deemed as credible, and needs to be sustained on a regular basis and not succumb to media cycles. Smart meters are good example of providing people with detailed information about their energy consumption and enables them to reduce their consumption as they can see clearly what uses lots of energy.

We can be made to appear to care is via reward substitution. This makes us care about something else which makes us act as if we care about saving the environment. People who drive hybrid cars are rarely driving them because they care about global warming. They are driving them because it gives their ego a boost as they get to think what a good person they are. He quotes an example of a game where people's emails were sent along with a number That number corresponded to that individuals Co2 levels. As people care what others think of them they care about the number and so try to reduce their CO2.

Another method is by targeting systematic decisions can be targeted. These are decisions that you make once but have long term consequences, such as buying a new fridge or new windows. As we cannot make people think about the environment all the time then we need to target them here. When they buy these appliances they need to be reminded about it. If they make an environmentally conscience decision for that one moment it will have lasting impacts for several years.

Financial rewards a are in essence the same thing- we are taught to care about the money. These can be carrot or stick measures, although carrot measures are a lot more popular. Examples are the tax levy on plastic bags and high subsidies for micro-generation. The OECD highlights that financial measures are necessary and not sufficient to bring about behaviour change. Infrastructure upgrades allowing people to act are a pre-requisite for financial incentive being effective.

Be that as it may a growing body of experimental evidence indicates that monetary incentives can be a deterrent to cooperative behaviour(Frey, 1997; Frey and Oberholtzer-Gee, 1997). An often cited example is the finding that paying blood donors significantly reduces blood donations (Titmuss, 1971). This indicates that financial incentives can crowd out feelings of civic responsibilities and discourage the types of behaviour needed to counter climate change. In contrast to the policy recommendations of most economists, relying on monetary incentives to tackle collective choice problems can have perverse effects. As environmental philosophers have argued (O'Neill, 1993; Norton, 2005) giving people a shared responsibility and appealing directly to a sense of the common good can be an effective way of gaining acceptance for environmental policies. This suggests carbon taxes may be ineffective. If as a consumer I feel I have paid my contribution to the global warming effort then I will not try and reduce by impact in other ways. However Frey also acknowledges that money can "crowd in" civic motivations when it is used to acknowledge the social worth of individuals' contributions. This is relevant to channelling financial aid to ease the climate change burden on the developing world. Monetary compensation and technology transfers to the developing world would represent an acknowledgement of the responsibility of the developed world for driving upCO_2 levels during the past 100 years. Therefore tax revenue from a carbon tax can be put in a pool to help developing countries and this could encourage contribution.

Some government schemes to encourage alternative energy use or generation are generous, to put it mildly. State Governments pay up to 60 cents per KWh for electricity from domestic photovoltaic-generated power, which, when combined with Commonwealth credits for small systems, provides a tax-free return on investment in the order of 13 percent. The payments 75are not indexed, but even so the real annual return is in the order of ten percent. These financial incentives for investing in energy-efficient appliances or motor vehicles do change behaviour in the expected directions, but the effect is usually much smaller than economic models predict. This so-called energy efficiency gap—the difference between actual behaviour and what a simple economic theory of cost minimization would predict—is quite large (McKinsey, 2007) and also varies widely with the behaviour (e.g., which appliance is being purchased; Ruderman, 1985). A main reason for this is again human discounting. Many od the savings gains are over the long term and so the net saving is not in the short term and so is not as valuable.

There are many positive schemes to incentivise people such as those with electricity grids. However with a future of more austerity we need other solutions. The problem with many penalties is that they are regressive as the rich can afford to pay. However penalties for excessive consumption can be a very effective way of reducing consumption and can be progressive. Consumption of basic goods such as water and energy could be supplied at affordable fixed rates up to a threshold and thereafter have steeply rising charges, much like income tax.

As discussed earlier a problem with acting on climate change is the rebound effect. One solution to this is personal carbon credits. People are allocated an equitable share of emissions and much like the EU trading scheme can buy or sell emissions as required. The total number of emissions would be reduced over the years in line with targets. Although a fine theoretical model

Governments should promote eco-groups. Groups enable people to work together as citizens and have other benefits. Unfreezing of bad habits is better in groups, overcoming social lock in requires groups, new social norms are created in groups and social learning in groups is an effective tool for encouraging new behaviour. Community based based management of social goods has a long pedigree. Successful examples include walking groups and weight watchers which have both helped people overcome the barrier between wanting to act and acting. Eco groups need commitment from the government to help them become main stream.

Companies also do not think long term and are even more short term than people. For instance the wall street rewards every quarter, and so how do we make companies care long term. The first way is what the EPA are trying now and regulating companies. However governments should also try to place internal and external pressure to change. Internal pressure can be applied by employees and external pressure from customers. People immediately care more when something is measurable. Therefore if firms are forced to measure their carbon footprint and then report it in their financial statement every quarter. Workers will take pride in working for a company that produces less CO_2 and workers may try micro initiatives to cut down their pollution at their factor or office. Also if companies are aware of their pollution levels then it means they may look at ways to cut down. Customer demand can be created by placing the carbon footprint of product on the packaging. Much research has already been done on the effective ways to do this. There is little point in placing absolute values of co2 emitted for that product as consumers will have no relative scope of if it is clean or not. Therefore a coding system is much more effective, much like with the traffic light system for food. Another example is the A-G labelling on fridges and freezers. This was very successful after price incentives led to a large increase in the percentage of A-grade models. Companies then stopped stocking the lower grade models. For instance Comet chose not to stock anything below a C-grade.

The Sustainable development Commission in their report 'I will if you will' offer several demands people have of government policy.

Firstly policy should be fair. The main tenant of this is the polluter pays. On top of this it means it is not open to abuse by free-riders, which as discussed earlier can heavily impede action. It should also not be open to manipulation by rich people or powerful companies; this is a concern with carbon trading schemes. At the same time low income groups need to be protected. In their study people were happy to pay more for planes if it went to subsidies inner city transport. Boyd and Richerson (1992) make a strong case that almost any type of human behaviour can be called forth through social punishment mechanisms. Henrich et.al(2006) argues further that cooperation and punishment go hand in hand. People are willing to make sacrifices for others when they are assured that (free riders can be punished if they take advantage of altruistic behaviour by others. They found in their research that all population showed a willingness to punish free riders and costly punishments were positively correlated with altruistic behaviour. At an international level Stiglitz (2006) calls for using the international trade framework to impose penalties on countries that refuse to cooperate in reducing CO2 emissions. He suggests that Japan, Europe, and other signatories of the Kyoto agreement should bring a WTO case against the U.S. for unfair trade subsidization arising from U.S. energy and environmental policies.

Government policies need to help people act together. There is a default assumption that people would be making an individual sacrifice for no guaranteed benefit. Governments need to make new interventions social norms. There was a lot of support in the study by the Sustainable Development Commission for voluntary paying to offset their carbon on the assumption it would become a social norm and people would be ashamed into paying it. Work by Stewart Barr (2003) analysed the factors affecting recycling rates and found the norm to recycle was very significant. The green box reminded people to recycle and the simple act of leaving the box out for kerbside collection places social pressure on other residents to recycle.

Governments need to offer incentives for people to take positive, tangible action. Micro-generation through mini wind turbines and solar panels because it is a positive move that offers tangible benefits and results of their effort and it is also very visible and so gives people an ego boost as discussed above with hybrid cards. This visible approach also has the benefit of convincing people they are not acting alone and other people are not free-riding and so people are more likely to become involved.

Importantly governments need to win trust. Many people see fiscal penalties as another tax that is based on revenue raising over environmental concern. This can be solved through greater levels of transparency. The money from any green taxes can be ring-fenced for a 'green fund'. Governments can win this trust by setting an example; putting their money where their mouth. For instance they can reduce flying and travel more sustainably or they can invest themselves in micro-generation. Many government departments have aimed to reduce their carbon footprint but the individual politicians doing this would go a lot further.

There are many barriers that affect humans acting to stop climate change. Psychologists are beginning to understand this and are helping governments introduce policies to engage people.
These government policies can be summarised by the 4 E's:

Enable – remove barriers, give information, provide facilities, provide alternatives to the norm
Engage- community in action, personal contact

Exemplify- lead by example

Encourage- tax system, reward schemes, punishment, recognition, league tables

References

http://www.apa.org/science/about/publications/climate-change-booklet.pdf

Ajzen, I. (1991). The theory of planned behavior. Organizational Behavior and Human Decision Processes, 50, 179-211.

Ajzen, I. (1991). The theory of planned behavior. Organizational Behavior and Human Decision Processes, 50, 179-211.

Maio, G. R., Verplanken, B., Manstead, A. S. R., Stroebe, W., Abraham, C. S., Sheeran, P., & Conner, M. (2007). Social psychological factors in lifestyle change and their relevance to social policy. Social Issues and Policy Review, 1, 99-138.

Krosnik, J. A., Holbrook, A. L., Lowe, L., & Visser, P. S. (2006). The origins and consequences of democratic citizens' policy agendas: A study of popular concern about global warming. Climatic Change, 77, 7-43

MacGregor, D., Slovic, P., Mason, R. G., & Detweiler, J. (1994). Perceived risks of radioactive waste transport through Oregon: Results of a statewide survey. Risk Analysis, 14, 5-14.

Eilam, O., & Suleiman, R. (2004). Cooperative, pure, and selfish trusting: Their distinctive effects on the reaction of trust recipients. European Journal of Social Psychology, 34, 729-738

Goldenberg, J. L., Pyszczynski, T., Greenberg, J., & Solomon, S. (2000). Fleeing the body: A terror management perspective on the problem of human corporeality. Personality and Social Psychology Review, 4, 200-218.

Vess, M., & Arndt, J. (2008). The nature of death and the death of nature: The impact of mortality salience on environmental concern. Journal of Research in Personality, 42(5), 1376-1380.

Jakobsson, C., Fujii, S., & Garling, T. (2000). Determinants of private car users' acceptance of road pricing. Transport Policy, 7(2), 153-158.

Gifford, R., Iglesias, F., & Casler, J. (2009, June). Psychological barriers to pro-environmental behavior: The development of a scale. Paper presented at the meeting of the Canadian Psychological Association, Montreal

Schiffman, L. G., Kanuk, L. L., & Das, M. (2006). Consumer behaviour. Toronto: Pearson Education.

Diekmann, A., & Preisendörfer, P. (1992). Personliches umweltverhalten: Diskrepanzen zwischen anspruch und wirklichkeit. Kölner Zeitschrift Für Soziologie Und Sozialpsychologie, 44, 226-251

Schultz, P. W., Nolan, J. M., Cialdini, R. B., Goldstein, N. J., & Griskevicius, V. (2007). The constructive, destructive, and reconstructive power of social norms. Psychological Science, 18(5), 429-434.

Lindenberg, S., & Steg, L. (2007). Normative, gain and hedonic goal frames guiding environmental behavior. Journal of Social Issues, 63(1), 117-137

Arctic Climate Impact Assessment. (2004). Impacts of a warming Arctic.Cambridge, UK; New York, NY: Cambridge University Press.

Damasio, A. R. (1994). Descartes' error. New York, NY: Avon Books.

Loewenstein, G. F., Weber, E. U., Hsee, C. K., & Welch, E. (2001). Risk as feelings. Psychological Bulletin, 127, 267-286.

Weber, E. U. (2006). Evidence-based and description-based perceptions of long-term risk: Why global warming does not scare us (yet). Climatic Change, 77, 103-120

Gowdy, M, Behavioral economics and climate change policy, Journal of Economic Behavior & Organization, Volume 68, Issues 3–4, December 2008, Pages 632-644

Lorenzoni, I;Nicholson-Cole,Sophie;Whitmarsh,L. (2007) Barriers perceived to engaging with climate change among the UK public and their policy implications. Global Environmental Change 17 (2007) 445–459

Kempton, W., 1997. How the public views climate change. Environment 39, 12–21

Swim, J.K., (Chair), Clayton, S., Doherty, T., Gifford, R., Howard, G., Reser, J., Stern, P., & Weber, E. (2009). Psychology and Global Climate Change: Addressing a multi-faceted Phenomenon and Set of Challenges. A Report by the American Psychological Association's Task Force on the Interface between Psychology and Global Climate Change

5.4 Cultural Psychotherapy: Beyond Pride and Ecocide[144]

Alastair McIntosh

Introduction

My thesis is that climate change cannot be approached only through political, economic and technical responses. It is, at a much deeper level, a psychological and depending on one's worldview, even a spiritual issue. Here I abridge some thoughts that explore climate change in relation to what we understand a human being to be. I suggest that the hubris of climate change is a function of violence, and I show that far from being modern or postmodern, such an analysis is profoundly premodern. It was a dominant concern in ancient wisdom. I move on to suggest that in early modernity violent or competitive interpersonal relationships lead to a reduction in empathy. This left a nihilistic emptiness of which consumerism is an addictive masking. A case study of British cigarette advertising is used. Finally, akin to Alcoholics Anonymous, I suggest a 12-step programme towards a cultural psychotherapy to reach the parts that consumerism fails to reach. From within the psyche and not just through outward actions, this sets a stage from which to challenge consumerism a key driver of climate change.

---

144 This chapter draws heavily on the author's *Hell and High Water: Climate Change, Hope and the Human Condition* (2008) – a book described as 'profoundly important by the then Scottish environment minister Michael Russell, as notable for 'its psychological and spiritual insights' by Jonathan Porritt, and by Rowan Williams when Archbishop of Canterbury as inspiration for his address on climate change at COP15 in Copenhagen. We are grateful to McIntosh's publisher, Birlinn Ltd of Edinburgh, for permission to incorporate material from Part 2 of the book.

Consumerism and the False Self

I situate this discussion in the field of ontology – the study of being. If, as a latter-day cultural icon suggests, all we are is material beings – egos walking on legs of meat – then consumerism makes rational ontological sense. As Madonna puts it: ''Cause the boy with the cold hard cash/ Is always Mister Right, 'cause we are/ Living in a material world/ And I am a material girl.'[145]

The trouble is that such unmitigated materialistic hedonism is all very well while the lamp of life remains filled with the birthright oil of youth, but as that runs out the drive of consumerism becomes more and more urgent and, ultimately, nihilistic, as if hell itself tightens up around the soul.

Consumerism as Fromm's psychology of 'to have is to be' reveals itself over time to be a false satisfier of fundamental human needs as the soul, deprived of authentic nourishment form within, atrophies into a false self. As R.D. Laing suggested in *The Divided Self*, this drains libidinal life energy from an increasingly shrunken and shrivelled true self and that, to him, is the definition of mental illness.[146] As a great English theologian expressed the syndrome: 'I can't get no satisfaction/ 'Cause I try and I try and I try and I try.'[147]

Theologically speaking this is the problem of idolatry. Idolatry is the *worship* (from the Old English: 'worth-ship', *the showing of worth towards...*) of a false god, a false reality. Consumerism rests on a false sense of what gives satisfaction in life and therefore, is an idolatrous force that progressively destroys both the Earth and the soul captured by its addiction.

The Ancients, Violence and Consumerism

The Greeks derived the word *hubris,* meaning excessive pride and all that comes with such narcissism, from their word *hybris* meaning 'wanton violence'. From a review of ancient writings we might derive the qualitative formula:

---

145 Madonna, *Material Girl*, 1984, http://www.azlyrics.com/lyrics/madonna/materialgirl.html
146 R.D. Laing, *The Divided Self*, Pelican, Harmondsworth, 1969.
147 Mick Jagger (with Keith Richards), *Satisfaction*, 1965, http://www.metrolyrics.com/i-cant-get-no-satisfaction-lyrics-rolling-stones.html

Hubris = pride → violence → ecocide

A prime example is the world's oldest book, *The Epic of Gilgamesh* which attributes the ecological devastation of Mesopotamia – the turning of parts of the Fertile Crescent into the deserts of modern-day Iraq – to Gilgamesh's vanity and its consequent destruction of the cedar forests. In a closely related epic the Biblical story of Noah's ark portrays an extreme weather event as the hubristic result of a position where:

> God saw that the wickedness of man was great in the earth, and that every imagination of the thoughts of his heart was only evil continually … and the earth was filled with violence….[148]

Plato in *The Critias* and *The Timaeus* gives several instances, including the legend of Atlantis, of the earth being inundated or desertified as a consequence of human hubris. In both *The Laws* and *The Statesman* he describes the increasing tendency towards corruption of lowland city-based cultures that the gods then periodically destroy. The population of these wasted areas would then be slowly replenished from virtuous-living pastoral stock that survived in the mountains.[149]

Plato's most explicit analysis of hubris yielding to hybris with devastating consequences for social justice and ecological sustainability comes early in his greatest work, *The Republic*. This depicts his mentor, Socrates, as hanging around with the privileged young men of the city discussing the meaning of life. Repeatedly they touch on a quality called *areté*, usually translated as justice, virtue or excellence but really meaning the fulfilment of human potential – the fullest all-round expression of what a person can become.

The group wishes to understand wherein the virtues that are linked to *areté* in the soul reside. They agree to approach their discernment by analogy, examining the

---

148 *The Bible,* Genesis 6, King James (Authorised) Version.
149 For full discussion of Gilgamesh, Genesis, Plato and Shakespeare's *Macbeth* see chapters 5 ("Pride and Ecocide") and 6 ("Dissociation of Sensibility") in *Hell and High Water.*

question first on the macro scale of the state or republic and then applying such 'outer life' principles to reveal the 'inner life' dynamics of virtue.

Socrates kicks off by laying out his table. His ideal city state is the rustic idyll. In our sense today what he describes is more of a village than a city. Men and women would spend their time in honest pastoral and craft work, living simply, caring for their children, guarding against poverty and war, eating a humble but wholesome vegetarian diet, drinking in moderation and, in their spare time, singing hymns to the gods. Socrates warns that 'ambition and love of money are . . . something to be ashamed of', and the test of right livelihood is that people 'leave their children to live as they have done.' In this way he presages the definition of sustainable development that the United Nation's Brundtland Commission came up with two-and-a-half millennia later: namely, 'Sustainable development is development that meets the needs of the present without compromising the ability of future generations to meet their own needs.'[150]

But the most petulant of the city sloanes, a young man called Glaucon, is aghast at these suggestions. He tells Socrates that he and his fellows expect meat plentifully on the table, homes furnished with gold, ivory and art, perfumes and adornments for the wives and courtesans, clothes and shoes, entire classes of servants and nannies (both wet and dry) for the children. He says: 'If you had been founding a city of pigs, Socrates, this is just how you would have fattened them,' and he demands what he calls the 'ordinary dishes and dessert of modern life.' To this the master replies: 'Very well. . . I understand. We are considering, apparently, the making not of a city merely, but of a luxurious city. And perhaps there is no harm in doing so. From that kind, too, we shall soon learn, if we examine it, how justice and injustice arise in cities. I, for my part, think that the city I have described is the true one, what we may call the city of health. But if you wish, let us also inspect a city which is suffering from inflammation. . .'

---

150 The World Commission on Environment and Development, *Our Common Future*, Oxford University Press, 1987, p. 19

And so, with his sword now suitably blooded, the Platonic Socrates turns to his famous question and answer method, ruthlessly teasing out the contradictions in Glaucon's aspirations.

'Then I dare say even the land which was sufficient to support the first population will be now insufficient and too small?'

'Yes,' he said.

'Then if we are to have enough for pasture and plough-land, we must take a slice from our neighbours' territory. And they will want to do the same to ours, if they also overpass the bounds of necessity and plunge into reckless pursuit of wealth?'

'Yes, that must happen, Socrates,' he said.

'Then shall we go to war at that point, Glaucon, or what will happen?'

'We shall go to war,' he said.

'And we need not say at present whether the effects of war are good or bad. Let us only notice that we have found the origin of war in those passions which are most responsible for all the evils that come upon cities and the men that dwell in them.'

'Certainly.'

'Then, my friend, our city will need to be still greater, and by no small amount either, but by a whole army. It will defend all the substance and wealth we have described, and will march out and fight the invaders.'

. . . 'Yes'. . .

'Then, Glaucon. . . with such natures as these, how are they to be prevented from behaving savagely towards one another and the other citizens?'

'By Zeus,' he said, 'that will not be easy.'[151]

The terrible reality is that a willingness to take by the sword slices its pound of flesh from the soul. *For violence hollows out the capacity to have an inner life.* It does so by desensitising the ability to feel and to relate to others beyond the formalised tenors of seemly conduct.

Dissociation of Sensibility

Anthropological studies suggest that different societies under different conditions in their history may shift towards or away from patterns of behaviour that are conducive of violence. T.S. Eliot brings us to a similar place as did the Platonic Socrates by examining our own society, resting on the foundations of early modernity. His essay, *The Metaphysical Poets*, published in the *Times Literary Supplement* in 1921, puts forward a theory of the *dissociation of sensibility*. He means by this the breaking up (dissociation) of the ability to feel and relate to life (sensibility), thus:

> In the seventeenth century a dissociation of sensibility set in, from which we have never recovered. . . It is something which had happened to the mind of England between the time of Donne. . . and Tennyson and Browning; it is the difference between the intellectual poet and the reflective poet. Tennyson and Browning are poets, and they think; but they do not feel their thought as immediately as the odour of a rose. A thought to Donne was an experience; it modified his sensibility [and] these experiences are always forming new wholes. . . While the language became more refined, the feeling became more crude. . . [in some cases exposing] a dazzling disregard of the soul.[152]

---

151 Plato, *The Republic*, trans. A.D. Lindsay, Everyman, London, 1936, II:372-74.
152 T. S. Eliot, 'The Metaphysical Poets', *Times Literary Supplement*, 20 Oct 1921.

In Scotland, the Hebridean poet Iain Crichton Smith endorsed T.S. Eliot's appraisal and added that 'some irretrievable damage was done to the Scottish poetic psyche. . . as far back as the Reformation.' Smith draws this into his lament for the decline in what he calls 'the feeling intelligence'. We will 'not allow the intelligence to be other than that of the relentless logician' and this is 'because the feelings have been lost, it is because *we are afraid of our feelings, and we have substituted a dead intelligence in their place.*' When that happens, he says, the culture loses lose touch with the 'feminine' and so becomes bereft of *tenderness.*[153]

This, then, is how hubristic violence destroys the inner life. It strips sensibility not just from the violent but also from those who suffer violence. It's lie is to represent the inner life as a lie. The outcome is more than merely nihilistic. At its most extreme the symptoms, as with other causes of addiction, are necrophilic.

Colonisation of the Soul

Addiction is a fitting description. Writing over half a century ago in *The Affluent Society,* John Kenneth Galbraith used these sombre terms:

> The general conclusion of these pages is of such importance for this essay that it had perhaps best be put with some formality. As a society becomes increasingly affluent, wants are increasingly created by the process by which they are satisfied. . . Increases in consumption, the counterpart of increases in production, act by suggestion or emulation to create wants. . . It will be convenient to call it the Dependence Effect.[154]

More recent writers like Clive Hamilton and Richard Denniss have named it *Affluenza.* As they see it, rich societies: '. . . seem to be in the grip of a collective psychological disorder. . . We have grown fat but we persist in the belief that we are thin and must consume more. . . Affluenza describes a condition in which we are confused about what it takes to live a worthwhile life. Part of this confusion is a

---

153 Iain Crichton Smith, *Towards the Human: Selected Essays*, Macdonald Publishers, Loanhead, 1986.
154 John Kenneth Galbraith, *The Affluent Society,* Marner Books, NY, 1998, pp. 128-29.

failure to distinguish between what we want and what we need.'[155] Similarly, in May 1925 when addressing the conference of the Associated Advertising Clubs of the World in Manhattan Herbert Hoover, then the US Secretary of Commerce, articulated the manufactured spirit of the age: 'The older economists taught the essential influences of "wish", "want" and "desire" as motive forces in economic progress. *You have taken over the job of creating desire.* You have still another job-creating goodwill in order to make desire stand hitched.'[156]

Vance Packard documented this process as it took root in the 1940s and early '50s. *The Hidden Persuaders* cites the front page of *The Wall Street Journal*: 'The business man's hunt for sales boosters is leading him into a strange wilderness; the subconscious mind.' Packard explains:

> Ad men began talking about the different levels of human consciousness. As they saw it there were three main levels of interest to them. The first level is the conscious, rational level, where people know what is going on, and are able to tell why. The second and lower level is called, variously, preconscious and subconscious but involves that area where a person may know in a vague way what is going on within his own feelings, sensations, and attitudes but would not be willing to tell why. This is the level of prejudices, assumptions, fears, emotional promptings, and so on. Finally, the third level is where we not only are not aware of our true attitudes and feelings but would not discuss them if we could. Exploring our attitudes towards products at these second and third levels became known as the new science of motivational analysis or research, or just plain M.R.[157]

Pushing this ethos along was a new kid on the block. What Edward Bernays had been to the advertising industry after the First World War,[158] Dr Ernest Dichter was to the Second. Dichter was only the most prominent amongst a loosely knit school

---

155 Clive Hamilton & Richard Denniss, *Affluenza: When Too Much is Never Enough,* Allen and Unwin, Sydney, 2005, pp. 6-7.
156 TIME, 'Associated Advertising Clubs of the World', 25 May 1925, my emphasis.
157 Vance Packard, *The Hidden Persuaders*, Penguin, London, 1960, pp. 27-28.
158 Edward Bernays, *Propaganda*, Ig Publishing, NY, 2004.

known as the 'depth boys'. Scouring the works of depth psychologists, especially Freud, Jung and Adler, these men set about trying to convert therapeutic insight to commercial gain. Only Jung, writing just before his death in 1961, could clearly see saw what was happening:

> Modern man does not understand how much his 'rationalism' (which has destroyed his capacity to respond to numinous symbols and ideas) has put him at the mercy of the psychic 'underworld'. He has freed himself from 'superstition' (or so he believes), but in the process he has lost his spiritual values to a positively dangerous degree. His moral and spiritual tradition has disintegrated, and he is now paying the price for this break-up in world-wide disorientation and dissociation.[159]

Like Bernays, Dichter pushed the idea of the augmented product with disarming charm. 'To ladies, don't sell shoes. Sell them sexy feet.' He was a master at motivational manipulation. In his 1947 book, *The Psychology of Everyday Living*, he describes how soap is basically just lanolin, but it can be sold by 'extensive advertising campaigns to convince the male of the species that he suffers from body odour, and that this is why most girls reject him.' Similarly, women are shown 'moving picture stars, who stress the fact that they acquired their beauty primarily by using Lux toilet soap.' With astonishing candour Dichter adds: 'The psychologist is not interested in the truth or falsehood of such claims. He is interested in the fact that a simple everyday commodity like soap has been advertised as a means of satisfying the important human need for beauty and happiness.' The circularity of the argument seems to have escaped him. Was it not the psychologist in the first place who created the need by stirring up insecurity? The name of the marketing game, then, was to 'trigger' buying behaviour. The advertiser baits the emotional hooks – freedom, love, sex, fear, envy, greed. He drops them deep in the psyche and waits for the little fish to bite.

Both Eddie Bernays and Ernest Dichter worked extensively with the automotive industries, big oil, and tobacco. Bernays first demonstrated the marketing power of

159 Carl Jung, *Man and his Symbols,* Picador, London, 1978, p. 84.

the publicity stunt during the Easter Parade through New York in March 1929. Led by a lady called Bertha Hunt, a group of women who appeared to be suffragettes passed the Baptist church attended by John D. Rockefeller and each pulled from their suspenders a Lucky Strike cigarette. In front of flashing press cameras that just happened to be placed there, they lit up, telling reporters that in so doing they were lighting up 'Torches of Freedom'. They said they wanted to 'smash the discriminatory taboo on cigarettes for women' and pledged that their gender would 'go on breaking down all discriminations.'

What the public didn't know was that Bertha Hunt was Bernays' secretary. He had set the press up for a photo opportunity complete with product placement. His stunt made smoking look 'cool' for women and linked Lucky Strike to freedom. Later, Ernest Dichter would follow on in similar vein. 'Smoking is fun,' Dichter wrote, in presenting his research for the tobacco industry. 'Smoking is a reward. . . I blow my troubles away. . .. With a cigarette I am not alone.'[160] Here smoking becomes an antidote to anxiety, to loneliness; an emotional anaesthetic.

Dying for a Slash – British Cigarette Advertising

In 1980 when I studied marketing as part of an MBA at Edinburgh University none of this was on the core curriculum. The world guru was and remains Philip Kotler, Distinguished Professor of International Marketing at the Kellogg School of Management. To this day his bland tomes are the staple diet of most management schools. Back in the 1980s Kotler at least made passing reference to Dichter. Today, in almost a thousand pages of *Principles of Marketing* co-published with the *Financial Times,* there's not a glimpse, still less of Eddie Bernays or the use of an expression like 'motivational manipulation'. There's only squeaky clean descriptions of the 4 Ps – product, price, place and promotion – like eating a dry Weetabix with the box still round it. My suspicion is that the industry no longer wants to embarrass itself by teaching the revealing stuff. In any case, the industry already embodies the values that we have been looking at, but unconsciously. They arise spontaneously from the culture that marketing has normalised. Let me give an example and, in so doing, suggest just how far colonisation of the soul can go.

---

160 Ernest Dichter, *The Psychology of Everyday Living,* Barnes & Noble, NY, 1947.

Some years ago I carried out research into the advertising of Gallaher's two main cigarette brands in Britain – Benson & Hedges and Silk Cut. The findings were published as an occasional paper of the Centre for Human Ecology in 1996. They were picked up on by the BBC, *The Sunday Times*, *New Statesman* and *The Wall Street Journal* – with the latter featuring the paper as part of a front-page lead story.

My attention was first grabbed by a series of surreal ads for B&H that seemed to defy all the norms of advertising. They'd picked up an array of industry awards. No fewer than five of them had been chosen by three dozen industry experts for inclusion in *The World's 100 Best Posters*. These showed (and the images can be viewed on my website):[161]

The pack sitting like a trap outside a mouse hole.
The pack perched like a bird inside a cage.
The pack underwater, opened like a tin of sardines.
The pack forming one of the great pyramids of Egypt.
The pack against a torrid sunset, being carried away by ants.

The only printed message on each ad was the government warning: 'Cigarettes can seriously damage your health.' Equally bizarre were ads for Gallaher's Silk Cut range. These became surreal from 1983, starting with a poster that simply showed the health warning and a length of purple silk with a slash in it – silk cut. A relentless campaign that followed on lasting nearly two decades used a stream of images, typical of which were:

A human figure showering behind a purple silk curtain.
Surgical scissors with a wisp of purple silk lined up against a prison wall.
A Venus flytrap monstrously ripping the crotch from purple silk trousers
Four purple silk figurines shaped like stubbed-out cigarettes with chess pawns for their heads, lined up outside toilet door that has a knife hanging on it.
During the Edinburgh Festival that Silk Cut were sponsoring, purple bagpipe-like haggises, wandering in a bleak landscape of open-jawed mantraps.

161 http://www.alastairmcintosh.com/images/silkcut.htm

Again, the only wording – the only indication of the nature of the product being advertised – were the government health warnings. What could be going on here?

What caused my paper to make a media splash is that I suggested that sadomasochistic psychology was being exploited. The B&H sequence were made by the advertising agency Collett Dickenson Pearce. It was almost as if CDP were saying: 'Smoke these, and be. . .

> *trapped* like a mouse,
> *caged* like a bird,
> *canned* like sardines,
> *mummified* like the Pharaohs, and,
> *consumed* as carrion by the ants.'

Silk Cut's images from Saatchi and Saatchi seemed even more morbid. Masterminded by Charles Saatchi, the marketing man credited with bringing Margaret Thatcher to power, the campaign was unceremoniously dubbed 'Silk Cunt' by industry wags. But it seemed to be about more than just sex. There was an undertone suggestive of rape; even, like with the B&H ads, of death. Yet the adverts for both brands were outstandingly successful. A 1996 study by the Cancer Research Campaign showed that both brands had higher recall than any of its competitors amongst girls. Silk Cut topped the league with girls who had never smoked before. The ads may have been bizarre, but something about them was compelling too.

It's always fun in this kind of research to speak to the kind of people who are paid to tell you nothing. I therefore contacted Gallaher and spoke to Colin Stockall, their Media Services Manager. 'What's going on here?' I asked, not flinching from posing a leading question in the short opportunity during which time I hoped to hold his attention before he rumbled me. 'What's the meaning of, for example, the purple curtain? Is it an allusion to Hitchcock's *Psycho* where she's stabbed in the shower?'

'Well,' he said in a heard-it-all-before tone, 'I know some people interpret it that way but I can't say that's our view of it.'

It wouldn't be, so I chanced my luck elsewhere. This time I got on to the creative executive at M&C Saatchi – a spin-off company of the Saatchi brothers which had devised the haggis advert. 'What's the story with these extraordinary haggii?' I asked. 'Might this be how Gallaher sees its customers?'

He, too, had heard it all before but was less guarded. 'I think people would have to be either very negative in their view of life or overanalysing it to create a sub-plot that doesn't really exist,' he told me. 'I mean, the idea really is that these are not people, these are not living breathing animals. They're just objects that look funny. That look although they almost want to get trapped because that's what man traps do. They trap things. And that's what animals do. They step in things. You know, especially like dumb sheep-type animals. But these are more than that. They're just odd looking, bagpipes, which have been made to look like haggises. It's a fantasy. It's just an odd image, and because it's odd it looks interesting. It captures people's attention.'

Duly reprimanded for my negative view of life and yet fascinated by the confused tension in his account, I asked about the shower curtain image. 'Oh yes,' he acknowledged, '. . . people recognise the connection between the advertisement and *Psycho*, the thriller, so people think they're quite clever. It's smart arse. It affirms their intelligence and their wittiness. It strikes a chord with them.'

'And the pawns outside the door with the knife?' I ventured. 'It looks to me like they're dying for the loo. . .'

By now he sounded remote, lackadaisical, ready to get back to whatever he'd been working on. 'We call it *dying for a slash*,' he said.

Pedlars of Death

My penetration of the bastions of CDP was also lackadaisical, indeed, serendipitous. Some of the finest anti-war advertising copy of the First Gulf War had been run by Amnesty International and Friends of the Earth. These full page newspaper spreads had been drafted by an Anglo-Indian advertising creative, Indra Sinha. We met in the course of campaigning against the war over the internet and he invited me to visit when next in London. Imagine the surprise as I went into a plush office block to see all Indra's right-on stuff there on the wall and, alongside it, ads promoting the British Army and B&H!

'I'm sorry, Alastair,' he said with a knowing shrug, 'but something has to pay the bills.' Indra was only one of a much larger team. His was just one voice in the composition of some of the ads. But he told me how they'd hit on the idea of using surrealist images after the government had tightened the rules making it impossible to show cigarettes in much of a positive light. Apparently one of the CDP chiefs described the campaign as 'very Jungian', but nobody imagined that the images were doing anything more than just being 'clever'.

I replied that 'clever' doesn't just come from nowhere. In 1924 the French psychiatrist and cultural critic, André Breton, had defined surrealism as 'pure psychic automatism by which one proposes to express. . . the actual functioning of the mind.' It is 'the future resolution of. . . dream and reality. . . into a kind of absolute reality, a *surreality*.'[162]

My question was about the 'actual functioning' of these macabre images. I told Indra what my theory was. In the final stages of Sigmund Freud's thought in the early 1920s he arrived at a stage that embarrassed even many of his supporters. His medical work treating the battle neuroses of traumatised soldiers led him to conclude that, in addition to *Eros* – the life force – there was also its counterpoint expressed as a 'death instinct'. This was later called *Thanatos* after the Greek god of death. 'In the end we came to recognize sadism as its representative,' Freud wrote, 'and life itself would be a conflict and compromise between these two trends.'[163]

---

162 André Breton, Manifestoes of Surrealism, University of Michigan Press, Ann Arbor, 1972, pp. 26, 14 (retranslating 'thought' as 'mind').
163 Sigmund Freud, 'The Ego and the Id', *On Metapsychology*, Penguin, London, 1984, pp. 380-81.

Was it possible, I wondered, that at some level in Gallaher's creative hierarchy, minds had wandered where no advertiser would have previously thought or dared to venture? Was it possible that the advertising industry, having worked all the more conventional motivating forces to death, had hit on death wish as the final frontier? The *Silk Cut* ads make it even plainer than those from the B&H stable. With *Silk Cut*, death, sex and the scatological unambiguously interweave. I wondered if such surrealism could be capitalising on the nihilistic roots of addiction in the gnawing emptiness of the hollowed-out soul? After all, there is a well-recognised mystic link between sex and death. Mythology is full of it. The French call orgasm *'la petite mort'* – the little death. There can be a sense of release in the prospect of death. Some analysts of women's erotica suggest that rape fantasies can provide an excuse to liberate an inhibited imagination. Could Gallaher, wittingly or unwittingly, be turning the government's health warnings into a unique selling point? Could the adverts be saying, in effect, that smoking offers everything they've ever warned you against. Cigarettes kill. And if you want *la petite mort* big time, then why not just die into the ecstasy of Gallaher's arms? As the Roberta Flack lyrics put it, 'Strumming my pain with his fingers | Singing my life with his words | Killing me softly with his song | Killing me softly, with his song.'

Indra was fascinated. He said that they never discussed the ads in terms of 'meaning'. The guys who design these things are creatives who come up with images, not intellectual propositions. But now that I mentioned it he could glimpse something possibly there. He said that maybe the very reason why he and his colleagues were good at their jobs is that they don't think too much. They just get given a brief and follow their gut feelings.

Indra was perhaps more open than many would have been to what I was suggesting. One of his other claims to fame is that he had translated the *Kama Sutra* from the original Sanskrit. In the Tantric traditions of esoteric Hinduism, the connection between sexual love and death is celebrated. One is seen as being the flip side of the other. Both are equally sacred. In a similar vein, but without overt sexualisation, the great mystics of the world talk of 'dying into love'. Mystical death is the essence of advanced spiritual experience. The outward form of this varies between traditions, but inwardly it's the meaning of the Cross. As the Spanish mystic St John of the Cross said in one of his poems: 'In hope I now begin to die | My destiny I seek, for I | Am dying, so as not to die.'[164]

That last line is the essence of it. Mystical death is not about running into the buffers of terminal morbidity. Mystical death is the small self of the ego letting go into the great Self that is grounded in the divine. It is the soul's marriage to God. Such is the apogee of *liminal* experience – the crossing of a threshold of consciousness into higher reality. But consumerism, the wares of tobacco companies and other forms of addiction, don't offer real liminal experience. They just offer a transient glimpse. They merely offer the *liminoid,* which is a false semblance of the liminal. As the Franciscan spiritual teacher, Richard Rohr describes the distinction: 'The liminoid is a movement into trance and unconsciousness so nothing real will be revealed. . . The liminoid feels like the real thing, it feels momentarily renewing, but it is just a diversion and actually reaffirms our ego. . . and our capacity for denial. It is not a threshold at all, only more of the same.'[165]

Here lies exposed what consumerism blocks us from. It interrupts the very journey of life. It keeps us narcissistically at a child-like level of immaturity, seeking only the next fix. We bypass challenges that might heal our emptiness and give birth to human potential. Indra is exceptional. He phoned me up a year later and said, 'I just wanted you to know I've left CDP. I've decided to stop being a peddler of death.'

Let me be clear that my argument is not with those who smoke cigarettes. It is with the pushers. If one Googles 'Silk Cut' my paper on 'Eros and Thanatos' in Gallaher's ads comes up immediately alongside the company's own website. They must be right pleased! I also noticed that, after the blaze of publicity surrounding the paper's publication in August 1996 through until February 2003 when cigarette

---

164 Kathleen Jones (trans), *The Poems of St John of the Cross*, Burns and Oates, Tunbridge Wells, 1993, p. 53.
165 Richard Rohr, *Adam's Return: The five promises of male initiation,* Crossroad, NY, 2004, pp. 140-42.

advertising was finally banned in Britain, most of Gallaher's ads were fairly muted. But one of them did bring a wry smile to my face. It was February 1997. There, on a huge billboard by a football stadium, I saw the familiar cigarette pack. It had been cut in half and sewn back together again with big purple silk stitches as if it had gone through a surgical procedure. I admit that my imagination ran a bit wild. For a moment it felt as if old Charles was conceding something; as if he was saying, 'stitched up'!

I have chosen tobacco here as a case study. But examples also abound with the alcohol, food, fashion, travel and automotive industries. From an environmental point of view the health warning on tobacco products could be more widely replicated. Here's my suggestion for the wording:

This product can seriously damage
your planet causing loss of life
and species extinction

12 Steps Towards a Cultural Psychotherapy

Just as when an individual experiences psychological suffering it can be helpful to understand the forces that configured their psyche, and how life's deepest desire may have been frustrated or contorted, the same applies to whole cultures. When dealing especially with psychopathologies driven by mass communications I believe that we need what might be called a cultural psychotherapy for we are faced today with a collective neurosis. As Jung wrote, 'People who know nothing about nature are of course neurotic, for they are not adapted to reality.'[166] That maladaption is both psychological and ecological: ecopsychological. As such, we need to be able to take a long deep look out ourselves, individually and collectively, and measure this against our greatest hopes and aspirations for what it could mean to be most fully human. Only then can we chart a humane and human course ahead, as First Nations people say, 'For all our relations.'

---

166 Carl Jung, *Memories, Dreams, Reflections*, Fontana, Glasgow, 1967, p. 190.

I live and work in an area of Glasgow, an area stricken by poverty where many people find help from the services of such organisations as Narcotics Anonymous, Gamblers Anonymous and Alcoholics Anonymous. AA teach that addiction can only be conquered by confessing the problem and seeking help from a 'higher power'. It aims, as it were, at a reconnection of the human with the divine that involves the renowned '12-step' recovery programme. I ask: 'What might a 12-step programme to counter the addiction of consumerism look like?' What steps might we and our societies consider to heal the dissociation of sensibility that has left so many struggling in their lives to find satisfaction?

I recognise that for some people talk of a 'higher power', 'God' and 'spirituality' is all so much 'woo-woo'. Worse, my position is interfaith but with a bias to Christian teaching. Here there is not space to discuss why I accord this reality status. Permit me, therefore, to speak from within my own worldview, but feel free to borrow and adapt anything that might speak within you, the reader's, worldview. If nothing speaks, then I am sorry to have wasted your time.

In *Soil and Soul: People versus Corporate Power*, my book about community empowerment and land reform, I suggested that there needs to be a *re-membering* of that which has been dismembered. A *re-visioning* of alternative ways in which things could be. And a *re-claiming* what is necessary to bring that vision to fruition. The steps that follow are attempts to reconnect with reality, with the subjects and objects of sensibility. I have written them up in 'we must' form. That way adds rhetorical oomph. But they are only suggestions, faltering and contestable at that.

1. We must re-kindle the inner life
This is where it all must start. The inner life is our most fundamental resource. It is the realm of thought, creativity, imagination, veneration, visions and dreams. It falls both within and beyond our conscious ken, starting in the individual mind but anchored to the eternal Spirit. We will not be able to live sustainably on Earth nor deepen human dignity unless we learn how to be resourced from such roots. I have suggested that violence historically destroyed the inner life and has subsequently limited it from re-emerging. The antithesis of violence is empathy –

felt connection in loving relationship. Rekindling the inner life is therefore about opening to empathy. That includes its expression through family, friends, community, work, the arts, nature and psychospiritual development.

Whether we are aware of it or not, spirituality is the powerhouse of the inner life. It is the inner reality or *interiority* of all things, akin to the role of energy vis-à-vis matter in the outer world. Like any form of power, spirituality can be corrupted. Religious history is full of it – tormenting inquisitors, mad mullahs and paedophilic priests. But always the name of the game, as Walter Wink's writing so powerfully shows, is to call 'fallen' power back to its higher, God-given vocation.[167] The aim is not to destroy but to redeem. This is where spirituality is revealed as that which gives life and, specifically, life as love made manifest.

I believe that none of us can force love to happen. It doesn't come from an act of will mandated from the ego. Love is an opening, a gift of Grace. It comes from the Spirit that animates the soul, and is within conscious intent but beyond conscious control. We can ask for it, but usually we must wait. In the waiting we have to sit with our emptiness. That's where courage is called for. The courage to face the truth without resorting to the masks of lies and addiction.

Awakening others to the inner life is perhaps the most important contribution that the artist can make to present times. Rekindling it is a process that takes many years in most people. It happens in fits and starts, sometimes seeming to run more backwards than forwards. But gradually, steadfastness develops. A person with a well-developed inner life finds grounded strength within. This is what the violent can neither stand nor understand, but this is what sustains the world and living things.

2. We must value children's primal integrity
Our children are shaped partly by their intrinsic potential – both genetic and spiritual – and partly by the social and natural environments that surround them (including consequent epigenetic interactions). When either of these are degraded

167 Walter Wink, *Engaging the Powers*, Fortress Press, Mn, 1992.

or marred by violence, the child is at risk of becoming a product of a damaged world.

Each child is a seed waiting to flower into its own destiny. That seed is the child's primal integrity, its innermost soul. Caring for this means neither neglecting nor indulging the child. It means helping to birth its *areté* – its all round potential – across a range of competences that integrate head, heart and hand. It means, above all, communicating empathy by expressing respect and, equally, graciously accepting its reciprocation.

Psychologically speaking as Jung and Richard Rohr have suggested, the 'first half of life' is about developing an ego identity. Here we learn to wash our face, express what we're about, and make a living in the world. What distinguishes a child where the primal building blocks are well positioned is the ease with which transition can later be made into the 'second half of life'. This is the deepening into the soul – the realisation, as we saw earlier, that one is not just the cork but also integral to the river that carries it. Such inner-resourced adults make bad addictive consumers. Their sense of wellbeing comes mainly, though never entirely, from things that cannot be bought or sold.

All children need safety and stability, social networks where they can make well-formed attachments in relationship, and contexts where they can express without fear what is happening in their lives. The provision of these things should be the cornerstone of public policy and family practice. Neither should attention to these needs in one another cease as the first half of life matures. Children can remind us that such principles remain important even in the 'second childhood' of old age. That means honouring primal integrity all the way from the cradle to the terminal letting go that, one day, will signal the 'passing' of a life fulfilled.

3. We must cultivate psychospiritual literacy
Implicit to what has been said so far is a framework of understanding of what it means to be a human being. In the past, religion defined this with its creeds and dogmas. At their best, these express profound truths. But spiritual abuse within

politicised religious structures has too often soured them. It has left many potential followers allergic, fuelling the rise of secular humanism since at least the Enlightenment.

The bridge between rationality and spirituality started to be rebuilt during the twentieth century by depth and, laterally, transpersonal psychology.[168] Depth psychology was pioneered by Jung, and transpersonal psychology is its late twentieth-century flowering into a spiritual psychology that is built upon the psychic interconnection of all things. Since the turn of the millennium, words like 'psyche' and 'spirituality' have become increasingly acceptable in mainstream public discourse. This has been helped along by many people now drawing a distinction between religion and spirituality.

At its best, religion is the socially organised structure of communally expressed spirituality. The religions of the world should be the culturally appropriate trellis up which the living vine of spirituality can grow. But where religion has become dysfunctional and the trellis no longer leads towards life, the vine is perfectly capable of growing wild. That is what we commonly see happening today. It is a healthy development – provided that sight is not lost of the fact that spirituality does concern the dynamics of interconnection. *Community* is therefore a key part of it, whether we name it 'Sangha' (Buddhist), 'Ummah' (Islamic) or 'Church' (Christian). Spirituality does require withdrawal and private retreat, but this must interplay with a social context. There can be no such thing as a wholly private or privatised spirituality.

In my own work speaking to many different types of group – environmental, church, corporate, military, governmental – I often find it useful to communicate a basic structure and terminology of the psyche. It is only a model and a simple one at that, but I find it invaluable for creating a shared starting-off point. This is what I mean by psychospiritual literacy. What I do is to hold up the back of my hand and say:

---

168 Stanislav & Christina Grof, *Spiritual Emergency: When Personal Transformation Becomes a Crisis*, Tarcher, NY, 1989.

The structure of a human being can be modelled like this. Here's a finger nail. That's my ego self – my small self which is the *outer self* that is Alastair McIntosh. It's centred in my field of consciousness. It's the me who's giving you this lecture, who has done this and that in life and, oh yes, hopes to flog you one of his books afterwards! That's ego for you! We've all got one and actually, we all need one. It's our face in the outer world and building it is the psychological task of the first half of life. It's like something that my friend Djinni of Scoraig did. Once she stood outside a potentially fraught community meeting holding a box marked *Ego*. As people arrived she enquired jauntily: 'Do you need some, or would you like to leave some of yours here?'

Right at the base of my finger is the hand. Where the finger joins the hand is my deep Self, the great Self or the soul. The capitalisation there is deliberate to distinguish from small self. Here is the part of me that connects to the undercurrent of the Spirit, the animating fire that is 'God' within. The deep Self is the ultimate grounding of who I am; the deepest me and the crucible of inner life. It sits, at the boundary of space and time, at the juncture of the personal and the collective unconscious. We are not normally aware of these realms, but notice that there's several spread fingers on this hand. They're one another. The deeper we go the closer they come. At the level of the collective unconscious – down at the bottom - they're all joined, like islands beneath the sea. That's the nature of mystical interconnection. It is the ultimate basis of community.

But don't get your harps out yet! In the middle, right between the small and the great selves, is my finger's *knuckle*. That's my shadow self. It sits at the level of the personal unconscious – the realm that's specific to my life but of which I'm not very aware. For the shadow is the flip side of the ego's light; it's the murderous Mr Hyde that gives the lie to the charming Dr Jekyll. The shadow complex is charged up with all the hurts going back to infancy, all the things I've done or have had done to me that I've repressed, but also, all that I could be but have never yet become. Really, I'd mostly rather pretend the shadow's not there. Unfortunately, if you ask my close colleagues or my wife, they'll tell you it's there!

The integration of these three layers of being is called 'self-realisation' or 'individuation'. The name of the game if we want to become not 'perfect', but whole, is for the ego self to settle down to being held in the deep Self. Psychologically this is the work of the second half of life. Some people start working on it as early as their teens and others might reach their seventies but still be no more than uncentred teenagers. What makes it tough is that this journey requires coming to terms with the shadow self. Psychospiritual development always requires facing the darkness. Anybody telling you that spiritual development is all positive vibes and sweetness and light hasn't yet faced their own shadow, and a shadow unacknowledged is a shadow that gets projected out onto the world. A shadow that hits out in what I call *shadowstrike*. That's why psychologically naïve groups are always infighting. A shadow that is faced, on the other hand, becomes the lode from which gold is gleaned. It becomes the coal face of both inner and outer growth. Humbled in our own humanity and tenderised towards others, the fullness of who we are can be gradually realised.

I am aware that some Buddhist would take issue with the schema presented here. They would say that there is no self or Self, therefore rather than creating psychospiritual literacy I am compounding the delusion. I suspect that there are depths of mystery here that surpass understanding, and that even their concept of no-self would collapse when pushed far enough – perhaps into 'Buddha nature'! Let me just emphasise that the simplified Jungian model I have presented is just that – a model. I find it useful, but that doesn't make it one size to fit all shapes.

4. We must expand our concept of consciousness

As we have seen in our exploration of advertising, the spirituality of consciousness matters because its hijacking is nothing less than a dangerous theft of life. Theologically speaking, to have consciousness captured is to fall into the hands of 'false gods' – those of money, power, fashion and insatiable want. When marketing substitutes real needs with artificial wants, it becomes idolatry – it requires the sacrifice of our lives' efforts for ends that can never fully please.

Western psychology and philosophy presumes that consciousness, as Professor Hans Eysenck personally put it to me in 1975, 'is just an epiphenomenon of brain activity.' So far neurological research has failed to establish how such an 'epiphenomenon' comes about. Eastern philosophy would argue that it never will be established. That is because the East considers the brain to be an epiphenomenon of consciousness, or 'mind', rather than the other way round! It is as if the brain is the radio receiver, but consciousness is everything that goes on in the recording studio that makes the programmes we listen to. The brain, of course, regulates consciousness. It has been described as a 'reducing valve', just as a radio set can regulate the volume or tone of what the programme it plays. But to look for the source of consciousness within the brain is like trying to find a studio full of performers hidden inside a microchip.

The idea that consciousness has no intrinsic existence is the root of nihilism – the idea that everything is meaningless. One of the problems with nihilism is that it removes all ethical constraints on behaviour. It permits open house in the manipulation of consciousness and thereby feeds both the degradation of human dignity and mindless consumerism. It is to counter such dehumanisation that re-humanisation, in the form of spiritual practice that acts upon consciousness, lies at the heart of all great religions.

In outward form spiritual practice involves such activities as prayer, meditation, yoga, dance, poetry, study, work, engagement with nature, singing and sacrament.[256] What all these share in common is a requirement for *presence* – the process of becoming mindful to that which is real as distinct from that which is 'virtual' or a facade. This stimulates values that are more than mere ethical choices. It opens realms of motivation driven from inner essence. In some religious outlooks this is thought of as being 'moved' or 'led' by the Spirit.

There is no rocket science in all this. Sages have taught it for millennia. Yet the faculty of consciousness is the first casualty of hubris. Conversely, hubris cannot bear to be exposed by mindfulness. It cannot prosper in awakened *Homo sapiens*, the 'knowing human'. That is why violence, the adjutant of hubris, is described by such adjectives as 'senseless' and 'mindless'. Violence can only arise in mindless ignorance of reality, thus Hinduism, for example, attributes evil to *maya* or 'ignorance'.

The development of consciousness is the antithesis of violence. It connects us with the fullness of reality, as we have seen, through empathy, which is love. Such is the shift from the liminoid to the liminal – the threshold that distinguishes deathly nihilism from life-giving Being.

5. We must shift from violent to nonviolent security

Psychological advances since the end of World War II have opened new insights that offer hope for how violence can be reduced. But these insights are emotionally challenging to those who persist with a punitive approach, and so they have yet to be adequately integrated into public policy. 'Violence,' says James Gilligan, former director of psychiatric services in the Massachusetts prison system, 'is the ultimate means of communicating the absence of love by the person inflicting the violence. . . The self cannot survive without love. The self starved of love dies. That is how violence can cause the death of the self even when it does not kill the body.'[169]

Because those who have been desensitised by violence will be predisposed to its perpetration, Gilligan describes violence as a 'social epidemic'. The late Brazilian Roman Catholic bishop, Dom Hélder Câmara, first popularised this idea in his classic 1971 text of liberation theology, *Spiral of Violence*.[170] He said that social violence starts with the level 1 violence – the primary violence of *social injustice.* This leads to secondary violence – *rebellion* by the oppressed. That in turn invokes tertiary violence – *repression* by the powerful. And that further impoverishes the state and so completes the spiral by feeding back into more primary violence.

The only antidote to the spiral of violence is the spiral of love, or what Desmond

---

169 James Gilligan, *Violence: Reflections on a National Epidemic*, Vintage, London, 2001.
170 Helder Camara's *The Spiral of Violence* is out of print but scanned as a PDF at
http://www.alastairmcintosh.com/general/spiral-of-violence.htm .

and Mpho Tutu calls 'the Spiral of Forgiveness.'[171] This is the power of nonviolence, not as a passive 'pacifism' but as vibrant 'truth force' as Gandhi called it. Nonviolence has played a major part in bringing liberation to India, Portugal, the Philippines, South Africa, countries of the former Soviet Union, minority groups such as black Americans and dozens, if not hundreds, of other examples.[259] Is it not time to study peace and not just war? That, at least, is what I've said over the past decade in addressing some 4,000 senior officers from nearly 100 countries who have been through the Advanced Command and Staff Course at Britain's foremost school of war – the Joint Services Command and Staff College. A couple of hours each year are now devoted to exploring such a message in the curriculum. We live in strange times that can offer strange openings.

6. We must serve fundamental human needs
As we have seen, the cutting edge of consumerism is the insatiable generation of wants. 'To be' becomes equated with 'to have' – what J.K. Galbraith called the 'dependence effect' of a cancerously corpulent economy. In contrast, a sustainable society, a sane society, is one that seeks to meet fundamental human needs in life-enhancing ways.

Such needs are called 'fundamental' because happiness only requires a certain level of materiality before the balance of fulfilment shifts from outer acquisition to the inner capacity for appreciation. A sane society would be one that satisfies fundamental needs for shelter, food, water, education, healthcare and so on, but which also stimulates people onwards into realms of life what money cannot buy.

The Chilean economist, Manfred Max-Neef, has undertaken simple but life-giving work on this. He suggests that fundamental needs are the same the world over and throughout history.[172] They include the needs for subsistence, protection, affection, understanding, participation, creation, identity, recreation and freedom. In a

---

171 Desmond & Mpho Tutu, *The Book of Forgiving*, William Collins, London, 2014.
172 Manfred Max-Neef, 'Development and Human Needs,; in Paul Ekins (ed), *Real-life Economics,* Routledge, London, 1992, pp. 197-214.

matrix he analyses each of these for what they entail being, having, doing and 'interacting' (the nature of the relationships incurred).

For example, the need for identity means *being* in a sense of belonging, esteem and confidence. It might mean *having* a place of home, language, religion, sexuality, occupation, values, a set of memories and social reference groups. In terms of *doing,* it entails growing up, learning, working, worshipping, playing and, one day, dying. Some supposed satisfiers are *violators* of others. For example, the arms race supposedly satisfies the need for protection, but it violates needs for subsistence, affection, participation and freedom. Others are *pseudo-satisfiers*. For example, prostitution is only a surrogate for affection. Others are *inhibiting satisfiers*: television targets our need for recreation but can inhibit creativity. Some are *singular satisfiers*: they satisfy only one need rather than many, for example, food hand-outs that satisfy subsistence needs alone. And lastly, the ideal is to try and achieve *synergic satisfiers*. These satisfy a wide range of needs in ways that stimulate the creation of whole networks of wellbeing. An example is how babies are fed. Bottle-feeding is singular. It satisfies little more than the need for subsistence. But breast feeding additionally satisfies needs for protection, affection and identity.

In such ways Max-Neef's model challenges the conventional idea that a society should *maximise* economic growth. Instead it shows how outer and inner aspects of consumption – being, having, doing and interacting – are interwoven. The sane society, he says, is one that would assess socio-economic policies to *optimise* the satisfaction of fundamental human needs synergistically.

7. We must value mutuality over competition
Without the competitive ethic, modern life would be a very sluggish affair – perhaps not unlike the former Soviet Union. Competition both motivates and challenges towards perfection. However, competition becomes a destructive force if not held within a wider framework that is cooperative. Today, obsessive competitiveness is pushed in government policy, industry and even at children in

the classroom from the most tender age. In theory it does not have to be aggressive in this way. The original meaning of 'competition' derives from the Latin, *competere*, from *com* meaning 'together' and *petere* meaning 'to strive or seek.' *To compete* therefore originally meant, 'to strive in common.' But it is a sign of the times that this sense has largely been lost. Instead an expression of behaviour has evolved that has become injurious to the soul and destructive to the environment. People are encouraged to compete and consume not out of need, but to keep up – ever fearful that if they don't run faster and faster on the racetrack of success they'll be trampled by those coming up from behind.

The counterpoint to such competition is cooperation. At a commercial level this finds expression in cooperative and mutual business entities. But how can such cooperation be kept on its toes? Do we not need a bit of both qualities? Like Plato's image of the soul as a chariot drawn by two horses, one passionate and the other reasonable, could there be a higher synthesis by which such opposites can pull together?

I recall discussing this question with my friend, Thierry Groussin, head of training in the French cooperative bank, Groupe Crédit Mutuel. We were driving around on the single track roads of South Harris. Being the kind of place it is, as cars met in opposite directions, they'd typically pull in and flash one another to move ahead. Sometimes they'd cause mini traffic jams playing 'You go. No, you go'!

'There you are, Thierry,' I said. 'This is the community where people compete to cooperate!'

8. We must make more with less

One way that social and environmental justice movements have learned from the marketing world in recent years is in their understanding of product augmentation. This shows in the growing market for products with social or environmental 'kite marks' – *Fair Trade* for better prices to the poor, *Soil Association* for organic foods, *RSPCA Freedom Foods* for animal welfare, and so on. The added value accrues because *values* are built in. For example, as much as we can in our home, we buy certified organic meat from the local farmer's market. It costs double what we'd pay for the generic product in a supermarket so we eat smaller portions and a little less often than might otherwise have been the case. But it pleases us more, because we know it treats the soil, farm workers and the animals better. You're not left feeling tainted afterwards like you might with a leg of cheap imported battery chicken. As such, less becomes more. You don't just buy food. You buy something consistent with your understanding of right relationship.

One of the trade indicators that most gives me hope for the future is that, worldwide, the market for Fair Trade certified products grew 42% in 2006. It directly benefited more than 7 million producers. To my mind, paying for things like that is better than giving to charity. It embodies justice and so upholds dignity. None of the genuine ethical products require coercion or manipulation to make them leap off the shelves. Demand simply comes from people's growth in consciousness; from a growing activation of the inner life.

9. We must regenerate community of place
Ecology is the study of plant and animal communities in relation to their environments. Human ecology does the same with people. It studies human community in relation to its social and natural environments. Research in ecopsychology – ecological psychology – has repeatedly shown that we need to be able to attach to places as well as to other people.[173] We tend to be most at ease within ourselves when we have a sense of 'home' that is both emotional and geographical. As such, communities of place – our country, town, village or a bioregion such as an island or a watershed – tend to be very strong markers of identity. Bioregional identity is very often present in ways that we hardly notice. For example, when we speak of the 'Thames Valley Police' we are describing a bioregionally-defined organisation. How strange that crime can follow ecology even if other walks of life can't.

---

173 See Theodore Roszak et al, *Ecopsychology: Restoring the Earth – Healing the Mind*, University of California Press, Berkeley, 2002.

Usually communities of place are stronger than socially constructed communities of interest. There is an asymmetry here. Communities of interest are nested within communities of place, not the other way round. That is because place is physical: it is our grounding in nature. Some postmodernists will challenge this. They say that nature, too, is a mere social construction. Well, this particular premodernist has a penchant for inviting extreme postmodernists to stop eating, hold their breath, and then we'll see how long their social construction of nature lasts!

'Place' is a very warm word. It is the product of both *environment* and *culture*; of nature and society. There is a sequence of reconnection with place that I have observed from my work with community regeneration in both Scotland and Papua New Guinea. I call it *the Cycle of Belonging.*

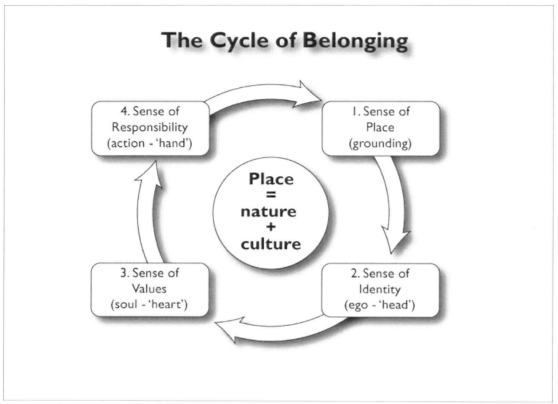

(From the author's *Rekindling Community: Connecting People, Environment and Spirituality*, Schumacher Briefing No. 15 (with WWF International), Green Books, Totnes, 2008.)

If the cycle is broken at any point, both human community and natural ecology are damaged – it becomes a vicious cycle. Conversely, if it is strengthened, people and place regenerate.

10. We must build strong but inclusive identities
The IPCC considers that by the middle of this century, 200 million people could be forced from their homes. These may lose all sense that they ever had of belonging to place. In a cool hilly country like Scotland where the impacts of climate change are likely to be less pronounced, pressure will grow to accept climate change

refugees. What will happen? Will the privileged pull up the drawbridge to try and keep at bay the human consequences of their consumer profligacy? Or might we be able to think more humanely about who belongs to where? Specifically, can we bring to the cultural foreground constructs of identity that are inclusive rather than exclusive? Can we emphasise civic rather than ethnic identity: not 'blood and soil' but 'soil and soul'?

To answer this we might start by looking at what a nation is. I believe that a nation is more than just a state. A state is a mechanism of government, but a nation, over and above that, is a cultural entity. In a celebrated address at the Sorbonne in 1882, the great Breton theologian and Celtic scholar, Ernest Renan, pushed this even deeper. He said: 'A nation is a soul, a spiritual principle,' and he continued:

> A large aggregate of men, healthy in mind and warm of heart, creates the kind of moral conscience which we call a nation. So long as this moral consciousness gives proof of its strength by the sacrifices which demand the abdication of the individual to the advantage of the community, it is legitimate and has the right to exist.[174]

This affirms that identity, including national identity, but only where it encodes a moral consciousness that can yield to principles supportive of community. Where people may lose their homes because of global warming, it begs the consideration that we who might be more fortunate have a special responsibility to take them in. Indeed, the legitimacy of our own claim to identity would depend upon it. It is for each nation to work out its own rationale, but in Scotland that might be built on existing cultural principles that define identity inclusively. For example, hospitality has traditionally been considered a 'sacred duty' for the short term and fostership, or adoption, for permanence. The fosterling must be protected, just as Joseph fostered and protected Jesus. As a Gaelic proverb says, 'The bonds of milk (i.e. nurture) are stronger than the bonds of blood (i.e. nature).' And another: 'Blood counts for twentyfold; fostership a hundredfold.' My own way of expressing this is

---

174 Ernest Renan, *What is a Nation?* The Sorbonne, 1882, http://ig.cs.tu-berlin.de/oldstatic/w2001/eu1/dokumente/Basistexte/Renan1882EN-Nation.pdf

that 'a person belongs inasmuch as they are willing to cherish and be cherished by this place and its peoples.'

The Scottish Government expresses it in the slogan: 'One Scotland; many cultures,' and often I think of some words by Iain Crichton Smith, a poet from my home island, the Isle of Lewis, that sees nothing less than the 'meta' behind or beyond the physical, the sacred inherent within the material:

> Sometimes when I walk the streets of Glasgow I see an old woman passing by, bowed down with shopping bags, and I ask myself: 'What force made this woman what she is? What is her history?' It is the holiness of the person we have lost, the holiness of life itself, the inexplicable mystery and wonder of it, its strangeness, its tenderness.[175]

11. We must educate for elementality

In *A Sand County Almanac,* the classic work of ecology published in 1949, Aldo Leopold described conservation as 'a state of harmony' between people and the land. He proposed a 'land ethic' based on the principle that, 'A thing is right when it tends to preserve the integrity, stability, and beauty of the biotic community. It is wrong when it tends otherwise.'

The 'biotic community' is the whole web of life. People need to understand and be motivated to preserve it if they are to accept stringent action to combat climate change. In Britain since the 1990's considerable progress has been made in advancing environmental education. But education at the level of the 'head' alone is not enough. The head is very good at making decisions. But it is the passion of the heart that pumps blood both to the head and to the hand that puts action into effect. That is why Leopold's emphasis on *beauty* stands out.

---

175 Iain Crichton Smith, 'Real People in a Real Place' in *Towards the Human* op. cit., online at http://www.alastairmcintosh.com/general/resources/1982-Iain-Crichton-Smith-Real-People-Real-Place.pdf

At the end of the day, when the glitter of the shops has worn off, the packaging transmogrified to garbage, and the credit card bill slips through the door, the world of consumerism is sad and tawdry. Except where economic growth serves the fundamental needs of the poor, it measures little more than the rate at which natural beauty and human effort is trashed. Consumerism only goes skin deep, which is why it is always so obsessed with cosmetics, fashion and keeping up appearances. In contrast, true beauty is experienced when inner values harmonise with outer action. This is why right relationship with nature makes us whole. It salves our neurosis; it is a form of 'salvation'.

I am convinced, especially from my own experience growing up, that children both young and old need an *elemental education* fully to be able to appreciate reality. They need contact with nature where they can learn about matter and energy, cosmology, the atmosphere and its weather, the soils and the rocks, and the rivers, lakes and seas and their flora and fauna. They need to experience nature's beauty and the sheer *fun* of it, for nature absorbs children in so many different ways.

We adults must be careful in our shouldering of the burden of awareness not to instil in our children the kind of eco-hypochondria that so often afflicts jaded greens – moaning about all that's wrong with the world, but forgetting to notice the magic of the crocuses pushing up and into blossom for yet another year. Children need to have a positive hands on engagement with the ancient four 'roots' or 'elements' of reality – *fire, air, earth* and *water*. They need to know them in all their dangers – in their wild vicissitude that demands respect and courage on the Hero's Journey. And they also need to know them in all their sensitivity and vulnerability – in the filigree of frost on a winter's morning leaf – the hallowed loveliness that brings a tear to the eye.

12. We must open to Grace and Truth
My father used to say that kindness is what matters above all else. Even when there is little else that can be done – when the actual or metaphorical floodwaters are rising all around and hope gets put to the test – even then, we can still try and be kind. Gratitude is what sustains and completes such grace. It is the essence of

'worship' – an Old English word meaning the celebration of 'worth'. If in our pride we neglect gratitude, or confuse it with sycophancy, there can be no hope of building true community because the doors of life's deepest gifts will stay closed.

The American environmental educator, David Orr goes so far as to believe that gratitude is the single most important quality needed to address climate change. He says that only in such a spirit can we be freed from the loveless illusion of independence, and discover the sustaining truth of interdependence. This applies both for our relationships with one another and with the natural world. It is the flow of grace that opens the doors of 'providence', which is to say, *provide-ence,* in all walks of life. Such is what it means to find blessing. Orr quotes the great twentieth century rabbi, Abraham Heschel, who said: 'As civilisation advances the sense of wonder almost necessarily declines. . . humankind will not perish for want of information; but only for want of *appreciation*.' And Orr concludes, 'In our universities we teach a thousand ways to criticise, analyse, dissect and deconstruct, but we offer very little guidance on the cultivation of gratitude – simply saying "Thank you."'[176]

Grace – both given to us and shared by us – walks hand in hand with another quality, Truth. The first verse of the Hindu gospel, the *Bhagavad Gita*, reads in Juan Mascaró's beautiful Penguin translation: 'On the field of Truth, on the battlefield of life, what came to pass, Sanjaya…?' The minutiae of that which comes to pass in each fleeting moment is thereby revealed as being staged on the battlefield of life, which in turn plays out on a much greater stage – the Dharma, cosmic Truth, the opening of the Way. And who was Sanjaya? but the eagle-eyed charioteer to the blind king, Dhritarashtra. We see here that political power on its own is blind without spiritual vision and so, as an old Quaker woman told me, 'It is perilous to neglect your spiritual life.'

The lie of consumerism as with all addictions is that consciousness itself is hijacked. Our sense of aliveness diminishes, and there's only the ache left behind – the lacuna in the soul – the promise of what could otherwise be that it's so

---

176 David Orr, 'The Rhythm of Gratitude', *Resurgence,* 247 Mar/Apr 2008, pp. 10-11.

tempting to try and reach through everyday addictions. As one of our community at the GalGael Trust in Glasgow's hard-pressed district of Govan told me, 'Heroin took away my pain, but it also took away my soul.' If we are to address climate change we must address consumerism, and to address consumerism requires nothing less than what the healers of indigenous cultures refer to as 'calling back the soul'.

5.5 Gifting: the New Approach to Economy

Manan Jain

Introduction: Capitalism and the ideology of overproduction

According to Marx, in capitalism, improvements in technology and rising levels of productivity increase the amount of material wealth. Capitalism, the economic system is based on the principles of maximizing the shareholder's wealth. Thus, it is a system based on the private interests of a few. In capitalism, the motive for producing goods and services is to sell them for a profit, not to satisfy people's needs. Thus, overproduction became one of the ideology of this system and it is believed that the more one produces, more are the profits. Though, economists argue, that overproduction results in lesser profit as greater supply reduces the profitability of the goods. However, with innovative marketing, latent needs are created among the mass, which ensures a good demand for the products. The concept of overproduction makes sense, if it is to satisfy the needs of people, but not, when it is for the profit motive. Man's greed knows no bounds and if not for the physical and capacity constraints, there would have been no ends to the production levels.

Going back to the history, the concept of overproduction started from the agriculture, which brought a revolution in the society. Agriculture satisfied the basic need of hunger of man, who was a hunter. It is to be noted that this overproduction was not for any profit motive. It was just to give food security to man and for the greater good of the community and the society. However, in today's world, agriculture has been restricted as another means of livelihood. Crops are grown and harvested to generate profits by selling it in market. Thus, land is exploited to get as much produce as possible.

Excessive use of pesticides and fertilizers has put a toll on the fertility of the soil.

However, it is not the agriculture which is to be blamed for this; it is the present socio-economic system to which the society has evolved to, resulting in the capitalist mindset of the people.. Apart from overproduction, it can further be debated that capitalism also results in increasing the divide between the rich and the poor. Increase in production does generate employment opportunities for the working class, but the value that is generated for the capitalists, far exceeds that for the workers. The gap only widens and at times the worker's farewell is neglected, which only adds to the growing frustration and creates a rift in the society. For instance, the jasmine revolution saw massive protests.

Effect of capitalism on environment

Overproduction of goods has put a lot of toll on the environment and the natural resources. Be it agriculture or manufacturing, each and every industry adds to the consumption of the natural resources, with most of them being non-renewable. As stated above, the quest for producing more and more has resulted in the soil becoming barren and infertile. Excessive use of pesticides and fertilizers has changed the soil chemistry and has made it devoid of minerals and nutrients.

No development can take place without the use of natural resources, and one needs to meet up with the incessant growing energy requirements to keep up the pace of the economic development. Energy is required for exploration and extraction of resources, and also to transform it to the finished goods. Further, energy is required for the transportation of these goods to the end consumers. Thus, every good that is produced has a significant carbon footprint. Though, the models to calculate the precise carbon footprint still needs to be researched upon, but the manpower used in the process also adds to the carbon footprint, which needs to be considered. Thus in nutshell, every good is costly and is of much more ecological value than its economic value as precious natural resources have been used, which are limited in nature.

However, this ecological value is not being realized at all, and one only looks at its economic value. Majority of these goods are not reused or recycled and end up being dumped in the landfills. This waste is only piled up and it takes a lot of time for biodegradation. Additionally, it's not just the resources that are limited, but also the land, which is being used as dumping sites. Besides, without proper disposal techniques harmful and toxic chemicals from the waste find its way into the soil and air, thereby affecting the food-chain and disturbing the natural equilibrium.

The cradle to grave system that is followed is not sustainable unless we return back all the constituents to the nature, in its natural form. The need of the hour is to follow a cradle to cradle approach, wherein we take the responsibility of the consumption of the energy and resources and ensure that we maintain the balance in nature by returning back what we take.

Furthermore, in the pursuit of profits, one seems to flounder all rules and regulations to minimize costs. Illegal mining of minerals, dumping of waste into rivers and seas are to name a few of these practices and form the tip of an iceberg.

The unsustainable consumerist culture
The rise of the capitalism along-with overproduction has been fuelled by a change in the consumer behavior as well. No longer are we satisfied by what we have and it is the human tendency to always aspire for more. This has no end, and is precisely the reason for the thriving consumerist culture.

Food, shelter and clothing form the basic necessities of a man, categorized in the bottom level of Maslow's hierarchy of needs. The basic human requirement is to have clothes to protect the body from the extreme weather. However today, it's more of a fashion statement. One aspires to have clothes as per the latest fashion, which gets outdated with each season. Wardrobes are filled with latest designer clothing, only to be dumped in the next season, to make space for the latest trends. It's an irony, that in-spite of so much of cloth production; so many people in the world still don't have anything to cover their naked bodies. The advances in technology has further proliferated the increasing wants of consumers. Such is the advent that latest gadgets and gizmos, which were being introduced in the market couple of years back, are getting obsolete. The shelf life of these products is decreasing with each passing day. Maybe this is one of the ways of being in the business, by introducing gadgets with fancier features.

But one needs to stop here and ponder, is this what is really needed? For instance, televisions provide a great source of entertainment. With technological advances, LCD televisions are replacing the Cathode Ray Tube models. These are further being replaced by the LED TV's. Though not a basic necessity, but this need is being replaced by want, and marketers are finding innovative ways to tap these latent needs of the consumers. This is also complemented by the increasing purchasing power, but then there would be no end to this madness. Some other technology will further replace this, and the process is endless. What one fails to realize is the ecological consequences of this consumerist culture which is unsustainable at its core.

We need to slow down our rate of consumption. But won't that mean slowing down the development? After all the more the goods and services are produced, the more the employment, and the more the wealth and thus more the prosperity.

Effect of consumerist culture on society
With this consumerist culture, and the capitalist mindset, it can be argued that earth has become a better place to live in, with all the so called development. In comparison to our ancestors, we have a better education system, higher life expectancy, advanced medical facilities, better communication and transport infrastructure. The world has become a place with no boundaries. One knows what is happening in other parts of the world and can travel anywhere in the world. The evolution of mankind to the present day and the growth story has been prolific. However, one needs to look at the complete picture.

The current system has bred an atmosphere of tension and worries. CEO's are worried about the top and the bottom-line, government is worried about managing the growth amongst all the economic turmoil, corporates are worried about hikes and bonuses they will be getting, parents are worried about managing the household with the rising prices and inflation. Everyone is in a rat race to acquire more assets, more wealth and more money, hoping to get a sense of security out of it. But what results is growing discontent, dissatisfaction, disharmony and lack of prosperity. We might become rich, but there is no communal harmony as that wealth is at the expense of others, and only widens the economic gap. This widening of the gap further leads to frustration among the lower halves and creates enormous pressure in the society. This pressure is released in the form of protests, social uprisings and revolutions that have changed the course of the mankind. One does not have to go far in the history for such examples.

Poverty, unemployment and political repression were the reasons which led to the Tunisian revolution of 2010-11 in the Arab country of Tunisia. Again, the world witnessed the Egyptian revolution wherein people frustrated by the rising unemployment, high food inflation, low minimum wages and increasing corruption toppled the government in 2011. 2011 also witnessed Wall Street protests, where people stood against the issues of social and economic inequality, greed, corruption and undue influence of corporates on governments.

Though the technology is bringing people close together, yet there is no closeness within the society. Had it been the case, people would have stood for each other, helping each other out to ensure that people meet at-least their basic needs. This wouldn't bring affluence to lives of poor, but contentment to lead a peaceful life.

Ideologies of Gift Economy

In this context, Gift economy seems to be a very constructive and innovative solution. Gift economy is an economy based on giving in the context of relationship rather than making transactions simply for profit or personal material gain. Valuable goods and services are regularly given without any explicit agreement for immediate or future rewards.

The foundation of a sacred economy, then, is gift consciousness. It is based on the following principles:[1]

1. Over time, giving and receiving must be in balance. The internalization of ecological costs ensures that we will take no more from earth than we can give.

2. The source of a gift is to be acknowledged. The restoration of the commons means that any use of what belongs to all is acknowledged by a payment that goes to all.

3. Gifts circulate rather than accumulate.

4. Gifts flow toward the greatest need. A social dividend ensures that the basic survival needs of every person are met.

Let's discuss these one by one. The first principle tries to bring the human civilization in harmony with nature. All the natural resources are a gift of nature to man. It doesn't differentiates humans based on demography or geography. As put by Mahatma Gandhi, earth has everything to satisfy man's need but not for man's greed. To pay back to the nature, is paying out of gratitude and to ensure that the same gifts are enjoyed by one and all, including the future generations. It also encompasses the cradle to cradle approach of production and ensures that whatever is taken, is given back to the nature, thus ensuring that the system, the growth and the development are sustainable.

Additionally, today, pollution and various other activities that degrade environment are at the expense of society and future generations. Shifting these costs to polluters will guarantee that they pay back entirely for all the pollution caused by them. This further keeps a tab on the pollution levels and ensures it to a level which is under control and has been offset.

The second principle acknowledges the source of the gift, be it nature or a fellow human being. The acknowledgement brings closeness in the community and meaningful relationships develop as there is no selfish or profit motives. The receiver overwhelmed with gratitude, in turn strives to pay back to the society and gifts to others in need. One looks towards helping others, and these feelings create close associations.

This further lowers the social and economic disparity. In a capitalistic economy, the goods and services are paid up with money. It leaves no obligation to help the society in return for the goods and services rendered, even though they may be at the expense of society. For instance, production of good, results in pollution which affects the society equally, but the money is paid only to the producer. The second principle helps in ensuring that all the stakeholders are acknowledged and gifted back. Moreover, it eliminates the divisions in the society based on one's wealth and tries to bring in equality, social as well economic.

The third principle is based on the ideology of non-accumulation. One receives gifts, and in turn gives gifts back to the society. This translates to non-hoarding of material. One is well versed with the evils of hoarding in a capitalistic society. Hoarding creates artificial scarcity which causes price rise and inflation, giving profits to the hoarders at the cost of the common man. The continuous flow of gifts ensures that needs of all are met, and a greater circulation of goods gives the sense of security that capitalistic minds seek in accumulation of materialistic wealth. Moreover it gives a peace of mind in not having to indulge in a rat race to acquire these material possessions.

A thing can be want for one and need for other, or in other words, a luxury for someone may be a need for another. For instance, a person might have hundreds of designer labels in his/her wardrobe, while at the same time, clothing is a necessity for someone else and he might not have even a single piece of clothing to cover his body. The fourth principle ensures that the benefits of the gifts are enjoyed by those who need it the most. Furthermore it also tries to bring in economic and social parity by ensuring that basic survival needs of all the persons are met. In this world, in spite of all the growth and developments, millions die of hunger and malnutrition, and millions do not have access to proper clothing and shelter. Wouldn't it be nice if our fellow brothers and sisters are all able to live a better life, satisfying all their basic needs? Imagine, if you yourself was fighting to get two square meals a day, and if someone gifts you enough to eat, how much happiness it would bring to you. Imagine, if there is so much of happiness, contentment, harmony and prosperity within the society, then will there be Wall Street protests or Egyptian or Tunisian revolutions?

Gift Economy initiatives

There are various ways to promote this concept and put these ideologies into practice. A lot of initiatives have already been put into practice and the results are promising.

Seva café, in the city of Ahmedabad in India is one such example. A diner at Seva café is not viewed as a customer, but instead as a treasured guest, as part of a family. When someone dines at Seva Café, the meal is offered as a genuine gift, already paid for in full by previous guests, and one has no obligation to pay. One becomes part of a Circle of Giving, which is modeled more closely to that of a family. Thus there are no bills and the diner is free to pay anything or nothing, without any obligation. the wholesome vegetarian meals are cooked and served with love by volunteers and by a small, modestly paid staff - mostly graduates from Manav Sadhna's Earn N' Learn program.

The menu changes daily and they offer a delicious variety of options, both Indian and continental. They believe that everyone - volunteers, staff, and guests alike - all should leave the space feeling more nourished - body, mind, and spirit - and that together they can help set in motion, a more abundant, more generous mode of interacting that leaves everyone feeling happier and more closely connected. The inequities of the world derive from our own internal walls of separation from one another, and Seva Café strives to leave these walls behind. All their costs and income are made clearly transparent, and 100% of any profits that they take in, are used back in the community through Seva Cafe.[2]

Application of gift economy to solve current socio-economic issues

A probable application of this concept of gift economy could be to have an organization, primary goal of which is to provide a platform for the gifting. A non-profit organization, it would bring together people from all walks of life and apprise them of various gifting opportunities. It would be a medium wherein people can gift goods and services to be used by other in need. Today, the desire is there to donate or give to the society, and there are several NGO's for this as well. For instance, there are toy banks, there are NGO's which collect and distribute old and used clothes and so on. However, this is limited to the domain in which the organization operates, and the operations are usually localized in nature. These organizations fail to connect the giver and the receiver. Thus we need a medium which connects the giver and the receiver by providing them a common platform.

Moreover, we need to build an organization, which can also further the reuse and recycling of goods. Thus doing a value-add to the good and increasing its shelf life. Very often, a small problem in the working of an electronic gadget, or availability of fancier gizmos forces us to dump these goods into the waste bin. However, with small repairs, these become good enough to be operational for some more time. A person, who can't afford such a good, would be very happy if he gets to have that product in working order. A small personal example, I had an old desktop at my home in a good condition, lying unused. With small repair, it was gifted to a sweeper having a meager monthly salary of $100. His joy knew no bounds as he now had access to a computer, which fulfilled his dreams.

The point to be made is that there is a lot of scope for re-use and recycle of products and goods. Besides, this value addition to the goods has the potential to generate employment opportunities for people as well, and this could be supported by government welfare schemes. Based on a not for profit model, this organization can be run by volunteers, who can gift their time and render their services. For instance, people can gift their fully functional or part-functional devices. These can be further refurbished by people with suitable skills and gifted to the needy people. These skilled persons can be the individuals who have the required technical know-how and have volunteered. Additionally, corporates under their CSR initiatives can impart technical know-how to refurbish the goods and add more value to them. Today, the leaders talk of the need to transfer the technical know-how from the developed nations to the developing ones in order to solve the climate issues. The solution, the vision for an organization that is presented in this chapter can very well be a means to achieve that.

Conclusion

Thus with the participation of corporates, the government and the individuals, one can hope to achieve the desired objectives of the gift economy. This would further help in achieving sustainable consumption by the virtue of sharing of goods, thus reducing demand at-least for the goods which are sparingly used in daily life. Initiatives like Seva café, Karma kitchen[3] have shown to the world that such initiatives are sustainable as well as practical. What is needed in today's world is an understanding of the various issues at hand and a shift in the mindset to achieve a solution for that. Gift economy, with its ideologies offers a practical and sustainable solution, which is for all to uncover..

References and supporting tables are available on request.

5.6 The Attitude-Behaviour Gap and the Committed Volunteer

Craig Duckworth

Introduction

A discrepancy between expressed attitudes and actual conduct has long been observed in psychological and sociological research (LaPiere,1934, DeFleur & Westie, 1958, Campbell, 1963, Deutscher, 1966, Fishbein & Ajzen, 1975). What is commonly called the attitude-behaviour gap has more recently come to the attention of researchers in marketing and in business ethics. The main locus of interest is the evident tendency for people to profess favourable attitudes towards ethical consumption[177], while failing to act on those attitudes when making actual consumption choices. Evidence for the gap can be found in the shortfall between consumer survey evidence that indicates a prevalence of ethically minded consumers, and actual consumption data that shows the continuing, relatively weak performance of ethical goods (Devinney et al., 2011, 2010, Co-operative Bank, 2012, European Commission, 2009, Smith, 2008, Vogel, 2005, Auger & Devinney, 2007, p. 361, Carrigan & Attalla, 2001, p. 564, Boulstridge & Carrigan, 2000, Roberts, 1996, Pew Research Centre, 2010, pp. 71-72, D'Astous & Legendre, 2009, pp. 255-6, Barr, 2004, Lane & Potter, 2007, see also Skapinker, 2012). It is important to attempt to understand the nature of the attitude-behaviour gap, as it presents a challenge for public policy intended to encourage more sustainable consumption patterns. The gap also carries implications for corporate strategy designed to promote goods that are the product of sustainable production processes and fairer supply chains. Wider policy issues relating to ethical consumption – for example, in relation to development and global poverty - are discussed in Singer 2002, 1972,

177 I understand by ethical consumption here a wide range of consumer behaviours. They include the purchasing of goods for moral reasons, but also recycling, and political boycotts (Harrison et al., 2005, p. 2).

Marchand et al, 2010, p. 1432, Barnett et al 2005, Soper & Lynn, 2005, Boivin, 2011, Smith, 2008).

In this chapter, I identify the dominant conception of agency in the literature on the attitude-behaviour gap, and suggest that it misconstrues the relationship between personal commitment and incentive. According to the dominant conception, the underlying commitment associated with a favourable attitude towards ethical consumption, can be expected to result in the relevant kinds of choices unless countervailing considerations, or material obstacles, stand in a person's way. This conception sets up the expectation that people will, in the absence of such countervailing forces, act on their professed attitudes. This, I argue, is a mistaken view in important respects. When a person commits to something their commitment is necessarily contingent. It is contingent on them having the resolve to act in the relevant kind of way. If they do not possess the requisite resolve this need not be a sign that their commitment is not genuine. It may be a sign that what was needed to enable them to act on prior commitment - some form of encouragement or enabling condition - was absent. Being in need of incentive in order to bolster resolve is consistent with being genuinely committed, given the inherently contingent nature of commitment.

However, while a person's requiring incentive is consistent with genuine commitment, this does not mean that a person can require *any* amount of incentive to encourage his or her resolve. To claim a level of incentive that is greater than that which is necessary to procure resolve is, I argue, a mark of *moral failure*. The agent is not to be blamed for failing to overcome certain hurdles, such as prohibitively high search costs. However, the committed individual cannot claim just any amount of incentive without being charged with moral failure - a failure to show sufficient resolve, given his or her prior commitment. I consider that the dominant conception of the person, in discussions of the attitude-behaviour gap, lets people off the moral hook too lightly. In the context of ethical consumption there ought to be a recognition that moral weakness is, in part, to blame for the attitude-behaviour gap. How public policy and corporate strategy address this is a further question. In what follows I limit myself to a characterisation of the difference between the dominant conception of agency, in the context of ethical consumption, and the alternative I want to defend. Central to the argument is a contrast between two ways of viewing the relationship between commitment and incentive. The dominant conception presumes that ethical consumers are voluntarily committed, and can legitimately withdraw or not act their commitment if incentives are insufficient. The conception I defend makes central the idea of the *committed volunteer*. While people voluntarily commit, once they are committed there are restrictions on the amount of incentive they can legitimately require.

Ethical Consumption and Discretion

A good place to begin is with the indelible role of discretion in the conception of the ethical consumer. If consumers did not possess personal discretion with respect to their consumption, at the point of choice, then their behaviour could be wholly controlled. The difficulty a governmental authority or a corporate strategist has is that they do not possess full control over the behaviour of the people whose choices they would like to affect, and abolishing discretion is not a normatively desirable nor a realistic option. The contrast I have mind here is that discussed in connection with the principle-agent problem (Shapiro (2005) contains a helpful review). The role and implications of discretion in differing institutional contexts is discussed also in, for example, Williamson (1975, 1996). And the theory of liberal paternalism, more popularly known as the nudge thesis (Thaler & Sunstein, 2008, 2003), recognises a need to use mechanisms to influence choice at the individual level. This is, in part, an attempt to secure individual discretion, but it is also a recognition of the difficulty of controlling individual actions by force. One consideration is that personal or agential discretion is viewed as having independent value in market economies. Consumers' personal discretion is one of the key determinants of the competitive pressure that supports the claimed efficiency properties of a free market system. It is also the case, however, that in economic systems in which the free market is not the dominant allocative mechanism, it is, nonetheless, prohibitively costly to monitor and control all personal consumption choices. The discretion that the consumer has to determine his or her own final consumption choices is an abiding constraint on governmental and corporate attempts to engender ethical consumption.

The capacity of the consumer to exercise personal discretion has important implications for how we conceptualise the agent in relation to ethical consumption. The ultimate control an agent has, the capacity to ultimately reject or accept reasons for choice, ought to be captured, or accommodated, by our conception of agency in this context. But these considerations bring to light a difficulty for the dominant conception of the agent in this area.

As is well known, it is possible to identify two broad approaches to the attitude-behaviour gap. One approach focuses on the self-directed character of personal choice (D'Souza et al 2007, Augur et al, 2003, p. 299, see also the findings in Carrigan & Attalla, Carrigan & Attalla, 2001, p. 564. See also Hausman, 2005 for a discussion of self-direction in the form of *considered preferences*). Notable, under this heading, is the influential *theory of planned behaviour*, due to Ajzen (1991), who builds 'perceived behavioural control' into the earlier *reasoned action* model of Ajzen and Fishbein (1980), (see Ajzen, 1991: 183). In this model the emphasis is placed on interfering factors at the point of choice, factors that the agent can potentially, self-consciously overcome (see also Hines et al, 1987). A second approach emphasises the determining role of factors that are outside of the agent's control (Blake, 1999, OECD, 2008, pp. 10-11, 122-135, Young et al, 2010, p. 29, Vanhonacker & Verbeke, 2006, 2009, Wyer & Srull, 1986, Starr, 2009. For discussion see Kolmuss & Agyeman, 2002). The former category includes accounts that identify price, search costs, and risk perception as being among the factors that are most influential in preventing a person acting on his or her positive evaluations. Positions that stress items that bypass the agent's conscious control, point to factors such as peer pressure and community ethos as significant influencers.

In addition to these two broad categories there are also holistic approaches. For example, personal choice in Bray et al. (2011) involves, in part, the application of considerations that bring to awareness underlying causal factors. This research agenda promises a comprehensive account of agency that may illuminate the reasons for the attitude-behaviour gap. It also hooks up to a rich vein of existing research in social theory. In a holistic approach, the agent is conceived as able to articulate personal principles of which she is aware and that have an extra-agential origin in factors such as social mores and cultural expectations. In Osterhus (1997) a framework is presented that integrates economic, normative, and institutional determinants of choice. A central aspect of this are personal norms that are, in part, the reflexive analogues of social norms and institutional rules. A reflective appreciation of choice-shaping factors is central, also, in Cherrier's work (Cherrier, 2005), whose broadly narrative approach has an interesting affinity with Archer's response (Archer, 2003) to the structure-agency question. Archer identifies a realm of personal narrative that places a deliberative, reflexive wedge between conditioning factors and personal choice (see also, Vitell, 2003, p. 34). Holistic approaches often, in addition, turn to Bordieu's much discussed account of practical deliberation (Bordieu, 1977). According to Bordieu, self-governed choice is possible, but what a person takes into account in practical deliberation is restricted by his or her socio-cultural setting, and, in a deeper way, her *habitus* (see also Hodgeson, 2004, Giddens, 1986, Wrong, 1961, Granovetter, 1985). A similar, explicitly Aristotelian, approach is that of John McDowell, for whom the cultural origins of personal preference need not be seen as a limitation on their openness to reasoned critique (McDowell, 1996, esp. Lecture IV).

A particularly noteworthy holistic approach, that attempts to incorporate self-directed and external factors as complementary aspects of choice formation, is Carrington et al. (2010). Drawing prominently on Belk (1975), Carrington and her co-authors extend Ajzen's theory of planned behaviour to incorporate situational factors that are specific to the particular choice setting. These site-specific environmental factors include subliminal influences, that have an unconscious impact on choice (Carrington, 2010, p. 148). It is the importance of these that Carrington et al emphasise. However, also present in their theory are the agent's perceptions and interpretations of environmental factors (ibid.). These factors, of which agents are cognisant, form a component of self-directed choice.

It would seem that these approaches carry sufficient emphasis on self-direction to secure a place for discretion in the application of personal, evaluative reasons for choice. A person may or may not, for example, give up searching for recycling opportunities when the search costs go beyond a certain level. A person may or may not balk at the relative price of an energy efficient electrical appliance. Even in holistic models, whether a person does or does not act on personal evaluations is in the control of the agent, and so personal discretion, it would seem, is accounted for in extant analyses of the attitude-behaviour gap. However, the way in which existing approaches accommodate discretion is not unproblematic.

Note that discretion requires that a person be understood to be at liberty to change his or her mind at any moment prior to choice. The corollary of discretion, at the point of choice, is that we must understand or conceptualise an agent's extant attitudes as playing, at most, a contingent role in his or her decision making. To accommodate discretion in our conception of agency we must view evaluations, attitudes, conscious beliefs, and so on, as *potential* determinants of choice. We cannot understand them to be psychological items that will irrevocably determine choice in the absence of countervailing factors, or constraints. If we do so understand them then the ultimate control an agent has - his or her personal discretion at the point of choice - will not be accommodated in our conception of the ethical consumer. If we understand attitudes as having ineluctable causal efficacy in the absence of constraint we could, in principle, produce behaviour that accords with the relevant attitude by removing the constraints. This implication must be prevented if we are to accord the individual personal discretion, or ultimate control over what he or she does, whether constraints are present or not.

Existing approaches do not do enough to avoid the suspicion that their interpretation of the motivational force of attitudes undermines the discretionary control agents must possess over their choices. Consider Carrington et al. (2010). In their holistic model of consumer choice Michal Carrington and her co-authors are wary of approaches that simplify the choice process. They concur with critiques that question the determining role of attitudes and intentions in personal choice (ibid., p. 142). They question also the assumption that perceived behavioural control will always coincide with actual behavioural control (ibid., p. 143). It would appear then that agential discretion is well accounted for in their model.

Central to their thesis is the idea of an *implementation plan*, this being a plan that specifies what will be done in particular circumstances in order to carry out an intention to consume ethically (ibid., p. 144). The danger in Carrington et al's thesis is that discretion not be accorded the priority that is needed in order to accommodate complete discretionary control. They say: 'Implementation intentions/plans protect and maintain intentions by enabling the individual to pass control of their behaviour over to the situational environment.' (ibid., p. 144). Through the implementation of implementation plans, individuals are able to 'switch from conscious and deliberate control of their behaviour to a state of 'automaticity' where their behaviour is effortlessly guided by the situational cues.' (ibid., p. 144). The implementation plan is invoked as a means to overcome limitations on personal control. It is, at first sight, a promising way to introduce discretion, as it enables people to overcome even ingrained routines. However, implementation plans accord power to the person over his or her actions in a way that subverts discretion. The successful implementation plan, it seems, is one that enables a person to satisfy her intentions without deliberate reflection. Discretion does not have a primary role to play in this account of ethical agency.

Discretion and Commitment

So far I have emphasised the tendency to presume a determinate role for factors other than discretion, in the standard view. The roots of this tendency are in a particular understanding of the relationship between a professed positive attitude towards ethical consumption and the associated commitment. The standard view and the one I am here defending agree that a favourable attitude derives its motivational force from an underlying commitment. However, the standard view holds a mistaken understanding of the nature of commitment, and, further, how commitment relates to incentive.

Consider, for example, Augur & Devinney's (2007, p. 365) critique of survey techniques. Survey questions, they suggest, are typically asked in a context in which it is easy, and so tempting, for interviewees to claim to possess convictions that they do not in fact strongly hold, and that they are unlikely to act on. What Augur and Devinney are not claiming is that surveys are unable to uncover attitudes. What surveys fail to identify is not attitudes *per se*. Interviewees may *believe* themselves to be expressing attitudes they hold. What surveys do not do, rather, in Augur and Devinney's view, is to reliably identify *genuine* attitudes, where attitudes that are genuine are understood to be those that are backed by a relevant commitment. What Augur and Devinney's critique implies is that if only we could identify genuine attitudes, then the accompanying commitment would ensure attitude consistent behaviour. On the interpretation I am offering, as we will see, it is possible for a person to express a genuine attitude, and to have a genuine commitment, and yet fail to act in a concomitant way, without that casting doubt on the authenticity of the commitment.

Similarly, Carrigan & Attalla (2001, p. 572) acknowledge that consumers' apparent prioritisation of price and value over ethical considerations, in their actual purchasing behaviour, justifies the doubts that many have about the reliability of consumer surveys. But it is not surprising that a person might possess a genuinely favourable attitude towards ethical consumption, and yet find it too challenging to pay a higher price at the checkout. The response to this need not to be to cast doubt on the credibility of commitment, once we fully recognise commitment's inherently contingent nature.

Further evidence for this weakness in the standard view can be found in consumer research that explicitly incorporates the idea of commitment. Pimental and Reynolds (2004) consider consumer devotion to beloved goods, and, centrally, the similarities between fanaticism in sport and consumer loyalty. They identify overlap between the kind of commitment shown to football teams and the loyalty that is shown to product brands. A distinction is made in their paper between *calculative* and *normative* commitment. These, for Pimental and Reynolds, represent degrees of commitment, normative commitment being a stage at which the object, relevantly the football team, has become venerated or *sacralized* (ibid., p. 10). The devotion that is shown to a football club, sometimes by entire families, is viewed as reflective of normative, superstrength commitment. It is evident that in many families the role (typically) of the father is to engender commitment through linking family identity to the football team. Pimental and Reynolds take this to imply that the father is engendering strong commitment, a commitment that will perforce create sustained loyalty.

What is arguably missing from this analysis is a distinction between commitment and commitment devices. Familiar from the work of Elster (2000) and Schelling (1984), for example, is the identification of a range of commitment devices that people use to overcome short run temptations. In the example that Pimental and Reynolds draw on, it is more appropriate to see the expression of norms in the family context as a commitment device. It is because of the importance to the father of family loyalty to the team that he creates, albeit unwittingly, a powerful commitment device. There is a threat that failure to obey the family norm - that the family's team be shown unfailing allegiance - will result in the offender being rejected by the family. It is not strength of commitment that is doing the work in Pimental and Reynold's example but the commitment device. Underlying the behaviour of the family that is loyal to a particular team is commitment, but it is commitment that is best understood as, of its nature, contingent. It is an unspoken recognition of its contingency that makes the aggressive expression of family norms, and the sacred status of the team, so important. The latter are commitment devices.

Commitment appears, then, in standard accounts, to be viewed as a motivational characteristic that will, in the absence of countervailing forces, result in choice that accords with the expressed attitude. Addressing this cannot be a matter of importing into a discussion of the attitude-behaviour gap a ready-made conception of commitment from elsewhere. It is common elsewhere to understand commitment similarly, as a compelling motivational factor. This is the conception of commitment that we find in the important work in this area of, for example, Michael Bratman (1987), Edward McClennen (1990), and Amartya Sen (2007a, 2007b, 1977)). Bratman (1987, p. 109) considers commitment to be a characteristic of intention. Intentions, in Bratman's account, enable planned behaviour. Acting on prior intentions simplifies and so lowers the costs of deliberation. It also facilitates co-ordination among actors. What makes an intention a reliable guide to a person's future choices, and gives an intention purchase on personal conduct over time, is an associated commitment, a commitment to behave as intended. On this interpretation, the more credible intentions are those that are backed by less personally onerous commitments. This is an implication of the contrast Bratman makes (ibid., p. 2) between intentions that require strategic control (a padlocked fridge to encourage dieting, recalling Elster and Schelling, ibid.), and intentions that are easier to carry out, and that require less will power. An implication of this understanding of the nature of commitment is that it is possible to have an intention that requires no effort to carry out, but that is nonetheless backed by an attendant commitment. What is mistaken here, I would argue, once again, is that Bratman's interpretation fails to recognise the inherent contingency of commitment. It is appropriate to talk of commitment only where there is a possibility that the commitment may fail to inform actual choice. Compare what Roger Trigg says here (Trigg, 1973, Ch. 3) with regard to belief. For Trigg, to be committed to a belief entails the possibility of doubt, the possibility of the discovery of contrary evidence. Similarly, to be committed to a course of action, a political cause, and so on, is to recognise that countervailing forces may result in choices that do not conform to the commitment. The possibility of failure is what makes it appropriate to speak of commitment.

The inherent contingency of commitment is missing also from Edward McClennen's account. For McClennen, it is legitimate to work with commitment in, what he calls, an ideal sense (McClennen, 1990, p. 202). Once we set aside the possibility of weakness of will, it is legitimate to view commitment, in McClennen's view, as a resolve that will, with certainty, result in the kind of choice to which the person is committed. However, even if we set aside external and psychological obstacles, it is a necessary aspect of commitment that it might not successfully translate into actual choice.

Amartya Sen, in his work on commitment, presents it as a type of motivation, a type that need not derive its motivating force from a person's personal goals. It is possible, on Sen's account, to be committed to behavioural rules (see, in particular, his reply to Pettit in Sen, 2007b, pp. 349-352), and to be so committed in an unquestioning fashion. This, again, is a view of commitment that doesn't see the need to accommodate its inherent contingency. It is also interesting that in Richard Hare's work the idea of commitment is shorn of its contingent nature. For Hare, a genuine, positive evaluation of an object commits a person to the choice of that object if the occasion arises, and there are no obstacles (Hare, 1952, p. 20). While Hare's claim might be a legitimate logical thesis, concerning the logic of evaluation, we cannot, on the basis of this, help ourselves to an empirical thesis about the implications for actual commitment (cf. Wolff, 2011, pp. 32-33). Hare's thesis works only if we assume that it is legitimate to think of commitment as non-contingent, but this, I suggest, is something we cannot assume.

The Committed Volunteer and Moral Failure

By 'commitment' I understand the strength of resolve a person may have to remain faithful to an intention. Commitment is not, as in Sen's work, understood to be a kind of motivation. There will be an associated motivation but this accounts for the resolve, and the strength of the resolve. Motivation is distinct from commitment so understood. Indeed, the motivation for a particular resolve will be grounded in the positive evaluation, or *pro-attitude* a person has. The emphasis on commitment as strength of resolve carries with it the idea that the resolve, and so the commitment, may fail, and an intention not be carried out. Of course, it may be that no obstacles appear, so as to weaken or to challenge a person's resolve. However, it is, as I have suggested, inherent in the very idea of having a commitment that challenges may, indeed are expected to appear. Commitment is *necessarily* contingent in this sense. If it is the case that obstacles - temptations, and the pull of inclination, for example - are unlikely to stand in the way of a person carrying out her intentions, then it is inappropriate to speak of commitment. There is no need to be committed to something that can be achieved with ease.

What follows from the inherent contingency of commitment is the following condition: there must exist a level of incentive that makes a commitment at least in principle credible. The in principle credibility of commitment is to be distinguished from actual credibility. In the literature on pre-commitment (e.g. Elster, op. cit.), and on the commitment that is associated with the conduct of central bankers (Barro & Gordon, 1983) it is *actual* credibility that plays a central role. If a commitment is *in principle* credible, however, there is no presumption that the agent will in fact ultimately commit. On the other hand, if there does not exist any level of incentive that can, in principle, ensure committed choice (choice that is consistent with the commitment) then the commitment has no practical significance. Were a person to claim commitment to a course of action, and also say that no incentive could encourage that commitment in the face of, say, temptation, then the claimed commitment would have no bearing on the person's actual choices. It would be merely an empty claim, without practical import.

There must be a minimal incentive that makes a commitment, at least in principle, credible. Let us call this a minimum effective incentive (M). M represents an incentive that is just sufficient to secure commitment, in the face of countervailing forces. It is worth noting that M need not be financial. It might be an evocation of an initial ambition as a powerful reminder of the reason for the commitment. A person training for a charity marathon, for example, may need this kind of evocation on freezing cold mornings. If no amount of evocation of, say, the joy of completing the marathon is likely to secure continued commitment (if nothing will, in difficult moments, bind the person to the prior commitment) then the professed commitment has no practical significance.

This argument has implications for the way that we view the role of incentives in relation to personal commitment. The standard view tends to see incentives as a necessary evil, to be employed only when attitude and its attendant commitment have failed. The view I am recommending makes incentives a necessity even when positive attitudes are backed by genuine commitments.

All this points to the need to conceptualise the ethical consumer as a *committed volunteer* (cf. Foot, 1972, p. 315). Where there is commitment the agent volunteers it, she is not forced to commit. However, once a person is committed the nature of her engagement with ethical consumption changes. On the one hand the contingent nature of her commitment entails a need for incentives, but on the other hand it entails that a degree of personal responsibility must be accepted by the agent. To see this, note that the agent cannot legitimately require just any amount of incentive in order to remain faithful to her commitment. Her commitment entails a restriction on the level of incentive she can require. If she requires or demands greater incentive than M then she is claiming incentives that are greater than those that are needed to keep her committed (cf. Cohen, 1997). Incentives in excess of M ought to be unnecessary, given that the person claims to be committed. A person can, of course, withdraw her commitment (it is voluntary), but so long as she is committed she is, we should say, a committed volunteer - one who is constrained in the extent to which she can require incentives to ensure her attitudes inform her behaviour.

Equipped with the notion of the committed volunteer, we are in a position to introduce ethical considerations into our conception of agency. The dominant, we might say, *obstacle-based* view that we began with failed to make a place for ethical considerations, because of the way it characterised the agent. Reducing the attitude-behaviour gap to a conflict between discretion and compelling motivations made the removal of obstacles and the creation of incentives the natural response to the gap. Failure to act in a relevant way is, on the dominant view, due to a failure of incentives or disingenuous motives. It does not leave open the possibility of moral inconsistency or, what I am calling, moral failure on the part of the individual. The distinctions that have been brought into play in the characterisation of commitment allow for the possibility of moral failure.

Moral Failure

A central idea in the view of commitment being defended here is a minimum effective incentive, M. This is a necessary incentive, in the sense that anything less will not, even in principle, encourage the relevant behaviour. An associated distinction is that between a necessary incentive, M, and a non-necessary incentive. If the latter is required by an agent then he or she is asking for an incentive that is greater than that which is necessary to maintain the commitment. The justification for the additional incentive cannot appeal to a need for incentives per se. This is because only M can be appealed to as necessary from the point of view of incentives. The requirement of extra incentive must be supported by other another kind of reason. But what kind of reason might this be? It cannot be the same reason that supports the commitment, because this is consistent only with the person requiring the necessary incentive. The person must either reject this reason and so reject the prior commitment or else acknowledge that the reason for the extra incentive is inconsistent with his or her prior commitment. Once a person is committed he or she becomes a committed volunteer: someone whose appeal to incentives is constrained by prior commitment, and who is open to the charge of moral failure when he or she fails to act in a way that her attitudes lead us to expect.

Conclusion

A positive attitude towards ethical consumption will only lead a person to make ethical choices if he or she has an accompanying commitment. How we understand such commitment has implications for how we characterise and respond to a person who acts in a way that is inconsistent with his or her positive attitude. If we understand commitment as a compelling motivational factor then we will expect it to inform choice whenever countervailing considerations are absent. Where commitment does not ensue in relevant conduct we ought, on this account, to either doubt the credibility of the commitment or seek to secure greater incentives, to support the agent's resolve. What this does not make room for is moral criticism of a person who professes commitment yet fails to act in a concomitant way. The view that I have defended aims to make good this deficiency in the standard account. It is important to b able to accuse a person of moral weakness where that is the source of the behavioural discrepancy. If the conception of the agent, for purposes of analyses of the attitude-behaviour gap, does not allow for the possibility of moral failure, then an important aspect of people's conduct, in relation to ethical consumption, will be left unconsidered.

References Available on Request

Part 6 THE ROLE OF THE CORPORATION

6.1 Psychopaths, Inc.: On Corporate Personhood[178]

Joel Bakan

The bizarre notion that corporations are "persons" and thereby entitled to constitutional rights is under attack, thanks in part to Occupy Wall Street activism and the Supreme Court's controversial campaign finance decision in *Citizens United v. Federal Election Commission* (2010). New York and Los Angeles have passed resolutions condemning corporate personhood, joining a growing number of cities, and Senators Bernard Sanders (I-VT) and Mark Begich (D-Alaska) have proposed a constitutional amendment that would exclude for-profit corporations from the rights given to natural persons by the Constitution. Democracy is well served by these initiatives, but more is needed to curb significantly the power and malfeasance of corporations: we need to go beyond the *fact* that corporations are legally conceived as persons and address the *kind* of persons—psychopaths—that they are created by law to be.

> *We the People, Not We the Corporations*
> (Sign at an Occupy protest)

Through a strange legal alchemy, courts decided in the late nineteenth century that corporations deserved the same constitutional rights as human beings. Until then, corporate personhood had been understood as a mere legal fiction, a limited device for enabling companies to operate as economic actors. "A corporation is an artificial being, invisible, intangible, and existing only in contemplation of law," as

---

178 From The Occupy Handbook (Back Bay Books, 2012)

Chief Justice John Marshall held in 1819. "Being the mere creature of law, it possesses only those properties which the charter of its creation confers upon it."

The artificial being magically came to life in 1886, when the Supreme Court decided that corporate persons—"[no longer] imaginary or fictitious, but real; not artificial but natural," in the words of a contemporary lawyer—should have constitutional rights. Over the next two decades courts considered 288 Fourteenth Amendment claims by corporations (compared to just nineteen by African Americans, whom the Amendment was originally designed to protect). Well into the 1930s, the courts routinely nullified laws at the behest of corporations claiming constitutional rights violations. This era of pro-business judicial activism—called the Lochner era, after the 1905 case *Lochner v. New York*, which exemplified it—ended in 1937, when President Franklin D. Roosevelt threatened to add five judges to the Supreme Court in order to shield his reforms from judicial attack.

Citizens United heralds the Court's return to its Lochner-era ways. The case, which invoked the First Amendment to nullify restrictions on corporate political spending, "elevate[s] corporations to a level of deference which has not been seen at least since the [*Lochner*-era] days when substantive due process was regularly used to invalidate regulatory legislation thought to unfairly impinge upon established economic interests," according to Justice John Paul Stevens in his dissenting opinion (quoting, in turn, from Justice Byron R. White's dissenting opinion in *First National Bank of Boston v. Bellotti*, a political spending case decided in 1978). As such, *Citizens United* reflects a broader judicial trend. Sixty-one percent of the Roberts Court's decisions have been pro-business, according to a study by Lee Epstein, William Landes, and Richard Posner, compared to 51 percent for the Rehnquist Court (1986–2005), 47 percent for the Burger Court (1969–86), and 29 percent for the Warren Court (1953–69). "The Roberts Court is undeniably conservative," says Steven Shapiro, national legal director of the American Civil Liberties Union, "but it is a particular kind of conservatism. This is not a libertarian court. It is not a states' rights court. It is a pro-business court."

Amending the U.S. Constitution to bar corporations from having constitutional rights would help curb pro-business judicial decisions. But, importantly, the impact would go little beyond that. The United States would become more like other nations, where corporations have no, or very limited, constitutional rights; nonetheless, ill-gotten corporate gains would remain. The fact is that corporate power and malfeasance are not rooted in the Constitution, which is why excluding corporations from the benefits it confers can have only limited effects.

The *corporations'* constitution, on the other hand, its legally mandated character, is a major source of corporate-caused ills in the world today—and that is where the real work needs to be done.

Corporations are Psychopaths
(Sign at a rally on the first day of Occupy Wall Street)

Law not only confers personhood on corporations; it imbues them with unique personalities as well. The "best interests of the corporation" principle, a pillar of corporate law, compels managers and directors to prioritize corporate interests above others, to exploit anything in any way that might yield profits, and to ignore whatever ill effects befall others. Self-interest, in other words, is the overriding imperative for corporate action. That characteristic well equips corporations to create wealth for shareholders, and jobs and useful products for society, but it also makes them extremely dangerous institutions. Unable to feel genuine concern for others, experience guilt or remorse when they act badly, or have any sense of obligation to obey laws and ethical norms, corporate persons are, in effect, psychopathic beings.

Despite corporations' dangerous character, governments, especially over the last thirty years, have been in retreat from regulating and overseeing their behavior. Beguiled by free market ideology, and naively trusting corporations will do right, governments have rolled back regulatory restraints and promoted self-regulation as an alternative. The results have been disastrous, and include two recent crises— the 2008 financial meltdown and the 2010 Gulf of Mexico oil rig explosion—each a consequence of government's failure to rein in reckless corporate behavior. In hindsight, it was no surprise that financial institutions, driven by promises of huge profits and with few regulatory constraints in place to stop them, would carelessly grant risky loans, repackage the resulting debt as securities, and build exotic derivatives schemes. Nor was it a surprise that British Petroleum, a company with a string of serious environmental and safety infractions dating back at least to the 1990s (though strategically hidden by its carefully cultivated green image), would, if it could, cut corners to save money when constructing and operating its deep-sea wells. The same harmful dynamic has played out across numerous other areas—workers' rights and safety, children's well-being, consumer protection, and democratic processes, to name a few—as governments continue their retreat from effective regulatory roles.

That retreat is fueled in part, I believe, by dangerous misconceptions about the corporation's true nature. The concept of corporate social responsibility has evolved to suggest that corporations can care about social and environmental interests, not only profits. This has, in turn, fostered a belief, widely held among activists, governments, and business groups, that corporations can be trusted to regulate themselves and refrain from causing harm. They can, the logic goes, therefore be freed from regulatory restraints—deregulated—without risking bad behavior. "There has been a transfer of authority from the government to the corporation," as Samir Gibara, former chair and CEO of Goodyear Tire, describes it, "and the corporation needs to assume that responsibility; needs to really behave as a corporate citizen of the world; needs to assume the self-discipline that in the past, governments required from it." The notion that corporations, psychopathic at their institutional core, *can* be responsible, self-disciplined, and citizens of the world is oxymoronic. Yet it powerfully serves today to sugarcoat, and hence justify, governments' continuing retreat from regulation—the "transfer of authority from the government to the corporation," as Gibara calls it.

Psychopaths are notorious for masking their dangerously self-obsessed personalities with charm, and corporate psychopaths have made an art of it with social responsibility. It is crucial not to confuse the charm (carefully constructed by marketers and public relations practitioners) and the reality. Corporate social responsibility is—can only be, in light of the corporation's legally mandated nature—a *strategy* for serving corporations' ends, whether by warding off regulators, deflecting criticism, or attracting customers. It can never be an end in itself. That would be illegal. As a result, assuming a mantle of corporate social responsibility is, in essence, "like putting a good-looking girl in front of an automobile to sell an automobile," as the late Milton Friedman once told me. "That's not in order to promote pulchritude. That's in order to sell cars."

That helps explain why flagrant social *irresponsibility* is so often the handiwork of social responsibility's loudest advocates. Enron and AIG were paragons of corporate social responsibility before they collapsed, in 2001 and 2008, respectively, under the weight of reckless greed and criminality. Pfizer, a company intent on doing "more good for more people than any other company on the planet," as its former CEO Hank McKinnell once stated, was later revealed to be one of the world's worst corporate criminals. BP, a social responsibility leader—"Can business be about more than profits?" asked a prominent ad campaign, "We think so"— blatantly and routinely ignores safety and environmental standards, most destructively in connection with the above-mentioned oil rig explosion. And on it goes.

Governments, and the citizens who elect them, must give up on the fantasy of corporate benevolence and treat corporations for what they really are— psychopathic institutions, incapable of genuine social responsibility and unable to regulate themselves. That means requiring, *by law*, that they be socially responsible, not trusting and hoping that they will be. Restoring the ability and will of governments to protect public interests through democratically created and effectively enforced regulatory laws is, I believe, the best way to push back against corporate rule and malfeasance. To that end, I offer the following general prescriptions:

Government regulation should be reconceived, and relegitimated, as the principle means for bringing corporations under democratic control and ensuring that they respect the interests of citizens, communities, and the environment.

Regulations should be made more effective by staffing enforcement agencies at realisticlevels, setting fines sufficiently high to deter corporations from unlawful behavior, strengthening the liability of top directors and managers for their corporations' illegal behaviors, barring repeat offender corporations from government contracts, and suspending the charters of corporations that flagrantly and persistently violate the public interest.

Regulations designed to protect the environment and people's health and safety should be based upon the precautionary principle, which prescribes that corporations be prohibited from acting in ways that are reasonably likely to cause serious harm, even if definitive proof that such harm will occur does not exist.

Regulatory systems should be reformed to improve accountability and avoid "agency capture" by industry, which currently serves to undermine their integrity; and the "revolving-door" flow of personnel between government and business should be stopped. Though corporations have a place in representing their concerns to government and cooperating with government on policy initiatives, their current status as "partners" with government endangers the democratic process. At a minimum, their influence should be scaled back to a degree commensurate with that of other organizations, such as unions and environmental, consumer, and human rights groups.

Elections should be publicly financed, and corporate political expenditures phased out (in light of *Citizens United*, this would require a constitutional amendment, such as Senators Sanders and Begich propose, or a reversal by the Supreme Court in some future case). Additionally, electoral reforms that might bring new voices into the political system and encourage disillusioned citizens to return to it, such as a move to proportional representation, should be pursued.

Most importantly, we need to embrace a subversive truth—that corporations are our creations. They have no lives, no powers, and no capacities beyond what we, through the governments we elect, give them. That is why it is our fundamental right—indeed, our duty as citizens in a democracy—to limit their actions in the name of public interests.

Bibliography

 The bizarre notion that corporations are "persons": Most ideas and some key passages in this essay are based upon passages in *The Corporation*; one or two passages draw upon *Childhood Under Siege*.

"The Roberts Court is undeniably conservative": ACLU, "Supreme Court Ends Pro-Business Term with Important First Amendment Rulings,"Senators Bernard Sanders (I-VT) and Mark Begich (D-Alaska): Senate Joint Resolution 33; see http://thehill.com/images/stories/blogs/flooraction/Jan2011/sjres33.pdf.

 one of the world's worst corporate criminals: Pfizer received the largest criminal fine in history, $1.3 billion. Collins v. Pfizer Inc., 04-11780, U.S. District Court, District of Massachusetts. See, for instance, Cary O'Reilly, "Pfizer Pays Record $1.3 Billion Penalty for Drug Misbranding," Bloomberg, October 17, 2009.

Sixty-one percent of the Roberts Court's decisions: Lee Epstein, William M. Landes, and Richard A. Posner, "Is the Roberts Court Pro-Business?," December 17, 2010, http://epstein.usc.edu/research/RobertsBusiness.pdf; see also Adam Liptak, "Justices Offer Receptive Ear to Business Interests," *New York Times*, December 18, 2010.

Photo by Miriam Kennet during Occupy Protest, St Pauls Cathedral

6.2 Mergers, downsizing and labor relations: rebalancing global business power

Maria Alejandra Caporale Madi

Among the main changes in the global financial scenario, the emergence of private equity funds as major transnational employers has resulted from new global business models where companies are managed and traded in order to get short-term returns (Klier et al., 2009).   . Private equity funds currently centralize endowments from banks, institutional investors - also pension funds- and high net worth individuals in order to assume a key-role in high profit investment buyouts.

These new investment practices have been overwhelmed by the financialisation of wealth that has reinforced "short-termism" in American and European business. As a consequence of a global wave of mergers and acquisitions, workers have been confronted with over more than U.S. $ 1 trillion in concentrated buyout power (IUF, 2007). In Great Britain, for example, 1 of every 5 employees has been working for a company owned by private equity funds since the middle 2000s (BVCA, 2006).

This chapter fosters a greater understanding of the social and economic challenges to rebalance the global business power. Why private equity matters to think alternatives to rebalance the economy? Private equity funds have significant impact both on how companies are run and in the current business environment. On behalf of the role that private equity investors play in many companies' board of directors, higher expectations for short-term profits subordinate the evolution of labor relations. Among larger companies, private investment funds have been mainly responsible for mergers and acquisitions—a process that can also favor increasing unemployment. Besides, as the private equity fund - as an investment group- decides to sell a business, managers of private equity firms can adopt downsizing strategies with layoffs and other cutbacks to improve the balance sheet and make the company's short- term profits more attractive to potential buyers. Indeed, short-term returns under this model can come at the expense of good jobs, secure pension plans, higher investments in operations and product development, and the upskilling and training of workers (Blum, 2008).

First, we give a brief overview of the global business model based on mergers and downsizing. Secondly, we present the scope of downsizing policies. In the third section we discuss the challenges to rebalance global business power and wealth.

1. Private equity funds and a new global business model

Private equity funds are a global financial phenomenon. These funds use a combination of equity and debt to access pension funds, insurance companies and endowments of wealthy people to invest in companies that are not traded publicly. Private equity funds articulate the operation of firms and, consequently, affect the competitive features of different markets. Their business strategies, based on capital centralization and high leverage, have been favoured by the expansion of global liquidity since 2003.

Looking backward, since the end of the 1980s, Michael C. Jensen (1989) encouraged the emergence of private equity firms to resolve the longstanding conflict of interests between owners and managers in corporate control issues within public companies. As a matter of fact, Jensen believed that takeovers and leveraged buyouts by private equity funds can favor the emergence of new business models where resources could be managed more effectively. Indeed, in his view, the monitoring role of private equity investors could exert pressure on underperforming managers in order to achieve targeted goals.

Our concern relies on those views that understand the emergence of private equity industry as revolutionizing corporate ownership by creating new funding options and corporate governance structures, as well as by providing investors with attractive, long-term investment opportunities. Indeed, buyout investment decisions by private equity funds must be analyzed in a context of capitalist speculative finance where the accumulation of private wealth is the targeted goal of investors. Assets, debts, cash flows, mergers and acquisitions overwhelm the investment decision process where private equity firms are viewed as a set of assets in which operation divisions may be bought or sell in order to pursue short-term profits. Indeed, in the context of the assets of a private equity fund, a company acquisition (investment buyout) depends on expectations on the extraction of short-run cash-flows, mainly anticipated dividends and non–equity based fees soon after the buyout transaction. To achieve this goal, the typical private equity buyout firm *presents a business plan characterized by cost reduction* (Tannon and Johnson, 2005). Besides cost reduction, a higher debt ratio aimed to improve short-term cash flows before selling the firm three to five years later, either publicly or to another investor. Indeed, the private equity business model shortens the maturation of investments since the relevance of exit conditions reveals that investors are looking after capital mobility and high returns.

2. The scope of rationalization strategies

As private equity firms are responsible for employment standards among tens of millions of workers worldwide, the impact of private equity investments on working conditions has been raising growing concerns. Indeed, the deleterious social impacts of "rationalization" strategies have been less explored by academic researchers while most studies developed by private companies and organizations have only reported cases of success (Cressy et al, 2007). Labor unions and many academics have a less favorable view on private equity funds—criticizing buyouts for job losses and lower benefits for workers. A leveraged buyout differs fundamentally from a traditional merger or acquisition in two important ways. First, the acquired company pays the cost of its own acquisition through debt and fees (Table 1). Secondly, as private equity investors are aggressive in pursuit of short-term profits, managers are committed to restructuring programs (Montgomerie, 2008). Indeed, as downsizing practices are not implemented by investors (owners), the expected financial targets put pressure on managers. As a result, this business model favors downsizing and cost reduction at the expense of employment. While labor costs are frequently considered large expense items, managers must tightly control those costs in order to minimize risk of non-achieving the investors' expected goals.

Table 1 U.S. acquisitions: leverage ratio

Private Equity Firm	Leverage Ratio
Madison Dearbon Partners	11.8
Providence Equity Partners	11.0
Blackstone Group	10.6
Thomas H. Lee Partners	10.3
Carlyle Group	9.6
Goldman Sachs Group	9.5
Apollo Management	9.1
TPG	8.2
Bain Capital	7.8

Note: (1) US acquisitions: more than US$100 million from January, 1, 2005 to September, 12, 2007; (2) Leverage ratio: Average amount of debt committed to an acquisition relative to the target´s EBITDA.
Source: Jason Kelly, "Madison Dearbon Beats Blackstone, Goldman Sachs as Deals Stall", Bloomberg, Oct. 1, 2007.

As managers are committed to short- term profits and the payment of debt, the private equity firms must subordinate labor and employment relations to efficiency targets. Under the private equity firms' business model, the generation of cash flows to pay non–equity based fees, dividends and debts after the takeover has usually require growing cost reductions with deep effects on labor relations, employment trends and social rights and benefits. As a matter of fact, the changing working conditions result from a *continuous restructuring* in order to generate cash outflow. In this downsizing setting, the levels of productive investment fall while sell-offs and closures turned out to be decided regardless of productivity and profitability. Besides, those restructuring programs reshape workers' tasks, promoting turnover, outsourcing and casual work (IUF, 2007). Workforce displacement and the loss of rights are also part of the spectrum of management alternatives aimed to cost reduction. Montgomerie (2008) gives outstanding examples of the changing investment and working conditions in Germany and the UK. Evidences show that managers generally use operating cash flow to repay the debt and this fact lead to a declining investment in research, development and new capital equipment. In addition, labor is the main focus of cost saving measures, first through longer working hours, then the abolition of holiday pay and finally through the reduction in the workforce and the displacement of workers.

3. Current global business and labor relations
Private equity funds´ ability to acquire control of underperforming corporations has fostered the   control over the global production of products and services. Managers of private equity firms have constantly reshaped the degree of monopoly and productive capacity in a variety of industries. Consequently, investment and employment trends have been subordinated to ownership changes, financial restructuring and company efficiency. As Keynes warned, finance regulates the pace of investment, while the pace of investment determines income and employment. Thus, the dynamics of investment and employment is currently being discussed primarily in financial terms. Private equity firms are viewed as a set of assets that has to be financed and in which operation divisions may be bought or sell in order to pursue short-term profits, while the portfolios of product lines follow the same rule. The adjustment on the labor force, in the context of rationalization strategies, aims to improve next quarter´s profits. Thos e workers who are left are supposed to carry the burden by increasing productivity.

Analyzing the general transformations in the capital accumulation process, Bauman (2000:122) states:

"The downsizing obsession is, as it happens, an undetachable complement of the merger mania…. Merger and downsizing are not at cross-purposes: on the contrary, they condition each other, support and reinforce. This only appears to be a paradox….. It is the

blend of merger and downsizing strategies that offers capital and financial power the space to move and move quickly, making the scope of its travel even more global, while at the same time depriving labour of its own bargaining and nuisance-making power, immobilizing it and tying its hands even more firmly."

Indeed, in spite of the euphemism of "rationalization strategies", the outcomes are not socially acceptable since the restructuring programs have put pressure on social and economic protections for all workers (IUF, 2008). Trade union organizations and social allies have been committed to fight for regulations that safeguard the public interest, support quality employment and generate productive jobs. As a result, metalworkers and their unions have developed strategies to counteract the potential excesses of leveraged buyouts and to protect the interests of workers and their communities. For example, affiliates of the International Metalworkers' Federation (IMF) have developed counter strategies through collective bargaining to defend employment and working conditions, maintain pensions and secure investments, and to influence conditions of potential leveraged buyouts. These approaches have evolved over time as trade unions carefully account for institutional, legal and industry factors in order to enhance their effectiveness (IUF, 2008)

Besides, important features of these approaches have also been used in the automotive, aerospace and mechanical engineering industries, After Dana filed for bankruptcy in the U.S. in 2006, the company tried to cancel labor contracts. In this scenario, the UAW (United Automotive Workers) and the United Steel Workers (USW) avoided a labor dispute (Blum, 2008). The bargaining led to successful outcomes which included the limitation of the leverage ratio of the company; expansion of the rights of unorganized workers, among others.

Other examples also show the importance of counteracting the global business power of private equity firms. In 2007, in the context of the acquisition by Cerberus of Chrysler, in which Daimler retained a 20 per cent stake, the United Auto Workers (UAW), Canadian Auto Workers (CAW) along with IG Metall insisted on the importance that the new ownership and company structure contribute to a sustainable future for the Chrysler Group. As a consequence of these demands, collective bargaining ensured continuity of negotiated protections of workforce terms and employment conditions - including pension and healthcare provisions (Blum, 2008).

In the UK, among the trade unions' initiatives, Unite have set out concrete demands upon the sale by Ford of Jaguar and Land Rover in order to impact the decision of the eventual buyer. As a result, within the conditions of sale to Tata Motors in 2008 we can highlight a) the continuation of existing arrangements for trade union bargaining; b) the protection of workforce terms and employment conditions- including pension arrangements; c) the protection of long-term production, development, investment and sourcing commitments from Ford and Tata.

Rebalancing global business power: an agenda

The apprehension of the meaning and dynamics of the recent spread of private equity funds is decisive to the understanding of the social impacts of a new business model in contemporary capitalism. Beyond our argument is that capital accumulation driven by profit and competition involves social relations. As private equity investors search for liquidity and short-term profits, managers' decisions have turned out to challenge social and economic sustainability. In this scenario, mergers, acquisitions and downsizing strategies have submitted the livelihood conditions of millions of workers around the world. As Bauman warned, livelihood conditions turn out to be overwhelmed by uncertainly because of the flexibility required by mergers and downsizing strategies. In his own words,

"Flexibility is the slogan of the day, and when applied to the labor market it augurs an end to the " job as we know it", announcing instead the advent of work on short-term contracts, rolling contracts or no contracts, positions with no in-built security but the "until further notice" clause. Working life is saturated with uncertainty" (Bauman, 2000:147)

Considering this background, rebalancing the current global business power requires changes in the business model under the private equity funds. Globally, although the number of people living in absolute poverty has decreased, income inequality has increased both between countries and within countries. Indeed, strategies and practices of private equity firms support a business model where the concentration of private wealth configures social interactions for the continuation of surplus extraction, obtained from the working population (Foster, 2006).

Among the main issues of an agenda to change the global business scenario, we can highlight:

1) **Transparency on key aspects of business operations**. There are needs to be transparency in reporting on performance, risk management and fee structure. There are also needs to be transparent on rewards and executive pay. In the context of takeovers, transparency must mean full access to:

a) The private equity business plan: exit strategy; plans for selloffs/closures; utilization of company cash-flows and reserves, financial assets and intangible assets; sale and possible lease-back of real estate; availability and sources of funds for investment in plant and equipment, research and training; projected changes in employment relations, pension funds/ retirement benefits and collective bargaining.

b) Audited financial accounts disclosing: the total amount of the debt incurred in purchasing the company; the types and maturities of the debt; the rates (floating or fixed) and schedules; the identities of the lenders/holders of the debt securities if they are not publicly traded; the fees paid for the takeover operation (IUF, 2008).

2) **Tax regulation** needs to be reshaped to avoid a bias toward short-term investor behavior - including tax deductibility of debt service, tax on capital gains made of the sale of assets and tax havens.

3) **Corporate governance** should favor long term value creation and reinforce the responsibility and powers of the boards of directors to preserve long-term interests of companies under private equity regime. Such regulation could include the following: measures to discourage short-termism; greater transparency and public reporting requirements; more supervision by public authorities; limits to levered credit; taxation of capital gains made on the sale of assets; enforcement of relevant employer obligations (ITUC, 2007).

4) **Financial stability** should be fostered by improving open information and by the reduction of leverage ratios in private equity firms (Amicus, 2007).

References

Amicus (2007) Memorandum of Evidence to Treasury Select Committee Inquiry into Private Equity.

Bauman, Z. (2000) *Liquid Modernity*. USA. Polity Press.

Blum, R. (2008) *Leveraged buyouts, private equity and restructuring in the metal sector.* Special Report. Metal World , Available at
 http://www.imfmetal.org/files/08090411533679/special_report.pdf

BVCA, 2005. *The economic impact of Private Equity in the UK 2005*. British Venture Captial Associaton Report, London.

Cressy, Roberto, Munari, Federico and Malipiero, Alessandro (2007)   Creative destruction? UK Evidence that buyouts cut jobs to raise returns. (October 30). *Working Paper Series.* Available at SSRN: http://ssrn.com/abstract=1030830

Foster, John Bellamy. "Monopoly-Finance Capital." *Monthly Review* 58 (December 2006): 1-14.

Hill, James M. and Gambaccini, John S. (2003) The Private Equity Paradox: When Is Too Much Control a Bad Thing?. *Journal of Private Equity.* Summer,   Vol. 6 Issue 3, p37.

International Union of Food, Agricultural, Hotel, Restaurant, Catering, Tobacco and Allied Workers´ Association –IUF (2007) *A Workers´Guide to private Equity Buyouts*. Geneve.

International Union of Food, Agricultural, Hotel, Restaurant, Catering, Tobacco and Allied Workers´ Association –IUF (2008) Private Equity Buyouts: A Trade Union View. Public Hearing on Hedge Funds and Private Equity - Committee on Economic and Monetary Affairs of the European Parliament. Brussels.

ITUC- CSI   (2007) Labour and the Shifting Power Equation: Statement of Labour Leaders to the World Economic Forum Annual Meeting Davos, 24-28 January. Available at http://www.ituc-csi.org/IMG/pdf/WEF_Statement_-_Labour_and_the_Shifting_Power_Equation_-_Rev_EN.pdf

Jensen, M. (1989) The eclipse of public corporation. *Harvard Business Review.* (Sept.-Oct.), revised 1997.

Klier, D., Welge, M and Harrigan, K. (2009) The Changing Fface of Private Equity: How Modern Private Equity Firms Manage Investment Portfolios. Journal of Private Equity. Vol. 12 issue 4, Fall

Montgomerie, J. (2008) Labour and the Locusts: Private Equity's Impact on the Economy and the Labour Market, *Conference Report of the Seventh British-German Trades Union Forum*, London, Anglo-German Foundation for the Study of Industrial Society, July.

Tannon, Jay M. and Johnson, Robin (2005) Transatlantic Private Equity: Beyond a Trillion Dollar Force. *Journal of Private Equity*, Summer, Vol. 8 Issue 3, p77-80.

Tate, A. The Effect of Private Equity Takeovers on Corporate Social Responsibility, International Officer, Australian Council of Trade Unions   16 May 2007 available at http://www.accsr.com.au/pdf/pet_speech_Alison_Tate.pdf

Uni Global Union (2008). *Pension Fund Investment in Private Equity*. Report.

6.3 Sustainability Reporting Requirements as a Value Added Tool: Do Stakeholders Really Care About the Environment?

Constance J. Crawford, MBA, CPA

Introduction

The world has embraced green as the desired color of the overall economy…..green for the environment, that is, and not green for the color of money. Business leaders point to the importance of sustainability and the resulting value created by the implementation of environmental and societal goals as a means to corporate success. Corporations are essentially blending sustainability initiatives into their corporate strategies as an indication of their commitment to environmentally sound business practices. The issues are varied and include topics ranging from climate control to clean technology. The stakeholders range from financial to regulatory to social and, all of these disparate users, have very different goals. In addition, the descriptions used in the reporting process are as disparate, alternating from Corporate Social Responsibility to Triple Bottom Line Reports relating to people, planet and profit (O'Rourke, 2011). But what do these terms and concepts really mean to the investor? Are they really leading indicators of the long-term sustainability of the corporation issuing the report? Or are these entities merely complying with socially acceptable behavior in response to government mandated reporting requirements?

In 2002, reporting guidelines stemming from the Global Reporting Initiative, provided the foundation for corporate sustainability reporting requirements (Ballou, Heitger, Landes, 2006). The Global Reporting Initiative was in response to a worldwide outcry by stakeholders demanding disclosure pertaining to environmental issues. The importance of nonfinancial data in helping to assess the future viability of an entity became what has been termed: "The Value Reporting Revolution: Moving Beyond the Numbers Earnings Game" (PriceWaterhouseCoopers, 2012). At this point, the accounting industry created triple bottom line reporting which infused corporate sustainability factors into their bottom line.

Sustainability reporting requirements

The purpose in providing stakeholders with information relating to the impact the green economic initiative has had on a particular company is the goal of sustainability reporting. Unfortunately, the reporting process is complex and confusing according to many in the worldwide corporate arena (Wilson, 2012). The primary concern of many in the sustainability reporting world is the fear that many reports are merely "green washing" the impact of environmental issues on corporate bottom or triple lines (Wilson, 2012). The ability of corporations to interpret vague guidelines to provide the appearance of transparency is a continuing concern for all stakeholders. The role of the report is to enable analysts to ascertain how value is being created through compliance with government mandated requirements. The impact of burning carbon, overusing fresh water supplies and climate change issues need to be woven into the reporting process accurately (Baue, 2013).

Unfortunately, Wall Street and the worldwide economy does not provide positive incentives to the self-reporting of "bad news." Corporations have historically been rewarded by the financial reporting community to "accentuate the good and disguise the bad". Sustainability issues pertaining to the environment, social and employee matters, human rights and anti-corruption and bribery are the broad spectrum of topics that fall under the sustainability reporting spectrum. How a corporation or reporting entity accurately reports these varied issues and their resulting impact on value continues to be debated throughout the worldwide economy. The need for the report to be forward looking is one of the universally agreed upon guidelines. Unfortunately, due to disparate international reporting requirements and guidelines the ability for stakeholders to effectively compare sustainability reports among various entities is limited at best. In addition, there is no standardized reporting framework in place, which further undermines the sustainability reporting process (Passant, Hewitt, 2013).

In March 2014 the Investor Network on Climate Risk issued a report entitled: Investor Listing Standard Proposal: Recommendations for Stock Exchange Requirements on Corporate Sustainability Reporting with the following disclosure requirements:

1.   Governance and Ethical Oversight

2.   Environmental Impact

3.   Government Relations and Political Involvement

4.   Climate Change

5.   Diversity

6.   Employee Relations

7.   Human Rights

8.   Product and Service Impact and Integrity

9.   Supply Chain and Subcontracting

10.   Community and Community Relations

The report stated that the disclosure should include both quantitative and qualitative information to better provide the transparency desired. These topics were selected because of the perceived risk and opportunity associated with each of these broad spectrum areas.

Most large corporations throughout the worldwide economy have abided by the reporting requirements first mandated in the beginning of the 21st century and continue to willingly participate in providing sustainability reports. But whether these reports provide the most accurate and transparent data continues to be a problematic issue for all the varied stakeholders.

Sustainability Reports: Do they Add Value

Stakeholders need assurance concerning the future viability of a reporting entity regarding profitability, growth, value, rights and obligations. Integral to the reporting process is the assurance provided by the independent auditor regarding the financial information provided by the reporting entity. Clearly, relevant and accurate financial data pertaining to revenue, expenses, assets, liabilities and net worth provide value to the stakeholders. But, does sustainability reporting provide equally valuable financial data to the investment community? Social responsibility and the need to think "green" is a popular worldwide sentiment from a social perspective but does it provide valuable information during economic downturns? Prior to the 2007 United States financial collapse, the cost to comply with a greener environment was viewed as a necessity. However, once corporate profits began to decline, that cost was no longer a necessity but rather became a luxury. The relative cost of the public good at the expense of economic growth has become a focal point to stakeholders in a problematic economy. The support for environmentally sound policies diminish when the economy falters. Stakeholders view the environment as a public good which should be paid for by businesses through government regulations (Jacobe, 2012). Unfortunately, once businesses decline and their ability to underwrite the cost of the public good is diminished, public support declines accordingly. As unemployment rates rise, public support of environmental sustainability costs dissipates (Jacobe, 2012).

Therefore, it appears that stakeholders and society, in general, only really care about sustainability issues pertaining to the environment when the overall economy can support the additional costs necessitated by compliance. Once the economy falters and businesses can no longer afford to comply with costly government regulated mandates, the public no longer perceives these mandates as a priority. The cost of environmental compliance fades when society stumbles as the worldwide economy struggles. The previous thirty year trend in society prioritizing "the environment, even at the risk of curbing economic growth" disappeared when the worldwide economy began its downward descent beginning in 2007 (Jacobe, 2012). Apparently, once the economy declines, the perceived value added by sustainability issues disappears along with corporate profits. If sustainability issues were truly perceived as value adding corporate initiatives that value would not evaporate merely because profits were on the decline.

The risk associated with non-compliance of sustainability issues is one of the primary drivers in the reporting process. However, once an economy is in decline, the risk factors pertaining to ineffective sustainability reports are no longer the focus of the stakeholders as risk factors change from environmental to economic. Clearly, the fickleness of the international financial community pertaining to the importance of sustainability reporting in a declining economy undermines the concept of sustainability issues as a value added component to the financial statement report.

Conclusion

The concept of sustainability is an extremely important one for the long term viability of all members of society. All aspects pertaining to both environmental and societal issues are captured under this broad yet vague term. The only way corporations will continue in their efforts to provide a sustainable environment for their entities is if society, as a whole, demands such behavior. These concerns cannot become less significant as profitability comes into question. The idea of sustainability as a mandate for corporate success must become an integral component of determinants of success regardless of whether the bottom or triple lines are negatively impacted (Wilson, 2012). Until society demands sustainable behaviors on the part of all corporations...the effort will ultimately fail. Many US based corporations opt for "off-shore manufacturing" as a more affordable venue in light of the stringent manufacturing restrictions placed upon domestic manufacturers. This cost reduction techniques enhances the corporate profitability, yet clearly undermines the intent of a sustainable environment.

 A corporation should not merely comply with a regulation, but rather embrace the concept for its intended goal. This lofty ideal cannot be accomplished unless there is a reward for acceptable sustainable behaviors rather than merely a reward for cost reduction and profit enhancing activities. It is essential that sustainability reporting requirements contain specific standards so that the stakeholders can assess actual compliance rather than mere future intentions. Currently, sustainability reporting focuses on ideals and strategy rather than the ultimate impact corporations' activities have on the achievement of a sustainable environment for all mankind.

References

Ballou, B., Heitger,D., Landes,C., "The Future of Corporate Sustainability Reporting, Journal of Accountancy, Dec 2016.

Confino, J., "What's the Purpose of Sustainability Reporting?" The Guardian, May 2013.

Edwards, J., "Critically Discuss the Value of 'Sustainability Reports' and the Need to be Accountable for Environmental Impacts," Feb 2014, http://jamieedwards1.hubpages.com/hub/

Jacobe, D., "Americans Still Prioritize Economic Growth Over Environment" Gallup Poll, March 2012, http://www.gallup.com/pol/153515/

Koehler, D., "How Materiality Drives Improved Sustainability Reporting" GreenBiz.com, Jan 2014, http://www.greenbiz.com/print/56041

Margolis, J., "A First Look Inside the New GRI G4" Grenbiz.com, May 2013. http://www.greenbiz.com/print/52371

Minan, P., Hickox, J., Gimigliano, J., "Sustainability Reporting-What You Should Know" www.KPMG.com

O'Rourke, J., "Getting to Green Profit: The Executive's Guide to Oracle Applications", Oracle's Solutions for Sustainability Reporting, May 2011.

Passant, F., Hewitt,G., "What Do Investors Expect From Non-Financial Reporting?", The Association of Chartered Accountants, June 2013.

PricewaterhouseCoopers LLP. "Do Investors Care About Sustainability? Seven Trends Provide Clues," 2012. http://www.pwc.com/en_US/us/corporate-sustainability-climate-change/assets/investors-and-sustainability.pdf

Wilson, A., "Adding Value Through Sustainability Reporting" Corporate Citizenship, July 2012

Part 7 Globalisation and Trade

7.1 The WTO: friend or foe in the process of re-greening?
Its origins, mechanisms and potential

Helene Albrecht

'Arguing against globalisation is like arguing against the law of gravity'
Kofi Annan, UN Secretary-General

Introduction

The level and impacts of globalisation we are facing today had never happened was it not for a sophisticated and comprehensive backing-up through the World Trade Organisation (WTO) and its Agreements. The preambles of the latter reflect genuine hopes and aspirations further trade liberalisation was meant to achieve. While non-discrimination and equal treatment as traditional key principles of free trade have been realised to some extent, globalisation for many has turned to be associated with increasing unemployment, recession and degradation of our natural environment. (World Trade Organisation, 1999)

This chapter seeks to trace the origins of the WTO in its economic-political context while summarising the main historical stages and referring to sources which allow for a deepened understanding of the described developments. It then explores the working mechanisms of some of the agreements which have been negotiated in the course of the Uruguay Round 1994 , focussing on those that are most relevant in respect of green economics, their interconnectivity and inherent conflicts as they are reflected in case law. Though within these trade disputes rifts and cracks in the system become notable and were apt of achieving most striking paradigm shifts in response to past lacks in transparency, legitimacy and accountability of the WTO if properly recognised and managed by society at large. In particular the SPS Agreement, TBT Agreement and the Safeguard Agreement point to the need for new insights and call for interaction of different legal regimes. While for many the global economy bears nothing but chagrin, multinational trading partners are confronted with returning regionalism, the renaissance of sovereign confidence and the appreciation of cultural differences. In this context a body of critical and progressive writing has evolved which seeks to explore the WTO's potential for sustainable economic activities and prudent management of our global resources. The chapter will provide an overview about these new approaches, point to potential translations into concepts of green economics and conclude with some philosophical considerations of the evolutionary value and mission the WTO has imposed upon the global community.

Some general remarks on international trade

The endeavour to organise and regulate international trade in modern Western societies dates back to times of mercantilism and becomes most obvious in the second half of the 19th century: the progressive removal of trade barriers and tariffs in order to allow for the undistorted movement of goods resulting from industrialisation brought unexpected economic expansion with the side effects of unforeseen wealth creation and increasing social division within European nations. (Gerber, 1998) Several precursors of contemporary trade management can be traced: a preferential regional pact between England and France, increasing pressure on Germany as main trading partner and provider of capital, Corn Laws to protect cereal producers in England and Ireland from foreign imports and exportable surpluses of foodstuff which resulted in disproportionate population growth without being able to establish long term food security were accompanied by the rise of protectionism and corresponding competition law.(Keynes, 1920)

After the First World War the League of Nations launched further attempts to beware from cartelisation and monopolies; however, from a contemporary perspective the aggressive powers of a failing economy were devastatingly underestimated and inevitably resulted into the next catastrophe. The never completed attempt to establish the Havana Carter in 1947 after World War 2 for the economic benefit of all nations unified for a short period of time socialist, Marxist, republican and liberal concepts of many shades and variations before left and right, East and West moved apart and left Western countries with the General Agreement on Trade and Tariffs 1949 which would though re-negotiated in several subsequent rounds and govern trade as a de facto organisation until 1994. (Gerber, 2010; Lang, 2011) The Uruguay Round setting up the WTO Agreement coincided with the breakdown of the Cold War regime and subsequently rather reacted to new market opportunities than to simultaneous international calls for economic re-thinking following findings of the Brundtland Report 1987 and the Rio Declaration in 1992 (Scott, 2004). What is more: looking at the drafting process which eventually started with trade inefficient shortcomings following the Tokyo Round in 1973, the Uruguay Round can rather be understood as intensifier of the widening rift between trade and environmental priorities. (Lang, 2012; Kulovesi, 2012)

The trade and environment divide

Since the establishment of the GATT economic activities have been strictly separated from environmental considerations, a fact that interestingly is also mirrored in the division between human rights and trade. Two of the most illuminating conflicts are the *Tuna-Dolphin* (1991) case and the *Shrimp-Turtle* case (2001) which set trade and environmental protection ambitions into direct confrontation and found their resolution in the further deepening of a divide as will be illustrated below. Serious environmental concerns had also addressed the impacts of chemicals as food additives and main pollutants of air, water and soil while at the same time the latter were building blocks of post war economies and conferred strength and economic power in particular to Europe and the US. While Rachel Carson and her 'Silent spring' experienced fierce opposition and accusations, the UN Stockholm Conference in 1972 and a concurrent first 'Communication of the European Commission on the Protection of the Environment' were able to put environmental protection on the official Agenda. Success became soon obvious and has repercussions until these days: the river Rhine today invites to bathing and fishing and several European countries are pesticide free zones. However, the oil crisis in 1973 raising serious energy security concerns distracted attention: an increased reliance on nuclear energy and better coordination of OECD countries permitted re-enforced business as usual. The incapacity to link one problem with the other, in other words to establish correlative or causal relationships between the environmental and the economic crisis tragically returned back into conscience after the major incidents of Chernobyl and Seveso and urged the well known Brundtland Report in 1987 which in essence reiterated and expanded on a prognosis the Club of Rome had announced under the heading 'limits to growth' as early as 1969. While growing population, the choice of energy, environmental degradation, desertification and pollution clearly appealed to politicians and civil society across the Globe at the same time Europe became overwhelmed by the end of the Cold War and the US experienced a political shift both having sharp implications on domestic legal systems and the emergence of new forms of global governance. (Lynch and Vogel, 2001)

Culmination in the Uruguay Round: the making of a new global economic order

'Globalisation by itself is morally neutral', it can be good or bad, depending on the kind of content we give to it.'
Vaclav Havel, former Czech President

The US fierce commitment to environmental protection throughout the 60s and 70s has been almost forgotten since the country refuses to ratify Multilateral Environmental Agreements such as the Kyoto Protocol, the Convention on Biodersity, the Protocol on Biosafety and others. Keleman describes the former position as 'leading' and gives accounts of the extent of its engagement which from 1990 onwards was continued by the EU, the latter turning its environmental commitment even into a comparative advantage with harmonising effects on its trading partners (Keleman, 2010) However, early case law under the GATT describes the circumvention with which the US Government tried to protect scarce and exhaustive resources and the limitations which were imposed on this endeavour for the benefit of unrestricted free trade. In the case of *Dolphin-Tuna* the Panel was asked to decide about compatibility of the Marine Mammal Protection

Act 1972 which imposed import bans on tuna products which were not caught with dolphin saving fishing methods. From a legal perspective the case challenged the breadth of Art XX of the GATT which allows for 'general exceptions' from the obligations under the agreement. Providing an exhaustive list of headings including protection of human health and public moral permits derogations, the 'US stood virtually alone in its insistence that Article XX allows scope for unilateral trade measures to protect the environment'.(Hudec, 1996) Mexico and Venezuela won the case in 1991 and 1992 on grounds that the US import restriction were neither justified nor necessary to 'protect human, animal or plant life or health', or 'relating to the conservation of exhaustible natural resources if such measures are made effective in conjunction with restrictions on domestic production or consumption.' The reasoning was expanded on in *US –Gasoline* when 'clean air' was acknowledged to be an 'exhaustible natural resource' and discussed the validity of a US measure setting a baseline for refined petroleum adversely affecting imports from Brazil and Venezuela. The AB required that even though a measure would qualify as one of the exemptions under Art XX of the GATT, it must not result in 'arbitrary and unjustified discrimination' between domestic and imported goods and be a 'disguised restriction on international trade. Having decided the case in direct succession of the Uruguay Round the AB insisted that 'not [...] the ability of any WTO Member to take measures to control air pollution or, more generally, to protect the environment, is at issue.' Though in *EC-Asbestos* and *US-Shrimp 21.5* the environmental exceptions under the GATT Art XX were invoked by the AB, for Sanford Gaines the cases reflect 'the larger controversies over the trade-environment relationship [...]' The author associates public reactions and clash of values as expressed in Seattle in 1999 with most politicians' decline to 'exercise strong leadership to bridge the differences on the domestic as well as the international level.' Because the issues were complex and divisive on the domestic as well as the international level, most politicians had declined to 'exercise strong leadership to bridge the differences.'

The preamble of the WTO Agreements mentions the goal of sustainable development; it is also reiterated in the Doha Development Ministerial Declaration and in documents constituting cooperation between the WTO and the United

Nations Environmental Program (UNEP). As regards environmental or social protection measures designed by members must not come into conflict with the substantial provisions of the Agreements under the WTO. In this respect the WTO exceeds boundaries imposed by the GATT: as its rules aim at trade liberalisation, violations even though for legitimate objectives are not easily tolerated.

It will be worthwhile to return to *Tuna-Dolphin* at a later stage as the final decision has just been circulate and sheds new light on the trade-environment divide which will be even better understood when having analysed some recent developments pointing more precise to conflicts of different legal systems representing trade and environmental protection. For now trade conditions under of those Agreements shall be introduced which had the most significant implications on sustainable economical activities.

The Agreement on Agriculture, SPS and TBT Agreements: restrictions onself-regulation

With the establishment of the WTO the creation of a Dispute Settlement Mechanism (DSM) came also into being which most spectacular set benchmarks for economic developments in the field of agriculture through its emanating jurisprudential body of trade dispute.

The Agreement on Agriculture has as its main aim to eliminate trade distorting measures. Hence it obliges member States to commitments to gradually reduce subsidies in order to fight protectionism and has set out disciplines for market access, export competition and domestic support. Trade disputes such as *Canada-Dairy*, *EC-Sugar*, *Korea Beef* and *US-Cotton* have explored the range of potential clashing of interests and re-shaped attitudes towards domestic support. The Agreement continues to stand in the centre of ongoing tensions: it sits at the crossroad of biotechnology in agriculture and organic farming practices, trade relations resulting from colonialism and transnational agribusiness. Further tensions arise out of the demand for more sustainable agricultural practices in developed countries and dependency on exports of agricultural products of lesser standards by developing countries such as India, China, the Philippines and potentially Russia. The overall picture is patchy: African countries keep themselves as GM free zones and fight for support of small farming, whereas investment in biotechnology is still of major interest to economies such as China, India and Brazil. In negotiations under the WTO it is not clear who will be winner and loser within trade battles: while countries such as the Philippines and Brazil pledge for tighter rules on domestic support, negotiations in the Doha Round 2008 were meant to reduce significantly the scope for domestic support by developed countries to the advantage of developing countries. This means de facto that while in developed countries the taste for organic and green agriculture is growing, both on the field of GM crops cultivation and animal welfare, developing countries, up and foremost members of the Cairns group will have better market opportunities to enter markets of developed countries through price competition and to intervene consumers' desire for more sustainable and environmentally friendly agriculture. Looking at food scandals, resistance to GM crops and deteriorating climatic conditions consumer across the globe will probably continue to feel that food safety and security concerns are dissatisfactory addressed in current trade organisation.

However, under the Agreement on Agriculture some policies are tolerated in the three categories exempted from expenditure commitments. Measures under the 'green box' are considered to have at most minimal trade distorting effects. They pursue desirable social policies rather than the exclusion of competitors and may have beneficial environmental outcomes. However, problematical remains decoupled income support, in other words payments made to farmers which neither depend on nor affect current prices or production. They are domestic policy choices which may stimulate production through easing of credit constrains, coverage of fixed costs or the reward of future production. This kind of stimulation may depress world prices to the detriment of producers in other countries, in particular in large agricultural markets such as cotton, bio fuel, soya and rice. In addition market pressures arising in the face of climate challenges will provide more distortions: the increased demand for bio fuel and climatically induced variability in agricultural production encourage countries to provide more subsidies without obeying notification procedures under the Agreement on Agriculture adequately.

In the debate around reforms of the Agreement benchmarks for food quality are wanting; international economic law is used to measure on global scales rather than to pursue a 'from- the- bottom- up- to -the top' line. While calls for spatial justice are familiar in the community of environmentalists and ecologists, spatial assessments which would inform first a regional, than a global assessment as to sustainable food supply step back behind observations of global grain, bio fuel and soya bean markets. This has further implications for valid assessments as regards the improvement of overall environmental conditions as specific farming practices have beneficial impacts on climate, water and soil conditions. In summary, sustainable farming practices and their success stories do not form the matrix of negotiations under the Doha Round although they are captured in studies and research.

The Agreement on Sanitary and Phytosanitary Measures (SPS Agreement) which co-acts with the Agreement on Agriculture is concerned with the protection of human, animal or plant life through Member States' regulatory measures. The protective measures must not arbitrarily and unjustified discriminate between trading partners and must be based on scientific evidence. It is considered to be one of the most intrusive and controversial agreements (Echols, 2001) and has soon entered the stage after the establishment of the WTO in major cases such as *EC-Hormones I*, three poultry cases and most recently in the *EC-Biotech* case, the latter eventually raising profound questions as to interpretative methods and competences of the WTO panel and as regards the interactivity of different legal systems.(Young, 2007) The Agreement itself derives its legitimacy from harmonisation of sanitary and phytosanitary measures under the auspices of international standard setting bodies and from reliance on scientific expertise in the assessment of risk which can be obtained at national or international level. (Gruszcynski, 2011) Criticism has been stated against the working mechanisms of international authorities (Livermore, 2006), insensitivity towards different perceptions of risk and the ignorance of wider contextual factors opposing unrestricted imports of hormone-treated meat, foreign fruits and vegetables and genetically modified organisms.(Jasanoff et al., 2005)

Some release for puzzles and resulting inconsistencies under the Agreement on Agriculture and the stringency of the SPS Agreement is provided by the Agreement on Technical Barriers on Trade (TBT Agreement) which again balances Member's regulatory autonomy with rights and benefits other contracting parties obtain under the GATT and the Marrakesh agreements.(Marceau et al, 2001) The TBT Agreement allows for technical regulations that pursue legitimate objectives such as 'national security requirements, the prevention of deceptive practices and the protection of human health and safety, animal or plant life or health, or the environment' as stated under Art 2.2. Hence it has become practice to accommodate non-trade aims under the Agreement which may otherwise fall short within global trade organisation, up and foremost labour rights and high environmental standards. Through certification and licensing any international organisation may set labour or environmental standards which meet customers' ethical expectations with the effect of widening markets for some while restricting access for others(Joshi,2004). Though the TBT Agreement has not been able to work towards an international approximation of socio-economic rights or protective environmental regulation; the recent *Tuna-Dolphin* decision rather suggests an engraving of the enduring trade-environment divide. Of particular concern is the fragmentation of technical barriers through private standard setting bodies that raise questions as to credibility and accountability.(Ghandi, 2007) The TBT Agreement in case law occurs in the context of consumer welfare, and is invoked by WTO members in order to circumvent the inexorable science based requirements of the SPS Agreement.

Before plotting the evolution of case law under all three Agreements and approaching the complex cultural and political problematic of food production and regulation the article wanted to illustrate the Safeguard Agreement shall not be unmentioned. It enables states to apply safeguards in the case of serious injury or threats of serious injury to their domestic industry due to the unforeseen increase in imports. The components of the safeguard agreement have often been explored in agricultural disputes such as *US-Lamb* and *US- Wheat Gluten* whereby again it became clear that domestic dynamics and conditions, mostly unpredictable for a variety of reasons were not compatible with commitments under the international trade obligations of the GATT and the WTO. (Sykes, 2003)

Nature fights back: animals and plants as potential reformers

As explored above the recent dispute around biotechnology not only points to limits of the WTO's almighty reach and jurisdiction but also to the rise of regionalism and comeback of state sovereignty and national cultural values. The major dispute of *EC-Hormones* which firstly left the EC with retaliation costs about 116 million Euros as it had not based it 'genuine concerns' on a risk assessment as required under the SPS Agreement was recently decided in favour of the EU while revising the standard of review of the DSB and admitting EU scientific expertise to the stage.(Du, 2010) In *EC-Biotech* the inconsistent and controversial ruling of the panel pointed to the unacceptable fragmentation of different international legal regimes: while the decision-making body over-included international rules of international organisations such as the Codex Alimentarius and the International Convention on Plant Protection (IPPC) it excluded non-WTO sources such as the Convention on Biodiversity, the Protocol on Biosafety and the Precautionary Principle, the latter being a recognised norm in international customary law. The panel based its decision on principles of the interpretation of Treaties (Vienna Convention on the Law of Treaties, Art 31(1) and (3)(c)and reasoned that as one of the disputing parties, namely the US is not a ratifying party of the Biodiversity and Biosafety Agreements, the latter could not be considered in the dispute. (Young, 2007) The result of the dispute which ended with the authorisation of 10 GM crops in EU countries raised not only awareness of the International Law Commission but also of the legal community at large who seriously questions the relationship between law and economics as it has developed in recent years. (Benforado, Hanson 2008)

However, before the two major cases of *EC-Biotech* and *EC-Hormones* severely unhinged WTO values which were taken for granted, disputes aggressively impacted on WTO Member States traditional and culturally anchored farming and trading practices as can best be traced in the case of GMO release in marketing in the EU. The case had been brought against the EU as entity, the latter having exclusive competence according to Art 3 of the treaty on the Functioning of the EU in common commercial policy and the conclusion of international agreements 'in so far as its conclusion may affect common rules or alter their scope.' (Foster, 2012) In this tension field EU Member states fierce opposition against GMO production and use clashes with the interests of investors in biotechnology which has at the one hand has brought wealth and development to countries of the Cairn group but simultaneously raised anxieties and questions of risks and liability been in the context of the Biosafety Protocol 2000 and put any investment into these technology onto a controversial if not instable footing. Maria Lee dedicates her research to the democratic and substantial difficulties which EU Member States associate with the deliberate release of GMO products and their use in agriculture which goes beyond concerns of cross-pollution of organic and modified crops and irreversible environmental harm. (Lee, 2012) The cases of Poland, Greece and Austria against the Commission illustrate how EU legislation restricts Member States own competences in deciding on contested technologies: national claims expressing concerns against the incompatibility of GM release with national policies on religious, economic-social and ecological grounds respectively failed in the face of the strict regime under Art 114 TFEU which provides for the 'approximation of laws'. However, in January 2012 Martin Sieker gave a comprehensive statement as to the future of GMOs in the EU which signifies a determined and differentiated turn away from universally decided policies towards individual decision-making and room of manoeuvre. (Sieker, 2012) Rectifying the argumentation of GM food producers that GM crops are able to appease the world's hunger, Sieker counters that 'the global food crisis is a problem of distribution rather than production as global production is equivalent to over 150% of global consumption) He pledges for a 'European farming model, which has a positive impact on biodiversity and is envisaged in the future Common Agricultural Policy (CAP)' by requiring that not just natural scientists but also social scientists, lawyers, ethicists and representatives of civil society interest groups should be involved, so that decision-making is informed not only by scientific evaluation of risks to humans and the environmental, but also by 'other legitimate factors', including for example socio-economic, cultural and ethical considerations and societal values.' His calls as they are supported by further opinions of the Economic and Social Committee (Kienle, 2012) and widely comply with ideas and aspirations of green economics should fall on preferential grounds as the European Commission itself is increasingly concerned with resource-efficiency and sustainability achieved through regional efforts. (EU Commission, 2011)

On the world's political stage similar movements may result in favourable sustainable developments through a movement which is described by Adrian M. Johnston and Michael J. Trebilcock as 'the proliferation of preferential trade agreements'; however, potential benefits and harms depend on many factors. In general it is acknowledged that by 'advancing trade liberalisation and performing certain functions of deep integration that cannot be achieved through a global multilateral institution' PTA's can play a benign role: a further question is whether they might also be apt to release WTO members from the straightjacket the Agreements currently impose and may allow for more individual forms of trade, knowledge and technology transfer and new forms of cooperation in the furtherance of sustainable economies. (Trebilcock, 2012)

Using fragmentation as basis for a reset

The crisis consists precisely in the fact that the old is dying and the new cannot be born: in this interregnum a great variety of morbid symptoms appear.'
Antonio Gramsci, prison Notebooks (Gramsci, 1975)

The WTO can be seen as success story in eliminating discriminatory and selective trading policies dating back colonial times and historical preferences (Bartels, 2007). However, new trade areas have introduced the threat of neo-colonialism whereby the dealing with IP rights under the WTO imposes particular problems: in particular seeds and plants are protected under the Agreement on Trade – Related Aspects of Intellectual Property Rights (TRIPS) and create dependencies in particular of developing countries from multinational investors and agribusinesses. (Marin, 2002) While countries have aimed for domestic solutions and regulations which get around the IPR problem the battle might not be over: multinationals are still seeking to spread their restricting merchandise to the disadvantage of small farmers and biodiversity; this will in particular be true for newcomers to the WTO such as Russia. Gillian Moon has envisaged another potential solution for democratic and sustainable shortcomings by linking human rights protection and free trade obligations with the provisions of the Agreement on Agriculture. Having established that ethnic minority groups and women in Nicaragua and Ghana are particularly affected by subsidy reduction requirements and prohibition of export subsidies under the agreement, the author suggests that this form of 'indirect discrimination' may urge the acceptance and exceptions of 'special products' which would allow small farming to produce and export outside of the stringency of the Agreement of Agriculture. Referring to linkages with Human Rights jurisprudence, the de facto discrimination of women and ethnical minorities violates the Convention on the Elimination of Discrimination against Women (CEDAW) and the Convention on the Elimination of Racial Discrimination (CERD) under the UN System for Human Rights Protection. (Moon, 2011)

A new linkage between human rights and trade is also subject in Andrew Lang's analysis of 'World Trade Law after Neoliberalism': he identifies the need for a redefinition of the boundaries and relationship of legal regimes, the international human rights system and the international economic law order. (Lang, 2011) While attributing their division and separate developments to historical predispositions crossing the post WW 2 time and the neoliberal turn of the 1990s he makes away with an doctrinal trade and human rights divide as proclaimed by Petersmann and Alston as advocates of both sides (Cottier et al, 2005) and rather calls for the establishment of a 'collective responsibility regime.' According to Kati Kulovesi this requirement may well meet the limits of 'present WTO norms and the present mandate of dispute resolution mechanism' which are 'not equipped for the task at hand'. (Kulovesi, 2012) After past improvements through 'Greening the GATT' and 'GATTing the Greens' (D C Esty, 1993, 1994) the current system faces a crisis of legitimacy as expressed in challenges through environmental disputes. Conflicts affect climate change in the clash between the UNFCCC and the WTO (Scott, 2011), and the abovementioned encounters between interests in biodiversity and biotechnology(Young, 2011) An attempt to resolve political controversies as expressed in the fragmentation of international legal regimes through the institution of the Dispute Settlement System (DSS) is in Kulovesi 's eyes unrealistic and undesirable for obvious reasons: together with the International Law Commission she agrees that 'when conflicts emerge between treaty provisions that have their home in different regimes, care should be taken so as to guarantee that any settlement is not dictated by organs exclusively linked with one or the other conflicting regimes.' (ILC, 2006) The need for a holistic view on human's life conditions and its diffusion into all areas of political, economic and legal organisation cannot become more apparent. (A R Migiro,)

Conclusion

As the manifold provisions of the WTO Agreements and the disputes brought before its settlement system suggest the WTO can well be understood as major stumbling block in the advancement of fair and sustainable development and economics. This chapter has not yet mentioned controversies under the Trade-Related Investment Measures (TRIMS), the imbalances and controversies arising under the General Agreement on Trade in Services (GATS) and the Subsidies and Countervailing Measures Agreement (SCM Agreement) and does neither comprehensively refer to the increasing importance of NGO participation as reflected in the evolutionary use Amicus Curiae letters in during litigation. The current economic crisis may have unpredictable outcomes on world trade: in the worse case resources for scrutinising criticism and reform may diminish; established trade relations, most recently including Russia, may result in further deregulation and destabilisation, unemployment, environmental degradation and business as usual and lead to the fragmentation of a meaningful new global economic order. The crisis can also mean that environmentally motivated changes are starting to bite: a theory which would have to be evidenced by green economists through the provision of empirical and statistical analysis. In this apparent new surrounding the WTO would have to give space to substantive reforms embracing modification of the provisions of its agreements, new standards of review and extension of its interpretative scope; overall it would have to move towards greater admission of economical empirical evidence and environmental protection requirements. As the WTO disposes over functional instruments of three branches, the legislative, executive and judicial branch, it is enormously powerful and cannot be ignored in its force; in contrast, Multilateral Environmental Agreements (MEAs) at the time of writing have no dispute settlement bodies and were only able to create few direction giving decisions. Recent case law confirms the willingness of the Appellate Body to at least acknowledge countries' concerns as regards environmental protection.

For the proponents of green economics these developments would require raising awareness for and understanding of the mechanisms operating in contrary motion to own aspirations but also awareness and cooperation as regards profound changes that happens in adversarial camps. A clear measurement of influential success stories of green economics would be helpful and strengthen the potential of our global community. In the end true sustainability can only be achieved when every earth-dweller is integrated in the process of its realisation. This article sought to bridge mainstream economic organisation and wants in environmentally friendly developments. It can thereby provide only a small contribution: intuitive and wise economic claims and actions from civil society will continue to deliver essential pushes to the system's flexibility and fragility whereby mutual understanding for the mechanisms and practices of each side must enhance dialogue, trust, patience and the sharing of common responsibilities.

Bibliography

J M Keynes (1920),' The Consequences of the Peace', New York: Harcourt, Brace and Howe p 9-26

D J Gerber (1998), 'Law and Competition in Twentieth Century Europe- Protecting Prometheus', OUP

D J Gerber (2010), 'Global Competition-Law, Markets, and Globalisation', OUP p 24-38

A Lang (2011),' World Trade Law after Neoliberalism', OUP

K Kulovesi (2012), 'The WTO Dispute Settlement System-Challenges of the Environment, Legitimacy and Fragmentation', Wolters Kluwer

J Scott (2004), 'International Trade and Environmental Governance: Relating Rules (and Standards) in the EU and the WTO', 15 European Journal of International Law 2, p 301-354

D Lynch and D Vogel (2001), 'The Regulation of GMOs in Europe and the United States: A Case-Study of contemporary European regulatory Politics', Council on Foreign Relations Press, available on http://www.cfr.org/genetically-modified-organisms accessed on 9 June 2012

R E Hudec (1996), 'GATT Legal Restraints on the Use of Trade Measures Against Foreign Environmental Practices' in R Hudec and J Bhagwati (Ed), Fair Trade and Harmonisation, MIT Press (1996) Vol 1

S Gaines (2001), 'The WTO's Reading of the GATT Article XX Chapeau: A Disguised Restriction on Environmental Measures', 22 University of Pennsylvania Journal of International Environmental Law 4, p 757-62

M A Echols (2001), 'Food Safety and the WTO: The Interplay of Culture, science and Technology', Kluwer Law International

M A Young (2007), 'The WTO's use of relevant rules of international law: An analysis of the *Biotech* case', 56 International and Comparative Law Quarterly 4, available on www.law.cam.ac.uk/faculty-resources/10004248.pdf accessed on 9 July 2012

S R Gandhi (2007), 'Voluntary Environmental Standards: The Interplay Between Private Initiatives, Trade Rules And The Global Decision-Making Processes', available on http://www.iilj.org/GAL/documents/Ghandienvironment.pdf accessed on 9 July 2012

Joshi, 'Are Eco-Labels consistent with World Trade Organisation Agreements?' 38 Journal of World Trade 1, 2004, 62-92.

L Gruszczynski (2011), 'Regulating Health and Environmental Risks under WTO Law' OUP

S Jasanoff (1986), 'Risk Management and Political Culture', Russell Sage Foundation

Marceau and Trachtman (2002), 'TBT, SPS, and GATT: A Map of the WTO Law of Domestic Regulation', 36 Journal of World Trade 811

M M Du (2010), 'Standard of Review under the SPS Agreement after EC-Hormones II', International and Comparative Law Quarterly, Vol. 59, pp. 441-459

Sykes, A O(2003), 'The Persistent Puzzles of Safeguards: Lessons from the Steel Dispute', 7 Journal of International Economic Law 3, p 523-564

A Benforado and J D Hanson (2008), 'The Great Attributional Divide: How Divergent Views of Human Behavior are Shaping Legal Policy', 57 Emory Law Journal

World Trade Organisation, 1999. *The Legal Texts-TheRresults of the Uruguay Round of MultilateralTrade Negotiations.* Cambridge: Cambridge University Press.

Foster N (2012), 'Blackstone's Law on EU Treaties and Legislation 2012-2013', OUP 2012

Lee M (2011), 'Beyond Safety? The Broadening Scope of Risk regulation' Current legal Problems, Research Paper of the University College of London, available on http://papers.ssrn.com/sol3/papers.cfm?abstract_id=2088170 accessed on 9 July 2012

Sieker, M (2012) 'Opinion of the European Economic and Social Committee on 'GMOs in the EU' European Union Preparatory Acts (additional opinion), Official Journal C 68, 06/03/2012 p 56.

Trebilcock M (2012), 'The proliferation of free Trade Agreements: The Beginning of The End of the Multilateral Trading System?' paper is with the author; information available on http://www.ucl.ac.uk/laws/global_law/content.shtml?events accessed on 9 July 2012

Gramsci, A, (1975) 'Prison Notebooks', Columbia University Press 1975

L Bartels (2007) 'The trade and development policy of the European Union', 18 European Journal of International Law 4 (715-756)

P L C Marin (2002), 'Providing Protection for plant Genetic resources-Patents, Sui Generis Systems, and Biopartnerships' Kluwer International

G Moon (2011),'Fair in Form, But Discriminatory in Operation—WTO Law's Discriminatory Effects on Human Rights in Developing Countries' 14 Journal of International Economic Law (3) p 553-592.

T Cottier, J Pauwelyn, E Bürgi (Ed) (2005), ‚Human Rights and International Trade' OUP

EU Commission (2011), 'Communication from the Commission to The EU Parliament, the Council, The European Economic and Social Committee and the Committee of the Regions- a resource-efficient Europe-flagship initiative under the Europe 2020 Strategy', COM(2011) 21, Brussels 26 January 2011

Kienle, A (2012), Opinion of the European Economic and Social Committee on 'Agriculture and crafts — a winning combination for rural areas' (own-initiative opinion) (2012/C 143/07) available on http://eur-lex.europa.eu/LexUriServ/LexUriServ.do?uri=OJ:C:2012:143:0035:0038:EN:PDF accessed on 9 July 2012

A R Migiro (2011), 'The Green Economy: A Pathway to Sustainable Development-A Holistic View of Environmental, Social and Economic Well-Being', available on http://www.dubuquepresentations.org/UserFiles/documents/green_economy.pdf accessed on 9 July 2011

'Greening' World's Economies Debated As Viable Pathway To Development Destination As General Assembly Considers Shortcomings Of Prevailing Growth Models' http://www.unep.org/greeneconomy/Portals/88/documents/news/UNGA.pdf

Part 8 Sustainable Development

8.1 Green growth: reconciling economic growth and environmental protection

By Martin Koehring (Senior Editor, The Economist Intelligence Unit, writing in a personal capacity)

Introduction

It is often said that economic growth and environmental sustainability are irreconcilable. There are good reasons to support this hypothesis. After all, the exploitation of natural resources has fuelled economic growth for centuries. Deforestation, dwindling biodiversity and human-induced climate change are only a few examples of the devastating environmental consequences of an economic growth model that has paid little attention to the environment. And government measures to protect the environment are often associated with undermining economic growth.

However, the notion that there must be a trade-off between economic growth and environmental sustainability is a myth. As this chapter will argue, economic growth can—to a degree—also have positive effects on the environment. There is an interesting link between economic prosperity and certain indicators of environmental health, for example biodiversity. But governments would be ill-advised to simply rely on economic growth to magically provide environmental benefits; they could design policies that provide the conditions for "green growth", that is growth which is "efficient in its use of natural resources" (World Bank 2012). A government that wants to future-proof the economy will have to design policies that do not only reduce the negative environmental externalities of rising economic output on the one hand, but that also provide incentives for green growth on the other hand.

This chapter will set the scene by briefly looking at the downsides of the relationship between economic growth and the environment. It will then look at some of the benefits that economic growth can have on the environment, with a focus on forests and biodiversity. Finally, the paper will focus on the potential of green growth as a way to reconcile economic growth and sustainability, both in the developing-market and developed-market contexts.

The adverse effects of economic growth on the environment

At first glance the link between economic growth and the environment seems obvious. There are many examples that suggest that economic growth is bad for the environment. The economic growth sparked by the Industrial Revolution since the 18th century has relied on mass production, with polluting machines and factories causing environmental degradation. Population growth, urbanisation and mechanisation—all strongly linked to industrialisation—have had major effects on global air, water and land pollution levels.

Air, water and land pollution

Emissions such as carbon dioxide (CO_2), nitrogen oxides and sulphur oxides, for example from vehicles, factories and power plants, have had a damaging impact on air quality. Moreover, greenhouse gases (GHGs) such as CO_2 and methane have played a major role in global warming. Rapid economic growth has also tended to go hand in hand with population growth and a concomitant rise in food demand, which, in turn has led to the expansion of farm land—often to the detriment of forests, leading to deforestation. According to the Food and Agriculture Organisation of the United Nations (FAO), the livestock sector contributes 18% to total global GHG emissions, primarily caused by nitrous oxide, methane and CO_2 (FAO 2014). Meanwhile, deforestation is a major contributor to global warming as forests are vital for storing carbon emissions and cleansing water supplies, for example. Moreover, the destruction of forests can cause species extinction and the irreversible loss of biodiversity.

The earth's water bodies have long been mistreated by humans. Water Pollution has occurred as a result of industrial processes associated with economic growth in the industrial age, as harmful chemicals are released into water bodies from sludge and domestic waste, for example. These make the aquatic ecosystem increasingly toxic. The state of the global oceans is even worse. Concentrations of chlorophyll are falling—a phenomenon that has been linked to global warming—and two-thirds of the fish stocks in the high seas are over-exploited (*The Economist* 2014b), while the global appetite for fish is rising further (World Bank 2014).

Finally, there is also a strong link between economic growth and land pollution. As a side-effect of industrialisation and urbanisation, the disposal of urban and industrial wastes, including non-biodegradable materials, have caused the release of harmful materials into the land. Exploitation of minerals and agricultural practices such as the use of pesticides have also contributed to land pollution.

Steady-state economy
Will it get worse? As developing countries seek to catch up with the developed world, the demand for non-renewable resource is rising sharply. Since the turn of the century, real commodity prices have risen by around 150% (Dobbs et al 2011). According to Achim Steiner, the Executive Director of the United Nations Environment Programme (UNEP), "this explosion in demand is set to accelerate as population growth and the increase in incomes continue to rise. More than 3 billion people are expected to enjoy 'middle class' income levels in the next twenty years, compared to 1.8 billion today" (UNEP 2014). This reality makes it highly unlikely—and also difficult to justify from the point of view of historical economic justice towards the developing world—that the world will transition to a "steady-state economy", as advocated by ecological economists such as Herman Daly (Daly 1991).

Some environmentalists warn that growth cannot be sustained as it has overly relied on fossil fuels, so that growth becomes a myth: "the inescapable failure of a society built upon growth and its destruction of the Earth's living systems are the overwhelming facts of our existence", says George Monbiot (Monbiot 2014).

However, despite the negative impact that the resource-intensive economic growth model of the industrial age has had on the environment over the centuries, economic growth and the environment can be reconciled, especially as many parts of the world have already entered a post-industrial age. In the next chapter we will look at the notion that economic growth can actually spur stronger environmental protection, and we will then examine how governments can actively encourage a transition to a new green growth model.

The benefits of economic growth for the environment

Some economists argue that economic growth—and its associated increases in industrial production and consumption—causes environmental destruction only up to a point, namely once incomes reach a certain threshold at which demand for environmental goods such as clean air and fresh water, as well as for more efficient infrastructure, increases. At this point, further economic and income growth is associated with falling levels of environmental degradation. In this hypothesis, the relationship between economic growth and environmental degradation is described by an inverted U shape, or a so-called "environmental Kuznets curve", based on the income-inequality relationship explored by Simon Kuznets (Kuznets 1966).

Empirical evidence of the environmental Kuznets curve is inconclusive. But there are indications that such a growth-environment relationship exists for some pollutants such as sulfur dioxide and particulates whose levels have fallen in OECD countries at a relatively low income threshold as a result of regulatory changes. There are also indications that the relationship holds for other pollutants such as nitrogen oxides, lead and sewage (Panayotou 2003; Zhang 2012, p.6).

Evidence from forests

A similar relationship can be seen in the case of deforestation, although it may not strictly follow an environmental Kuznets curve. Here, a so-called "forest transition curve" has been observed; a reverse J, whereby forest cover falls rapidly in the early stages of development as countries clear their forests for fuel and farms, before forest cover bottoms out and then recovers slowly (*The Economist* 2014c). Encouragingly, the rate of global deforestation has decreased over the past decade —although it remains alarming in many countries—with South America and Africa recording the highest net annual loss of forests between 2000 and 2010 and Asia recording a net gain (FAO 2010).

Forests are a good proxy for biodiversity. And there have been positive developments in biodiversity too. There is increasing evidence that economic growth and biodiversity follow a relationship that could be described by the environmental Kuznets curve, especially in countries moving towards a post-industrial economy. The contrasting fortunes of forests in relatively poor North Korea, where the environment is on the brink of collapse (McKenna 2013), and relatively richer South Korea, where forest cover has been stable for some time, are an example of the prosperity-biodiversity relationship mentioned above. As countries become richer they tend to become more innovative and technologically advanced—including innovations in environmentally friendly technologies—with populations that have fewer children (usually following an initial period of rapid population growth) and that are more concerned about the health effects of environmentally destructive growth and about future generations and other species. Moreover, as agricultural production becomes more efficient and the agricultural workforce declines, more people move to towns and cities, while abandoned land can be turned back to forest, for example (*The Economist* 2013b). All these factors are beneficial for biodiversity.

The importance of political will
Why are some countries more successful in moving from environmentally destructive economic growth models to more sustainable ones? Mexico and Costa Rica, for example, have made some progress along the forest transition curve, with Mexico having cut its deforestation rate even more than Brazil (which has had ambitious official deforestation targets for more than a decade), while Costa Rica has increased its forest cover to over 50%, from only 20% in the 1980s; both

countries have pioneered "payment for ecosystem services" (PES) models, although it has been challenging to create markets for clean water downstream from forests (*The Economist* 2014c). PES is a market-based mechanism to encourage the conservation of natural resources by offering incentives to farmers or landowners in exchange for managing their land or watersheds to provide an ecological service (IIED 2014).

The example of PES illustrates an important point about the link between economic growth (and rising incomes) and the environment: it is government policy, rather than income *per se*, that tends to lead to better environmental outcomes. The notion of an environmental Kuznets curve assumes that economic systems will innovate and come up with clean technologies as economies reach a certain income threshold. But these changes cannot happen automatically, without policy-makers providing incentives via enacting environmental policies (Zhang 2012, p. 7). Hence, a certain level of economic prosperity, plus political will, appear to be crucial for making economic growth and environmental concerns more compatible.

Environmental turning-points
Sometimes the trigger for change can be an environmental wake-up call, such as the Beijing smog of January 2013 when air pollution rose past levels considered hazardous by the World Health Organisation (WHO) (BBC News 2013). The government was forced to show a sense of political urgency with regard to the pollution crisis, culminating in China's premier, Li Keqiang, declaring a "war on pollution" in early 2014 amid plans to introduce environmental tax legislation that would penalise heavy polluters (FT 2014). Much of this response is born out of necessity as public anger at the health effects of pollution threatens the Chinese government's stability.

It seems the Chinese government has not only passed the point at which it feels it can afford to deal with some of the most pressing environmental consequences of its rapid growth trajectory, but it seems to also have reached the point at which the costs of environmental destruction are becoming unbearable. Indeed, according to the World Bank, environmental and natural-resource degradation cost China the equivalent of around 9% of GDP, among other things as a result of health costs associated with air pollution as well as soil erosion and fisheries loss (World Bank and Development Research Center of the State Council, the People's Republic of China 2013). China may now have reached its "environmental turning-point" akin to America in 1969 when the polluted Cuyahoga river in Ohio caught fire, prompting the creation of the Environmental Protection Agency a year later (*The Economist* 2013a).

Moving towards a new green growth model

How many wake-up calls will the world need to move to a more sustainable model of economic growth? Despite the potential benefits that economic growth can have for the environment when an economy reaches a certain level of income (see discussion on the environmental Kuznets curve above), it is clear that a transition towards "green growth" has to occur as soon as possible—globally, and not just in countries that have reached a certain income threshold.

Moving beyond "grow first, clean up later"

Green growth is often seen as a route for emerging economies to industrialise and develop in an environmentally sustainable way, in the knowledge that the path taken by developed economies in Europe and America—based on the principle "grow first, clean up later"—would lead to environmental disaster (*The Economist* 2012).

In a sign that green growth is becoming increasingly important in development strategies, the World Bank has been a strong advocate of the concept. The World Bank believes that a central tenet of any green growth strategy is to include the valuation of ecosystem services in national accounts. Such a "green accounting" approach would enable governments to make much better cost-benefit analyses when coming up with environmental policies.

At the moment, governments tend to regard environmental policies as costly for the economy and beneficial for the environment. Such a distinction would not be made in a green accounting framework, in which the economic benefits of environmental policy can be assessed much better. For example, if an environmental regulation reduces productivity, this can be more than compensated for by a reduction in externalities, e.g. by preserving ecosystem services (World Bank 2012, p. 39). Likewise, an infrastructure project, such as the construction of a road through the rainforest, can be much better assessed from an economic point of view if environmental assets are assigned economic values to make them comparable to other economic values (Ibid., p. 52). Green accounting is still in its infancy; hence, the economic benefits of a country's natural capital are often not taken into account when governments are faced with tough decisions that appear to pit purely economic benefits/costs against purely environmental benefits/costs, when in fact environmental considerations can have measurable economic benefits and costs too.

However, green accounting has caused controversy because of bringing nature into an accounting framework, although the environment clearly has an intrinsic value that, many argue, goes far beyond its economic value. This is one of the reasons why green growth has been dismissed by some environmentalists as "greenwashing capitalism" (*The Economist* 2012).

In addition to green accounting mechanisms and other measures that enhance decision-maker's access to information, the World Bank's green growth approach also entails a variety of incentive-based market instruments to reduce environmental degradation, including environmental taxes, tradable permits, subsidies, deposit refunds schemes and refunded emission payments (World Bank 2012, pp. 47ff.). Such price-based mechanisms are generally preferable to regulations and rules, as these tend to entail higher costs and risks (for example favouring incumbents in an industry and creating additional barriers to entry into markets for smaller firms). However, they may be useful in spurring green growth when there are market failures and difficulties in establishing appropriate prices, for example in the case of the absence of a carbon price, which means that fuel-efficiency standards may be the favourable second-best solution to price-based approaches on vehicle fuels (Ibid., pp. 58 ff.).

As mentioned above, green growth is gaining traction in many developing countries, with green growth strategies in place or in the process of being designed in a diverse range of countries such as Brazil, China, Ethiopia, Indonesia, Kenya, Mexico, Morocco, and Tunisia (Ibid., p. 30). Another manifestation of the emergence of a green growth agenda in the developing world is the Global Green Growth Institute (GGGI), an international organisation founded in 2010 "on the belief that economic growth and environmental sustainability are not merely compatible objectives; their integration is essential for the future of humankind" (GGGI 2014). The GGGI is driven by the needs of developing countries and aims to support "the development, implementation, and diffusion of green growth strategies", including by engaging policy-makers and the private sector (Ibid.).

But green growth is not just a new development paradigm, it has also become more important in the developed world, notably Europe. This is partly in response to soaring commodity prices and a desire to reduce dependence on energy from unstable sources (such as Russia and the Middle East), but also as an opportunity to create a competitive advantage in a world in which resource efficiency will become increasingly important. For example, the OECD has developed a green growth strategy (OECD 2011). The elements of the strategy are similar to the World Bank's, but more geared towards richer countries, with a focus on productivity, innovation and new markets. Like the World Bank approach, the OECD's policy framework for green growth highlights the importance of market-based instruments, regulations and investment.

Europe's struggle to adopt green growth policies
The EU is also a good test case for the move towards the new green growth model. Its experiment with its emissions trading scheme (ETS) as a market-based instrument to move towards a greener economic model has been disappointing so far. The ETS was launched in 2005 with high hopes of reducing GHG emissions and setting a standard for the rest of the world; however, poor policy design, too many exemptions, the European economic crisis and an oversupply of carbon allowances have led to a sharp fall in the carbon price since 2008 (*The Economist*

2014a). Hence, the scheme has so far failed to discourage the use of fossil fuels in the energy sector, particularly coal. The European Commission's policy framework on energy and climate for 2030 aims to revive the ETS: in order to ensure more stable carbon prices and support low-carbon investment, the Commission wants to establish a market stability reserve in 2021.

But the European Commission continues to advocate market-based approaches to environmental challenges in order to spur economic growth. In early 2014, the Commission unveiled a study that showed that moving taxes away from labour towards pollution could bring in revenues of around €35 billion in 2015, potentially rising beyond €101 billion by 2025, especially if environmentally harmful subsidies were removed (European Commission 2014a). This could allow lower taxes on labour and reduction of budget deficits, thus freeing financial resources for environmentally friendly investment projects.

Apart from market-based instruments, green innovation and technology will be crucial in determining the success of green growth in the EU. In theory, the 2030 policy framework provides several incentives for the EU to speed up innovation in eco-friendly technologies. The European Commission wants the EU's GHG emissions to be reduced by 40% by 2030, while raising the share of renewables in total energy consumption to at least 27% by 2030, up from around 13% currently. In mid-2014 the Commission also unveiled a plan for the EU to raise energy efficiency by 30% by 2030 (that is, reducing energy consumption by 30% below the levels projected for 2030 in 2007). It is important to keep in mind that the European Council still has to decide on the exact targets ahead of international negotiations on a new global climate agreement, due to be concluded in Paris in late 2015. However, it is likely that the EU will adopt significantly tougher targets than the other major global economies, including the US and China. This could prove challenging, but could also provide incentives to speed up the technological transition to a low-carbon economy.

Elements of the green growth agenda are part of the EU's biggest research and innovation programme ever, called Horizon 2020, which provides almost €80bn of funding from 2014 to 2020 (European Commission 2014b). Among other things, the funding programme aims to boost secure, clean and efficient energy; smart, green and integrated transport; and climate action and resource efficiency. Green growth opportunities could therefore arise in areas such as green transport, low-carbon technologies and energy-efficient buildings.

Conclusion

Economic growth and its hunger for resources have had a devastating effect on the environment since the Industrial Revolution. But that does not necessarily mean that the only option now is to move towards a "steady-state economy". Instead, there is growing evidence that economic growth and a concomitant increase in incomes can help to make economies more likely to address environmental concerns, for example in the case of various pollutants and deforestation. In addition to a certain level of economic prosperity, political will also appears to be crucial for making economic growth and environmental concerns more compatible —and major environmental turning-points such as the Beijing smog of January 2013 can sometimes nudge policy-makers to muster the necessary political will to move towards a more sustainable growth model.

This paper has argued that the notion of "green growth" has emerged as a viable contender to provide a conceptual framework for practical action to reconcile economic growth and environmental concerns. Green growth is a model both for the developing and the developed worlds. Green growth offers developing countries that aspire for developed-world prosperity a development path that promises to avoid the pitfalls of the "grow first, clean up later" mantra that many in Europe and America adopted in the past. For developed countries, particularly in the EU, green growth offers opportunities and risks. Some mechanisms that were supposed to help Europe on its path to become a leader on green growth, such as the emissions trading scheme, have been a failure so far. But market-based approaches will remain important, for example highlighted by attempts to move taxes away from labour towards pollution. Green innovation and technology hold some potential for Europe, especially as the policy framework will entail more ambitious targets for greenhouse gas emissions, renewable energy and energy efficiency than in most of the rest of the world. Europe could become a champion of green growth—and this could allow the region to emerge more strongly with a more fundamentally sound economy, especially in light of the recent economic and financial crises that were built on an unsustainable economic growth model.

Bibliography

BBC News (2013) "Beijing smog: When growth trumps life in China", January 27th 2013, www.bbc.com/news/magazine-21198265 [accessed on September 4th 2014].

Daly, H. E. (1991) "Steady-State Economics", second edition, Washington DC: Island Press.

Dobbs, R., Oppenheim, J., Thompson, F., Brinkman, M., Zornes, M. (2011), "Resource Revolution: Meeting the world's energy, materials, food, and water needs". McKinsey Global Institute, November 2011.

European Commission (2014a) "Environment: New studies strengthen the case for boosting flood protection and switching to greener taxes", europa.eu/rapid/press-release_IP-14-202_en.htm, March 3rd 2014 [accessed on September 4th 2014].

European Commission (2014b) "What is Horizon 2020?" ec.europa.eu/programmes/horizon2020/en/what-horizon-2020 [accessed on September 4th 2014].

FAO (2010), "World deforestation decreases, but remains alarming in many countries", www.fao.org/news/story/en/item/40893/icode/ [accessed on September 4th 2014].

FAO (2014), "The role of livestock in climate change", www.fao.org/agriculture/lead/themes0/climate/en/ [accessed on September 4th 2014].

FT (2014) "China declares war on pollution", March 5th 2014, www.ft.com/cms/s/0/5c9b4d18-a437-11e3-b915-00144feab7de.html [accessed on September 4th 2014].

GGGI (2014) "Overview", gggi.org/about-gggi/background/organizational-overview/ [accessed on September 4th 2014].

IIED (2014) "Markets and payments for environmental services", www.iied.org/markets-payments-for-environmental-services [accessed on September 4th 2014].

Kuznets, S. (1966) "Modern Economic Growth". New Haven, Yale University Press.

McKenna, P. (2013) "Inside North Korea's Environmental Collapse", PBS, March 6th 2013, www.pbs.org/wgbh/nova/next/nature/inside-north-koreas-environmental-collapse/ [accessed on September 4th 2014].

Monbiot, G. (2014) "It's simple. If we can't change our economic system, our number's up", *The Guardian*, May 27th 2014.

OECD (2011) "Towards Green Growth", May 2011.

Panayotou, T. (2003) "Economic growth and the environment", in UNECE (ed.) *Economic Surveys of Europe*, No. 2, United Nations Economic Commission for Europe, pp. 45-72.

The Economist (2012), "Shoots, greens and leaves", June 16th 2012.

The Economist (2013a), "The East is grey", August 10th 2013.

The Economist (2013b), "The long view", September 14th 2013.

The Economist (2014a), "Europe's energy woes", January 25th 2014.

The Economist (2014b), "The tragedy of the high seas", February 22nd 2014.

The Economist (2014c), "A clearing in the trees", August 23rd 2014.

UNEP (2014) "Decoupling 2: technologies, opportunities and policy options. A Report of the Working Group on Decoupling to the International Resource Panel". Nairobi: UNEP.

World Bank (2012) *Inclusive Green Growth: The Pathway to Sustainable Development*, Washington DC: The World Bank.

World Bank (2014), "Raising More Fish to Meet Rising Demand", www.worldbank.org/en/news/feature/2014/02/05/raising-more-fish-to-meet-rising-demand, February 5th 2014 [accessed on September 4th 2014].

World Bank and Development Research Center of the State Council, the People's Republic of China (2013) "Seizing the Opportunity of Green Development in China", in: *China 2030*, March 2013, pp. 229-291.

Zhang, J. (2012) "Delivering Environmentally Sustainable Economic Growth: The Case of China", Asia Society, September 2012.

320

8.2 THE GLOBAL TRANSITION FROM THE INDUSTRIAL ERA TO THE SOLAR AGE

Hazel Henderson, RichardSpencer, Tony Manwaring
Excerpt from *Mapping the Global Transition to the Solar Age*
(ICAEW and Tomorrow's Company, 2014)

This global transition requires, and is generating, innovation based on principles of equity, social inclusion and ecological sustainability. This shift, already underway, will no longer be powered by digging fuels from the Earth's crust but harvesting the Sun's rays as our free daily income and is now widely evident: north, south, east and west. Breakthroughs in efficiencies of solar cells now achieve 43.5% conversion to electricity[179] while costs continue to drop – falling by over half in 2013. Much of this innovation occurs outside the official money-denominated GDP measured sectors in the unpaid 'love economies'.[180] Some 50% of all production and services in OECD countries and up to 75% in many developing and traditional societies are invisible to economists.

Main Street local economies starved of credit and facing a collapse in the domestic money supply are re-building local enterprises with voluntary groups, credit associations, time banking, local currencies, farmers markets, holistic, preventative health cooperatives and constructing community-owned wind turbines and solar collectors.[181] In 2012 the cooperative MOSAIC financed three community centre solar rooftops in 24 hours using crowdfunding sites online.[182] Energy efficiency is the fastest payback and thousands of small companies now offer these services to

179 'Solar PV's Efficiency Record, Thanks to NREL and Solar Junction', Cleantechnica.com, 30 December, 2012.
180 Love Economies – the term Hazel Henderson coined to describe all unpaid work, sharing, caring. See Fig. 6.
181 www.ethicalmarkets.com/category/community-development-solutions/

large companies and big retailers, including Wal-Mart, because they also save money.[183] To capture these changes missed in formerly 'externalised' costs, accountancy is evolving towards 'triple bottom line' and ESG (environment, social, governance) standards[184] and the six types of capital used by the International Integrated Reporting Council, the Natural Capital approach,[185] as well as models by the Sustainability Accounting Standards Board.[186] Novethic reports that 'norm-based exclusion' from pension and sovereign wealth portfolios reached €2.3tn in 2013.[187] New research finds $13.6tn of assets now managed by such new metrics.[188] A new method, 'confidence accounting' moves from a bookkeeping paradigm toward a scientific measurement using ranges and broader auditing criteria as in the proposal by the Association of Chartered Certified Accountants (ACCA), ICAEW, the Chartered Institute for Securities and Investment, and Long Finance.[189] The UN has hosted several conferences on sustainable stock exchanges and reforms are promoted by the Network for Sustainable Financial Markets (one of our partners). Many foundations and charities, are also held to new standards to assure that their portfolios are aligned with their missions. Although this seems obvious, many of these foundation portfolios are still focused on financial returns and hold investments that actually undermine their social mission. The Jessie Smith Noyes Foundation in the USA led by Stephen Viederman pioneered aligning its entire portfolio to its social mission.[190]

182 Woody, Todd, 'Startup Launches Online Platform to Let Individuals Invest in Solar Projects', Forbes, 7 January, 2013.

183 Clinton Global Initiative, New York, September 2012.

184 Global Reporting Initiative, www.globalreporting.org.

185 'Is natural capital a material issue?' ACCA, Fauna & Flora International, KPMG, 2012.

186 Sustainability Accounting Standards Board, www.sasb.org.

187 'Blacklisting controversial companies helps responsible investors curb excesses', Novethic Research newsletter, Paris, 18 June, 2013.

188 'Global Sustainable Investment Alliance Issues First International Assessment Of The Sustainable Investment Landscape', ASRIA, 28 January, 2013.

189 Mainelli, Michael, 'The Battle for Accountancy Has Begun', *Financial Times*, 29 July, 2012.

190 Johnson, Keith L. and Viederman, Stephen, 'The Philanthropic Fiduciary', Cambridge University Press Fiduciary Handbook, forthcoming, June 2013 draft.

Tracking the green transition worldwide

By Q3 2013, the Green Transition Scoreboard® (GTS) totalled private investments in green sectors since 2007 worldwide at $5.2tn. We intentionally exclude nuclear power, 'clean' coal and carbon sequestration and agricultural-based biofuels. Carbon sequestration is best achieved through better land and forest management[191] as well as development of seawater agriculture of halophyte (salt-loving) plants, while biofuels can be made from algae on sea water. We are carefully evaluating nanotechnology and 3D printing and manufacturing, which so far have not been assessed for their social impacts and are still unregulated. Proliferation of drones, especially small ones, often for trivial purposes such as Amazon's plan for delivering packages, now pose pressing social and environmental concerns. Meanwhile, companies in these fields rapidly develop products with little regard for the public interest.

Our Green Transition Scoreboard®, tracking healthier trends, confirms our view that this transition is on track to reach $10tn by 2020. The International Energy Agency projects a $6.4tn total investment in renewable energy during the 23-year period 2012–2035, or an average of $280bn per year. This $6.4tn comprises 33% in wind power, 24% hydro, 20% solar PV, 12% geothermal and biomass with another 6% in biofuels, which may be reduced as transport is further electrified.[192]

This global transition follows many earlier phases of human societies' evolution as our technologies evolved from the Iron and Bronze Ages through the energy transitions from wood to coal, whale oil to petroleum. This current transition from fossil fuels to greater efficiency and renewable energy and resources is simply the next stage in human knowledge and scientific progress, auguring the post-Cartesian scientific worldview.[193] This has been forecast since the 1970s by the US Office of Technology Assessment.[194] John Elkington, co-founder of SustainAbility

---

191 See for example, Savory, Allen, *Holistic Resource Management*, Island Press, 1988; Jackson, Wes, *Consulting the Genius of the Place*, Counterpoint, 2011; 'The Grasslands Project', The Capital Institute, www.capitalinstitute.org.

192 World Energy Outlook, International Energy Agency, Paris, 2012.

193 www.ethicalmarkets.com/reports/2011GTSFebruaryReport.pdf

194 Hazel Henderson served on the US Congress Office of Technology Assessment Advisory Council from 1974 until 1980. All its studies are archived at Princeton University, the

consultants and Volans Ventures, sees such systemic shifts in his latest book, *Zeronauts* (2012), as does architect William McDonough and chemist Michal Braungart, co-authors of *Cradle to Cradle* (2008) and *The Upcycle* (2013). As OECD Secretary-General Angel Gurria recently stated, 'Green growth strategies focus on ensuring that natural assets can deliver their full economic potential.'[195] The World Economic Forum's Green Investment Report 2013 estimates investments required for water, agriculture, telecoms, power, transport, building, industrial and forestry sectors by 2020 stands at about $5tn.[196] The Green Growth Alliance calls for $700bn for sustainable infrastructure investments annually.[197]

Since the 2011 GTS report, increased concern by governments and United Nations agencies in promoting the global green transition[198] culminated in the Declaration of 191 countries at the UN Rio+20 Summit. Private markets and financial sectors ride roller-coasters and global geopolitical risks, many self-inflicted: from political wrangling in the USA to the failure of EU politicians to address the travails of the euro and restructure budgets. All this fuelled rising civic anger over bailouts of too-big-to-fail banks while imposing cuts and austerity on their citizens, echoed worldwide in the 99% facing the concentrated power of the 1%, verified by ETH.[199] New levels of concern by institutional investors at the CERES-UN Foundation Investor Summit on Climate Risk and Energy Solutions at the United Nations in New York appear in their report on "Inaction on Climate Change: The Cost to Taxpayers" released November 2013.[200] Secretary-General Ban Ki-moon

University of Maryland and in the Henderson-Kay-Schumacher Library at Ethical Markets Media, St. Augustine, FL, USA.

195 'Green Growth: Making It Happen', OECD, Paris, 7 February, 2012.

196 'The Green Investment Report', World Economic Forum, Geneva, 2013. www3.weforum.org/docs/WEF_GreenInvestment_Report_2013.pdf

197 Berthon, Bruno, 'A call for $700 billion in sustainable infrastructure investments', GreenBiz.com, 23 January, 2013.

198 See, for example, Clark, Helen, et al, 'Human Development Report 2011', United Nations, New York, 2011 and Appendix 3, Green Transition Scoreboard, February 2012.

199 Stefania Vitali, James B. Glattfelder and Stefano Battiston, 'Network of Corporate Control', *New Scientist* , ETH (Swiss Federal Institute of Technology), Zurich, Switzerland, 22 October 2011, 8-9.

200 www.ceres.org/investor-network/investor-summit/investor-summit-2012

commissioned a high-level panel on global sustainability which endorsed his 'Sustainable Energy For All By 2030' initiative in its report 'Resilient People: Resilient Planet: A Future Worth Choosing,' 2012. Ban Ki-moon urged these investors, who represented some \$10tn assets under management, to step up their investments in renewable energy and greater efficiency since governments were struggling with budget cuts 'while there is no lack of capital in the world.' Speakers from Deutsche Bank, Goldman Sachs, GE, Bank of America and other mainstream financiers previously had spoken little about the green transition. A host of new funds using ESG criteria are now offered by Bank of America, Morgan-Stanley, Goldman Sachs, Deutsche Bank and others jumping on the bandwagon. New pledges by signatory companies of the UN Principles of Responsible Investing at Rio+20 evidenced further concern by these institutional investors managing some \$32tn in assets[201]. They pledged to include natural capital reporting as 'material' to asset valuation. These terms, 'material' and 'materiality', which crop up in all such reports, betray 'rearview mirror' thinking based on earlier industrial models of material productions. Today, some 70% of production in OECD countries is services, while in modern corporations, some 80% of their asset value is intangible.[202] Private investor members, including AQAL in Germany, launched a €100m pledge fund for green companies,[203] based on its founder's integral investing model.[204]

Meanwhile, the global notional value of derivative contracts rose from \$600tn prior to 2009 while GDP was only \$65tn to now \$1.2qn while GDP remains in the \$65tn range.[205] Risks of investments in coal reserves of companies comprising 25% of London's FTSE Index are rising as they are seen less as assets than future liabilities in a carbon-constrained world. A high-level group warned the Bank of England

---

201 (UNPRI.org)
202 IIR Report, op. cit.
203 AQAL's new fund is led by Dr. Mariana Bozesan, a member of Ethical Markets Advisory
   Board, and for full disclosure, I serve as an AQAL advisor.
204 Bozesan, Mariana, 'Demystifying the Future of Investing: and Investor's Perspective',
   AQAL Investing, 2011.
205 Cohan, Peter, 'Big Risk: \$1.2 Quadrillion Derivatives Market Dwarfs World GDP', *Daily Finance*, June 9, 2010.

and the European Central Bank that these are now 'sub-prime' assets, posing a systemic risk to pension funds and economic stability.[206] In conventional financial models, risk has referred to financial loss, and therefore maximising financial returns has been paramount. Since the 2008 crises, the focus shifted to overlooked systemic risk. The broader view of risk includes climate, loss of species, biodiversity and ecosystem services (still often unpriced) as well as social risk of ecological refugees, costs of floods, fires, etc., leading to massive insurance losses. A framework for global risk analysis, the Principles for Sustainable Insurance was launched in June 2013 by UNEP-FI, endorsed by many global companies based on ESG factors and the UN Principles of Responsible Investment.[207] At its November 2013 conference in Beijing, UNEP FI launched its Online Guide to Banking & Sustainability to help bank employees integrate ESG issues.[208]

New courses for asset managers and democratizing education

A course on triple bottom line accounting was offered at St. Andrews University in Scotland to retrain asset managers, addressing the lag in updating portfolio analysis models still mired in traditional 'efficient markets', 'rational actors', obsolete asset-allocation models and business school curricula, exacerbating agent-principal conflicts of interest and creating an atmosphere of intimidation by portfolio managers and consultants toward asset owners and trustees.

While many institutional investors have focused on climate risk (mostly pension funds, endowments and mutual funds), they now have made the leap to seeing opportunities in the global retooling for the inevitable green transition, estimated by venture capitalists and others as a $45tn new global market.[209] Thus, our GTS thermometer is calibrated for a realistic annual global private investment of $1tn until 2020, so as to secure this transition. Shale fossil fuel extraction may involve additional wasted investments. Natural gas (methane) from shale is still seen as

---

206 'Coal Occupying the London Stock Exchange', Investor Watch, Carbon Tracker, London, January 2012; 'Unburnable Carbon 2013' op. cit..

207 Principles for Sustainable Insurance, UNEP-FI, www.unepfi.org, June 2013.

208 UNEP FI Newsletter, November 2013, and www.unepfi.org/bankingguide.

209 Doerr, John, Kleiner Perkins, Caufield and Byers, Palo Alto, CA, 2009.

providing a bridge to retiring coal plants – if the process of 'fracking' can control methane release, pollution and be made less destructive to water supplies and the environment.[210,] Methane itself is a powerful greenhouse gas and its theoretical claim to produce 50% less CO_2 than coal and oil is now questioned.[211] Extracting oil from shale or tar sands is unjustified on thermodynamic and environmental grounds and, when 'externalities' are fully internalised, extracting these fuels and the unwise investments in more coal plants proves uneconomic, as well as unnecessary. Many of the studies we cite confirm that renewables and efficiency can provide 100% of the world's energy, even as global population increases.

Power shifting to Asia

Meanwhile, global geopolitical shifts rearranged power toward Asia, particularly India, China and Indonesia, and the rising influence of developing countries, especially Brazil, China's major trading partner. Now the world's sixth industrial economy, Brazil is the natural resource-rich 'green giant' and a leader in hydro and wind power as well as flex-fuel cars. The mature economies of Europe and North America stagnated, all on various forms of life-support from their central banks and rebellious citizens. Japan joined in central bank money-creation under President Shinso Abe, with predictable rises in its Nikkei Index. Lobbyists and special interests maintained their grip on politicians.

In 2013, Asia experienced nature's wrath added to 2012's unprecedented series of crises: Japan, Chile, China and New Zealand suffered earthquakes followed by tsunamis in Japan and Chile and two devastating typhoons in the Philippines, all situated in the Pacific and on its ocean's Ring of Fire. Pakistan, Thailand and Australia suffered devastating floods, followed by record heat in Australia. The USA also experienced droughts, a wave of destructive tornadoes, massive flooding along the Mississippi basin and in the North-east due to unprecedented devastation from hurricane Sandy. The global loss of life and disruption of

---

210 Liroff, Richard, '5 ways to clean up fracking's chemical act', GreenBiz.com, 21 September, 2012; Romm, Joe, 'Bridge to Nowhere? NOAA Confirms High Methane Leakage Rate', ThinkProgress, 2 January, 2013.

211 Jacobson, Mark Z., Robert W. Howard, Mark A. Delucchi, et al, op. cit.

production was massive as were the costs estimated by Munich Re – \$378bn for 2011.[212] In the USA, Hurricane Sandy costs estimated for New Jersey and New York reached \$60.4bn, a fraction of yet to be calculated liabilities for 2012. While sceptics pointed to a slowing of atmospheric warming in 2013, the world's oceans were absorbing the heat, leading to rising sea levels in the Pacific Ocean.

Coming out of climate denial in North America

Those denying scientific consensus on Darwin, evolution and anthropogenic (ie, human) effects on our planet's biosphere (including the 75 members of the US Congress in 2012) have been exposed as largely funded by fossil fuel interests. 350.org found US citizens lag behind 26 other advanced countries in their belief in evolution. Backlash legislation and more 'rebound effect' studies to protect coal and oil interest are still pushed by Republicans in Congress. Meanwhile, the UK's Parliament launched the Green Investment Bank, and the Environmental Audit Committee began its inquiry on green finance to explore institutional investors' decision making; to what extent a 'carbon bubble' exists and how to re-direct finance toward green sectors.[213]

Media and public debate is now surfacing in the USA and Canada on the need to shift to a more ecologically sustainable, socially just, cleaner, greener economy. Coverage of the heat waves, fires and storms, finally caused wider public recognition of global warming's effects.[214] The influential Centre for American Progress' 'Fulfilling the Promise of Concentrating Solar Power' and the US Department of Energy's Sun Shot programme urge ramping up solar CSP.[215] Canada's Conservative government is challenged by new opposition groups. Geothermal energy, long overlooked, is now growing as a clean alternative,

---

212 *The Economist*, 14 January, 2012, 60-62.

213 'New Inquiry Launched on Green Finance', media release, Environmental Audit Committee, UK Parliament, 14 June, 2013.

214 Borenstein, Seth, 'Climate Change', AP, 3 July, 2012 and Lacy, Stephen, 'Media Connecting the Dots on US Storms, Heat and Wildfires', ThinkProgress.org, 3 July, 2012.

215 'Fulfilling the Promise of Concentrating Solar Power', Center for American Progress, Washington, DC, June 2013.

promoted in the USA by the Geothermal Energy Association.[216] The reporting in our GTS still comes as a surprise to most mainstream media and public opinion driven by advertising revenues from incumbent fossil-fuelled sectors. At last, a high-profile US TV series 'Years of Living Dangerously', will arrive in 2014,[217] as well as the new SeeGreen® app based on the PBS TV series 'Earth: the Operating Manual'.

Emerging economies, led by China, India, South Korea, Brazil and many other countries, are advancing apace in shifting to greener economies.[218] A report now shows how little land is required in developing countries such as, Indonesia, Madagascar, India, Mexico, Morocco, South Africa and Turkey, to provide 100% of their electricity with solar at utility scale, i.e., able to provide across larger areas and grids.[219] The Asian Development Bank-UNESCAP report sees Asia emerging as a green economy leader now reflected in China's new 5-year plan moving toward a circular economy able to provide electricity nationwide on a large-scale.[220] Research by Pew found that among the G-20 the USA still lagged far behind.[221]

Momentum for the global green transition was accelerated by the OECD group of 37 advanced economies. Their Towards Green Growth reports[222] (and many others) indicated greater efforts to 'de-carbonise' their economies and grow green sectors

216 'Promoting Geothermal Energy: Air Emissions Comparison and Externality Analysis', Geothermal Energy Association, Washington, DC, May 2013.

217 'Showtime to Air 'Years of Living Dangerously', a Multi-Episode Documentary Series on Climate Change', Showtime, 3 December, 2012.

218 'A Guidebook to the Green Economy', UNDESA, November 2012, and 'Renewables Global Futures Report', Ren21, January 2013.

219 'Solar PV Atlas: Solar Power in Harmony with Nature: Toward 100% Renewable Energy, eds. Jean-Phillippe Denruyter and Lettemieke Mueder, WWF, First Solar, 3 Tier and Fresh Generation, Gland, Switzerland, 2013.

220 'Green Growth, Resources and Resilience', UNESCAP/UNEP, Bangkok, 16 February, 2012.; 'China's xx, *The Economist*, November xx 2013.

221 'Who's Winning the Clean Energy Race', Pew Charitable Trust, Washington, DC, 2010; 'Everygody who loves Mr Xi, say yes', *Economist,* November 16, 2013

222 www.oecd.org/greengrowth/towardsgreengrowth.htm

simply to modernise, create jobs and invest in more energy and resource efficiency.[223] Also, the International Monetary Fund's working paper: 'Who's Going Green and Why?' appeared in December 2011 and the global Katerva Awards have identified through their scientific networks many brilliant new technologies and approaches to sustainability.[224] A leading research group's list of 'Top Emerging Technology Companies in 2012' is replete with cleantech companies in solar, grid storage, bio-based materials, energy efficiency as well as health, wellness and infrastructure.[225] The world's cities now compete on these new metrics, including the C-40 group of over 63 cities worldwide sharing knowledge, led by New York City's former Mayor Michael Bloomberg in partnership with the William J. Clinton Foundation.[226] London already has 300 diesel/electric buses with a further 600 due for delivery in 2013 and 1000 electric car charging stations.[227] This green progress is tracked in the USA by the US Metro CleanTech Index.[228]

The need for new metrics

Mainstream financial markets confronted with reports from Carbon Tracker[229] show that mal-investments in fossilized energy sectors and reserves again illustrate the need for new metrics, not only to internalise externalities in prices and investment models, but also to correct GDP.[230] Such metrics include the Ethical Markets Quality of Life Indicators pioneered with Calvert in 2000 and the OECD's

---

223 See for example, 'Vision 2050: the New Agenda for Business', WBCSD, Conches-Geneva, 2011; 'Global Trends in Renewable Energy Investment', UNEP-Bloomberg, 2011; 'The Energy Report: 100% Renewables by 2050', WWF, ECOFYS, OMA, 2011. Full list in Appendix 3, Green Transition Scoreboard, February 2012.

224 Adams, Susan, 'The World's Best Sustainability Ideas', *Forbes*, www.katerva.org, 30 January, 2013.

225 'What Were the Top Emerging Technology Companies in 2012?', Lux Research, Inc., 18 December, 2012.

226 www.C40cities.org

227 Milton, Chris, 'Hydrogen Fuel Network In London Expands', CleanTechnica, 15 February, 2013.

228 US Metro CleanTech Index, Clean Edge, October 2012.

229 'Unburnable Carbon 2013: Wasted capital and stranded assets', Carbon Tracker Initiative and Grantham Research Institute, 2013, and others.

230 See for example, Capra F. and Henderson, H, 'Qualitative Growth', ICAEW, 2009.

Better Life Index. Many countries are now shifting beyond GDP to such more comprehensive indicators. The Sustainable Society Index (SSI) 2012 takes a similar broad approach.[231] A new Inclusive Wealth Index (IWI) was launched by the United Nations University at Rio+20, June 2012.[232] The UN Report 'Happiness: Toward a Holistic Approach to Development' calls explicitly for a new development paradigm.[233] Since 2008, large majorities in 22 countries agree that the move to renewable energy is critical to prevent climate change.[234] The Green Growth Knowledge Platform, launched January 2012 by OECD, UNEP and the World Bank, will help governments design and implement green growth policies.

In 2012 impetus for green growth also came from the United Nations. Its 193 member nations submitted their plans for the green transition and 191 signed the Declaration at Rio+20. Only two countries remain sceptical about this global transition to a green economy: Venezuela and Bolivia. Both see it as a capitalist takeover of environmental resources to commodify them for private profit. The Green Economy Coalition (GEC) is the largest global coalition of NGOs tracking these definitions of the inclusive global green economy. Indeed, agricultural land is described as the newest 'asset class' in an April 2012 conference for hedge funds, sovereign wealth funds and other institutional investors. The US pension fund TIAA-CREF and Sweden's AP2 are developing standards for farmland investing.[235] Ethical Markets believe that food should not be traded as an 'asset class,' since speculative positions have caused prices of staples to rise around the world, causing unnecessary hunger.[236] In particular pension funds should refrain from

---

231 Sustainable Society Index 2012 (SSI-2012), Sustainable Society Foundation, The Netherlands, 2012, www.ssfindex.com.

232 IWI, UNU-IHDP and UNEP, 2012.

233 Ban Ki-moon, op. cit.

234 Mountford, Sam, 'The Green Economy Global Public Opinion Briefing', original data from 2008, Globescan, Green Economy Coalition and IIED, 2010. greeneconomycoalition.org

235 Gilbert, Katie, 'Institutions Seek Long-term Value in Responsible Farmland Investing', *Institutional Investor Magazine*, December 2012.

236 Paramaguru, Kharunya, 'Betting on Hunger: Is Financial Speculation to Blame for High Food Prices?', *Time*, 17 December, 2012, which cited the NECSI computer model,

holding long positions in commodities futures and ETFs. US subsidies to ethanol produced from corn proved environmentally harmful and were reduced in 2012 but are still mandated in gasoline. They divert so much agricultural land and resources from food production that this also contributed to higher prices.

Wide debates continue in 2013 seeking to define the 'green economy' from the report of the Green Economy Coalition to those scheduled in the UN General Assembly in 2013.[237] Pakistan, Mexico, Ghana, Egypt and Argentina expressed reservations that poor people and the social dimensions of development would be short-changed while Costa Rica has become a green economy leader. Meanwhile, 27 EU countries increased their share of renewable energy consumption from 11.5% in 2009 to 12.4% in 2010.[238] A GlobeScan survey of experts found 72% saying that the green economy was the right theme for Rio+20 while 76% agreed that socially responsible investors would be the most important influencers, along with NGOs (69%) and labour unions (57%).[239] Closer focus on the successes of standards of energy efficiency and requirement for feed-in tariffs and renewable energy percentages for electricity utilities show that such government mandates are effective, as are labelling of appliances, products and building projects. Eco taxes, pollution and carbon taxes can keep any 'rebound effects' to a minimum, as well as a tax on financial transactions, all now on agendas in many countries.[240]

Leapfrogging old technologies

The developing countries of the southern hemisphere have specific advantages in the race to green the world's economies.[241] UNEP-FI reports on financing

---

mentioned earlier and the link with the tragic 'Dust Bowl' in the US mid-west during the 1930s.

237 'Summary of the Thematic Event on Employment and Inclusive Growth in the Post 2015 Development Agenda', Post-2015 Development Agenda Bulletin, IISD Reporting Services, vol 208 no 11, 14 June, 2013.

238 'The State of Renewable Energies in Europe', EurObserver, February 2012.

239 Survey on Activism and Rio+20, GlobeScan, London, January 2012.

240 Henderson, Hazel, 'Financial Transaction Taxes: The Commonsense Approach', Responsible Investor, 19 October, 2010.

renewable energy in developing countries focus on Africa[242] where countries are rich in solar resources. Here, infrastructure can be designed to support green, inclusive sustainable development as outlined in 'Infrastructure for a Changing World.'[243] These countries have fewer legacy and incumbent industries in fossilised sectors, less obsolescent infrastructure and fewer stranded assets (eg, aging nuclear plant decommissioning, mal-investments in proven fossil-fuel reserves which are unlikely to be recovered for multiple reasons: net energy costs, prices, additional pollution, etc.).

Transmission lines may shift from AC to DC and grids may be more regionalized and localized in many countries. The DESERTEC project is planned by 12 EU companies to bring electricity from solar facilities in North Africa over a high-voltage transmission line under the Mediterranean into Europe's grid. Another shift is occurring in electricity and transport in the USA and Europe which reverses the assumptions of big power plants that renewables (solar and wind) are too 'intermittent' and cannot be integrated into base-load generation.[244] The new paradigm is that renewables are developing to bypass or 'leapfrog' big plants and are growing locally via micro-grids, rooftops and cooperatively owned and municipal generators. All this is making 'big project finance' unprofitable.[245] By 2011 the boom in solar installations was driven by cost reductions rivalling coal plants and utility-size solar projects are close to grid parity. Bloomberg estimates that such projects will cost $1.45 per watt to build by 2020 – half the 2013 price.[246] A

---

241 'Sustainable Emerging Markets', Conference Report, *Responsible Investor*, London, March 2010.
242 'Financing Renewable Energy in Developing Countries', UNEP-FI, Nairobi, February 2012.
243 Clements-Hunt, Paul, et. al, 'Infrastructure for a Changing World', Sustainable Infrastructure Financing Forum and Summit, Global Energy Basel, 2013.
244 Baseload - varying as often as hour to hour, the minimum amount of power a utility must make available to customers in order to meet expected minimum demands.
245 'Renewables Global Futures Report', Ren21, January 2013.
246 Gossens, Ehren, 'Solar Power May Already Rival Coal, Prompting Installation Surge', *Bloomberg*, 6 April, 2011.

2013 report finds that 100% renewable energy could be closer than we think – particularly in coal-rich Australia.[247]

Thus, the 'technological leapfrog' strategies are preferred, particularly by China, Brazil, India and many other emerging giants, including those in the DESERTEC initiative. This 'leapfrog' takes many forms eg: mobile phones, leapfrogging costly landlines; distributed, local solar, wind, geothermal, low-head hydro leapfrogging wasteful national grids and costly centralised power plants; more energy and resource efficiency leading to re-designing of cities for pedestrians, cycles and mass transit, LED-municipal lighting and locally sourced solar and wind generators. As noted in many studies,[248] not only do developing countries now have these leapfrog advantages, costs are lower, allowing the 1.6 billion people who live far from electricity grids to enjoy simple solar electricity thanks to such innovators as Philips, mentioned earlier, Swiss-based DT Power and others.

Most developing countries cannot afford nuclear power or big central power plants and grid systems. However they are abundant in solar and renewable resources and culturally attuned to conservation and efficiency. For example, India uses its domestic coal inefficiently. Its future choices concern whether to increase imports and build more costly coal plants, or to ramp up renewables, particularly wind and solar.[249] Nuclear power's future is cloudy even in industrial countries, due to huge cost over-runs even after massive government subsidies and the disaster at Fukushima-Diachi which spurred a shift to renewables and Japan's plentiful

247 Parkinson, Giles, '100% Renewables Could Be Closer Than We Think', CleanTechnica, 16 February, 2013.

248 See for example G-20 High Level Panel on Investing in 3rd World Infrastructure, Cannes, France, November 2011; 'Towards a Green Economy: Pathways to Sustainable Development and Poverty Eradication', UNEP, Geneva, 2011; 'Toward an 'Energy Plus' Approach for the Poor', UNDP Asia Pacific Regional Center, Bangkok, Thailand, September 2011; and others in Appendix 3, Green Transition Scoreboard, February 2012.
    .   Chase, Jenny. *Bloomberg BusinessWeek*, 9 January, 2012.

249 'Renewables Global Future Report, op cit., p49.

geothermal energy sources.[250] As the *Financial Times* special report shows,[251] the idea of rich countries funding development in poor countries is becoming a thing of the past. Emerging markets are as much sources of cash as they are recipients, especially the sovereign wealth funds of China, Singapore and OPEC member countries. Many employ public development banks, such as the Brazilian Development Bank – BNDES, which finances innovation in all sectors. Others fund domestic entrepreneurs with community-based banks such as Grameen and BRAC in Bangladesh and ACLEDA in Cambodia.[252]

Biomimicry

The most efficient technologies are those employing the science of biomimicry (as for example, computer optimization for solar power plants, *The Economist*).[253] These new technologies mimic nature's designs for producing materials, conserving energy – optimised over 3.8 billion years of experimentation! Globally, companies are turning towards biomimicry methods in production.[254] Biomimicry is helping re-design many industrial methods and products such as dying fabrics using CO_2 instead of water.[255] Global clothes manufacturer H&M partnered with WWF to convert its suppliers to reduce water use.[256] Long overlooked agricultural technologies, pioneered by the Savory Institute[257] include the restoration of grasslands; the most efficient way to sequester carbon. In addition, innovations pioneered by The Land Institute in perennial plants and eco-restoration and

250 Henderson, Hazel, 'Nuclear Fission: the most wasteful, stupid and costly system for boiling water', Other News, 14 April, 2011.

251 'The Future of Development Banks', *Financial Times*, 24 September, 2012.

252 'The Bank that Likes to Say Yes', *The Economist*, 22 September, 2012.

253 'Flower Power', *The Economist*, 21 January, 2012.

254 'A Greener Footprint for Industry', UNIDO, New York, 2011; 'Tomorrow's Natural Business', BCI, Atos, Tomorrow's Company, London, 2011.

255 Makower, Joel, 'Color It Green: Nike to Adopt Waterless Textile Dying', Greenbiz.com, 7 February, 2012.

256 Stevens, Harry, 'Inside H&M's design for a new water management strategy', GreenBiz.com, 14 February, 2013.

257 Allan Savory, founder of the Savory Institute, and Wes Jackson, co-founder of The Land Institute, are members of the Ethical Markets Advisory Board.

seawater farming in desert lands using halophyte (salt-loving) plants for human and animal food.[258]

Helping companies re-tool offers safe biomimicry alternatives in many areas. These natural methods are distinguished from the more questionable "artificial life" methods including genetically-modified organisms for producing transport fuels and those using nanotechnologies which have not yet been assessed for their possible social and environmental impacts.

The potential for energy efficiency

Energy efficiency and reducing material throughput in all national economies target the lowest-entropy goals. For example, there is the potential in 120 million buildings in the USA to triple or quadruple their energy productivity with an average return of 33%.[259] Projections by the US Department of Energy, based on best available technology, show reductions in primary energy consumption are possible by 2030. 'The 3% Solution: Driving Profits Through Carbon Reduction' found that the US corporate sector can drive up to $190bn in 2020 and the net present value between 2010–2020 could be as high as $780b.[260] Demonstrable progress has been made in many countries and the potentials for huge efficiency improvements still exist worldwide. While some think tanks and economists still oppose energy efficiency, citing Stanley Jevons' 'rebound effect' from externalities allowing increasing consumption, this effect overall is reported at only 11%.[261]

---

258 Brown, Jed, Edward Glenn and James Leary, 'Irrigating Crops with Seawater', *Scientific American,* August 1998; Ho, Dr. Mae-Wan and Prof. Joe Cummins, 'Saline Agriculture to Feed and Fuel the World', www.i-sis.org.uk, 18 February, 2013; Bushnell, Dennis, 'Seawater/Saline Agriculture for Energy, Water, Land, Food and Warming', ed. Gad-el-Hak, Mohamed, *Large-Scale Disasters: Prediction, Control and Mitigation*, Cambridge University Press, 2008, p212.

259 US DOE AEO-2012.

260 'The 3% Solution: Driving Profits Through Carbon Reduction', McKinsey, CDP, WWF, June 2013.

261 ACEE 2012. (The rebound theory is based on economist Stanley Jevons' study of coal use in Britain in the 1800s and was reviewed inconclusively by the report of the UK Energy Research Centre.)

The decline in energy usage

ACEEE, ECEEE and the US Energy Information Administration's 'Annual Energy Outlook: Early Release Overview 2012' see energy use per capita declining at an average rate of 0.5% per year from 2010 to 2030.[262] A positive note on the advance of energy and materials efficiency is 'Long-term Efficiency Potential' report [263] which compares the 2050 USA energy-use forecast of 220 quads[264] with an Advanced Scenario using only 70 quads and the super-efficient Phoenix Scenario using a mere 50 quads which requires deeper 're-design.' These offer a net savings of $255bn per year and net 1.3 million jobs in the Advanced Scenario and net 1.9 million jobs in the Phoenix Scenario. All these advances are documented in *Cleantech Nation* (2012)[265] and in 'Renewables Global Future Report (2013) from Ren21.[266]

Information technology sectors

Another little-reported transition is the evolution of unpaid, voluntary, open-source sectors, based on sharing, cooperating and working for intrinsic satisfaction and personal development. These information age sectors are joining the traditional gift and love economy sectors of caring for families, elders, community volunteering, hitherto ignored in economic models and GDP statistics.. Canadian Don Tapscott describes these new trends in his *Macrowikinomics* (2011). The rise of barter, sharing and peer-to-peer production, lending and recently crowd-funding are covered on the Ethical Markets website in our Wealth of Networks, Crowdfunding and Community Development Solutions pages,[267] as well as in our TV programmes and by the P2P Foundation. These movements are expanding

---

262 US DOE AEO-2012.

263 ACEEE, Washington, DC, January 2012.

264 Quadrillion Btus—the U.S. consumed 98.081 quads in 2010 (Energy Information Administration).

265 Pernick, Ron and Wilder, Clint, *CleanTech Nation: How the US Can Lead In the New Global Economy*, Harper Business, New York, 2012.

266 www.ren21.net
     See for example, Shuman, Michael, *Local Dollars, Local Sense*, 2012; Cortese, Amy. *Locavesting*, 2011; Bauwens, Michel. *Collaborative Economies*, 2012.

267 www.ethicalmarkets.com

rapidly, and we follow the many continuing experiments to bypass fiat money circuits with local currencies, credit networks, cell phone banking and digital currencies, including bitcoin, qoin, ven and others.[268] Designs for currencies based on kilowatt hours from renewably generated electricity are in development by the Green Money Working Group and its conference in Split, Croatia, July 2012.[269]

Breakdowns and breakthroughs

Clearly, in spite of recessions caused by the financial crises, these breakdowns are also driving breakthroughs hastening the global green transition from conventional finance in fossilised sectors. China is now the global market leader in solar, wind and other low-carbon technologies in which they include nuclear. In spite of this, China provides a positive scenario for stabilising the global climate beyond the disappointments of focusing only on carbon emission reduction. Both China and India are still heavily reliant on coal – a huge challenge to scientists of the IPCC, highlighted in the failures of Kyoto Protocol trading regimes at Doha and Warsaw. Trading carbon on financial markets has proved inefficient in removing or preventing further CO_2 emissions, as described in 'From Rigged Carbon Markets to Investing in Green Growth'.[270]

---

268 'Filling the Bank-shaped Hole', Briefing on Non-Bank Finance, *The Economist*, 15 December, 2012.

269 'Energizing Euro', Declaration of the 1st International Social Transformation Conference, University of Split, Croatia, 2012.

270 Henderson, Hazel, 'From Rigged Carbon Markets to Investing In Green Growth', *Real World Economics Review*, Issue 57, 2011.

8.3 Renewable energy, sustainability and the valuation of natural capital

A.R.G. and W.H.Heesterman

Introduction

A successful and sustainable economy is unthinkable without an adequate supply of energy. Undoubtedly a healthy and stable society requires resources and facilities other than an adequate supply of energy. Nevertheless, the installation of renewable energy and its cost is a central topic of this paper. Here we focus on the relationship between renewable energy, a prosperous society and the threat of catastrophic climate change. Modern society needs energy. This is necessary, not merely for luxury consumption and the manufacturing of perhaps less than necessary gadgets, but rather more urgently for the provision of safe drinking water, irrigation, transport and storage of food. In the temperate and sub-Artic climate zones it is essential for heating and in parts of the tropical and sub-tropical climate zone where summer day time temperatures can be 40 degrees Centigrade or more, for cooling.

There is on current trends a real danger of catastrophic climate change. Thus, an increase in global mean surface temperature of no more than 1.5 degrees Centigrade above the 1850-1900 average is expected by IPCC (2013) in the case of only one of the emission scenarios (RCP2.6) considered; even though it could be more, up to as much as over 2 degrees, even for this particular scenario:

"Global surface temperature change for the end of the 21st century is likely to exceed 1.5°C relative to 1850 to 1900 for all RCP scenarios except RCP2.6. It is likely to exceed 2°C for RCP6.0 and RCP8.5, and more likely than not to exceed 2°C for RCP4.5. Warming will continue beyond 2100 under all RCP scenarios except RCP2.6."

What needs to be taken into account as well is the circumstance that a warming Artic could give rise to the release of large amounts of methane into the atmosphere. This relates not only to the methane hydrates i.e. methane locked in ice in so far frozen soil on land as well as below certain shallow areas of sea. The waters of the Arctic Ocean also contains large amounts of methane in a dissolved state likely to escape into the atmosphere when the water warms once the 24 hours sunshine beats down upon a seasonally open Arctic Ocean (Kort et al., 2012).

It is against this background that we come to the conclusion that the RCP2.6 scenario with the CO_2 concentration peaking at 500 ppm (parts per million) and then declining to about 400 ppm by 2100 is inadequate. We agree with Kevin Anderson (2013), who insists that to avoid dangerous climate change total decarbonisation is essential, i.e. zero CO_2 emissions by around 2040. To achieve this, emissions need to peak by about 2020 and then start reducing by around 20 percent per year. He is certainly not the only climate scientist pleading for rapid reductions in emissions (Le Quéré, 2104).

It is not widely known that an obvious way to meet this need for energy from renewable sources is perfectly affordable. We also argue that there are suitable means of implementing a programme to such a purpose in a market economy context, given the political will.

The technofix and the obstacles against implementing it

Whilst we argue that continuation of "economic growth" and increasing energy use is at least for some time technically possible it leaves other major issues unresolved. It is therefore no more than a technofix, although a relatively sound one. The onslaught of humanity on the earth is wider than climate change alone. Loss of biodiversity by habitat destruction and forms of environmental pollution other than emission of greenhouse gas are the most obvious additional threats. We do, however, defend resorting to this fix, because a more radical reorganization of society is impossible on the time scale required to avoid a catastrophe whilst also maintaining, respectively restoring full employment.

We also suspect that fast decarbonisation will bring the bankruptcy of the main energy companies and their specialised suppliers in their wake as long as these continue to rely on fossil fuel production. Known reserves of economically exploitable fossil fuel deposits already amount to several times the quantity we can afford to burn without running a substantial risk of exceeding the 2 degrees target (Carbon tracker, 2013; Berners-Lee and Clark, 2013). These authors refer to IPCC's 2 degrees target, i.e. RCP2.6, rather than the kind of more drastic action envisaged by Professor Anderson. Clearly measures to cushion the social impacts of such a development will be needed. Any such proposal is also bound to run into a climate change denial storm. The obstacle is much more political than technological or economic. And of course there is sheer inertia to be overcome. In this respect Michael Grubb's 2014 book *Planetary Economics* (359, see also 257*ff*, summary of societal obstacles against rapid decarbonisation) hits the nail on its head. Not only does the section emphasise the importance of inertia, existing technology and infrastructure, it also confirms the relevance of vested interest.

Earth rentals: the financial side of affluence without endless growth

There are statistical and conceptual difficulties in trying to express the value of activities which people may enjoy even if they are not paid to engage in. The distinction between the conceptual framework of statistically measured income and some measure of 'true' wellbeing and its measurability is, however, not as clear-cut as might be imagined.

To begin with, measured GDP is not quite as properly defined and accurate within its own conceptual framework as one might imagine.

Statistically recorded GDP is based on records of sales, that is to say *paid for*. That is an important limitation as maybe illustrated by the following two examples: (1) Increases in payments to 'fat-cat' senior executives give rise to increases in measured GDP, but it is debatable whether these payments represent any objectively useful work. (2) Changes in social structure. For example increased participation of women in the recorded labour market while services provided by firmsspecialised in floor and carpet cleaing. As well as purchased washing machines and dishwashers replace formerly unpaid chores by housewives, lead to payments and therefore constitute an increase in measured GDP. The same may, or may not apply to hired home helps … if there is any record, not if they are paid in cash without any record.

In addition there is a problem of complete statistical information on a global scale. The convention that income is identical to the value of production means that it needs to be corrected for speculative increases in asset prices. For example, a property developer may buy a bankrupt factory in an urban area for, let us say, £1 million and obtain planning permission to demolish it in order to build residential property on the land instead. The company may then leave it lying unproductive (keep it under wraps) for, let us say 20 years and sell it to another developer for £10 million. That is £9 million profit for filing the right pieces of paper to the appropriate authorities. Those nine millions are part of the first developer's taxable profit, but *not* of GDP, defined as the value of production only. GDP is corrected accordingly in the developer's country of residence by subtracting the increase in asset values from income, in order to obtain the value of production. However, if similar transactions are performed by a subsidiary operating abroad, the £9 million is rated as profit of the subsidiary company and booked as   export of financial services. This makes it a part of GDP.

Given the lack of precision in any figure of GDP or National Income obtained on the basis of records of payments, we have to admit to some scepsis in relation to correction this figure with a view to obtaining a meaningful figure for 'true' wellbeing. One might well argue that there is not even an open-ended possibility to increase true wellbeing, whether measurable or not. According to Wilkinson and Pickett (2010) there is an optimum level of affluence below which an increase in per capita GDP serves to reduce poverty, in particular, if inequality is reduced at the same time. In their view reaching this level is beneficial to social stability, whereas any further increase in material affluence is of questionable benefit.

To be sure, there are aspects of standard neoclassical economic theory which could conceptually justify corrections between measured total financial income and the 'utility' or satisfaction to which it gives rise, notably in relation to income inequality. For example Nordhaus (2008: 61) assumes that future generations will be less concerned about further even higher increase in income, as they are assumed to be more affluent. Therefore one percent increase in 'utility' requires 1.5 percent more measured income, If this proposition is accepted its generalisation to income distribution is straightforward. Taking one billion away in taxation from the 'fat-cat,' 1% highest income earners and spreading it equally out over the twenty-five percent of the population with the lowest incomes gives rise to a significant increase in total satisfaction. The problem is that while the basic proposition that more money is not as important to already wealthy people as it is to poor people is obvious, we lack any clear evidence regarding the value of this coefficient. The 1.5 percent rather looks like having been chosen so as to be consistent with a discount rate of an order of magnitude which this author thought suitable in the first place.

The balance of our judgment is to accept that any measure of 'true' income is inaccurate and to dispense with further attempts to correction. This conclusion, does, however, need qualifying when it comes to the providing incentives to business to act responsibly towards nature and the earth at the same time as decoupling social status from the requirement to engage in paid work.

There is a surprising similarity with what we referred to as compensated indirect taxation on p.183 of our *Rediscovering Sustainability*, and what James Hansen (2009a) calls 'Carbon Tax and 100% Dividend' and also refers to as the 'fee and dividend plan' (2009b). This would (at 2007 prices) amount to paying every US citizen aged 22 years or over $250 per month, and $125 per month for every youth aged 19-22. Hansen reckons this could be financed by a carbon tax equivalent to $1-- per gallon of gasoline (petrol).

Although we knew that James Hansen had urged the US authorities to take action on climate change when we wrote this section on compensated taxation, we were unaware of the details of his proposal. Perhaps we should have checked more carefully. In both cases the proposal is to start at a relatively low charge rate, which is then to be gradually increased. Both schemes also include a provision to correcting the cost of imported products that were produced with the support of a lower carbon tax abroad. Hansen refers to 'border taxes' and we to 'additional import duties' (Heesterman and Heesterman, 2013: 190). The one issue lacking in Hansen's discussion of this issue is an awareness of the relationship with global income distribution. If the rental value of the atmosphere is recognized as belonging equally to all citizens of the earth, the share of citizens of affluent high emission countries is much lower, as it needs to be distributed among a much larger number of individuals. We shall come back to this issue and to the alternative of tradable permits further down in this paper. Suffice it here to say that income which is allocated as part of the rental value of the earth could also be the financial basis of giving people the option of not doing any paid work. If so it ought to be accounted as original income and part of GDP even whilst being a gift of nature rather than the result of work or effort.

Once this point is recognized, two further comments arise. One is that any changes in charge rates, including their introduction from an initial situation of a zero rate cannot be classified as changes in income on their own.. The same comment applies to the act of re-defining an existing charge as a rental payment, so far booked according to usual rules of national income accounting as an indirect tax and hence a transfer payment, as a rental payment and hence primary income (Heesterman and Heesterman, 2013: 47), referring to the relevant official recommendation (United Nations 1964). The usual practice on this point in national income accounting is to report what is seen as the total amount produced as value in (year xxx) constant prices. A change in an environmental charge is therefore treated as a change in price. Note however, that a financial quantification of living beyond our means i.e. the consumption of environmental resources without replacing them, only arises if a separate sector 'collectively owned natural assets' (natural capital) with its own financial valuation is introduced into the national accounts. Otherwise the identity between income and production still means that the total valuation of investment in capital goods, etc., whether environmentally beneficial or harmful is identical to total savings.

We conclude this section with an admission of its limitation. Ideally, sustainability should ought to imply a non-reducing, presumably unchanging value of natural capital, which should have some kind of rate of interest type of relation with the total sum of taxation-type environmental charges. Well, that would be stylish and elegant. In practice we are, frankly, more concerned about directly practical issues like the climate crisis and (see below) reconciling a low rate of growth, (ideally zero for already affluent countries) with social stability. At this point we just note that assigning a cost to taking something from nature implicitly implies a valuation of its total value.

Renewable energy and its cost

The perception of high cost
There is, and certainly was, a perception that a more or less complete replacement of burning fossil fuels by renewable energy is particularly difficult or expensive. Consider the following quotes and references:

"To stabilise at 450 ppm CO_2e without overshooting, global emissions would need to peak in the next 10 years and then fall at more than 5% per year reaching 70% below current levels by 2050. This is likely to be unachievable with current and foreseeable technologies." (Stern, 2009: 218)

The Department of Energy and Climate Change, although not arguing that total decarbonisation is impossible with now known technology still emphasizes its cost.

"It would be unsafe to assume that renewable energy will become cheaper   than fossil fuel as a consequence of rising fossil fuel prices, especially   given   the additional cost of storage that will be need to deal with intermittency" (DECC, 2011)

Rosen and Guenther (2014) basically argue that given the horrendous risks of climate change, we should start with decarbonisation, even while we cannot know the cost.

Actual Prices charged are as yet also relatively high for renewable energy (The Economist 2014: Editorial)

Renewable energy is quite affordable

The view that renewable energy is horrendously expensive is seriously out of date in comparison with the available technological information and the costing thereof, if the most cost effective method of producing renewable energy is assumed.

Gregor Czisch (2005; 2011 English translation) carefully costed a range of technologies according to the information and references available in 2005. As the title indicates he took renewables only as the reference case for establishing the cost of supplying Europe, parts of adjoining central Asia and North Africa with electric power and then evaluated a number of alternatives. The only qualification with respect to the optimality by 2050 of an electricity supply based exclusively on renewables was (in 2005) gas fired Combined Heat and Power. What has since happened to gas prices and the further reduction in the cost of renewables since then strongly suggests that this caveat no longer applies.

Crucial to this conclusion is, however, the transmission of electricity over long distances via High Voltage Direct Current cables. The usual form of electric power supply on a city or regional scale is Alternating Current, i.e. the direction of the current changes all the time, usually 60 times per second. All transmission of electric energy via cables is associated with some losses, as electric energy is converted into heat. However, the energy loss due to this direct conversion of electric current into heat depends on the metal used and the thickness of the cable rather than the voltage. Thus, this form of energy loss per kilometre in a 25,000 volt overhead power line is the same as would arise if 250 volt were used, although the amount of energy transmitted is 100 times as much. There are, however, other forms of energy loss, which are AC current only (Electrical Engineering Portal, 2013).

Transport of energy over long distances via High Voltage Direct Current electricity cables is by now a well established technology and it has three distinct advantages.

• Renewable forms of energy can be harvested where and when they are naturally abundant, e.g. solar energy in deserts and in the middle of the day and geothermal energy in volcanic areas and used where required.

• Pooling of resources: supply over time zones reduces the maximum capacity needed to meet peak demand.

• Installations can normally be used at a level close to their maximum design capacity whenever the local supply of renewable energy such as sunshine is available. When the local supply exceeds local demand the energy can be used or stored elsewhere. In the event of insufficient local supply demand can be met by import of energy from somewhere else.

Czisch even envisages HVDC power lines under oceans, although that was not included in his costing.

Whilst the HVDC supergrid technology and its integration with AC was known, well tested and costed by the time the Stern Review came out, an alternative method of avoiding the investment cost of installing wind turbines for when there is wind, solar panels for when the sun shines and hydropower for when it rains now looks like becoming available: large batteries.

A letter in Nature (Huskinson et al 2014) makes it clear that although this is as yet not technology which simply needs rolling out, the possibility to store large amounts of energy locally is now well established physics.

Either technology integrates smoothly with a so-called smart grid which changes tariff and informs energy users of price changes according to the actually available supply capacity in tandem with timing the use of storable forms of energy such as hydro power (http://en.wikipedia.org/wiki/Smart_grid). For example battery powered electric vehicles should be charged and dish washers and washing machines should be switched on at times when there is a surplus of supply capacity over types of demand that are more difficult to postpone.

Financing the construction of HVDC supergrids

There are two main routes which both would achieve the aim of more or less completely eliminating the use of fossil fuels: taxation of emissions, i.e. a carbon tax, and direct public support for building supergrids. A third type of scheme, the tradable permit system, is clearly not suitable for completely eliminating the use of fossil fuels, and for reasons to be explained below although not the most cost effective method of a drastic cut in emissions.

Route 1: Taxation of emissions to an extent where burning fossil fuel becomes uneconomic in comparison with renewable energy even whilst the latter does not as yet have the support of a HVDC supergrid. If that route is chosen, the price of energy is high enough to make renewable energy price competitive with burning taxed fossil fuel, even whilst the capital cost of renewable energy has to support a capacity which is used only intermittently: solar panels for when the sun shines as well as wind-turbines for when there is enough wind, but if there is enough sunshine and also enough wind the total installed capacity exceeds demand. For reasons explained in the section on earth rentals above, we support compensated taxation.

Route 2: Direct support for building supergrids from public funds. There are two mean reasons why we would recommend this route as the more suitable under present circumstances even whilst a carbon pricing scheme might support it as well. Firstly, although this might possibly still apply to the indirect process of manufacturing a petrol or diesel like fuel via electricity from renewable energy sources, we don't think that as far as across the board energy costs is concerned, a carbon charge equivalent to as much as $1-- per gallon and then still rising further is needed to make renewable energy more cost effective than burning fossil fuels. However, in the broader context of making full employment for all those who want or are socially pressed to find paid work and the associated containment of exploitation, we reckon there are other suitable types of earth rental charges. Taxation of investment, unless it can be shown to be environmentally beneficial (Heesterman and Heesterman, 2013: 136) could fulfills the same role, even whilst it relates not currently known forms of natural capital.

In our opinion the main reasons why building of HVDC supergrids in high emission areas of the world is not yet proceeding at the speed at which it would be desirable are firstly the sheer inertia and lack of information (Grubb, 2014: 257ff). In addition there is a disproportional influence of vested interests, because of their ability to support political parties and candidates for election. The latter point is emphasized by Hansen (2009b: 2012ff) who blames the lack of action regarding his specific proposal on this situation. In our view that is a major part of the explanation of the paucity of any meaningful action on climate change so far. This is certainly a situation which we expect to aggravate with any serious attempt to phase out fossil fuel use (W. H. Heesterman, forthcoming). However, a project which would not lead to higher energy prices might not meet with quite as much opprobrium. In addition, there is the issue of scale economies, and more specifically of system scale economies. The supergrid does not itself produce energy, even whilst it facilitates the import of energy from areas where renewable forms of energy are naturally abundant to where the energy is needed. Further benefits of the supergrid resulting in an improved ratio between the maximum total design capacity of the individual installations and their effectively used capacity depend on its coverage of a large area. This situation gives rise to substantial once-for-all overhead costs before it is prudent to rely on supply via the grid rather than ensuring adequate local capacity under all weather conditions. These overhead costs are more effectively utilised under a market structure of monopoly than under competition. Public (national or multinational) ownership is the more efficient structure (Heesterman and Heesterman, 2012: 75ff). We also note that, as long as fossil fuels are at all cost effective at the prevailing false price structure, reaching the full potential of a partly completed supergrid, (i.e. exceeding the target,) may not be fully realisable in the presence of a system of tradable permits, as it does not encourage utilities to exceed the target.

Under the current situation of unemployment in industrial countries rapid build up of the renewable energy capacity (as well as better insulation) is also is the obvious form of Keynesian stimulation of employment (See also Campaign against Climate Change, 2014). Given the problems around public debt, we support finance of the HVDC supergrid by direct issue of money by central banks, notably the European Currency Bank (ECB) and the US Federal Reserve. That would still involve less of a risk of inflation than the current programs of Quantitative Easing, i.e. the purchase of government bonds by central banks from private banks, paid for with newly created money.

A realistic paradigm for the entire world?

A world where only the so-called developed part of the society has access to affordable energy would be subject to dangerous tensions. It would also be highly unethical to continue to ignore the needs of those less fortunate. By 2014 a fifth of the world population is still without any access to energy, while some 2.6 billion people lack clean cooking facilities (International Energy Agency, 2014). In consequence, many millions of women are destined to ruin their lungs by cooking on open wood, charcoal or dung fires, and so are millions of small children whose lives tend to be lived in company of women. This is a situation which a United Nations initiative intends to put right by 2030 through its 'Sustainable Energy for All' project (UNDP, 2012).

Energy is the golden thread that connects economic growth, increased social equity, and an environment that allows the world to thrive." (United Nations, UN Secretary-General Ban-Ki Moon, 2012)

The question is whether a programme of energy provision to currently poorer countries has to follow the same route as in the affluent parts of the world. Traditionally this has been disputed. Small-scale solutions are being implemented piecemeal, mostly by NGOs or governments. According to the Sussex Energy Group some 300,000 homes in Kenya have now been fitted with solar panels, presented as a major pro-poor achievement (Pearce, 2014). However, according to a recent report published by the Breakthrough Institute this type of power provision locks people into a future of low innovation, perpetuating disastrous neo-colonial policies. Countries where just thirty percent of the population currently has access to electricity, such as Kenya, need 'the latest technology' rather than 'appropriate technology.' "Thresholds are typically unacceptably low and far from equitable" (Caine et al. 2014). These authors criticise the narrow vision of the 'Sustainable

Energy for All (SE4all)' initiative, claiming that it relies on the premise that 'basic human needs' can be met with enough electricity to power a fan, a couple of light bulbs, and a radio for five hours a day."

But "what is the latest technology?"

Accordingly, Caine et al. interpret 'latest technology' as one that is only deliverable over a power grid. The authors do not dispute the need for low-carbon energy and are adamant that it should not be based on coal. They advocate a policy of large-scale solutions such as hydro-electric or nuclear instead. "High population densities require large-scale, centralized energy sources" (ibid.: 9). A large scale scheme they refer to in particular concerns the 'Grand Inga' project, to be built in the Democratic Republic of Congo.

In keeping with suggestions such as these, the World Bank has voted a grant of $73 million for the construction of the Inga 3 Dam, the first phase of the scheme (World Bank, 2014), less than two weeks after agreeing to postpone the project indefinitely (International Rivers, 2014). The final project promises to be the largest hydroelectric power installation in the world, capping even the power output of the Three Gorges Dam in China. Completion would have the potential to electrify a third of the entire continent and even some parts of Europe. Half of the expected output has already been reserved for South Africa. In addition, the build of this dam is expected to spur other infrastructure projects in Africa (Smith, 2014). In 2002, the New Scientist correspondent Fred Pearce referred to the opinion of "engineers" advocating an alternative non-dam Grand Inga project which would involve 52 separate hydroelectric power stations generating electricity from different sections of the river. Our inspection of the literature indicates that, whilst Showers (2012) warns of serious other, so far not adequately assessed environmental impacts of large hydro-dam projects, Helston (2012) describes an alternative system, the so-called 'Run-of-River' (ROR) which has been extensively applied in Canada. This involves diverting part of the river flow above rapids or cascades into a side channel leading to a turbine inlet pipe. There are however, two important limitations even to this version of hydropower:

Firstly, ROR does not harvest anything like the full potential of the amount of energy of the current. Only a relatively small part of the river's flow is diverted to the turbines, Helston also reports that it has so far proved for this reason to be significantly more expensive per unit of energy than dam-generated hydropower. In addition, her references to environmental impact refer to local ecosystems, ignoring the reduced silt supply. Presumably ROR also limits this effect to a large extent (see below).

Reservoirs give rise to several types of problems. In many cases land has been flooded without prior removal of the vegetation. In that case submerged woodland and peat may be a source of methane emissions, in particular in the tropical climate zone, which for a transitional period could make hydro power as climate disrupting as coal. (St. Louis et al., 2000). In fact, we have seen an example of this bad practice ourselves in Surinam: the sorry remnants of submerged trees still visible in 2002, sticking out from the Brokopondo Reservoir, one of the largest in the world. It was created between 1965 and 1970 by flooding 160,000 hectares of biologically valuable tropical rainforest (World Bank, 2003: 1). We just learnt that the valuable hardwood is now being harvested, more than forty years after it ought to have been. In the meanwhile decay of the undergrowth has, of course, led to extensive methane emission.

Clean electricity generated by hydropower from either version of the Grand Inga project would certainly benefit many urban households, although in particular in the case of the more substantial energy supply via dams, the bulk of the electricity could well go to industrial users or be exported. But to what extent would such a large-scale project profit those living widely dispersed in rural areas? Connection to a centralised grid would be virtually impossible. According to Grossman, this caveat applies to the majority of the 85 percent of people lacking electricity worldwide (2014: 20).

Environmental and social impacts of the Dam project
Sanyanga, Africa Director for the International Rivers NGO, claims that few of those currently living downstream from the future dams, realise what the impact

on their lives will be. In fact many are unaware of the size of the project (Pambazuka.org: 2014). The experience of those displaced by the earlier Inga dam schemes does not inspire much confidence. The author visited the Inga I and II dams, completed respectively in 1972 and 1982, which have been poorly maintained and urgently require repairs, estimated to cost $883 million, four times the 2003 World Bank estimate. As it happened, responsibility for maintenance lay with local authorities. In case of the Grand Inga project, intended to bring power to several countries, responsibility for maintenance would be with numerous bodies. This would apply even more if electricity were to be generated in the form of ROR hydro-electric plants.

There are reasons to fear that a project such as this, which would require extensive power grids to be constructed across large tracts of Africa, could be subject to corruption in a state such as the DRC, which experiences so much crime and violence. Many of those displaced by the earlier dams are living in 'Camp Kinshasa' even now, and are still waiting for compensation packages promised some forty years ago. In fact many people have been displaced worldwide by dam projects with resettlement efforts and compensation inadequate at best (Hathaway and Pottinger, 2008: 150).

Last but not least, CORAP (Coalition Reformes Action Publique), a coalition of some 31 DRC citizen organisations, sent a letter, signed by twelve chair persons to the World Bank in January 2014. The letter criticises the way in which the Inga Dam project had been conceived, without a prior inclusive assessment of the needs of the Congolese society nor of any alternative potential of energy supply. There had been no environmental impact assessment either. The writers also highlight the fact that the population of the areas concerned has not been consulted or even been properly informed of the proceedings. They also draw attention to the fact that those displaced by the earlier Inga projects had never received any comprehensive compensation. By disregarding these issues, the proceedings were in contravention of the Bank's own stated standards. The letter ends by making an appeal to the Bank to ensure that "The energy needs of the DRC population are prioritized in a comprehensive needs assessment."

The CORAP letter also refers to studies that treat the Inga 3 as separate from the overall Grand Inga scheme, yet sharing the same environment including the river mouth. According to the International Rivers NGO, the falls and rapids are in proximity to the estuary, where the river disgorges a massive nutrient-rich plume of silt, reaching as far as 400 km out from the coast, which currently acts as a major carbon sink, as it feeds large numbers of plankton. In consequence construction of the dam might well give rise to a serious aggravation of climate change. Note that this applies to the Inga 3 dam as well as to the dam version of the Grand Inga project. The alternative ROR version might not inhibit the outflow of silt to the same extent.

The scope of the potential solutions

As it is, we have been unable to verify the claim by the authors of the Breakthrough report that SE4all's objective would not go beyond the provision of 'basic needs,' consisting of "a couple of light bulbs, and a radio for five hours a day" to poor people in underdeveloped countries. We were unable to find the aforementioned expression anywhere on the Internet other than in that self-same report. Instead, we came across a January 2014 SE4All Country Action Agenda Template, specifically relating to Africa. According to this document UNDP "supports access to electricity (on- and off-grid, decentralized whenever possible and based on clean energy technologies), access to clean fuel and devices for cooking and heating and increased access to and use of mechanical power. The means of access to power could both by the provision of grid infrastructure and supply efficiency and distributed electricity solutions" (SE4All, January 2014: 2.1.3.1. & 2.). Already such solutions are being implemented, in the form of micro-grids, whether from micro-hydro-power plants constructed in fast flowing rivers or from wind turbines, some of these apparently cobbled together from scrap metal. Larger energy installations, such as, CSP plants (concentrating solar power) could be part of the energy mix. This type of power provision has even been welcomed as a potential model for rural communities in the rich world eager to switch to renewable sources. The downside is that distributed electricity tends to be more expensive. On the other hand, older centralised power grids are more vulnerable: if one component fails, the entire system may well go down

(Grossman, 2014: 20). Why is it that large-scale schemes are so eagerly embraced and funded by large institutions, while coordination of small projects by NGOs tends to be lacking?

In our view there is no clear one-or-the-other answer to the question whether small-scale solutions are always preferable. The grid has advantages which are not limited to affluent 'developed' countries. Accordingly DESERTEC, to whose plans we referred to on p. 245ff. of Rediscovering Sustainability, intends to build several HVDC lines in North Africa including an East-West connection. On the other hand, there are large scale renewable energy projects which are controversial and not always as environmentally desirable as might be thought. In particular large dams and reservoirs more often than not require people to be relocated, in many cases without provision for proper resettlement. In the absence of formally registered ownership this is likely to happen without compensation. Also, the creation of reservoirs tends to give rise to large scale methane escapes. To avoid this requires removal of all plant material rather than just harvesting commercially valuable timber before the dam is closed. A low population density also means that bringing mains electricity to remote villages is impractical whilst local installations to harvest renewable energy are more economic under these circumstances.

The rise of robotics

As long as labour continues to be seen as the main commercially relevant production factor commerce and industry will strive to increase production per worker. Hence maintaining full employment depends on a regular increase in production. Given that earning one's living by working for money is the accepted social norm, social stability requires opportunities for paid employment for a large section of the population during at least part of their adult lives. In view of current trends in technology security of employment may well require a faster rate of growth of material affluence than has been the norm in the last decades.

David Zeiler, writing in the US financial magazine Money Morning (2013) refers to a report by Kevin Kelly in Wired (2012) which forecasts that 70% of US current jobs will have gone by the end of the century. Ben Miller and Robert Atkinson of the (US) Information Technology and Innovation Foundation (2013) disagree pointing out that this is not what has historically happened with previous waves of technological innovation. They also comment that "human wants are close to infinite." Maybe that is the case and it may well be possible to use demand management to enable people to buy more luxury goods and to make use of the same number of staff to produce more, rather than producing the same amount while employing fewer workers. The problem with this approach is that there are finite limits to the earth's resources as well as to the absorption capacities for the debris of all those frills. Whilst it is possible to produce more GDP per worker by giving people the money to buy more, this keeps us hooked on indefinite economic growth. The only way this problem can be fully resolved in a market economy context implies separating the right to live as a respected member of society from the requirement to earn money by doing paid work. This is an issue reviewed in some detail in Chapter 11 of our book Rediscovering Sustainability (Heesterman and Heesterman, 2013). Whether individuals paid for being idle would be content with a lifelong holiday or might be willing and able to engage in some unpaid, but socially useful activity, is an issue we don't want to go into any further. The one point which is, however, useful to add here in particular in relation to robotics is that we have elsewhere (Rediscovering Sustainability pp. 136-137) defended a charge on commercial investment which cannot be shown to be beneficial to the environment. The primary purpose of such a charge is to slow down the growth of further luxury consumption in order to protect the earth from so far unknown forms of environmental damage whilst nevertheless maintaining full employment. However, it would undoubtedly also help to finance the relaxation of the requirement to earn money by doing paid work as discussed above.

Concluding remarks

Containing the risk of catastrophic climate change by means of a rapid replacement of the use of fossil fuels by renewable energy is technologically feasible and not even particular costly in financial terms. The controversy over large scale versus small scale energy provision is misleading: we need both, while it is quite possible to integrate them. However, due to the reluctance to take the threat to the climate seriously, resulting in unwarranted delays in taking action any real attempt to contain the danger of catastrophic climate change is likely to run into fierce opposition from vested interest who may well face bankruptcy. In addition, it leaves the longer time problem of the tension between maintenance of employment for the sake of social stability versus natural and physical sustainability unresolved. A more radical reconstruction of society, in particular of the status of people who do not engage in financially rewarded work is of the essence. Otherwise one is left with the choice of maintaining economic growth for the sake of employment whilst damaging the environment, or alternatively, risk serious social and political disorder. Above all, populations and most of all those affected by decisions, need to be consulted from the start, while compensation should be provided on the nail rather than pledged for some undefined future.

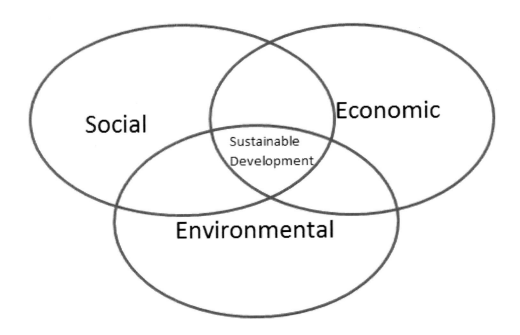

References

Anderson, K. 2014. http://kevinanderson.info/blog/wp-content/uploads/2013/01/EcoCities-presentation-for-distribution-.pdf

Caine, M., Lloyd, J., Luke, M., Margonelli, L., Moss , T., Nordhaus , T., Pielke, R. Jr., Román, Roy, M. Sarewitz , J.D., Shellenberger, M., Singh, K. and A. Trembath, 2014. Our High-Energy Planet: A Climate-Pragmatism Project. The Breakthrough Institute / the Consortium for Science, Policy & Outcomes, April 2014

Campaign against Climate Change, Trade Union Group, 2014. '1 Million Climate jobs, 2nd ed. Expected 20 September 2014. London: Campaign against Climate Change'

Coalition Reformes Action Publique (CORAP). 2014. Letter to World Bank http://www.internationalrivers.org/files/attachedfiles/corap_world_bank_ed_letter_0114.pdf

Czisch, G. 2011. Scenarios for a Future Electricity Supply. Cost-optimised variations on supplying Europe and its neighbours with electricity from renewable energies. London: The Institution of Engineering and Technology2011 (German source original: Thesis, University of Kassel, 2005)

DECC Science Advisory Group, . 2011. 3d Meeting: Minutes, 9 March 2011. Was available at: http://www.decc.gov.uk/assets/decc/11/about-us/science/2092-decc-sag-meeting-minutes-090311.pdf

The Economist, 2014. editorial "Why is renewable energy so expensive?" http://www.economist.com/blogs/economist-explains/2014/01/economist-explains-0

Electrical Engineering Portal. 2013. http://electrical-engineering-portal.com/advantages-of-hvdc-over-hvac-transmission

Grossman, L. 2014. 'Africa's power struggle,' New Scientist, 23 August 2014, p. 20

Grubb M. 2014. Planetary Economics, London/New York: Routledge

Hansen, J. 2009a Testimony to the Ways and Means committee of the U.S. House of Representatives on 25 February 2009 made available by Columbia University at http://www.columbia.edu/~jeh1/2009/WaysAndMeans_20090225.pdf

Hansen, J. 2009b. Storms of my grandchildren, London/New York: Bloomsbury Publishing, 2009

Hathaway, T. and L. Pottinger. 2008. 'The great hydro-rush: the privatisation of Africa's rivers' (Chapter 5) in Electric Capitalism: Recolonising Africa on the power grid

Heesterman, A.R.G. and W.H. Heesterman, 2013. Rediscovering Sustainability: Economics of the Finite Earth, Farnham: Gower Publishing

Heesterman, W.H. 2015. 'Disparagement of climate change research: a double wrong' (Chapter 6) in Ethical Engineering for International Development and Environmental Sustainability, ed. Dr M. Hersh, London: Springer (in press)

Helston, C. http://www.energybc.ca/profiles/runofriver.html

Huskinson, B., Marshak, M.P., Suh, C., Süleyman Er, S., Gerhardt, M.R. Cooper J. Galvin, C.J. Chen, X. Aspuru-Guzik, A. Gordon, R.G. and Aziz, M. J.. 2014. 'A metal-free organic–inorganic aqueous flow battery,' Nature 505, 195–198 (09 January 2014) doi:10.1038/nature12909

Intergovernmental Panel on Climate Change (IPCC). 2013 Summary For Policymakers Working Group I (Science), http://www.climatechange2013.org/images/report/WG1AR5_SPM_FINAL.pdf

International Energy Agency. 2014. Energy Poverty, http://www.iea.org/topics/energypoverty/

International Rivers 2013, http://www.internationalrivers.org/resources/congo %E2%80%99s-energy-divide-factsheet-3413

International Rivers, 2014. http://www.internationalrivers.org/resources/pr-%E2%80%93-world-bank-indefinitely-postpones-inga-3-project-8223

Kelly, K. 2012. 'Better Than Human: Why Robots Will — And Must — Take Our Jobs'. Wired, 24 December 2012, http://www.wired.com/2012/12/ff-robots-will-take-our-jobs/all/

Kort, E.A., Wofsy, S.C., Daube, B.C., Diao, M., Elkins, J.W., Gao, R.S., Hintsa, E.J., Hurst, D.F., Jimenez, R. Moore, F.IL., Spackman, J.R. and M.A. Zondio. 2012. 'Atmospheric observations of Arctic Ocean methane emissions up to 82° north', Nature Geoscience, April 2012 Abstract, http://www.nature.com/ngeo/journal/v5/n5/full/ngeo1452.html

Le Quéré, C. 2014. The scientific case for radical emissions reductions, http://www.tyndall.ac.uk/sites/default/files/le_quere_radical_emission_reductions.pdf

Miller, B. and R. Atkinson. 2013. 9 September 2012 at http://www.itif.org/publications/are-robots-taking-our-jobs-or-making-them

Pearce, F. 2002: 'Giant Congo hydroelectric project is a betrayal'. http://www.newscientist.com/article/dn2839-giant-congo-hydroelectric-project-is-a-betrayal.html#U_-WVMVdVNs

Pearce, F. 2014. Power to the people, NewScientist 2 August 2014, pages 26-27

Rosen, R.A and Guenther, E.,: The economics of mitigating climate change: What can we know? Technological Forecasting and Social Change, In Press, February 2014 http://www.diw.de/documents/dokumentenarchiv/17/diw_01.c.469665.de/tfsc %20paper%20-%20final%20published%20version%20-%2002-27-14.pdf

Showers, K. 2012, http://www.internationalrivers.org/resources/grand-inga-will-africa%E2%80%99s-mega-dam-have-mega-impacts-1631, pp. 10, 11, 15 (excerpt from Engineering Earth, the impact of megaengineering projects, ed. S.D. Brunn, 2011, Springer

St. Louis, V. Kelly, C., Duchemin, É., Rudd, J.W.M. and Rosenberg, D.M. 2000. Reservoir surfaces as sources of greenhouse gases to the atmosphere: a global estimate. BioScience 50 (9), 766–775

Sanyanga, R. 2013. Will Congo's poor benefit from world's largest dam project? http://pambazuka.org/en/category/features/88088

Smith, D. 2014. The Grand Inga Dam: A Risk to Powering Africa? Borgen Magazine, June 21, 2014

Stern N. 2009. The Economics of Climate Change: The Stern Review. Cambridge, UK: Cambridge University Press

United Nations (Department of Economic and Social Affairs, Statistical Office of the United Nations). 1964. A System of National Accounts and Supporting Tables (Studies in Methods, Series F, No. 2, Rev.2). New York: United Nations.

United Nations. 2011. Secretary-General to Global Development Center, http://www.un.org/News/Press/docs/2012/sgsm14242.doc.htm

United Nations. 2014. SUSTAINABLE ENERGY FOR ALL (SE4ALL) COUNTRY ACTION AGENDA TEMPLATE, http://www.se4all.org/wp-content/uploads/2013/10/ActionAgendaTemplate_AfricaHub_01032014.pdf

Wilkinson, R.G. and K. Pickett. 2010. The Spirit Level: Why equality is better for everyone. London: Penguin Books.

http://www.internationalrivers.org/files/attached-files/electric_capitalism_-_5_the_great_hydro-rush__the_privatisation_of_africa_s_rivers.pdf

World Bank. 2003. Good Dams and Bad Dams: Environmental Criteria for Site Selection of Hydroelectric Projects, http://www-wds.worldbank.org/external/default/WDSContentServer/WDSP/IB/2014/07/24/000470435_20140724121745/Rendered/PDF/303600NWP0Good000010Box18600PUBLIC0.pdf

World Bank. 2014. 'Press release: World Bank Statement on the Inga-3 Hydropower Development Project Appraisal Document,' 5 March 2014, http://www.worldbank.org/en/news/press-release/2014/03/05/world-bank-statement-on-the-inga-3-hydropower-development-project-appraisal-document
Zeiler, D. 2013. Money Morning, 4 February 2013
http://moneymorning.com/2013/02/04/robots-taking-jobs-from-every-sector-of-the-economy/

8.4 Inequality Matters: Responding to the Growing Wealth Gap

Chuck Collins

In April 2014, a French economist, Thomas Piketty, published his English language edition of *Capital in the Twenty-First Century*. The book climbed to the top of *The New York Times* best-seller list, along side Daniel Steele's steamy romance novel, *First Sight*.

How did a book about wealth inequality by an obscure French economist capture the imagination of U.S. readers?

One reason is that public alarm over growing U.S. income and wealth inequality has been building steadily for the last decade. From Presidential debates, to the "occupy movement," wealth disparity is now on the political agenda.[271]

In the fall of 2011, a website emerged urging people to share a photograph and story of their experience being in the 99 percent. One young woman wrote,

> I used to dream about becoming the first woman president. Now I dream about getting a job with health insurance.[272]

A twenty-seven-year-old U.S. veteran of the Iraq War described how he enlisted in the military to protect the American people but discovered he "ended up making profits for politically connected contractors."

> I returned to a country whose economy had been devastated by bankers

---

271 The primary resource for this article is the author's book, Chuck Collins, *99 to 1: How Wealth Inequality is Wrecking the World and What We Can Do About It* (Berrett Koehler, 2012).
272 We are the 99 percent website, http://wearethe99percent.tumblr.com/post/12556818590/i-also-wanted-to-go-to-a-top-university-which-i (accessed January 3, 2012).

with the same connections and the same lack of ethics. . . . This is the second time I've fought for my country and the first time I've known my enemy. I am the 99 percent.[273]

One handwritten sign simply says:

> I am twenty. I can't afford college. There aren't many jobs I qualify for, and the rest "just aren't hiring." Tell me, what exactly am I living for? I am the 99 percent.

On another website, organized to give voice to members of the 1 percent who support the 99 percent, an investment advisor named Carl Schweser wrote,

> I made millions studying the math of mortgages and bonds and helping bankers pass the Chartered Financial Analyst Exam. It isn't fair that I have retired in comfort after a career working with financial instruments while people who worked as nurses, teachers, soldiers, and so on are worried about paying for their future, their health care, and their children's educations. They are the backbone of this country that allowed me to succeed. I am willing to pay more taxes so that everyone can look forward to a secure future like I do. I am the 1%. I stand with the 99%. Tax me.[274]

These are the stories that are propelling a new conversation in the United States and the world. The underlying conditions of debt, despair, low-wage jobs, persistent poverty and a collapsing middle class standard of living are not going away. Along with the stories, there are statistics like these:

---

273 We are the 99 percent website, http://wearethe99percent.tumblr.com/post/12639892423/i-am-a-27-year-old-veteran-of-the-iraq-war-i (accessed January 3, 2012).
274 We Stand with the 99 Percent website, http://westandwiththe99percent.tumblr.com/post/11849022824/i-made-millions-studying-the-math-of-mortgages-and (accessed January 3, 2012).

• The 1 percent in the U.S. has 35.6 percent of all private wealth, more than the bottom 95 percent combined. The 1 percent has 42.4 percent of all financial wealth, more than bottom 97 percent combined.[275]

• The 400 wealthiest U.S. individuals on the Forbes 400 list have more wealth than the bottom 150 million Americans.[276]

• In 2010, 25 of the 100 largest U.S. companies paid their CEO more than they paid in U.S. taxes. This is largely because a few thousand global corporations use offshore tax havens to dodge their U.S. taxes.[277]

• In 2010, the 1 percent in the U.S. earned over 21 percent of all income, up from 8 percent in 1979.[278]

• Between 1983 and 2009, over 40 percent of all wealth gains flowed to the 1 percent and 82 percent of wealth gains went to the top 5 percent. The bottom 60 percent lost wealth over this same period.

• The world's 1 percent, almost entirely millionaires and billionaires, own $42.7 trillion, more than the bottom 3 billion residents of earth.

• While the middle-class standard of living implodes, sales of luxury items such as $10,000 wristwatches and Lamborghini sports cars are skyrocketing.

• Between 2001 and 2010, the United States borrowed over $1 trillion to give wealthy taxpayers with incomes over $250,000 substantial tax breaks, including the 2001 Bush-era tax cuts.[279]

---

275 Sylvia A. Allegretto, "The State of Working America's Wealth," Economic Policy Institute Briefing Paper #292, March 23, 2011.

276 Sam Pizzigati, "The New Forbes 400—and Their $1.5 Trillion," inequality.org, September 2012).

277 Sarah Anderson, Chuck Collins, Scott Klinger, and Sam Pizzigati, "The Massive CEO Rewards for Tax Dodging," Institute for Policy Studies, September 2011, www.ips-dc.org/reports/executive_excess_2011_the_massive_ceo_rewards_for_tax_dodging (accessed January 3, 2012).

278 Congressional Budget Office, "Trends in the Distribution of Household Income Between 1979 and 2007," October 2011, www.cbo.gov/doc.cfm?index=12485Name (accessed January 3, 2012).

279 Kathy Ruffing and James Homey, "Economic Downturn and Bush Policies Continue to Drive Large Projected Deficits," Center on Budget and Policy Priorities, May 10, 2011, www.cbpp.org/cms/?fa=view&id=3490 (accessed January 3, 2012).

For decades, U.S. culture has had a high tolerance for these growing inequalities — in large part because of the belief that everyone had a chance to climb the ladder to success. The economic crisis of 2008, the "occupy movement," and the eloquent cries of the "We are the 99 percent" movement have shattered this illusion of an opportunity society.

A Period of Extreme Wealth Inequality

For more than three decades, the United States has undertaken a dangerous social experiment: How much inequality can a democratic self-governing society handle? How far can we stretch the gap between the super-rich 1 percent and everyone else before something snaps?

The U.S. has pulled apart. Over a relatively short period of time, since the election of Ronald Reagan for U.S. President in 1980, a massive share of global income and wealth has funneled upward into the bank accounts of the richest 1 percent—and within that group, the richest one-tenth of 1 percent.

This has been not just a U.S. trend but a global tendency, as the wealthiest 1 percent of the planet's citizens delinked from the rest of humanity in terms of wealth, opportunity, life expectancy, and quality of life.

There has always been economic inequality in the world and within the United States, even during what is called the "shared prosperity" decades after World War II, 1947 to 1977. But since the late 1970s, we've entered into a period of extreme inequality, a dizzying reordering of society.

This radical upward redistribution of wealth was not a weather event but a human-created disaster. Segments of the organized 1 percent lobbied politicians and pressed for changes in the rules, rules governing such areas as trade, taxes, workers, and corporations. *In a nutshell: (1) the rules of the economy have been changed to benefit asset owners at the expense of wage earners, and (2) these rule changes have benefited global corporations at the expense of local businesses.* There has been a triumph of capital and a betrayal of work.

The story of the last three decades is that working hard and earning wages didn't move you ahead. "Real income"—excluding inflation—has remained stagnant or fallen since the late 1970s. Meanwhile, income from assets has taken off on a rocket launcher. The dirty secret about how to get very wealthy in this economy is to start with substantial assets.

Most educated citizens in industrialized countries are aware, on some level, that the rich have gotten steadily richer. We've seen the reports about mansions being torn down to build new mega-mansions. Or corporate CEOs who are paid more in one day than their average employees earn in a year. We've watched the middle-class standard of living collapse and we've intuitively sensed a shift in the culture toward individualism and the celebration of excessive wealth while also witnessing an erosion of the community institutions that we all depend on, such as schools, libraries, public transportation, and parks.

These extreme inequalities have distorted all the arenas of life that matter– health, education, the environment, culture, housing, and the amount of free time you have. These growing inequalities of wealth, power, and opportunity interact in a frighteningly dynamic way to contribute to a downward spiral of worsening social, ecological, and economic conditions. Compounding inequalities are like a black hole, sucking the life energy out of our communities, destroying our health, livelihoods, well-being, and happiness.

The "99 to 1" framework is a powerful lens for people to situate their experience and understand what happened in our society and economy over the last several decades. It is a real demographic we can pinpoint and picture as well as a symbolic reference to those primarily responsible for the polarization of wealth in the economy.

The "1 percent" icon has obvious limitations, too. It suggests we should focus on wealthy individuals when we should be also be thinking about the role that powerful global corporations and Wall Street. It also suggests that the 1 percent operate as a monolithic interest group. In reality, there are millions of people within the 1 percent are people who have devoted their lives to building a healthy economy that works for everyone.

The focus of our concern and organizing should be the "rule riggers" within the 1 percent—those who use their power and wealth to influence the game so that they and their corporations get more power and wealth.

Just as individuals in the 1 percent are diverse actors, the 1 percent of corporations are also not unified. There are several thousand multinational corporations—the Wall Street inequality machine—that are the drivers of rule changes. But they are the minority. There are millions of other built-to-last corporations and Main Street businesses that strengthen our communities and have a stake in an economy that works for 100 percent. We must defend ourselves from the bad actors—the built-to-loot companies whose business model is focused on shifting costs onto society, shedding jobs, and extracting wealth from our communities and the healthy economy.

The benefits and privileges that flow to the 1 percent are, of course, not limited to just the 1 percent. There are people in the top 2 percent and even the top 20 percent who saw their wealth expand dramatically by virtue of the rule changes benefiting the super-rich.

The data demonstrate that the closer one is to the top of the economic pyramid, the larger one's share of wealth and income. This is because income from investments, largely held by those in the top 1 percent, has been higher, whereas income from work and wages has stayed flat.

Who Are the 1 Percent?

So what does it take to join the 1 percent? How much wealth and income do they have? The U.S. population in 2010 was over 315 million people in 152 million households. So 1 percent of the population was roughly 3 million people in 1.5 million households.

There are a number of measures of what constitutes the 1 percent, including examining both annual income and wealth (the latter, also called net worth, being defined as what you own minus what you owe). These two groups—the top 1 percent of income and the top 1 percent of wealth—largely overlap, but not entirely. There are many with high incomes but low net worth. And there are many with vast wealth but relatively low incomes—at least according to their tax returns.

To join the top 1 percent of income earners, you must make over $500,000 per year. That's the entrance level for the club. The average income of the 1 percent is $1.5 million.[280]

To join the top 1 percent of wealth holders, you must have a net worth (assets minus liabilities) over $5 million. The average wealth of someone in the top 1 percent is $14.1 million, according to an analysis of Federal Reserve data conducted by the Economic Policy Institute.[281]

These Inequalities Are Reversible

Here's the good news: we can reverse these extreme inequalities. Indeed, we did this once before, in the last century after the first Gilded Age. The seeds of a new social movement to reverse these wealth inequalities are sprouting across the planet.

We must change the rules of the economy so that it serves and lifts up the 100 percent, not just the 1 percent. Starting in the mid-1970s, the rules were changed to reorient the economy toward the short-term interests of the 1 percent. We can shift and reverse the rules to work for everyone.

Three Types of Rule Changes

There are three categories of policy changes that we need: rules and policies that lift the floor, those that level the playing field, and those that break up the

---

280 Sylvia A. Allegretto, "The State of Working America's Wealth," Economic Policy Institute, Briefing Paper #292, March 23, 2011.
281 Allegretto, "The State of Working America's Wealth," 10–14.

overconcentration of wealth and unbridled corporate power. These are not hard and fast categories, but a useful framework for grouping different rule changes.

Rule Changes That Lift the Floor.

Such policies lift the floor, reduce poverty, and establish a fundamental minimum standard of decency that no one will fall below. The Nordic countries—Norway, Sweden, Denmark, and Finland—have very low levels of inequality, and they are also societies with strong social safety nets and policies that lift the floor. Examples of rule changes include:

- *Ensure the minimum wage is a living wage.*
- *Universal health care.*
- *Basic labor standards and protections.*

Rule Changes That Level the Playing Field

Policies and rule changes that level the playing field eliminate the unfair wealth and power advantages that flow to the 1 percent. Examples include:

- *Investing in education.*
- *Reducing the influence of money in politics. fair trade rules.*
- *Eliminating advantages for 1 percent global companies over 99 percent domestic businesses.*

Rule Changes That Break Up Concentration of Wealth and Unbridled Corporate Power

We can raise the floor and work toward a level playing field, but we cannot stop the perverse effects of extreme inequality without boldly advocating for policies that break up excessive concentrations of wealth and corporate power.

For example, we cannot pass campaign finance laws that seek clever ways to limit the influence of the 1 percent, as they will always find ways to subvert the law. Concentrated wealth is like water flowing downhill: it cannot stop itself from influencing the political system. The only way to fix the system is to not have such high levels of concentrated wealth. We need to level the hill!

Bold Rule Changes

There are far-reaching policy initiatives that must be considered if we're going to reverse extreme inequality. Some of these proposals have been off the public agenda for decades or have never been seriously considered.

Tax the 1 Percent

Historically, taxing the 1 percent is one of the most important rule changes that have reduced the concentration of wealth. Taxes on the wealthy have steadily declined over the last fifty years. If the 1 percent in the U.S. paid taxes at the same actual effective rate as they did in 1961, the U.S. Treasury would receive an additional $231 billion a year. In the 1950s, under Republican President Dwight Eisenhower, the top tax rate, only paid by millionaires, was 91 percent. Creating additional tax brackets for people earning $1 million or more per year could generate at least $79 billion a year. In 2009, the most recent year for which data are available, 1,500 millionaires paid no income taxes, largely because they dodged taxes through offshore tax schemes, according to the IRS.[282]

Break Up the Big Banks

Another set of rule changes would reverse the thirty-year process of banking concentration and support a system of decentralized, community-accountable financial institutions committed to meeting the real credit needs of local communities. We could limit the size of financial institutions to several billion dollars, and eliminate government preferences and subsidies to Wall Street's too-big-to-fail banks in favor of the 15,000 community banks and credit unions that are already serving local markets.

Reengineering the Corporation with Federal Charter

Federal laws should redefine the social contract between corporations and society through a new federal charter that gives other stakeholders the right to

---

282 Amy Bingham, "Almost 1,500 Millionaires Do Not Pay Income Tax," ABC News, August 6, 2011, http://abcnews.go.com/Politics/1500-millionaires-pay-income-tax/story?id=14242254#.TrwQYWDdLwN (accessed January 3, 2012).

fundamentally redefine the corporation. Most U.S. corporations are chartered at the state level, and a number of states, including Delaware, have such low accountability requirements that they are home to thousands of global companies. But corporations above a certain size that operate across state and international boundaries should be subject to a federal charter.

Tax Wealth, Not Work

We should tax income from assets and wealth the same level or lower than taxation of income from work and wages. Current law treats income from stock dividends and capital gains — the investment income that flows overwhelmingly to wealthier Americans—to a 20 percent tax rate. The tax on wage and salary income, by contrast, can now run up to 39 percent. This yawning gap is what inspired Warren Buffett to call on Congress to "stop coddling the super-rich" and institute higher rates on income from wealth.[9] We can end this preferential treatment on income from wealth.

Eliminate Carried Interest Deduction

One distortion our the U.S. tax system is the so-called carried interest loophole, which permits gazillionaires to pay only a capital gains tax rate (just raised from 15 to 20 percent) on the profit share (the carried interest) that they get paid to manage hedge and private equity funds. Ray Dalio of Bridgewater Associates raked in $3 billion in 2011, making him the highest-paid hedge fund manager in 2011. If his income were taxed like a doctor's wages and not investment income, he would have paid an extra $450 million in taxes.

Institute a Federal Maximum Wage

One "maximum wage" proposal is to levy a 100 percent income tax rate on incomes that exceeds a ratio of the federal minimum wage. So if the minimum wage is $10 an hour, a maximum wage could be tied to 100 times the minimum wage, say $1,000 an hour, or $2.08 million per year. During World War II, President Franklin D. Roosevelt called for what amounted to a maximum wage. FDR urged

Congress to place a 100-percent tax on income over $25,000 a year, a sum that would now equal, after inflation, just over $350,000.[283]

Rein in CEO Pay

The CEOs of the corporate 1 percent are among the main drivers of the Wall Street inequality machine. They both push for rule changes to enrich the 1 percent and extract huge amounts of money for themselves in the process. But they are responding to a framework of rules that provide incentives to such short-term thinking. An early generation of CEOs operated within different rules and values —and they had a longer-term orientation.

Ordinary taxpayers should not have to foot the bill for excessive CEO compensation at private companies. We can amend our tax code to deny corporations tax deductions on any executive pay that exceeds twenty-five times the pay of the firm's lowest-paid employee or $500,000, whichever is higher. Such deductibility caps were applied to financial bailout recipient firms and will be applied to health insurance companies under the healthcare reform legislation. Eliminating perverse loopholes that encourage short-term "take the money and run" financial decision making add up to more than $20 billion per year in lost revenue.[284]

Wall Street Financial Transaction Tax

A modest financial transaction tax on the sale of stocks, bonds, and other financial instruments such as derivatives would generate substantial revenue, estimated between $150 billion and $200 billion a year.[11] It would also discourage high-speed trading and financial speculation that destroys communities and destabilizes markets. High-frequency trading now comprises an alarming 55 percent of equity

---

283 Sam Pizzigati, "A Bold New Call for Maximum Wage"
http://otherwords.org/a_bold_new_call_for_a_maximum_wage/
284 Executive Excess, Institute for Policy Studies, September 2014.
http://www.ips-dc.org/obamacare-prescription/

trades in the United States.[12] At least eleven European Union countries are in the process of adopting a financial transaction taxes.[285]

Tax Inherited Fortunes

Since 2001, Congress has weakened the federal inheritance tax (technically called an estate tax), our nation's only levy on inherited wealth over $5 million. Fewer than 1 in 500 households will owe an inheritance tax and billions of revenue is lost due to aggressive avoidance and loopholes. A fixed and more robust inheritance tax would include graduated rates starting on wealth over $5 million and getting more steeply progressive on larger fortunes. A strong inheritance tax would a significant brake on the buildup of concentrated wealth over generations and raise substantial revenue from those most able to pay.[286]

Close Offshore Tax Havens

Hundreds of U.S. transnational corporations use offshore tax havens and subsidiaries in "secrecy jurisdictions" to dodge their fair share of taxes. A common gimmick of the corporate 1 percent is to shift profits to subsidiaries in low-tax or no-tax countries such as the Cayman Islands. They pretend corporate profits pile up offshore while their losses accrue in the United States, reducing or eliminating their company's obligation to Uncle Sam.

Companies like Apple, Verizon, Boeing, Pfizer, and General Electric shift their responsibility for paying taxes onto responsible businesses that operate within our borders, yet use our infrastructure, education system, courts, and military to defend their assets. Corporate tax dodging hurts Main Street businesses that are forced to compete on an unlevel playing field. Congress could close these escape hatches and eliminate incentives for tax shifting.

One strategic rule change would be for the U.S. Congress to pass the Stop Tax Haven Abuse Act, which would end costly tax games that are harmful to domestic

---

285 Sarah Anderson, "Giant Victory in Europe on Taxing Financial Transactions," http://www.ipsdc.org/blog/giant_victory_in_europe_on_taxing_financial_speculation
286 William H. Gates, Sr., and Chuck Collins, *Wealth and Our Commonwealth: Why America Should Tax Accumulated Fortunes* (Boston: Beacon Press, 2003).

U.S. businesses and workers and blatantly unfair to those who pay their fair share of taxes. The act would generate an estimated $100 billion in revenues a year, or $1 trillion over the next decade.

Cap Carbon and Pay Dividends

In order to slow the pace of climate change, we must raise the cost of carbon. A "cap and dividend" system would cap the amount of carbon dumped in the atmosphere and charge producers a dumping fee. The revenue would be paid out on a per-capita basis to consumers, in part to offset the impact of higher energy costs. Congress attempted to implement a "cap and dividend" regime in 2009, but the idea was still to new. But the urgency of the climate crisis, combined with stagnating standards of living for most people, will build support for the idea.

Dividends for All

The wealthy receive property income and rents from their ownership of private assets. The rest of society should also receive property income from what we own together. Our shared wealth includes the broadcast spectrum, the atmosphere, intellectual-property protections, and much more. We should charge for the use of common assets –and pay out dividends to every resident, one person, one share. Additional property income will help the vast majority of workers who have seen their incomes stagnate, while also addressing problems related to resource depletion and managing the commons.[287]

Taxing Wealth, Eliminating College Debt

The Gates Opportunity Plan, initiated by Bill Gates Sr., has three purposes: to 1) reduce excessive student debt in higher education; 2) put a brake on concentrated wealth and power –and its corrosive impact on our society; and 3) reweave the social fabric –through a massive voluntary national service program. The plan would establish an education trust fund to provide grants to any person who

---

287 See Peter Barnes, *With Liberty and Dividends for All* (Berrett Koehler, 2014). http://peter-barnes.org/book/with-liberty-dividends-for-all/

completes two years of national service. The fund would be capitalized by a progressive federal estate tax on wealth over $10 million.

Without a bold program to address the concentration of wealth and corporate power, efforts to "raise the floor" and "level the playing field" will not be sufficient to reverse a generation of inequality.

POSSIBLE BOX:
Low Wage Workers Lead Struggle to Reduce Inequality

On November 26, 2013, the people of SeaTac, Washington, enacted the highest minimum wage in the country, $15 an hour, almost double the federal minimum wage of $7.25 an hour.

On Black Friday, the biggest shopping day of the year, Wal-Mart workers at over 1,500 store locations conducted protests and informational pickets. Fast food workers in over 100 cities protested in front of McDonalds, KFC, and Taco Bell stores, calling for wage increases.

Across the U.S., a grassroots movement is blossoming to address the extreme inequality of wealth and wages. Led by low-wage workers and bolstered by faith community leaders, this movement is shinning a spotlight on the glaring disparity of wages, wealth and opportunity.

The wealthiest 1 percent of households, those with annual incomes over $555,000, now receive over 21 percent of all income. Meanwhile, millions of low-wage workers subsist on the federal minimum wage of $7.25 an hour, or $15,080 a year for a full time worker. As a result, many low-wage workers depend on charity and public subsidies to survive in the form of food stamps, Medicaid, and subsidized housing.

If the minimum wage had kept up with inflation since 1968, it would be $10.74, enough to boost a family of three over the federal poverty line, according to the Economic Policy Institute. If the minimum wage had increased at the pace of worker productivity, it would be $18.72 an hour.

Federal legislation has been introduced to raise the minimum wage over three years from $7.25 to $10.10. Polls indicate broad public support for this proposal. Seventy percent of Americans said they supported raising the federal minimum wage according to CBS News poll in December 2013, including 64 percent of independents, and 57% of Republicans. But this proposal faces bleak prospects in our gridlocked U.S. Congress.

Political paralysis at the national level has pushed organizing efforts to the state and local level, where living wage and minimum wage campaigns have won real results.

New Jersey, Connecticut, New York, and Rhode Island all passed laws in 2013 hiking the minimum wage. In nine states -- Arizona, Colorado, Florida, Missouri, Montana, Ohio, Oregon, Vermont and Washington –the minimum wage automatically increased with a legislated cost of living adjustment. Twenty-one states now have minimum wages higher than the federal minimum wage.

The next few years will see a lot of organizing around poverty wages. There will be ballot initiatives and campaigns to raise minimum wages in at least 11 states and the District of Columbia, according to the National Employment Law Project. These include ballot initiatives in Arkansas, Alaska, South Dakota and Massachusetts.

The primary opponents to minimum wage hikes include restaurant associations and some chambers of commerce. But not all business associations are opposed to increasing wages. The Business for a Fair Minimum Wage campaign has enlisted companies such as Costco, Eileen Fisher, ABC Home, and thousands of small businesses in state and federal minimum wage campaigns.

"Employers who pretend they can't pay a minimum wage equivalent to what their counterparts paid in the 1960s should be ashamed of themselves," said Jon Cooper, the owner of the New York-based Spectronics Corporation at a Capitol Hill press conference. "Fair wages are part of the formula for success at my company, the world's leading manufacturer of ultraviolet equipment and florescent materials."

Nicaragua Photo by Christopher Brook